Childhood, Youth and
Social Change:
A Comparative Perspective

Childhood, Youth and Social Change: A Comparative Perspective

Edited by
Lynne Chisholm
Peter Büchner
Heinz-Hermann Krüger
and Phillip Brown

RoutledgeFalmer
Taylor & Francis Group

LONDON AND NEW YORK

First published 1990
By RoutledgeFalmer, 11 New
Fetter Lane, London EC4P 4EE

Transferred to Digital Printing 2004

British Library Cataloguing in Publication Data
Childhood, youth and social change: a comparative perspective.
1. Young persons. Social development
I. Chisholm, Lynne
305.23

ISBN 1-85000-650-4
ISBN 1-85000-651-2 pbk

Library of Congress Cataloging in Publication Data

Childhood, youth, and social change: a comparative perspective/ edited by Lynne Chisholm ... [et al.].
    p.   cm.
Includes bibliographical references and index.
ISBN 1-85000-650-4 — ISBN 1-85000-651-2 (pbk.):
    1. Children — Great Britain — Social conditions — Congresses.
2. Children — Germany (West) — Social conditions — Congresses.
3. Youth — Great Britain — Social conditions — Congresses.
4. Youth-Germany (West) — Social conditions — Congresses.
I. Chisholm, Lynne.
HQ792.G7C47   1990
305.23'0943 — dc20   90-3740
                                                              CIP

Jacket design by Caroline Archer

Typeset in 10½/12 pt Bembo
by Graphicraft Typesetters Ltd H.K.

Contents

Contents

Acknowledgments

Firstly, we would like to thank the *Deutsche Forschungsgemeinschaft*, the *Wissenschaftsministerium* of the state of Hessen, and the University of Marburg for funding the Anglo-German conference in November 1988 which enabled us to open the dialogue which became this volume. But secondly, without the committed assistance of Helga Brühl, Bardo Heger and Matthias Burkholz, it would have been quite impossible for us to manage the complex tasks of double translation, editing and manuscript preparation successfully. We are indebted to their professionalism in what must have seemed like, at times, a never-ending maze of text.

Chapter 1

Childhood and Youth Studies in the United Kingdom and West Germany: An Introduction

Lynne Chisholm, Phillip Brown, Peter Büchner and Heinz-Hermann Krüger

The chapters in this volume were written for a bilateral United Kingdom (UK)-West German (FRG) conference held at the University of Marburg Institute of Education in November 1988. Our aim was to examine 'chidhood' and 'youth' as socially constructed stages of the life course in the context of contemporary social and cultural change. We wanted to assess and compare how theory and research in these fields had developed in recent decades, and to look at particular aspects of life conditions, experiences and transitions as these apply to children and young people. We also wanted to consider the direction of social and cultural change as understood and interpreted by researchers from each country. A consequence of engaging in comparative analysis is that it forced us all to question what we took to be sociological 'commonsense'. The study of youth and childhood in the UK and FRG stem from different sociocultural and academic traditions, and it is always easier (and perhaps more satisfying!) to point out the weeds, rather than the flowers, in a neighbour's garden. It was soon evident that productive cross-cultural communication and research needed to be grounded in an appreciation of the different national contexts and perspectives. Our hope, therefore, is that this volume represents part of a growing European dialogue, and not simply a collection of isolated empirical papers concerning childhood and youth in the FRG and the UK.

The need for pan-European studies of childhood and youth has increased in importance and not only as a result of the creation of a single market in Western Europe (1992) and the rapid thawing of East-West relations, but due to the increasing globalization of economic markets and communications. The expansion of international trade and consumer markets, along with the rapid advancement in mass communications and tourism, has contributed to an internationalization of childhood and youth in the advanced economies. They now have wider access to other cultures and different lifestyles. Although the UK has been a *de facto* multicultural society for some time, it is only particular groups in specific cities and regions who might be described as living in an internally cosmopolitan culture, so that satellite media and an increasingly accessible Europe may not simply be 'more of the same' for British children and young people. West Germans are yet to recognize themselves as living in a multicultural society, despite the established presence of guestworker minority communities from a range of Southern European countries, most notably from (rural) Turkey. Ethnic minorities live on the margins of West German society, with few links into the indigenous culture. West German children rarely have much contact with minority group children unless they live in specific areas (for example, Kreuzberg in West Berlin) or attend an urban *Hauptschule* (secondary school). On the whole, West German children are far more likely to know about Yugoslavia, Greece and Turkey as a result of family holidays rather than as a result of having friends amongst children whose families came from those countries to live and work in the FRG. There has, however, been some mild discussion about the rising insertion of 'American' ways of life and the English language into young people's lives and experiences. It is certainly true that 'slang' used by German youth is anglicized to a much greater extent than ten years ago. Blue jeans and Marlboro cigarettes exert a strong appeal, although they are being subjected to increasing competition from a more European champagne, silk and Lacoste style.

What this highlights is both the similarities and differences which exist within and between nation-states. The FRG is a more economically powerful and affluent society than the UK. Although all European countries have been hit by economic recession during the late 1970s and the early part of the 1980s, rates of adult and youth unemployment have always been higher in the UK (despite numerous attempts by the British government to massage the unemployment figures). In 1987 the official unemployment rate was 10.6 per cent in the UK and 6.4 per cent in the FRG. In the UK those under 25 years of age made up for a little over a third of this total, compared to a little over a fifth of under 25-year-olds to the FRG. In both countries there has been a further decline in the official rates of unemployment, in September 1989 the unemployment rate was 6.3 per cent in the UK and 5.6 per cent in the FRG.

Measured in terms of Gross Domestic Product (GDP) the FRG is the more productive and wealthier country. Annually, with 1967 hours, West German working hours are the shortest of all the industrial nations, and employees usually have six weeks' paid holiday (cf. Die Zeit, 1989). In the USA, annual paid holidays average two weeks and the working year measures 1912 hours (of the industrial nations, only the Japanese, at 2149 hours per year, work longer than this). The UK appears in the middle of the scale, with 1778 annual working hours and three to four weeks' paid holiday. However, in terms of productivity per hour worked, the UK performs very poorly in comparison with most other industrial nations. Average earnings per hour (in non-agricultural activities) were 17.68 DM in the FRG in 1987 compared to £4.27 in the UK. What *is* similar between the UK and FRG is income distribution. In 1984 the lowest 20 per cent of the population received 7 per cent and 7.9 per cent respectively, the top 20 per cent of earners received approximately 40 per cent of total income in both countries.

Despite the obvious problems involved in interpreting these data between countries, in purely economic terms the FRG is doing relatively well. This helps to explain some of the preoccupations of contemporary West German social theorists, who are writing about a society with a stronger economy and generally higher standard of living. It is no coincidence that in the FRG the debate about West German children and youth has focused on the declining importance of class cultural experiences and the 'curricularization' of youngsters' lives. In other words there has been an extension of formal participation in a wide range of sports, leisure and 'improving' activities outside school (this tendency is also noticeable in France, where there has been an explosion in summer schools and camps). West German youth experience; an almost universal post-school vocational education/training system, more 'leisurely' university studies, and an extended process of 'settling down' in adulthood often when they are in their mid-to-late twenties.

Economic factors are not, of course, the only reasons for socio-cultural differences between different Western European societies. Cultural traditions and values diverge, too, and in the case of the FRG continuity was overturned and broken in a particularly dramatic way by the Third Reich. The 'empty space' left by its destruction and the circumstances of its defeat was, and is, culturally problematic. One viable response was to emphasize the virtues of enterprise and materialism rather than a new political and moral consensus. In turn, it was the recoil from a materialist culture which fuelled the post-1968 'alternative' social and political movements that continue to be a strong feature of contemporary West German society. Again, the tension in West German social life between 'materialism' and 'culturalism' helps to explain the interest in lifestyles analysis, the idea of youth as a 'cultural fraction', and the role of cultural capital as expressed in the changing exigencies of children's and young people's lives.

At the close of the 1980s we stand on a narrow ridge. Behind us lies post-war Europe, ahead of us the unfamiliar terrain of post-1992, in which closer EEC political union will reshuffle the social and cultural cards. What implications change in Eastern Europe will have in this context are, as yet, unpredictable. One consequence is already apparent, however: the influx of (largely young and qualified) East Germans and other 'ethnic Germans' from various parts of Eastern Europe is helping to solve a number of social and economic problems confronting the FRG. Western European countries are undergoing a demographic shift towards an ageing population. This shift is sharpest in the FRG, where the birth rate is poised to drop below replacement rate. The newcomers provide an immediate source of consumer-oriented, skilled and semi-professional workers who require relatively little state or employer investment in comparison with the cost of retraining or upgrading the skills of the approximately two million unemployed West Germans.

The implications of the changing age structure of Western Europe and the consequences of what has been labelled the 'demographic time-bomb' has concentrated the minds of employers and policy makers in both the UK and FRG. However, a recent survey (NEDO, 1989) among UK employers found that a third of the construction firms canvassed thought that numbers of young people would *rise* in the coming years; but equally, only 20 per cent of all 2000 employers in the study were aware that, although there will be fewer school-leavers in the 1990s, the labour force *overall* is projected to expand. Similarly, there has as yet been little recognition within government or higher education that if the UK is to double its output of graduates by the year 2015 (as proposed by the former Secretary of State for Education and Science in early 1989), then there will have to be a significant increase in educational resources from the public sector. Moreover, an IMS (1989) report on how to achieve this aim concluded, firstly, that the proportion of young people staying on after 16 and attaining 'A' levels must be raised by a third (from approximately 14 per cent to 21 per cent). Secondly, the persistent social class and gender inequalities in educational opportunity and outcome must be eradicated, and alternative routes of certification and progression through to higher education must be developed. What such changes would mean for children's and young people's lives inside and outside the classroom or lecture theatre has not yet received serious consideration.

In West Germany, most people know that there are 'too few' (indigenous) children being born and that this poses a serious problem in the future, because there will be few economically active citizens contributing to the costs of pensions and health insurance. The state has begun to introduce social policy measures designed to encourage women to have more children, including parental leave carrying a 'salary' of (currently) £200+ per month for ten months (longer in some provincial states) and longer-term guaranteed rights to return to one's former employment. The reasons for the decline in the birth rate run much deeper than such measures can address; however it is common to hear West Germans lament the fact that children are at the bottom of societal concerns and priorities. There is also considerable professional and public concern about the level of stress to which many children and young people are subjected given a highly competitive schooling system in which formalized, continuous assessment begins at an early age. Children *and* their parents have come to see 'grades' as the most important thing about schooling. School success has become increasingly important not only as a determinant of future occupational status, but as a measure of social worth.

Given the similarities and differences which exist between European countries, the above examples offer some support for the view that the lives of children and young people are in some ways more homogenized and in others more polarized, both within their own societies and in comparison with others. The search for theoretical frameworks which can hold this kind of tension rather than produce mono-causal accounts which oppose each other is the major task of this volume. Individual contributions may position themselves differently within the terms of debate, but ultimately all are concerned to explore the structured and dynamic relations between institution and identity, collectivity and individualism, structure and agency, constraints and possibilities. There is little question that we must all begin seriously to venture beyond our national back gardens if we are to keep pace with understanding the course of social change. The coming generations of European children, at least in the EC, will no longer grow up, go to school, and become adults and workers under the same, nationally bounded conditions their parents knew. Wider social and economic changes may both draw lifestyles closer together across Europe and produce new patterns of regional and cultural differentiation. These are all very large themes for research to address, but the small beginnings of this volume are an attempt to place them firmly on the agenda.

Approaches to Childhood and Youth in the UK and the FRG

Over the last decade British and West German perspectives on childhood and youth have shown clear differences in emphasis. This is especially evident in the case of youth studies. The social science of childhood still remains in its own infancy. Writing on childhood has largely been confined to developmental psychology or as a subsidiary element of the sociology of the family, although a number of social historians have done much to release the study of childhood from this intellectual orthodoxy, and to open the way to more fruitful lines of enquiry (Gillis, 1980; Aries, 1962).

In this volume the chapters which address themselves specifically to childhood all draw attention to the underdevelopment of childhood studies. Diana Leonard provides a comprehensive review of the research literature, and goes on to suggest how we might approach the study of childhood in the future. She proposes that new insights into childhood experience can be gained by making more use of cultural anthropological and sociohistorical perspectives, drawing on Delphy's analysis of systematic social inequalities in family households. From this standpoint, the analysis of childhood cannot be separated from the question of gender oppression. John Hood-Williams adopts a similar line of argument in which childhood is understood in terms of the structured power relations which intersect patriarchy and generation. He interprets research findings about British children's lives in that light. Peter Büchner, however, places his assessment of contemporary childhood in the FRG into the context of processes of 'individualization' and biographical destructuring which are, it is argued, beginning to affect everyone's lives. He considers the positive and negative aspects of children's changing schooling, leisure and family lives, without making an ultimate judgment in either direction. His analysis implies that the social construction of childhood is in the process of qualitative change, and that this affects all children in the advanced societies. Jürgen Zinneker's analysis attempts to integrate the study of childhood and youth. His argument suggests not only that contemporary social change affects these two life stages in both similar and different ways, but also that the social constructions of childhood and youth are interdependent. The boundaries between childhood and youth are by no means self-evident or permanently fixed. What we understand to be the status, demands and activities associated with each can shift both in absolute terms *and* in relation to one another.

In the UK, the interest in youth (sub)cultures which emerged during the seventies gave way over the eighties to a focus on the problems associated with youth unemployment, education and training. Contemporary British 'youth studies' is characterized by the search for more sophisticated understandings of the reproduction of complex, differentiated forms of social inequalities. The concept of youth *transitions* occupies a central position in the attempt to find more satisfactory ways of understanding the relationship between social structure and action across time and space. Interestingly, the question of how fundamental changes beyond national boundaries (for example, the single European market) will affect the young in general has not been widely addressed.

Youth studies in the FRG has a rather longer history than in the UK and enjoys a higher profile as an established interdisciplinary research specialism. Writers can draw on a bank of data which now includes the possibility of historical cross-sectional comparison, thus enabling a more systematic tracing of youth and social change than is readily accessible from existing British material. In the late 1970s West German youth research came to be identified with the youth sub-cultural studies popularized by writers associated with the Centre for Contemporary Cultural Studies at the University of Birmingham. But the German researchers did not embrace the neo-Marxist brand of cultural studies characteristic of the Centre's work, and which guided the direction taken by British youth studies in the eighties (see chapter 3 by Chisholm). Critical theory in the

German context has led youth researchers to focus on critical modernization theory (Beck, 1983; Olk, 1985) and, increasingly, the recent work of Bourdieu (1986). In the FRG and the UK there has been a split between 'cultural' and 'school-to-work' studies, but an interest in the concepts of social biography and the life-course are beginning to draw together these two kinds of research in both countries, which suggests that this may be a promising channel for cross-cultural research.

The contributions from Peter Büchner, Heinz-Hermann Krüger and Jürgen Zinneker demonstrate the ways in which Beck and Bourdieu have been applied to the analysis of structural and cultural change in childhood and youth. Underlying Büchner's argument is the idea that childhood is becoming increasingly taken up with the acquisition of cultural capital. Children's lives are busier, chasing credentials in ever-expanding areas of their experience. Time and space come to be used, and controlled, differently, which in turn affects the children's relationships with parents, other adults, and peers. Heinz-Hermann Krüger compares the framing and sequencing of life-course events during the youth phase as this was typically experienced and normatively expected in the 1950s compared with the 1980s. He sees the differences between the two periods as providing empirical support for the proposition that the youth phase no longer consists of a standard sequencing of life events which mark transition stages to adulthood. Young people can no longer count on a secure labour market slot, they do not necessarily want to establish a 'conventional' family and the ages at which various transitions are accomplished vary widely. Jürgen Zinneker uses both the concepts of 'cultural capital' and 'individualization' to propose a series of changes in childhood and youth which are already identifiable and which will become more pronounced in the future. Essentially, he argues that the transmission and acquisition of cultural capital is now the main currency for reaching and reproducing favourable social positions. Leisure activities and life-style join education and training as the mediators of competitive and individualized acquisition of cultural 'credentials' both formal and informal. All may compete, but at the cost of making individuals more dependent and responsible for their own decisions, choices and biography.

The implications of constructing one's own biography are also addressed in Helga Krüger's chapter, but she places her argument very firmly within a framework which emphasizes the structure of constraints and possibilities confronting different groups of German youth. She describes the highly regulated youth labour market in the FRG, and why some researchers in her view have incorrectly interpreted youth unemployment and underemployment as an example of how economic change is fuelling the individualization processes because everyone is now vulnerable to market changes. Krüger's analysis suggests that education, training and employment in West Germany is locked just as tightly into the social reproduction of gender and class inequalities as is the case in

Britain. This is an important point. The broad sweep of critical modernization theory tends to neglect structural differentiations *within* generalized social groups, and the fact that cultural capital is acquired within unequal social conditions and power relations. Steffani Engler's chapter is interesting in this context. She reminds us, firstly, that university students also belong to the category 'youth', which prompts the reflection that research in this area has been rather neglected in the UK since the mid-seventies. But secondly, she too is particularly concerned to explore the reproduction of social inequalities through transition mechanisms. Her analysis begins to chart anticipatory socialization into subject-specific student cultures using Bourdieu's concept of social space, which combines both the economic and cultural aspects of capital resources.

Steffani Engler and Helga Krüger take up postions which are closer to those favoured by Phil Brown, Lynne Chisholm, and Gill Jones/Claire Wallace. All emphasize the complex structuring and dynamics of internal differentiation in societies marked by systematic inequalities. Lynne Chisholm sets the scene by reviewing the development of youth studies in the UK over the past twenty years or so, before moving on to consider both the theoretical weaknesses of dominant analytic frameworks and the direction of current social changes as these relate to young people's lives and prospects. She concludes that the evidence for the UK more readily supports a thesis of increasing social polarization than of an individualized distribution of social risks, but that in any event we shall only gain insight into the (structured) processes of social reproduction and change by mapping social biographical trajectories *across transitions*. Phil Brown takes his study of 'ordinary kids' to underline the internal differentiations within working-class young people's orientations to and uses of education as an entry route into the labour market and adult status. He shows how these orientations are very much *actively* constituted, relating to different understandings of social position and life chances which contain *both* collective *and* individualistic elements. Young people assess their prospects based on their social background in cultural context, their judgments of (local) labour market structure and opportunities, and their educational 'performance'. They decide what their goals might and will be under these circumstances, and act accordingly. Both Phil Brown's contribution and the chapter from Gill Jones and Claire Wallace point up some of the differences between the structuring of youth transitions from education, through training, into the youth (and then the adult) labour market in the UK and the FRG. Gill Jones and Claire Wallace combine their separate studies of young people in the transition to employment and adult family life to demonstrate that transition processes operate as multi-stage sorting mechanisms for ensuring that most destinations are class and gender 'appropriate'. Gill Jones' survey of young people's labour market trajectories is able to map a *generational* stratification system which filters newcomers over time from a more generalized youth labour market into a much more stratified adult labour market — but the filtering operates *indirectly* rather than directly. Claire Wallace's five-year study on the Isle of Sheppey was able to show how local, specific structures of opportunity and constraint steered young people into the reproduction of class and gender relations at work and in the family; whether they liked it or not, there really were few alternatives. Gill Jones and Claire Wallace conclude that neither critical modernization theory nor theories of social and cultural reproduction are particularly well-suited, as they stand, to account for the processes they were able to chart from longitudinal datasets. Once more, researchers are emphasizing the need to integrate time and space into the social analysis of life-course stages.

The continued lack of integration of race/ethnicity issues into childhood and youth studies in both countries remains a serious theoretical and empirical problem. Both societies are characterized by institutionalized and everyday racism and discriminatory practices against minorities; both economies sought (im)migrants to solve labour shortages in the years of post-war affluence through to the early seventies. Both governments responded with restrictive measures after the onset of economic recession and the accompanying indigenous opposition to large-scale (im)migration. Rationales for these measures were found in appeals for the preservation of 'national culture' and 'ways of life', apparently about to be 'swamped' by (non-white) foreigners and unfamiliar (i.e., undesirable) customs. But the scale, timing, nature and politico-legal context of (im)migration differs considerably between the two countries. This is reflected in the perspectives researchers bring to the issues involved, as well as in the extent to which race/ethnicity are even considered in their accounts.

Georg Auernheimer's review of the position of young Turkish people living in West Germany shows just how different the context is. Neither guestworkers *nor their German-born children* are accorded citizenship rights, unless they apply for naturalization (which not many do, for quite complex reasons). There is currently an active political and public debate over the idea of extending local/provincial election voting rights to foreign residents who have lived and worked in the FRG for a given length of time, as happens in Sweden and The Netherlands, for example. This debate has emerged largely in response to the broader discussions about what voting rights EC citizens will have post-1992 across the member states rather than as a response to the longstanding claims of guestworkers, significant numbers of whom have now lived and paid taxes in the FRG for some twenty years. The debate has been sharpened by the migration to the West of large numbers of East Germans and 'ethnic' Germans who, constitutionally, have full citizenship rights from the moment they arrive. Legal status is just one example of the highly ambiguous and conflictual position of second generation Turkish youth who have grown up in the FRG but who are socially and

9

politically marginalized. That marginality is reflected in the absence of Turkish children and youth from the literature on childhood and youth in West Germany.

The overwhelming majority of Commonwealth immigrants to the UK were British citizens and had full rights of abode and political participation. The Nationality Acts during the 1980s have curtailed these automatic entitlements, and asserted the need to preserve British culture and traditions. Nevertheless, this fundamental difference gives the minority communities a leverage that guestworkers (or any foreign nationals) in the FRG simply do not have. Roger Hewitt's account demonstrates that, despite inter racial and inter ethnic cleavages and tensions, there is some evidence of fragmentation and mixing of cultural traditions among the young. There is certainly considerable evidence for the development of positive, affirmative youth cultures within and between the various minority groups who are now an integral part of British society. He draws on his own research into language and music as cultural styles, but his analysis also contributes to what is a growing literature in youth studies and race/ethnic divisions. Georg Auernheimer, on the other hand, is forced to conclude that young Turkish people have not yet been able to develop confident, autonomous forms of expression which reflect their positioning between two cultural traditions. Rather, they are still firmly trapped in a double subordination to dominant indigenous German culture and to (rural) Turkish traditions in their private and family lives.

Finally, Mike Brake and Wilfried Ferchhoff pick up the threads of the youth cultural studies perspective and comment on current developments in each of the two countries. Mike Brake emphasizes the ways in which 'youth' in the UK has been interpreted as a social problem and has taken centre stage in contemporary moral panics about 'law and order'. This containment of youth has been backed up by an extension of police surveillance of groups defined as 'troublemakers', but also by the contraction and withdrawal of social welfare benefits to the young unemployed. At the time of writing in late 1989, information gathered both by the National Association of Citizens' Advice Bureaux and by Shelter suggests that young people between 16 and 25 years old can face severe hardship if they cannot find employment or a suitable Youth Training Scheme (YTS), and if they do not live at home with the support of their parents. Benefit changes introduced in 1988 mean that those under 18 years of age have at best short-term (and low-level) entitlements. The situation improves only slightly for those over 18 as they achieve adult status for the official purposes of claiming state benefits. Mike Brake's chapter presents the social polarization thesis as the most appropriate model for understanding the differences in life experiences and chances among children and youth in Britain today. Wilfried Ferchhoff, however, argues that youth culture, as this term has been understood in cultural studies, has lost its meaning in contemporary West Germany. Rather, young people occupy, at best, a semi-autonomous position in relation to the production and reproduction of culture and life-styles. Commercial media, leisure and consumer markets have taken over directing that (re)production, so that no youth culture can any longer be described as 'authentic'. Placed against each other, these two contributions are significantly different in their concerns, although it is clear that aspects of their accounts pick up on similar themes, such as the question of image and identity formation in the context of consumerism. It is perhaps on the investigation of teenage consumerism at the close of the eighties that the differences between the two societies are most evident.

Three themes can be identified in the attempt to summarize these cross-national differences in the study of childhood and youth. Firstly, in the FRG theoretical perspectives focus strongly (though not exclusively) on critical modernization and on cultural reproduction. In the UK, writers take up a variety of positions in relation to complex models of social and cultural reproduction and change, focusing on the material and ideological structures of power. Secondly, these perspectives lead British writers to place structured contradictions and differentiated systems of inequality at the centre of their analytic frameworks. This is markedly less evident in West German accounts, which place social biography and the life-course at the focus of analytic concern. British perspectives have only recently begun to consider childhood and youth more systematically along these lines. Thirdly, in the FRG institutionalized transition systems are long established and universally applicable and therefore it is commonly assumed that West German society is culturally homogeneous (apart from regional differences which are well recognized). By contrast, it is no longer possible to think of the UK as culturally homogeneous — it is a multiracial and multiethnic society, quite apart from the regional differences within the British Isles, which are beginning to reassert themselves in a variety of ways. Further, despite the current changes in education and training, British children and young people still experience the transition into the labour market and adulthood in significantly different ways. The 'institutionalized' terms of childhood and youth therefore are not identical in the two countries. Nevertheless, there are shared features, as the contributions to this volume show. It is the combination of similarities and differences which illuminate our respective understandings, and it is learning more about the relations between those patterns which can form a basis for future research dialogue.

Some Research Questions for the 1990s

We think that the core issues highlighted in this collection are neither restricted to the UK and the FRG, nor are they exhaustive of issues relating to children and youth in Europe. Therefore we want to pose a number of questions which we believe to be central to the development of *European* perspectives on childhood and youth over the next decade.

The current social, cultural and political transformation of Europe will undoubtedly have far-reaching implications for the experience of childhood and youth. A number of writers have discussed 'The end of organized capitalism', 'Farewell to the working class', and the shift from 'Fordism to post-Fordism'. All assume that the changes which are evident throughout Europe in the 1980s represent a new stage in social, economic and cultural development. In Lash and Urry's *The End of Organized Capitalism* (1987), for example, they argue that Western societies are entering a 'disorganized' phase of capitalist development. This they suggest can be characterized by the development of a world economy and an international division of labour. They also predict the further globalization of capitalism. The 'disorganized' phase of development also involves a decline in distinct regional/national economies and of industrial cities. Conversely, they foresee the growth of industry in smaller cities and rural areas, and the development of service industry. The systems of communication will also be transformed due to the fact that electronically transmitted information dramatically reduces the time-space distance between people and increases the powers of surveillance.

One of the initial concrete tasks will therefore need to be the development of a solid foundation of comparable *research* data which records and monitors social and economic trends and prospects in EC *and* non-EC nations and regions. Some progress is clearly being made here through EC initiatives, but much more is needed, especially in moving beyond the collation of official statistics, whose rationale lies in purely state-defined planning and policy requirements. The problems lie less in the availability of national data, but in their non-comparability across countries. This reflects more than simply disparate procedures, classification systems and priorities. The construction of comparative descriptive data is intimately linked to cultural meaning systems. What appears as a basic quantitative description already contains a measure of interpretation. In the FRG, for example, social inequality in educational opportunity is most commonly described using a threefold classification of socioeconomic background which at best represents an imprecise approximation to lower, middle and upper SES groupings (see chapter 5 by Engler, for details). Considerable 'cultural competence' is required before the nature and logic of the classification gains real meaning for non-Germans. Furthermore, simply to readjust the groups in line with, for instance, UK classifications of social and economic status would effectively obscure that element of cultural specificity which allows us to *make sense* of West German society. In other words, we need to develop much more sophisticated ways of bringing cross-cultural data together.

Two broad kinds of questions might then frame the direction taken by future research. Firstly, what are the specific similarities and differences in the social construction of childhood and youth within and between European nation-states? Secondly, are we moving towards a more open, democratic European society, or towards greater social polarization under a post-modern and dirigiste state apparatus? In both cases, it is the exploration of the interplay between identity and institutions which seems to be the central analytic task. Moreover, how will children and young people be positioned within the dialectic between the individual and the collective and its associated power structures? Were we to see, for example, the emergence of an underclass, how would children and young people be positioned in relation to it? In other words, what might be the articulation between class and generation? Were we, alternatively, to move towards a highly individualized society which allocates social positions and rewards on the sole basis of an open competition, what implications would this have for children's and young people's relationships with parents, siblings and for the kinship network itself? What will be the balance between generational conflicts (between the young, employed adults, and the old) over and against intragenerational conflicts (between race/ethnic, gender, class and other group interests)? Might we see the emergence of new collectivities, for example, on the basis of regional identities, that will foster new forms of intragenerational conflict?

These kinds of questions can be addressed in a wide variety of empirical settings. Our own 'shopping list' would include the following: education, training and labour market shifts in a post-1992 'deregulated' EC; new hierarchies of cultural resources and social positions in a multi-lingual Europe which encompasses an enormous range of economic prosperity and cultural diversity; the decline in welfare state provisions and its implications for generational relations and individual autonomy; the reconstitution of cultural identity along small-scale, regional cleavages; and the character and impact of social protest movements in Western and Eastern Europe.

As we go to press, the rapidity of change in Central and Eastern Europe defies the reflective powers of the speediest of analysts, certainly in print form. What will undoubtedly become clearer over the next months, once the emotional immediacy of the opening of the borders subsides, is that East and West Germany have been moving in different directions *culturally* as well as economically over the past decades. Young people in the GDR cannot be regarded primarily as 'deprived' versions of their western neighbours, as simplistic analyses might suggest, even though they would wish greater and freer access to elements of western consumer and youth lifestyles. Comparative studies between Eastern and Western European countries have suddenly become not only more feasible than they have been, but also especially attractive: we shall be able to observe processes of social and cultural change and 'cross-fertilization' as they happen.

Lynne Chisholm, Phillip Brown, Peter Büchner, and Heinz-Hermann Krüger

Conclusion

All these themes have direct implications for the organization and experience of the life-course. In the future we are likely to witness significant 'gaps' in generational experience. In pre-war Europe, most children and young people grew up in locally bounded, homogeneous social and cultural worlds. Childhood and youth were integrated into a stable network of generational and social relationships. The (re)production of gender and class divisions proceeded in a rather simple and direct way in comparison with today. This does not mean that there was no social change, but that it was accomplished rather differently, and arguably more slowly, than is now the case. This is a world we have most certainly lost over the course of the past four decades or so. There are few who would seriously mourn its demise. It was neither a just nor a compassionate world for the majority of people. No doubt most children and young people were positively integrated into their families and neighbourhoods, as they are today. But on the whole, most of them worked hard from an early age in the family and while still very young as cheap labour for local employers. Children were constrained within quite narrowly defined rules of behaviour, subject to considerable direct social control within and beyond the family. They passed through a short and generally unimaginative period of schooling which could do little to release their potential, and was not notably intended to do so.

Children born into affluent families may have avoided some of the worst aspects of all this, but by no means all of them. In a novelist's account of the life of the country gentry in central Europe during the 1930s, upper-class childhood is described as follows:

> [Margot has decided to leave her husband]
> — But the scandal of it, Miss Margot. And you won't be living like you used to now. I was told you got an ermine coat. Have you thought of it?
> — Of course I have. That's nothing ... I can go without luxuries.
> The agent's wife looked at her, doubtful and polite. She did not know that the young girl had spoken the truth. She had never come across the frugality which surrounds the childhood of the very rich. She had never seen the black wax-cloth and the linoleum, the white dimity and the cheap prints, the Spartan suppers of boiled egg and milk pudding day in, day out ... She had never been under the reign of those coveted governesses who ... spread their austerity in ... houses who can afford them, and she did not realise that they stand for getting up at six o'clock and a cold shower, only three presents at Christmas and chocolate

boxes locked away ... And it had never occurred to her that this rigid discipline, coupled with the knowledge that everything will be available in adult life, kills the craving for all which is beyond reach. (Templeton, E. (1950/1985) *Summer in the Country*, London, Hogarth Press, pp. 235–6)

Margot, incidentally, had colluded with her relatives in marrying her off to a man much older than she, who had no 'class' but was rich enough to save the family seat from bankruptcy. In another work of literary fiction Flora Thompson offers us a more optimistic and at times clearly romanticized glimpse of rural English childhood and youth in the decades around the turn of the century. She documents a very different set of conditions, but her description of the lives of agricultural workers' children would still be recognisable to those who grew up working-class before the Second World War:

Some of the cottages had two bedrooms, others only one, in which case it had to be divided by a screen or curtain to accommodate parents and children. Often the big boys of a family slept downstairs, or were put out to sleep in [another house]. Except at holiday times, there were no big girls to provide for, as they were all out in service. Still, it was often a tight fit, for children swarmed ... and ... beds and shakedowns were often so closely packed that the inmates had to climb over one bed to get into another ...

[The] asking of questions ... made them unpopular with their neighbours. 'Little children should be seen and not heard', they were told at home ... But no such reproofs could cure them of the habit ... In this way they learned the little that was known of the past of their hamlet and the places beyond ...

After the harvest had been carried from the fields, the women and children swarmed over the stubble picking up the ears of wheat the horse-rake had missed ... It was hard work, from as soon as possible after daybreak until nightfall, with only two short breaks for refreshment ... A woman with four or five strong, well-disciplined children could carry a good load home on the head every night ...

When the men came home from work they would find the table spread with a clean ... cloth. The vegetable would then be turned out ... and the bacon cut into dice, with much the largest cube upon Feyther's plate ... True, it was seldom that all could find places at the central table; but some of the smaller children could sit ... on the doorstep with plates on their laps.

Good manners prevailed ... and they were expected to eat ... in silence ... Father and Mother might talk if they wanted

to; but usually they were content to concentrate upon their enjoyment of the meal ... For other meals they depended largely on bread and lard ...
(*Lark Rise to Candleford*, Penguin, 1939/1984, pp. 18–9, 21 and 27–9)

The concern of many young parents in the early post-war years was to ensure that their children should not have to experience childhood in this way. Post-war Europe has been quite different, at least for those growing up in its industrialized North-West. By the 1980s children's and young people's worlds had expanded beyond local and national borders — although many still do not travel far, in reality or metaphorically. Racial and ethnic minority groups added a new dimension to everyday experience, at least in metropolitan Britain; race and ethnicity joined gender and class inequalities, all of which are now produced and reproduced in much more complex and indirect ways. Formal education now occupies more time and space, and its content and context have changed considerably. Transitions to the labour market and adult life are no longer straightforward. The hard work children and young people used to do has not disappeared, it simply takes on a different form. In this sense, images of a carefree childhood and youth were never realistic, nor are they ever likely to be so. To what extent the images of contemporary and future childhood and youth which take form in this volume are themselves realistic, we leave to others' judgment. What is unequivocal, however, is both the rich reservoir of ideas and fruitful intellectual exchanges which result from a comparative analysis of childhood and youth studies, and the fact that the economic and social changes taking place within Europe raise intellectual and policy questions which are in urgent need of systematic research and analysis.

Chapter 2

What Does the Future Hold? Youth and Sociocultural Change in the FRG

Jürgen Zinneker

Introduction

Along with the accelerated sociocultural changes typical of the twentieth century, especially of recent decades, concepts of childhood and adolescence, of education and socialization, have forfeited their general relevance. They have been placed into historical and cultural proportion, and have lost much of their normative power. Those disciplines which have traditionally addressed themselves to these concepts have responded to the changes by reformulating perspectives and research methods. So, for example, developmental psychologists reassessed dominant theoretical perspectives; sociologists became more involved in commissions and surveys; and educationalists adopted more explicitly social scientific approaches. The formulation of educational and social policy, together with the provision of associated social services, increasingly required research input; this itself attracted involvement in the field by a still wider range of disciplines. Social historians, for example, have raised their profile within the childhood and adolescence research community over the eighties. The same is true of sports studies, literature and linguistics, ehtnology, urban studies, social geography and political science (cf. Baader, 1979; Bauer and Hengst, 1980; Baur, 1987; Becker, 1982; Hengst, 1981; Henne, 1986; Hennig, Keim and Schulz zur Wiesch, 1984; Kaminski and Mayer, 1984; Kohr, Krieger and Räder, 1983; Lindner, 1983; Raschke, 1985; Sack, 1986; Striksrud, 1984; Tenfelde, 1982; Weber-Kellermann *et al.*, 1985; Wild, 1987). Such increased interest and strengthened field identity is clearly enriching: it expands the empirical base, raises new questions, supports the foundation of research centres, prompts policy-makers to use research input more regularly, and draws more media attention to the area. Nevertheless, there are some problems.

Firstly, research effort remains almost entirely contained within national, linguistic, cultural and political boundaries. Yet the *international-*

ization of childhood and youth cultures, life conditions, and problems is one of the very changes we are witnessing in late twentieth century Europe. Industrial societies and economies are becoming increasingly interwoven at the levels of organization, technology, communication and politics. At the same time, nationally identifiable values and patterns of education, socialization and cultural forms are increasingly exchanged. Researchers, however, continue to orient their perspectives and questions towards the public and policy concerns of their own countries. Official statistics, large-scale survey data, and conferences produce some level of interchange — particularly evident in connection with the International Year of the Child (1979) and of Youth (1985; and see Grootings, 1983; Grootings and Stefanov, 1988; Hazekamp *et al.*, 1988; ISA, 1985ff; Wiebe, 1988). We still stand at the threshold of more coordinated inter-cultural research in the field, however (cf. Jugendwerk, 1977).

For the FRG, the lack of a comparative political and cultural anthropological tradition in childhood and youth research adds a further obstacle. Cross-cultural psychological, social and political science is much more strongly developed in the North American and British research traditions, not only for the fields of our concern. Comparative educational research has emerged in the FRG since the early sixties (cf. for example, Froese, 1983; Forschungsstelle für vergleichende Erziehungswissenschaft, 1980ff), but until recently it was entirely directed towards the comparison between schooling systems and institutions (cf. for moves beyond this level, Kornstadt and Trommsdorf, 1984; Trommsdorf, 1988; Liegle, 1987).

Secondly, childhood and youth researchers have been reluctant to offer scenarios or prognoses for the future; studies are rarely directly towards long-term historical development processes and social structural change. In this context, the relative scarcity of sociohistorical studies and the practice of separating historical and contemporary research exacerbate this situation. Historical research itself is inclined not to be drawn into time periods close to the present-day — at present, it stops in the 1950s — and does not consider very closely (if at all) its questions and findings in relation to what is happening now, or may happen in the future. Psychological and sociological research, on the other hand, tends towards the theoretical and schematic, thus paying inadequate attention to empirical data and sources. An improved dialogue between the two camps is obviously necessary (and see here Dowe, 1986; Fend, 1988 for iniital attempts).

Thirdly, childhood and youth researchers do not notably communicate with each other. Further, both groups have been inclined to separate off the two life-phases from the rest of the life cycle and from age-specific social positionings and experiences. Since the mid-seventies this perspective has begun to break down as interest in the life cycle and biography as both perspective and method has revived (cf. for example, Baacke and

Schultz, 1979; Baltes and Eckensberger, 1979; BIOS, 1988; Fuchs, 1984; Heinze *et al.*, 1980; Hurrelmann, 1976; Kohli, 1978; Niethammer, 1980; Voges, 1987). It remains the case, however, that in research *practice*, productive integration through a more truly interdisciplinary and holistic approach to childhood and youth within the life cycle is under-developed.

Finally, research is increasingly dominated by the demand for rapid production of practical information oriented to immediate policy prior-ities and to the specific interests of those institutions concerned with children and young people. Under these circumstances, neither building up cumulative knowledge nor retaining the independence of the field's development are easy tasks. Where research becomes highly dependent upon social and political sectional interests, the development of the field becomes unstable and unsystematic. Effectively, the balance between short-term applied research and longer-term fundamental research be-comes disturbed. Youth research has been especially plagued with these difficulties in recent years. Despite the abundance of work in the field over the eighties, analysis and empirical investigation has not markedly addressed itself to the *general* social and cultural changes affecting children and young people.

Field Developments — A Review

By the seventies, developmental psychology had begun to move towards viewing childhood and youth in the framework of *spans*, or periods, of life (cf. Baltes and Eckensberger, 1979), accompanied by widening theoretical and methodological perspectives (cf. Silbereisen and Montada, 1983). These changes, in opening dialogue with, for example, the sociol-ogical study of socialization, prompted a reformulation of psychological understandings of individual and social development. The idea of univer-sal development processes leading to a fixed end-point gave way to that of differentiated, open-ended developmental processes characterized by high plasticity. This newer perspective increasingly recognizes that indi-viduals are active agents in these processes, so that human development results from intra-individual and inter-individual interaction in a dynamic environment. Cultural context and historical moment determine how *phases* of development are defined and understood, analogous to the recognition that classic psychological concepts like morality, emotion, cognition and memory are also variable across space and time (cf. Bron-fenbrenner, 1976; Ewert, 1983; Oerter, 1985; Olbrich and Todt, 1984; Walter and Oerter, 1979). In the FRG, these insights have still to work their way through to (much) research practice.

Educational research into childhood and youth has traditionally centred its attention upon the institutional environments in which children and young people spend so much of their time. In the first instance, the closest connections were made with psychology, through a concern with the teaching/learning process. The study of education from a humanities perspective, on the other hand, emphasized the history and philosophy of ideas — exploring the sets of values which underlie concepts of child and adolescent development and of proposals for educational reform. Once again, educational research found fresh impetus from the seventies as a consequence of intensified dialogue with sociological perspectives; and the DFG (equivalent to the ESRC) has supported two special research initiatives in the field, which have encouraged interdisciplinary approaches (cf. Breyvogel, 1989).

Youth and (even more so) childhood attracted sociological attention rather late on, and only then through the influence of cultural and social history. Childhood is that life phase most dependent upon the family of origin; its study has been largely submerged within the sociology of the family. Sociological perspective on youth began with the idea of adolescence as that phase of life in which individuals seek and formulate a self-concept and self-identity, on the basis that the formation of the subject is significant for social integration and aspects of social change. Mannheim's (1928) perspective was paradigmatic within the macro-social and cultural approach favoured in sociological analysis: he emphasized a certain universality of material and cultural context for the members of a *generation* (i.e., of an age-specified cohort). Particular groups of young people may construct specific self-definitions through alternative inter-pretations of their situation, but it is the contrasts between the *dominant* self-definitions of a cohort that generate cultural change.

It cannot be claimed that youth studies in sociology has in fact, to date, made much of a contribution to the explanation of social change; but it *has* contributed to describing successive generational profiles. Understanding social change at the macro-level is an ambitious project however we approach it; for sociologists of youth, it has been largely replaced in practice by attempting to describe and explain changes in adolescence as a social concept and cultural experience. As examples, we might refer to two recent West German survey-based studies which have incorporated cohort comparisons. The Shell Studies placed the findings of Schelsky's (1957) survey of fifties youth against those of a replication survey of young people in the eighties and their parents — who, of course, are members of the generation Schelsky studied in the fifties (cf. Fischer *et al.*, 1982 and 1985; Zinneker, 1987). Allerbeck and Hoag (1985) conducted a survey of West German youth in 1983, using the same questions as those used in a 1962 survey of attitudes and social relations amongst young people. The findings of both studies point to a dramatic change in young people's conditions of life, patterns of social relations, and in the ways institutions of social control impact upon them. At the same time, attitude patterns have remained relatively stable — in particular for those aged 15 to 19, less so for those in their twenties (cf. Sinus, 1984). It seems plausible to conclude that a decisive qualitative shift from a traditional to a modernized 'social model' of the youth phase occurred around the turn of the sixties to the seventies.

Sociological research into childhood both began much later and has remained sparser. Once the idea of the social construction of childhood had taken root in West German discourse, the way was open, firstly, for considering how parents' and teachers' understandings in this respect shape the quality of family life and socialization, and secondly, for the development of child-centred social policy (cf. Giehler and Lüscher, 1975; Kaufmann and Lüscher, 1979; Lüscher, 1975 and 1979). Once more, these changes in perspective have not wholly filtered through into research practice; their impact has been most noticeable in social welfare studies (as, for example, Lang, 1985). Ethnographic studies of children are markedly lacking (see Zeiher and Zeiher, 1987). There is considerable interest in recording and exploring the cultural traditions and artefacts of childhood amongst West German ethnologists, i.e., children's games and songs, toys and clothes, and rites de passage such as birth, baptism and puberty with their accompanying initiation ceremonies.

Spurred especially from France, sociohistorical research into childhood is enjoying a current wave of popularity, especially where linked with historical perspectives on the family, and especially focusing on the transition period between European feudalism and industrial capitalism (cf. Aries, 1962; Hardach-Pinke and Hardach, 1978; de Mause, 1977; Schlumbohm, 1983; Shorter, 1983; Sieder, 1987; Weber-Kellermann, 1979b). There is relatively little research into recent and contemporary historical periods, although studies of (generally) working-class childhood during the time of the German Empire are available (Behnken *et al.*, 1989; Saul *et al.*, 1982; Seyfarth-Stubenrauch, 1985; Sieder, 1984). We have virtually no research into childhood between 1920 and 1970, although museum historians and educationalists have plugged the gap to some degree (cf. Historisches Museum Frankfurt, 1984; Neue Gesellschaft für Bildende Kunst, 1980; AG Pädagogisches Museum Berlin, 1981). It has also been left to non-historians to trace the course of childhood through German history (cf. Büchner, 1985; Preuss-Lausitz *et al.*, 1983; Rolff and Zimmermann, 1985). A summary of the research *gaps* in this field would include: the significance for children's worlds of the demographic transition in early twentieth century western Europe; the history of living with children and the transition from street to domesticized family childhood (but see Niethammer, 1979; Schlumbohm, 1981; Teutenberg and Wischermann, 1985); changing family socialization patterns in the wake of the progressive education and social movements of the 1920s; and the formation of generations on childhood in the context of modernization processes in the family, schooling and everyday life.

Historical research proper into youth has developed remarkably over the eighties, both reinterpreting earlier accounts and eliciting new data, especially from oral history. We now have considerable information about the early twentieth century German youth movement, in both its working and middle class varieties — each of which maintain their particular traditions to this day; and there are several studies of youth in the post-war period (cf. Götz von Olenhausen, 1987; Hellfield, 1987; Koebner *et al.*, 1985; Musial, 1982; Neuloh and Zilius, 1982, Stambolis, 1982). We can expect further growth of research in this area with the current expansion of the German Youth Archive's activities to include youth cultures as well as youth movements. Little attention has been given, however, to comparative studies of youth movements in Western and Eastern Europe, or indeed in different industrial societies of all kinds (but see Dowe, 1986; Gillis, 1980). Similarly, studies of the general and specific life situations of young people as these unfold over the long term are sparse — though case studies of rural youth are now available (Gestrich, 1983; Herrmann, 1984; Mutschler, 1983), and the ways in which official concepts of youth and the youth phase have developed have also been explored (cf. Roth, 1983).

As far as cultural perspectives on youth are concerned, the CCCS school of the seventies (cf. chapter 3 by Chisholm in this volume) exercised considerable influence in the FRG, producing a spate of studies into (sub)cultural youth styles and their positioning between autonomous innovation and commercialized faddism. Just as in the British cultural studies tradition, West German youth studies — a decade later — explored the resistance potential of youth protest, the connections between youth subcultural style and class-specific traditional cultures, and the 'moral campaigns' directed against particular forms of youth cultural forms and behaviour (cf. Baacke, 1987; Becker *et al.*, 1984; Breyvogel and Krüger, 1987; Fischer *et al.*, 1982; Hartwig, 1980; Lindner and Wiebe, 1985). It is perhaps one of the few examples of intensive reception of a particular school of thought and research across a range of western European countries.

The Future of Childhood and Youth —
A Set of Propositions

In the remainder of this chapter I want to present a set of propositions about the ways in which the life situations and experiences of children and young people may develop in the coming decades. These propositions are founded upon the West German research we have available and, in particular, take their cue from what I see to be three current directions of Western European social structural change. These changes are, in my view, of key importance for the future of childhood and youth as social concepts and as life phases.

Firstly, the social wealth of Western European societies is developing upon the basis of high productivity and a relatively wide-ranging distribution of affluence amongst the population. At the least, the wealthy nations do not face a dramatic change in their position. This implies that we face a future characterized by *intensified mass consumerism*. Secondly, the distribution of the labour force and of occupations continues to shift towards the service sector; we are increasingly living in a *service society* (cf. Gershuny, 1981; Gross, 1983; Joerges, 1981). Thirdly, work, as we have come to understand it within the established system of paid employment, will become ever scarcer. We are moving towards a crisis of the employment society and the establishment of a system of *flexible underemployment* (cf. Beck, 1986).

What do these changes mean for children and young people as the twentieth century draws to a close?

Increased Pressure to Acquire Credentials

More and more groups have adopted a strategy of intergenerational transmission of social position which requires their offspring to absolve, in competition with others, a range of programmes for the acquisition of cultural resources. The future development of childhood and youth will therefore be very much determined by an individual obligation to amass as much cultural capital as possible during these life phases (cf. Bourdieu, 1982a and 1983; Zinneker, 1986). The acquisition of cultural capital occurs in the first instance through following particular trajectories, assisted with privileging 'titles' (Bourdieu, *et al.*, 1981; Bourdieu and Passeron, 1971). Participation in this system will become more generalized; the system itself will become more differentiated. Those trajectories and credentials which can be accessed through leisure and consumer activities will gain in significance, in addition to continued competition for educational qualifications. Competitive sport, creative arts diplomas, media production and participation, and consumer style 'performance' are examples of areas in which new varieties of cultural capital can develop.

Extended Childhood and Youth Phases as a Consequence of Competition for Credentials and Trajectories

The competitive acquisition of cultural resources has already extended youth into the third decade; transmission of cultural capital requires an increasing investment in young people's education and character development on the part of parents. Raising the stakes of the time and effort needed to succeed in that endeavour also has the effect of upgrading the desirability of the goals, i.e., favoured social positions.

Time itself is an increasingly significant variable in the game, accounting for the extension of the 'reproduction period' for successive generations. The planned length of time it takes to absorb the requisite cultural heritage itself becomes a form of social distinction. Once that length of time becomes the norm, i.e., what is expected for all social groups, a redefinition and differentiation occurs, creating and reserving an extra and *distinctive* period of time for the acquisition of cultural capital by one's own children.

Youth as Part of the 'Cultural Fraction'

As children and young people accrete ever more credentials and traject-ories, childhood and youth move ideologically and structurally closer to a social positioning as cultural fractions. This means that they become more similar to those adult social groups who possess high levels of cultural resources but are economically relatively constrained — for ex-ample, the producers and transmitters of culture (the 'educated classes' and the intelligentsia). Such groups see themselves as equipped with a certain savoir-vivre, space for thought, and articulated perspectives on self and society — but at the same time as cut off from the corridors of power and rather distant from the industrial and business world. I term this lifestyle and worldview as 'culturalism'.

For children, culturalism increasingly means that they are expected to develop and care about a sense of beauty, in the aesthetic sense. Supported and guided by educated women who have entered a profes-sionalized motherhood as 'cultural workers', the life phase of childhood busies itself with games, fantasy and aesthetic pursuits. Of all age groups, it is children who spend by far the most time on art, literature, drama, music, dance, exclusive sports and similarly culturalist activities. Thus children live in what Veblen would have called a 'conspicuous idleness', as proxies for adults too busy to indulge in these activities themselves. The lives planned for them are modelled on the ideal type of a privileged childhood drawn from the past.

For young people, culturalism includes a sociopolitical dimension in the acceptance of creating and participating in youth cultures, alternative life-styles, and social protest movements (cf. Raschke, 1985). An ex-tended youth phase of this kind calls forth and promotes new public forms of citizenship: action through discussion, interactive and symbolic competence take precedence over instrumental ends–oriented behaviour. We can expect that the youth phase of the future will be defined in three main ways. Firstly, the mythology of youth as a force for cultural innovation and change will return in a new, progressive guise (cf. Koebner *et al.*, 1985). Secondly, the youth phase for all young people — and not simply privileged young men — will essentially comprise an education and training trajectory. Thirdly, youth culture will be increasingly expressed through leisure activities and consumerism. This implies a differentiation of hedonistic, until now typically male proletarian, elements of our understandings of what youth is 'about'.

A Youth Moratorium in a Context of Underemployment

The crisis of the employment society is also producing an extension of the youth phase; it is young people who have been first affected by the growing scarcity of paid work (Grootings, 1983). Through to the sixties, the youth phase could have been accurately defined as that of transition to the labour force. At that time, more than four-fifths of young people left school at the age of 14 to take up apprenticeships, direct employment, or a job in the family business. In the interim, the educational system has replaced employing organizations as the setting in which young people 'work'. This does not mean that, in future, the youth phase will not include paid employment at all. Rather, it means that the emerging system of flexible underemployment, with its destandardized norms of access, will be in a position to turn the moratorium of youth to advantage in creating a peripheral and informal workforce. University students and school pupils, earning money to finance their studies or leisure and consumer pursuits, operate on this grey economy in much the same manner as do young workers, those pursuing alternative lifestyles, and the unemployed. Hence the three-fold *structural* backbone for extended youth comprises institutionalized education, leisure culture and flexible underemployment. In the future, young people will be constructing their social identities and establishing a stable way of life in the midst of *simultaneous* participation in all three fields.

The departure of young people from the employment system as we have known it is an historic event; it signals a shift in agencies of social control over youth (cf. Zinneker, 1987). Young people are moving away from the influence of adults in the economic fraction, i.e., employers and work colleagues, and towards that of adults in the cultural fraction, i.e., teachers, media figures, etc. We can expect to see increasing critical distance from the ideological principles of the employment society — though it is less likely that a general disavowal of work values and ethics will ensue (cf. Neidhardt, 1987; Fuchs and Zinneker, 1985). Rather, the concept of work will broaden to include study and consumption activities. Understandings of work will become more abstract, as in terms of a generalized willingness to achieve and to make an effort. Paid work, especially for men, will lose its monopoly as the central source of meaning and identity, giving way to competing values anchored in self-actualization and private life.

Life as Schooling

Understanding and organizing ever wider areas of children's and young people's lives as constituting a pedagogic process has become especially evident over recent decades. This does not automatically mean that educational institutions themselves are extending their realms of influence and responsibility — in relative terms, quite the reverse is the case. We can readily see that educational institutions have lost relative ground if we consider the way in which boarding schools, grammar schools and universities dominated the lives of middle class male youth in the past compared with the present. Credentials inflation as a function of wider educational access, together with the transformation of some educational sectors and courses into labour market waiting rooms and shunting yards, have further contributed to this process. At the same time, the 'pedagogization' of children's and young people's lives outside school is remarkable in its intensity. Many such 'extra-curricular' activities and leisure pursuits are explicitly founded on didactic principles — for example, piano lessons, junior fire brigade corps training sessions or sports club courses.

In the case of childhood, this pedagogization has taken place through a gradual 'backwards' extension — beginning in nursery education, then reaching down into playgroups and toddler circles, and now developing into pre-natal education (for example, courses in speaking/singing to the foetus, an activity in which the whole family can participate). This 'reverse extension' of schooling arises from the pressures of competition for the optimal acquisition of cultural capital: one cannot begin early enough, especially in lower middle class circles where financial resources are limited. It is in this kind of context that we should interpret the attempt to persuade mothers that they professionally qualify themselves as nursery nurses and infant teachers in order to bring up their own children, a view which was first heard in the early seventies (cf. Büchner, 1985). The kind of childhood culture specific to the families of the educated has been processed into didactic form — lower middle and working class mothers are offered seminars in parent education which encourage them consciously to adopt such patterns of socialization and upbringing. Current debates over the stress to which children are subject as a consequence of this comprehensive and demanding curriculum seem destined to intensify (cf. Rang, 1981).

Simultaneous Acceleration and Deceleration of 'Life-time'

The extension of 'educational work' into early childhood illustrates the acceleration of life history, in the sense implied by Elkind's (1981) term, the 'hurried child'. The extension of the youth phase illustrates the deceleration of life history by preventing transition to independent adult status. Taken together, we see the duality of movement affecting the pre-adult life-phase, which simultaneously begins both earlier and later, both speeds up and slows down (cf. Zinneker and Molnar, 1988). Whilst transition to paid employment is delayed, but access to adult behaviours occurs earlier. Thus on the one hand, the number of participants in the consumer society rises, and on the other, pressure on scarce jobs is reduced.

The Market as an Agency of Social Control

The goods and services market operates on the formal principle of equality and freedom of consumer choice; this extends to children and young people, too, so that it is the market which increasingly offers and controls the process of becoming independent. In this sense, the market emancipates childhood and youth from traditional agencies of socialization and control inside and outside the family, marking the close of these life phases as standing under the protection of parents and teachers (cf. Gillis, 1980; Trotha, 1982). Associated long-term trends include pre-adult access to adult activities (for example, drug use), independent access to services (for example, tourism), and encouraging early bodily and psychological self-management (for example, personal hygiene, making up the shopping list).

The dual system of education and consumerism in modern societies has the effect of removing children and young people from the intimate world of the family into confrontation with novel and generalized rules for behaviour drawn from a cultural code different from that operating within the parental home. Semi-autonomy is early acquired in this way, so that children and young people are held on a long rather than on a short lead (Zeiher, 1983 and 1988). Control agencies operate indirectly rather than directly. In the first place, the relative salience of family and neighbourhood as a source of immediate role models is diminishing in the light of increased availability of distant sources (such as media personalities). Secondly, behaviour is controlled anonymously: traffic lights instead of traffic police, card-regulated access to the swimming pool rather than people on the door, telephone helplines instead of well-known local adults to discuss problems with. Thirdly, immediate short-term controls are gradually giving way to longer-term self-responsibility punctuated by periodic monitoring. So, for example, busy parents may no longer ask children what they did in school that day, but rather request a glance at their exercise books every so often.

Early 'Biographization'

Many of these changes can be interpreted in Elias' (1939/1977) thesis of civilization as a process of moving from external to internal control systems. A further example of the expectation that self-control should develop early in life is the increasingly active involvement of children and young people in the shaping of their own biographies, termed here as early 'biographization' (after Fuchs, 1983). We might thus expect that the demand for child and youth advisers will expand in the years to come. In comparison with young people in the fifties, today's youth appear remarkably articulate and psychologically mature; they are well able to engage in reflective discourse about their identities and life situations (cf. Ziehe and Stubenrauch, 1982; Zinneker, 1985b).

Concurrently, children and young people are more exposed to a risk of individualized failure than formerly (cf. Hurrelman *et al.*, 1985). Avoiding failure involves skilful biographical manoeuvre, and in doing so they are adapting themselves to the individualization of social control by the strategy of flexible response to social and economic crises. It is precisely young people who are expected to soften the effects of allocation and succession turbulence on the training and labour markets by flexibly recharting their courses. The necessity for long-term flexibility inevitably implies that educational, training and occupational decisions are increasingly reversible — a privilege formerly restricted to those from the upper echelons of society. So, for example, interruption of schooling or of university study is increasingly acceptable as part of a standard biography. Such flexibility and manoeuvrability does bring a certain degree of independence; the decline in compulsory biographical elements and chronologies leads to a widening practice of negotiation between parents and children over what routes the latter will or should follow (cf. Büchner, 1983).

Post-adolescence and Internal Differentiation of the Youth Phase

There is every indication that a new institutionalized stage is crystallizing out which covers the third decade of life, a phase centrally marked by the attempt to manoeuvre one's way into full-time adult employment. The classic youth phase, which currently covers the years between 15 and 20, has accreted a suffix, which we might term post-adolescence (after Kenniston, 1970, in connection with youth in the USA). People in their twenties are thus unstably located in the labour market, manoeuvring on the underemployed periphery to gain access to secure jobs and careers. As a consequence, their obligations to family and state are reduced. In contrast to the under-twenties, post-adolescents are independent members of society exercising full adult rights, which indicates that adult status is becoming less dependent on secure employment and founding a family (cf. Mitterauer, 1983). Rather, adult membership is derived from a demonstration of competence in cultural, political and consumer life. As Baethge (1985) points out, whether post-adolescence is a personally and socially desirable development or an emergency response to the crisis of the employment society is likely to remain a controversial issue for discussion, given that the twenties have traditionally played a key role in maintaining social stability and in setting the course of personal biography.

The Significance of the Imaginary

The emancipation of childhood and youth from the bindings of tradition has brought with it an imbalance between what is desirable and possible over what is personally and socially realizable in an individual's life. Young people are increasingly inclined to orient themselves towards utopian (or dystopian, apocalyptic) scenarios of the future, of their self-identities, and of the course of their own lives (cf. Helsper, 1987). Adults, on the other hand, may engage in similar reflection and constructions, but they tend to project their unfulfilled and utopian wishes or their fears onto children and young people. (It seems to be generally the case that those fully incorporated into the duties and responsibilities of adult work and family life project hopes and fears onto those who are partially freed from social obligations and from employment.) Children's and young people's *own* wishes and fears tend to be then placed beyond the bounds of recognition; they are expected to take leave of these 'unrealistic' imaginings and manage themselves and their lives 'realistically'. On the other hand, the refusal to take young people 'seriously' in this way does serve as a motor for social-political dissent and for their participation in utopian oppositional movements.

Generational Tension and the Balance of Social Power

Demographic trends mean that children and young people are becoming numerically scarcer for the foreseeable future, which might lead to the conclusion that the balance of generational power will shift towards old people. Voting and consumer influence do depend on sheer weight of numbers, for example; and there are simply more older people than ever before to get involved with young people's education and socialization. However, it is also the case that as the young become a scarce resource, so will they become luxury articles. The qualitative changes in childhood and youth as life phases and social locations compensate for the effects of demographic patterns alone. Young people already act as opinion leaders or trendsetters in some areas of life (for example, in fashion and contemporary cultural expressions) and political power is not only a question of the strength of numbers (as the success of the Green Party shows). Young people are closely linked with the adult cultural fraction — with the media, the arts, educational and social welfare personnel, etc. This coalition is pressuring the adult economic fraction and political power elites into a legitimation crisis. Generational tensions are shifting out of the world of the family and into the public sphere, with the consequence that when such tensions do surface sharply within the family, both parents and offspring are increasingly likely to turn to extra-familial agencies for assistance and solutions. At the same time, intra-family generational tensions are less frequently interpreted as such: young people identify the 'enemy' in anonymous large-scale organizations and their representatives (for example, politicians, the police, functionaries), and their parents find the cause of the problem in spectacular youth subcultures whose members offend norms (for example, rockers, punks, skinheads and football hooligans).

Changes in Family Relationships

Shifts in the intergenerational balance of power are particularly evident in the private sphere. Over the course of this century children and young people have gained both more power and more independence from their parents' wishes. It is now acceptable for young people to live alone or with others, in a variety of relationships, rather than staying in the parental home until marriage. The ties that bind parents and children are becoming more elastic in character, permitting young people to take advantage of the support of their parents and relatives when in economic or personal difficulties, but not necessarily demanding from them commitments in return. One of the functions contemporary parents have for their children is that of personal trajectory advisers, a rather different role than the traditional one of handing on property or wealth, a business or a skill. As well as directly individualized support of this newer kind, parents increasingly lobby institutions on behalf of their children to secure improved educational and cultural opportunities.

Bringing up one's children 'on a long lead' and encouraging semi-antonomy from an early age has been made possible, *inter alia*, because parents are no longer obliged to ensure their offspring conform to the detailed normative expectations of a local milieu. The geographically and socially rooted intimate environment has given way to the family as a nomadic leisure and consumer cell in a cosmopolitan service society. For parents of the future, it will be more important to respond to the individual personalities of children and their cultural learning potentials rather than to ensure their offspring fit into the local social environment. The 'fine tuning' necessary to adjust to a particular social context can be left until much later, when it becomes clearer what a child's future may hold — and this future can be less readily determined in advance anyway, for trajectories may take several intermediate turns, loops and switches.

In this context, it is not surprising that the concept and practice of flexible qualifications and generic skills are to be found gradually creeping from the worlds of education and training into early childhood in the family, lending children and young people the potential for social mobility in its broadest sense. Socialization in the family is becoming 'abstracted educational stockpiling', available to be turned to a variety of social and cultural uses. The future of family upbringing thus holds a characteristic dual movement: on the one hand, abstracted achievement demands multiply; on the other, restrictive socialization practices are loosening. In the school system and in consumer society children must early take on responsibility for accumulating credentials; at home they can relax. The family sphere is taking on the attributes of a private leisure enclave not only for adults, but also for children. In this sense, the experience of familial socialization is losing some of its puritanical and work-oriented seriousness. This relaxation in patterns of upbringing is made possible to the extent that parents are surrendering some traditional duties (including disciplinary functions) to the educational system and the organizations of the service economy.

Revaluation of the Family and the Private

Young people, and especially young men, are increasingly inclined to place more value on the family and private life than upon activities and achievements in the public world beyond. Self-fulfilment is more important than doing one's duty; the meanings attached to private life have taken on a sociopolitical flavour. Bringing up one's children in a particular way, or consciously establishing a couple relationship under specific principles, have come to imply contributing towards a better society. Individuals establish a series of partner relations with adults and children in their family or household, rather than operating a range of differently institutionalized relations as a member of a family group.

Children, too, are expected to foster and support their parents' self-actualization; they also play a role in the construction and presentation of particular lifestyles (cf. Beck-Gernsheim, 1984; Rerrich, 1983; Schulz, 1983). Having children in the first place is a lifestyle statement

31

and a contribution to self-realization, rather than a decision related to ethical-moral considerations or what is traditionally expected. In this sense, having children is a matter of fashion, so that future demographic trends are increasingly difficult to specify. *Life-style discourse* thus extends or replaces former, religious or state motivated discourses about children and family life. We might conclude that the mother-child relationship will in the future comprise the dominant relational form; with which other people children live will be highly variable, although the bonds parents feel towards their children will continue regardless of the fate of the couple relationship which spawned them (Schulz, 1983).

The Weakening of Gender Polarization

The contemporary shaping of the youth phase relegates to the background family and work roles, the most significant carriers of a gender-specific division of labour. Educational system and youth cultural form dominate the youth phase, and these spheres are grounded in a formal gender equality. Hence, present day youth is playing a leading role in dismantling a gender polarization which has evolved historically since industrialization. The more extended the youth and post-adolescent moratorium becomes, the more insistently does this phase of life weaken the gendered division of labour and its corresponding psychology in subsequent life. This trend will inevitably lead to a weakening of gender polarization over the whole of the life cycle. It is girls and young women who will especially profit from the extension of the youth and post-adolescent phase — they gain in life perspective and room for manoeuvre. In contrast, boys and young men will find it difficult to come to terms with the crisis of the employment society, since their gender identity is so firmly anchored in a life-long paid work role. Having to juggle the demands of housework and childcare, flexible underemployment and full-time paid employment is closer to the life-course traditions and experiences of women.

In conclusion, we might say that girls and young women are rather special representatives of childhood and youth 'culturalism'. Once educational opportunities by sex had equalized over the course of the eighties, we can see that women are well integrated into a not insignificant range of cultural activities — for example, writing for private and public consumption, music, ethical discourse. It is foreseeable, then, that young women will emerge, in coalition with influential adult members of the cultural fraction, as the bulwarks and pioneers of progressive-liberal perspectives and sociocultural protest movements.

Chapter 3

A Sharper Lens or a New Camera?
Youth Research, Young People and
Social Change in Britain

Lynne Chisholm

Introduction

We have entered a new era in British youth research. The theoretically and methodologically innovative youth cultural studies tradition of the seventies was overtaken in the eighties by sobering descriptions and analyses of the nature and social consequences of youth unemployment; we now find ourselves on the threshold of structural changes which have implications for 'youth' as a social concept and for young people as a social category — at least potentially. Demographic shift, technological and economic change, and the reorganization of education and training provision are shifting and modifying the regulatory mechanisms of youth transitions. It remains a moot point as to whether and in what ways young people's values and attitudes to their lives and futures are similarly showing signs of shift; and, if so, whether such changes independently contribute to or are primarily a consequence of structural changes.

Against the backdrop of the last twenty years or so, this chapter first reviews critically the current state of play in British youth research. Currently, three elements contribute to a promising context for the focusing of interest around the concept of *youth transitions*: moves towards a greater degree of reconciliation of differing theoretical traditions, the direction of empirical attention to wider and more sharply defined constituencies, and a closer concern with dynamic processes. The changing climate of social research funding has been one factor, too, in a reappearance of larger-scale surveys furnishing quantitative data to add to the largely qualitative and ethnographic studies which have dominated youth research since the seventies. A positive aspect of this development is the impulse for productive rapprochement between qualitative and quantitative methodologies and techniques (cf. for example, Chisholm and Holland, 1986 and 1987; Roberts, 1989).

We might pause here to recall that the cohort of youth researchers itself is steadily ageing. The effects of current policies for social research and higher education mean that there are few coming in to take their places. We have to recognize that the dynamism of youth studies in the seventies and early eighties came from people who themselves were close to, and had been personally attached to, youth culture and subcultures as these had taken their contemporary post-war forms (cf. here Roberts, 1983, chapter 11). Slightly woundingly but unfortunately accurately, ageing researchers who cling vicariously to their own past through a falsely perceived symbiosis with young people become thereby neither younger, nor do they remain empirically effective. There are serious methodological issues here; ethnographic accounts generally include discussions of how the researchers gained good rapport with their subjects, but the intensity of such discussions in youth studies is noticeable. I do not subscribe to the view that only young people can effectively do youth research, but I do think that the kinds of research methods and the information researchers can access vary according to the subject positions and structural locations of the parties involved. In this sense, the increasing interest in youth research using historical sources and unobtrusive methods is, *inter alia*, an indication of recognition of this problem. The ways in which youth research has developed are connected with the social personae of the researchers who have led the field, just as the future styles of youth research will be influenced by the changing shape (*sic*) of these factors. I shall not be pursuing this particular strand further on this occasion, but it does offer food for methodological thought.

The second part of this chapter's discussion considers the possible effects of the kinds of social changes noted above for youth as a life stage, and for young people themselves, as we approach the end of the twentieth century. On the whole, there are a number of contrasts between the respective situations of young people in the UK and the FRG; these contrasts are reflected in both theoretical perspectives and images of youth in the two societies.

I have intentionally and pointedly placed the gender problematic at the centre of the discussion. It is not only that my own interests centre on this theme, but equally that it well illustrates systematic weaknesses in the development of research and thinking in the field of youth studies. My aim is, additionally, to frame the account in a manner which, where possible, mediates between the divergent debates in British and West German youth research. In this way, each may be better able to understand the concerns of the other.

British Youth Research: A Critical Review

Overview

The CCCS-dominated youth cultural studies school of the seventies is viewed in the FRG as 'the' (only) British tradition of youth research. This school did indeed dominate youth research in the 1970s and early 1980s, and it is not necessary to describe its perspective and the studies it generated in detail — extended accounts are readily available (see, for example, Brake, 1980). The cultural studies perspective took its initial lead in a critique of the universalistic and ahistorical perspectives on youth which had reached a peak of influence in the post-war decades. It was powerfully argued that youth is class-differentiated in nature, but that young people *per se* stand in a specific articulation with class structure. The precise quality of that articulation could be elucidated through re-searching youth (sub)cultures of different kinds (Murdock and McCron, 1976). In time, investigation of youth subcultures came to be understood and practised as a form of class analysis. This view constituted a decisive theoretical moment in the direction taken by British youth research over the last two decades, one which is only now beginning to break apart. As the perspective developed, youth sub-culture was more or less conceptually identified with the forms of male working-class cultural representation and action. Explicit debate ensued over the question of whether, in theoretical terms, there could be such a thing as *middle*-class youth sub-culture (Clarke *et al.*, 1976). Against such a background, we might question whether the youth cultural studies tradition was very concerned with *transitions* at all, despite Willis' *Learning to Labour* (1977). In the first place, its perspective was largely static; in the second place, interest centred on life outside school — but without taking the family into account. The exceptions here were the feminist-inspired *revanche* studies of girls' (sub)cultures, part of whose rationale was to point out the inadequacies of the field (cf. McRobbie, 1978 and 1980; McRobbie and Garber, 1976; Griffin, 1985).

A rather different kind of youth research, one which concerned itself with school-to-work transitions, had enjoyed a long-established tradition in both sociology and social psychology; it had slipped somewhat from view with the rise of the cultural studies tradition. The renaissance of this more disparate tradition over the course of the 1980s can be partly attributed to the application of theories of social and cultural reproduction in the study of schooling, but also to high youth unemployment and the resulting measures to contain this by changing the formal mechanisms of school-to-work transitions (cf. for example, Aggleton, 1987; Brown, 1987; Brown and Ashton, 1987; Cockburn, 1987; Jones, 1988; Raffe, 1988b; Roberts, 1984; Wallace, 1987). This 'other' youth research tradition had historical roots in occupational and industrial sociology, and until the 1980s tended to the macroanalytic. It was (until recently) no less dominated by male-oriented class analysis than cultural studies had largely been.

For the purposes of this account I have separated these two traditions rather more than they have been increasingly so in practice: contemporary youth studies draws on both. The cultural studies perspective was obliged to apply itself to the transitions problematic as youth unemployment rose; the school-to-work tradition profited from the theoretical and methodological advances in cultural studies. At the same time, the greater emphasis it placed on social structural perspectives was a timely reminder that the analysis of symbolic cultural representation is not in itself an adequate explanation for processes of social reproduction.

Sociological analyses of schooling and education have been an important mediating influence in the drawing together of the two traditions of youth research. Contemporary sociology of education is interested, firstly, in the qualitative analysis of pupil experience and educational process; secondly, in the role of educational system and pedagogic practice for social reproduction and change. Accordingly, it has taken a leading position in the theoretical development of a more widely-defined field of youth studies during the 1980s (cf. Dale *et al.*, 1981a and 1981b; Whitty, 1985). It also took up the neglected gender problematic in relation to youth — there has been a veritable explosion of feminist research in and around education over the decade (cf. i.a. Arnot and Weiner, 1987; Lees, 1986; Spender and Sarah, 1980; Walker and Barton, 1983, 1986; Weiner and Arnot, 1987). A youth research which is equally race/ethnic-specific in perspective and concern is gradually now emerging (cf. Mac an Ghaill, 1989; Cohen and Bains, 1988). Of particular interest is the way in which both North American (for example, Apple, 1986; Aronowitz and Giroux, 1986; Giroux, 1983) and Australian (for example, Connell, 1983; Connell *et al.*, 1982; Samuel, 1983) theory and research have become increasingly integrated into British debate.

The so-called 'critical modernization debate' (as in, for example, Beck, 1986; and see chapter 7 by Krüger in this volume), which has aroused considerable sociopolitical interest in the FRG, and which, together with the 'destructuring of youth' thesis (Olk, 1985 and 1988), has attracted marked attention in West German youth research circles, is absent from British discourse. In contrast, many in the UK view current educational and labour market policy as turning the tide back in the direction of the nineteenth century. Youth researchers are more inclined to emphasize the deep divisions *between* young people from varying social, ethnic/racial and regional backgrounds as well as gender-specific differences. This emphasis of difference arose initially in the spirit of a celebration of cultural autonomy; in other words, it marked a dismissal of deficit models. Hence it represents a positive commitment to cultural difference, *but* at the same time insisting that patterns of structured social

inequalities turn those differences into *divisions*. The recognition of profound divisions and fractions which run not only along *but also cut through*
the great social faultlines of class, gender and race/ethnicity does not
imply an abrogation of social reproduction theory. On the contrary, it
demands much more complex models and understandings of social and
cultural reproduction, although a Bourdieu-type (1979/1986) cultural
analysis has not (yet) played a central role in developing more appropriate
formulations. Whereas Bourdieu's habitus concept has been taken up
enthusiastically in the FRG (cf. Zinneker, 1986; see chapter 11 by Engler
in this volume), it has been viewed more circumspectly in recent British
youth research writing (for example, Aggleton, 1987). Bernstein (in
exemplar, 1982; most recently, 1990) offers an indigenous alternative for
those who favour a strongly structuralist approach to cultural analysis,
insofar as neo-Marxist formulations drawn from the CCCS tradition do
not suffice as a theoretical backdrop. Post-structuralist analyses of the
formation of subjectivity may in the UK (though much less so in the
FRG) appear on the more distant horizon of youth research 'proper' but
they are, in my view, relevant for the field; they in part draw their
inspiration from a reformulated psychoanalytic tradition (cf. Beechey and
Donald, 1985; Cohen, 1986 and 1988; Henriques *et al.*, 1984).

The consensus of opinion amongst British youth researchers probably favours an 'underclass' thesis (known in the FRG as the 'thesis of the
two-thirds-society' [*These der Zwei-Drittel-Gesellschaft*]) rather than proposing that fundamental social changes are occurring which bring generalized consequences for 'youth' as a unitary category. That social researchers sharing more nearly equivalent perspectives see the problem from
opposite ends is interesting — the British term emphasizes the losers, the
West German term the winners, so to speak. In the rather homogeneous
images of West German affluent youth emerging from some recent
accounts, I do not easily recognize the inner London working-class girls
and boys I got to know in the mid-eighties (see Chisholm and Holland,
1987; Chisholm, 1987; Holland, 1989). Metaphorically speaking, it is as if
West German youth researchers are in the process of changing their
camera, whereas in the UK we are seeking a sharper lens for the one we
already have.

Social-cultural Reproduction, Gender Problematics, and the Active Subject

For the purposes of youth research, to what extent is social-cultural
reproduction theory over-determinist; and to what sorts of problems has
it been applied?

To take the second question first: in that the perspective has been
primarily brought to bear on class analysis it is inevitable that gender
problematics have been marginalized, both as an independent analysis

field and where the aim has been to articulate gender with class on an equal basis (see here MacDonald, 1981). Equally and in parallel, the marginalization of gender problematics and the distorted image of girls in youth studies is no longer a matter for argument (see, for example, McRobbie, 1980; Griffin, 1985; and for the FRG, Bilden and Dietzinger, 1988). In the mainstream of contemporary youth research not a great deal has changed over the decade. Girls are more frequently included empirically and consciously, but the analytic perspectives still incline to the androcentric. In other words, masculinity and male patterns are taken as the 'neutral' or the normative; similarities are emphasized in a unidimensional way; girls are intermittently pinpointed or treated as a subsidiary theme (see, for examples Brown, 1987; Springhall, 1986; and various contributions to Bates *et al.*, 1984; Lauder and Brown, 1988; Walker and Barton, 1986).

This relative invisibility and lack of definition in the images of girls and young women is not so much a question of their actual or supposed participation in youth (sub)cultures. Nor can it be necessarily traced back to a lesser interest in, or more difficult access to, girls' perspectives and activities. In a theoretical sense the problem lies in the relative weighting of the sphere of *production* over against the sphere of *reproduction*. (In clear distinction to the term social-cultural reproduction I use the plain term 'reproduction' in its feminist sense, to refer to activities and spheres of life which are located in familial/domestic and household contexts, cf. Delphy, 1984). Usually, the starting-point for analysis is the public sphere of production. The sphere of reproduction (generally not so termed) effectively becomes *that which cannot be clearly allocated* to the production sphere. As a result, reproduction is treated analytically as if it were secondary to and dependent upon production. If, however, we begin by regarding the two spheres as *interdependent and of equal rank*, gender problematics are automatically integrated rather than tacked on. At the same time, we are placed in a better position to make sense of youth cultures and youth transitions, which means that we are also better placed to make sense of boys' as well as girls' experiences and social locations. Analytic integration is in any case an important consideration, given the evidently changing organization of production and reproduction in advanced capitalist social formations. I am not thinking here only of employment and household patterns, but also of a shift in the division of labour and distribution of tasks *between* production and reproduction — for example, the reprivatization to the domestic of various commercial and social services. In this context, a consideration of critical modernization theory in relation to individualization processes might enrich UK debate, and not only in youth research.

A provisional response to the charge of over-determinism in social-cultural reproduction theory has focused on the conceptualization and integration of the active subject. Agency and hegemony are linked together in an image of the active subject in constant struggle with structured and structuring contradictions; the struggles result in dynamic but systematic patterns of resistance and accommodation (see for example, Aggleton, 1987; Anyon, 1983; Chisholm, 1987; Connell *et al.*, 1983; Gintis and Bowles, 1981; Giroux, 1983; Kelly and Nihlen, 1982). A comprehensive understanding of these processes requires a systematic analysis directed to *how* social-cultural reproduction occurs, shifts its forms, and is remodelled — not merely *in whose interest* these processes operate. We thus need a youth research which encompasses *the full range* of social individuals, social positions, life contexts, strategies and consequences. Equally necessary, however, is a youth research able to extrapolate structuring principles which can provide sociological explanations for individual biographies.

Youth Transitions and Social Reproduction

Structuring principles and the analysis of their interdependence demand *both* historically specific anchoring *and* holistic, temporal contextualization. The concept of social-biographical transition offers a means to draw these strands together.

It is not coincidental that in Britain youth research has never really managed to establish itself as an independent specialism, but rather that youth researchers find themselves in a number of disparate professional discourse locations. In the conceptual ordering system of social science specialisms, what used to be termed the study of social organization (social class, bureaucracy ...) and social institutions (family, education ...) takes precedence over a temporal ordering of social life linked to social biography and life cycle. (Child development in psychology is an exception, but not a useful one for modern youth research, cf. Walkerdine, 1987.) In other words, we have prioritized a frame of analytic reference which favours a *horizontal* division of presumed areas of 'social life'. The theoretical rationales for these divisions and their foci may vary widely. In essence, though, individuals are seen to pass through and operate in these areas at different points in their lives, but the analytic perspective emphasizes isolation and sharp sequence rather than relationality and synchrony of experience (Kohlia, 1986, makes similar points). This horizontal ordering follows axiomatic divisions between the public and the private, production and reproduction spheres; simultaneously, processes of transition between social locations and life contexts are underexposed. These divisions have been carried over into youth studies. Its analyses have tended to be framed in ways compatible with the effects of subordinating gender to class; and have gone on to produce a rather static and isolated view of youth as a life-stage. The underemphasis of a *vertical* frame of reference grounded in the life-cycle has made it more difficult to access generation as a socially structured category of experience. The case of gender divisions is a classic example of the need for an analytic integration of the vertical with the horizontal. It is manifestly evident that women and men do not share similar social-biographical locations and trajectories, whether in the material or the normative sense. If we combine gender and generation, as, for example, in the study of adolescent girls, a primarily horizontal framework which also concentrates on the public and upon the production sphere appears inescapably inadequate.

I do not suggest that vertical frameworks should replace horizontal frameworks, but rather that youth research requires the two to operate together. If we then imagine this structure in the form of a Rubic cube moving through space and time, we see that youth research to date is largely located in the various 'boxes' of the lower rows and columns. It is, however, at the *intersections* of the boxes that contradictions and fields of tension are most visible and palpable; it is in negotiating the *nodes* that the active subject has to find and apply solution strategies. It is in this sense that the concept of transition is a productive one for youth research; the linked interfaces between education–employment and childhood–adulthood simply have to be a critical nervecentre for social–cultural reproduction, both its strength and its vulnerability (cf. Chisholm, 1987, for a more extended discussion). One task for youth research must be, then, to evince, historically and specifically, *where* divisions and intersections are placed and *how* active social subjects approach and negotiate these nodes. The social life cycle then becomes the medium–range analytic scaffold for this task (see chapter 11 by Engler in this volume, for a similar approach based on Bourdieu's concept of social space).

In the UK, we have yet to embark on a reproblematization of the concepts 'youth' and of the 'youth phase', probably because young people are not seen as a unitary category in the first place — i.e., the differences between youth fractions are seen to outweigh the similarities. To 'normalize' youth as a given stage in the life cycle certainly creates problems for gender-specific analyses; the social science literature on adolescence, for example, has been prone to take the male social life cycle as the norm, as the starting-point. In practical terms, it is remarkable how this androcentrism is embedded in the structures of the social institutions and organizations through which young people must pass. The organization of secondary education and vocational training, for example, bears much less relationship to girls' social and personal development trajectories than those of boys. Girls encounter sharp and critical struggles with the inevitable contradictions to which they are subject under modern patriarchy at a stage of social life in which they are highly vulnerable; the outcomes of those struggles set them on courses subsequently difficult to modify (see here the debate over coeducation, for example, Deem, 1984; Mahony, 1985; for the FRG, Faulstich-Wieland, 1987; Hurrelman, 1986;

Metz-Göckel, 1987). From this vantage point, we might conclude that a *destandardization* of the social life cycle or a *destructuring* of the youth phase could work positively in girls' favour. Unfortunately, we do not have an adequate empirical basis upon which we might make that judgment. It is not at all clear just how the 'institutionalized life cycle' has affected and currently affects women's and men's lives as a whole. Whether we are now facing processes of destandardization or, rather, new forms of standardization is hence an open question. In any event, we have not yet markedly succeeded in structurally integrating girls into our understanding of 'youth'. Insofar as this marginalization is not resolved, theses which propose a general destructuring of the youth phase are premature and unpromising.

Young People and Social Change: Trends and Prospects

Overview

British youth finds itself in a society which continues to be marked by structured systems of inequality along the divisions of class, gender, ethnicity and race, and, increasingly, geographical location. Institutionally, arrangements for youth transitions between education and employment have (until now) operated on the basis of a majority leaving full-time education at (now) 16+, i.e., immediately following the end of compulsory schooling, whereby a significant proportion of school-leavers possessed few or no marketable qualifications. Economically, except during the decades of post-war affluence (i.e., the fifties/sixties), this majority were channelled through a specifically youth labour market until the point at which they gained full adult worker status and, in particular, pay. They may or may not have received formal or informal training of some kind during this time, but their role was that of a cheap and low-skill labour force which was gradually socialized into appropriate attitudes and behaviour not only by employers but also by adult employees.

Culturally, over this century (and particularly from the fifties) young people have gained considerable autonomy of identity and expression. However, prolonged *dependence* upon parents has never been a feature of British industrial society, certainly not for the majority of its members, the working-classes. Until well into this century such families perforce pursued a strategy of economic cooperation — individual members contributed their wages to the family purse, and received funds back according to status, need and availability; this kind of arrangement can still be found in some family circumstances (see Allatt and Yeandle, 1986), but this is not economic dependence of the kind we usually mean today in connection with young people and their parents. In cultural terms, whilst the majority of young people have probably always enjoyed mutually

supportive and basically affectionate relationships with their parents, expectations have been that young people are economically and socially
responsible for themselves once they have left full-time education.

There have always been class and gender differences in these patterns; youth was extended for the more affluent, and differently constituted for girls. (Equally significant provisos apply in considering youth
transition patterns for *and between* minority ethnic and racial groups,
though we still know embarrassingly little here.) However, parents'
statutory responsibility to support their children economically dissipates
rapidly after the age of 16, even if their willingness to do so is increasingly
assumed in social security and educational policies and practices. Neither
parents nor young people are inclined to find such assumptions just.

Most centrally, then, 'youth' is not understood in the UK as a
unitary or homogeneous category; young people are viewed in culturally
autonomous terms, but the majority are economically vulnerable; 'youth'
as a life-stage has been a fairly short period (even university students will
be on the labour market by age 22/23 at the latest). Since the mid-
seventies youth unemployment has cut a swathe through young people's
landscapes, leaving an open wound filled with broken transitions, massive disillusionment, and smouldering resentment. Under these circumstances it is unsurprising that 'few areas of social and political research have
witnessed such a swift development ... than the study of the youth
labour market and youth unemployment' (Solomos, 1985, p. 343). In
many ways, this has been the very constitution of youth research in the
eighties, coupled with continuing study of the structures and processes of
schooling in relation to transitions and social reproduction. The material
we have available is on balance qualitative and cross-sectional, but is
increasingly shifting to incorporate both qualitative/quantitative and
longitudinal data. The *Scottish Young People's Survey* has been collecting
predominantly quantitative information on youth transitions regularly
since 1971, but for England and Wales this kind of baseline data is only
now beginning to be assembled, through the *Youth Cohort Study* and the
ESRC 16–19 Initiative.

The strength of the British empirical research on young people in the
last decade has lain in its close dissection of the specific realities and
experiences of increasingly finely-differentiated social groups; and whilst
many young people have found themselves stranded for long periods in a
social and economic hiatus (at high and often personally destructive cost),
the studies have been able to convey a sense of young people's agency and
resilience in finding a way through. In consequence, its weakness lies in
an unwillingness to formulate general perspectives on youth which might
engage with macro-social analyses of social change; and its empirical base
remains uneven. Our knowledge of young people from the *various fractions* of the middle classes, of those beyond the teenage years, or of those
on higher-level education and professional training routes, is currently

sparse and/or considerably out-of-date. We still know relatively little about young women and ethnic/racial minority youth — and very little indeed about how the major social divisions articulate together in material and cultural terms.

Prediction in the social sciences is an intrinsically high-risk activity; it also enjoys a dubious reputation on epistemological grounds, but any consideration of the directions and implicatons of social change inescapably entails interpretive extrapolation from a variably certain base. What are the main features of British society and economy as these have developed since the mid-seventies; in which directions is Britain now moving? What have been and will be the likely consequences for youth as a 'social condition'?

Demographic Change

If 'the child has become the quality product of industrial society' (Halsey, 1986, p. 113) then demand is about to outstrip supply: the number of 16–19-year-olds in the UK population will drop by 25 per cent between 1987 and 1995 (LMQR, July 1988). As in comparable European countries, Britain is moving rapidly towards an ageing population, and the uneven age-cohorts characteristic of our twentieth-century population history will accelerate the transition within a decade. The implications for all age-groups and for a range of social and institutional arrangements are of some moment, but in the short-term the possibility of an excess of demand over supply in the youth labour market has begun to be voiced. Indeed, some personnel planning absurdities have surfaced in this connection: recent health authority recruitment targets for nurses in England proposed to employ *half* of all female 16/17-plus school-leavers with five good GCSE or better passes in 1995! Youth unemployment, on this scenario, would disappear effortlessly; however, the reorganization of 16–19 education and training, in particular the introduction of YTS, has already shifted the nature and timing of youth transitions. Whether, however, demographic factors will work in young people's favour on the labour market is unclear given that general employment levels do not show signs of significant improvement and that young people may be competing with other groups. The health authorities have now revised their plans; they hope to recruit not only more young men but also mature entrants and women returning to nursing after childrearing breaks.

Social Inequality and Cultural Capital

Inequality has continued to be the outstanding feature of both income and wealth distributions in the UK (as it is in other similar societies), but Halsey (1988, p. 29) is able to show that since the mid–seventies divisions between a prosperous majority and a depressed minority have indeed deepened. Poverty has become more widespread: in 1983, 36 per cent of the British population lived at/around supplementary benefit level. The 'two nations' have been separating out residentially: the multiply-deprived are increasingly left behind to live under deteriorating conditions in the inner cities, those who can afford to do so move out to the fringes (Halsey, ibid., citing data from the *Faith in the City* commission report). The regional skew in affluence and opportunity has produced the so-called 'Roseland' phenomenon (= *R*est *o*f the *S*outh *E*ast land): its limits are acceptable high–speed BR commuter journey time from central London, currently around Grantham and Doncaster, where those seeking quality of life in provincial and rural England buy larger houses at cheaper prices and commute daily to lucrative London employment. Local house prices respond by rising out of reach of the borrowing capacity of local 'first–time buyers', largely young couples in their twenties trying to set up an independent household. However, migration in the other direction is at least as problematic in its housing consequences. The proportion of one–person households, a group composed of both the very young and the old, is increasing nationally: 23 per cent in 1983, compared with 17 per cent in 1971. Young people seeking employment are attracted in large numbers to the cities, especially London. London's housing stock has the worst index of overcrowding and well below average amenity standards; for young single people with limited financial resources private rents are high and council housing hard to get, so the young homeless are an expanding group in the inner cities (see also Liddiard and Hutson, 1989, for a Welsh study of young homelessness).

We have an abundance of research data on rates and patterns of social mobility in the twentieth century; once again Halsey has concluded that modern Britain combines a self–recruiting 'mature working class' with an 'arriviste middle class'. Although conventionally middle–class (i.e., routine non–manual and above) sectors of the occupational structure have expanded enormously, underlying mobility patterns have not changed: *relative* mobility chances are stable or increasingly unequal, *absolute* rates of upward mobility have increased. Inequality of relative educational chances by social class origin has remained stable; inequalities by gender have declined if achievement and participation levels are the measure, but not if patterns of participation (and their labour market consequences) are considered. In the mid–eighties, marked sex differences in subject choice both at school and for further/higher education courses still exist: young women choose languages, social and business administration, creative arts, biology and medical subjects; young men choose mathematics, engineering and physical sciences. Whilst at 16+ 41 per cent of girls but only 31 per cent of boys opt for a further education course at college, sex differences in the aspired level of 18+ higher education persist: a higher proportion of boys opting for the highest-status level, university (Youth Cohort Study, Sweep 2, 1989). Girls' take-up of further education has traditionally exceeded boys' for decades, but the reasons have lain in girls' poorer access to apprenticeship-linked employment at 16+. The introduction of YTS has not changed this situation either beyond or within its confines, where girls remain clustered in female-typed sectors and (together with black and Asian young people of both sexes) on the less desirable college-led schemes (see Cockburn, 1987; Clough *et al.*, 1988; Courtenay, 1988). There has been no shortage of studies which demonstrate how educational experience is gendered, and ultimately works to girls' disadvantage in the transition between schooling and the labour market, though space precludes further discussion here (see earlier references). Few studies document similar processes for ethnic/racial minorities (but see Barton and Walker, 1983; Carby, 1982a; Fuller, 1980; Mac an Ghaill, 1989; Troyna, 1987).

If we return to the topic of social mobility in relation to education and class origin, on which we have most research data (even if this is almost wholly restricted to white male experience), the difficulty of interpretation into the future becomes evident. It can be argued the evidence indicates that 'the social reproduction of generations is a reproduction of a hierarchy of cultural capital' and that there has been a shift from the transmission of material capital to that of cultural capital (Halsey, 1986, p. 115). This by no means implies a more open society for the *majority*, for whom the principle of intergenerational continuity of familial status applies. And although educational achievement improves chances of working-class upward mobility, it is equally so that the majority of the contemporary middle-class did not attend private schools or university, i.e., they did not achieve or retain their social status through the acquisition of distinctive educational credentials or titles. Education *per se* has not *yet* proved to be the main key to the reproduction of class relations in Britain, quite apart from the class-based inequalities which operate in the *process* of schooling to select out working-class children and young people. This suggests that to translate the concept of cultural capital into the acquisition of educational or quasi-educational credentials and titles in projecting how the life-phase of youth may be constructed in the future may well be misleading, at least for the UK. Raffe and Courtenay (1988) characterize the Scottish educational system as nearer to a contest-mobility model than is education in England and Wales, and thus *in some ways* more similar to the FRG's educational system. However, the patterns of differentiation between young people in the two countries are very similar. 'Far from being a homogeneous social group, "youth" finds its experiences and chances differentiated by gender, geography, social and ethnic background and educational attainment' (ibid, p. 39).

Where chances are unequal enough, where the cultural capital possessed by some families and groups has little overall social or market currency, it is difficult to see why these parents would continue to invest in their children's run for credentials. The UK, unlike the FRG, has never established a comprehensive system of formal links between levels and kinds of education/training and labour market/occupation sectors (see chapter 8 by Helga Krüger in this volume). In other words, formal qualifications regulate access to and practice of only a proportion of occupations, primarily towards the professional end of the hierarchy. It could be argued that current changes in the organization of education and training will encourage parents and young people to stay in the race for as long as they can and to compete as hard as they can. But this assumes that most parents and most young people do not already try long and hard. They do, but there simply are not sufficient opportunities at any level, and they run out of cash, never mind cultural capital, to keep going. In sum, 'it is clear that at present the trends are leading to increasing social divisions and increasing social injustice. Not only is the distribution of income becoming more and more skewed, but so is the distribution of work' (Watts, 1987, p. 9).

Work-values and the Distribution of Work

Except for statistics showing rises in the amount of overtime for hourly-paid workers we have little direct information, but it is plausible to suggest that the way in which the British economy has been regenerated since 1979 has not only resulted in high levels of unemployment but also in high levels of overwork for those in employment. This is in part a consequence of chronic understaffing, especially but not exclusively in the public sector, and of a labour force climate favouring employers in recruitment and job demands. Whether changing values have followed or have exercised an independent influence is a moot point. Nevertheless, the schism between apparent workaholics and the depressed, often long-term, unemployed is readily observable. Paradoxically, far from regeneration and technological innovation producing a redistribution of work and more leisure for all, the distinction between work and play is disappearing for both groups.

The response of young people to these changes is largely unknown in youth research terms. Willis (1986) has argued, on the basis of a mid–eighties policy study in Wolverhampton, that the broken transitions that follow from mass youth long-term unemployment are of enormous cultural and social significance. He tentatively poses the question of whether the generations of young people so affected since the mid-seventies constitute the germ of a new underclass, which will gradually establish itself as part of British social structure in the coming decades. The Wolverhampton study showed long-term unemployed young people to be interested in the same kinds of consumer goods and leisure activities as their employed peers, but that their actual participation in these was far more limited. Lack of money obviously severely restricts (even local) travel and use of commercial leisure facilities, but in principle the young unemployed have much more time than do their employed peers. Yet the majority were relatively socially isolated, spending much time in the home and doing 'more of the same', i.e., watching TV, listening to music. They were much more unlikely to use community facilities or to get involved in voluntary or political activities. Patterns of courtship, especially for young men, changed: they were less likely to have girl-friends, and saw them less often. Beuret and Makings (1987), in a study of a group of young women hairdressers aged 16–25 whose boyfriends were unemployed, described vividly how the girlfriends devised complicated strategies and manipulations to preserve their boyfriends' 'face'. Normative expectations for these (and many other) social groups are still that the boyfriend bears a higher share of the costs of courtship; this usually means they have more say in where to go and what to do, and on occasion can make (and finance) choices intended to 'impress'. The young women in this study went to great lengths to disguise the effective reversal of this pattern. Interestingly, the researchers suggest that such a situation weakens the female dependency syndrome which is conventionally part of the anticipatory socialization function of courtship, even though there is no *overt* challenge to convention. Willis' Wolverhampton study found that youth unemployment sharpened the gender-differentiation in activity patterns: young men became more involved in 'spectacular' youth cultures, young women's lives became more restricted to the home and to domestic labour in the service of their families (or their boyfriends/partners).

All studies of the young unemployed confirm that they are likely to blame themselves for their failure to find employment, and that despite the consequences of unemployment for their self-esteem, they have not ceased to place a high value on 'work' as an important part of life from which they do not wish to be excluded. A job may or may not be intrinsically rewarding, but only a 'proper job and a proper wage' gives access both to adulthood and to the consumer society. This is no surprise, given the work-centred and competitive values which are certainly strongly supported in public policy, although we do not know how far 'yuppie'-type values have *actually* been adopted by large sections of young people at school or at work. Aggleton's (1987) middle-class 'A' level college students were certainly not recognizable as 'yuppies' in the sense alluded to here, though they did show signs of individualization in their approach to life: they emphasized the personalized and personalizing nature of authentic commitment, and consequentially were distanced from commitment to collective cultural or political practices. Aggleton attributed this to the *form*, not the content, of the parental culture they had experienced; furthermore, these students underachieved at 18+, i.e., they did less well than they 'should' have done in their examinations. This suggests not only that familial context and educational achievement may work together in initially unexpected ways, but also that the class-cultural fractions which favour both educational success and 'yuppieness' may be quite specific.

If the phenomenon actually does exist, it is most likely to be found amongst the armies of young Londoners who have found lucrative employment in and around the City; and it is worth mentioning that in the financial service sector young people with comparatively low-level qualifications can earn comparatively high salaries, a development which is separate from the management/professional-level 'yuppiedom' of the highly-educated. It is impossible to say how far such values and their associated life-styles are heralds for the future as far as youth in general or particular social groups are concerned.

The Future of 'Work'

There is considerable *academic* discussion about the nature of post-industrial society and the social division of labour, but Britain has still to engage in a sociopolitical debate over the concept of work in the light of structural unemployment, technological innovation, and the distribution of rewards in the advanced economies. The future scenarios drawn together by Watts (1983 and 1987) offer a useful frame for consideration here. In the *unemployment* scenario, the 'two nation' pattern as it has developed in Britain since the mid-seventies would continue unchanged, with the socially weak constituting a flexible reserve labour force for the secondary sector of a dual labour market. The social risks associated with this scenario are manifest. The potential for youth unrest is but one of these, and the link with racial unrest explosive, since ethnic/racial minority youth are increasingly and reasonably inclined to see their particularly unfavourable situation as fundamentally attributable to institutionalized racism (see Willis, 1986; but for an understanding of the complexities surrounding this topic, see Gilroy and Lawrence, 1988; Solomos, 1988).

The *leisure* scenario would destigmatize the non-employed, who would form the basis of a new leisure class. There seems neither much prospect nor much evidence that contemporary British youth, whether underprivileged or 'successful', are moving in this direction. The *employment* scenario foresees a more even distribution of available employment and its associated income and status; the *work* scenario implies a reformulation of the concept of work to include both education/training/ regeneration cycles and all so-called 'non-productive labour' (in the family, voluntary work, etc.), on equal terms. Watts' view is that Britain has moved too far down the road of the *unemployment* scenario to change direction into the *employment* scenario. He favours a change of course into the *work* scenario, anchored in an individual right to a guaranteed basic income.

Given the contemporary economic and political situation in the UK, the wind does not stand fair for changing course in the foreseeable future. A comparison with the FRG is instructive. We might suggest that West Germany, too, has pursued the *unemployment* scenario during the same period, but the consequences have been somewhat milder. Despite similar fiscal and expenditure policies, the greater affluence of the West German economy has enabled containment and segmentation of unemployment. The much more highly-regulated mechanisms for transitions between education/training and the labour market and an established, large-scale vocational education/training sector have been particularly important in containing the scale and the consequences of mass youth unemployment. This does not mean that processes of economic and social polarization similar to those evident for Britain have not taken root, but they *have* been generally less stark; only now are the consequences of this trajectory becoming more evident (for example, the polarization of the vote in the 1989 local and European elections; the urban housing crisis). It could be argued that it is not too late for the FRG to switch direction either to the *employment* or to the *work* scenario, and indeed current sociopolitical debate reflects just this question. It is impossible to know how this debate will be resolved at the present time; there is little political consensus within the parties, or between policymakers, employers and the unions.

Speculatively, we might propose that were either the FRG or the UK to move to the *work* scenario, young people might well make gains: educational and quasi-educational activities would be relatively upgraded in terms of both status and reward, and their distinctive cultural creativity would play a more highly-valued role. However, it is more likely that the social division of labour will continue to be organized very much as it is now.

Education and Youth as a Cultural Fraction

The gradual extension of compulsory education and rising rates of post-compulsory participation are features of post-war and contemporary Britain as they are elsewhere. However, the proportion of the 18+ age-cohorts taken onto university or polytechnic degree-level courses has remained at around 13+ per cent since 1970 (but see below); extension of full-time education has occurred most significantly in the further education sector, i.e., for the 16–19 age-group at below degree level. The Youth Cohort Study (LMQR, January 1989) found 43 per cent of its 1985 17-year-olds in full-time education and a further 25 per cent on YTS, i.e., in full-time vocational training-plus-education. Only 20 per cent had full-time employment. This represents an enormous change since the beginning of the seventies, originating initially in educational policy but increasingly a consequence of youth unemployment — the acquisition of more qualifications to optimize labour market chances gradually merged into the take-up of courses and schemes provided for school-leavers unable to find an apprenticeship or simply a job.

The establishment of YTS effectively means that education or training through to the age of 18 has become the pattern for approximately 70 per cent of contemporary age-cohorts. It would be misleading to equate YTS with post-compulsory education in schools and colleges, in principle and (largely) in practice, but the divisions at 16+ do represent an educational as well as a social selection process. The less well-qualified, i.e., those with poorer public examination results, are more likely to move into YTS than they are to stay in full-time education *or* to find employment. Taken together with the curriculum and assessment reforms introduced during 1987/88, the trend towards a more strongly monitored standardization of educational provision and a proliferation of distinctions between levels and kinds qualifications is clear. Parallel developments in expanding access through new forms of accreditation and progression routes — still in a very early stage — imply not only a potential democratization of opportunity but also an increasingly individualistic form of engagement with education/training systems. Educationally, then, the stage is set for an intensification of individualized reproduction and production of social divisions and distinctions through the use and acquisition of cultural capital.

It has been suggested that the relative demand for university-level education will also rise: the correlation between social class and fertility is shifting from inverse to positive (i.e., the higher the social class of the parents, the *larger* the achieved family size), and the 'middle-class' proportion of the population is increasing due to occupational structure shifts (Coleman, 1988). Certainly current projections of future undergraduate numbers propose an age-cohort participation rate of 18 per cent by the mid-nineties (LMQR, October 1988). If credential inflation reaches further into higher education, we may witness an extension of university studies into postgraduate courses on a much wider scale than the UK has known to date — just at a time when comparable countries (for example, FRG, Finland) are devising means of *curtailing* the length of university study.

There is little likelihood, however, that a 'post-adolescence' life-phase extending into the thirties will crystallize as part of British culture, although a 'dinky' (*double-income-no-kids*) fraction might well establish itself should the trend to later childbearing continue and spread beyond the relatively well-educated. The kinds of post-adolescence life-stage described for the US and detected for the FRG depend on conditions not extant in Britain. In the UK, a relatively small proportion of young people have *extended* educational participation, university studies end relatively early, graduates are expected to 'settle down' into stable careers as soon as possible, and a post-'68' alternative political-cultural infrastructure' has never fully developed. Furlong *et al.* (1989), however, argue from Scottish data that expanding educational opportunities are likely to lead to a narrowing of sex and class divisions in leisure practices. Implicitly, this interpretation parallels the kind of arguments made by Zinneker (see chapter 2 in this volume).

Current UK policy on educational provision is, however, also moving closer to the American private enterprise provider-client model: parental choice within state-funded compulsory schooling, and individual 'investment expenditure' in a free mixed-economy market of further and higher education/training. If parents continue to be the major investors on behalf of their offspring, young people will be increasingly under pressure to bring a return on that investment. If opportunities for part-time study combined with peripheral employment expand, young people are likely to gain more personal autonomy and more influence over those agencies which regulate transitions. But how is the youth labour market developing?

Young People in Production and Reproduction

Raffe (1986 and 1988a) concludes from Scottish data that there has been no significant structural change in the *relationship* between youth and adult labour markets as a consequence of unemployment or of shifts in the occupational/industrial structure. Essentially, school-leaver employment in manufacturing has dropped very sharply, particularly for girls, because of the concentration of female employment in food, textiles and clothing manufacture, where the decline during the seventies was greater than average for the sector. In general, occupational and industrial segregation of employment by sex has *increased* since 1979. In this context, since the mid-sixties and especially between 1971–1981, the managerial/professional sectors have grown much more rapidly than the clerical sector; and since 1966 the absolute number of people employed as salespersons has fallen rapidly (Price and Bain, 1988). The feminization of the clerical sector had been largely completed by the fifties, but in the sales sector feminization was only fully established during the seventies — following retailing modernization and a consequent decline in the numbers of those employed. In other words, men moved out of this sector as opportunities contracted and the nature of sales occupations changed to reflect a more complex and fractionalized division of labour.

Trends in occupational segregation by sex are important for the youth labour market, since women and young people frequently find themselves similarly located. My own research on young people in relatively depressed areas of London in the mid-eighties indicated that 'sales assistant' was *not* seen as a female-typed *job*, though it was most definitely a female-typed *expectation*. In other words: boys do not want to become sales assistants, but both girls and boys know that many 16+ school-leavers do become sales assistants — archetypally in large supermarkets and department stores. Nevertheless, boys do not see this as an occupation they would want to continue in permanently — it is a 'fill-in' until something more desirable comes along. Girls do not generally rate sales jobs as a first-order or desirable aspiration either — they are more likely to see these as a fall-back should they not secure their first choice. The difference then is that *girls are much less likely to escape* from these sales jobs at a later date.

We could conclude that an emerging feature of *majority* youth transitions is to take a readily-available but relatively uninspiring job as a temporary measure, but that transition to more desirable sectors is regulated significantly by the usual factors of gender, race and class. In other words, we are describing here a dual-labour market mechanism as it affects young people: a generalized and cheap youth labour market is gradually transformed and sorted into a much more highly-stratified adult labour market. Retailing, a sector which is only part-way through a technological revolution, is a good example of strategic labour force utilization of this kind. The retail sales force as it is conventionally understood has no long-term future, and much of it has been progressively deskilled since the sixties — which is one reason why using a young and unskilled labour force is both feasible and attractive. A high proportion of retailing employees are now young people either working part-time well before leaving school or full-time as YTS trainees or as casual labour.

Buswell's (1989) study of a group of clerical and retailing YTS trainees' responses to their experiences in the workplace and at college describes the contradictions which arise: their jobs are located in the secondary sector, which is organized around low commitment, high turnover, and dependency, but at college quite the opposite values and traits are assumed and encouraged. She points out that recent and continuing service sector growth is based on part-time and temporary jobs, and that it is the pattern of employers' requirements for a flexible and expendable reserve labour base which has fuelled this expansion rather than young people's desire to combine employment with further education (or married women's assumed preference for part-time work). She concludes that 'marginal' occupations are now the site of work for both sexes; a quarter of the retail and clerical students on the course she studied were male — and this in a region noted for its traditional values. She suggests that the economic periphery may well be indicating the future, not the past, in this respect (ibid, p. 181).

On the basis of my own study, it would appear that this is not good enough for young people of either sex, but that young men are ultimately better able to avoid it as a permanent location. It may well be that *young people's* educational patterns and production locations are moving towards greater convergence. But the continuing divisions in their *reproduction* locations ensure that young women's educational achievement brings a relatively lesser return on the labour market and that as adult workers they are less able to escape from the secondary sector.

Young people from ethnic/racial minority groups are in a more complex, difficult situation. There is a marked trend towards above-average participation in post-compulsory education and training for these groups, which reflects a strong motivation to achieve upward social mobility via educational achievement. This applies equally and perhaps especially to young women. Education is traditionally highly-valued in Hindu culture, for daughters as much as for sons; in Muslim Asian families, educational achievement is an acceptable means for daughters to avoid early marriage. Young women from Caribbean backgrounds try to turn the 'double negative' of race and gender into a positive outcome by educational achievement and career commitment; the links between women's family roles and their employment status have been historically differently constituted than for white European women, so that combining the two is not similarly ideologically suffused. We could suggest that should the investments these groups of young people are now making not produce an acceptable labour market return, the potential for social unrest in the nineties will increase.

The changes in patterns of marriage, childbearing and household size and structure over the course of this century are both fascinating and are becoming increasingly complex, but the central point remains that kinship and marriage expressed through the life-cycle of the nuclear family still structures most people's domestic arrangements for most of their lives (Leonard and Speakman, 1986). Further, all studies of the domestic division of labour show that neither ideologies nor (still less) practices have changed with respect to gender roles. Regardless of their actual (typically low) level of participation, contemporary men give more assistance with childcare than with housework, but the ideology of mothering has not shifted; nor have the organization of employment or employer attitudes made the integration of work and family roles much easier for women *or* men. Young people's experiences of family life are unlikely to change dramatically in the near future, then.

It is not necessarily helpful to seek indicators of coming social change

53

in the voiced opinions and attitudes of young people themselves. Were I
to rely on what 11–16-year-old London girls told me in the mid-eighties,
I would have to conclude that marriage and family life are on the brink of
collapse: a majority of the (working-class) girls interviewed said they
neither wanted to marry, nor wanted to have children (as Lees, 1986, also
found). A notable minority wanted to have children, but to dispense with
husbands (who were viewed as generally irksome and lazy). They also
said that if they did marry/cohabit, they wanted to establish a more equal
sharing of the domestic load and certainly did not want to be 'chained to
the kitchen sink'. Boys of the same ages and backgrounds had no intention of practising domestic symmetry, quite the reverse. Other studies
have uniformly found that girls generally do more domestic work in their
parents' home than do their brothers, though teenage girls may not
realize that they too take their mother's domestic labour for granted (for
example, Griffin, 1985). Similarly, Hayes (1989) concludes from a study
of white middle-class youth that the future is unlikely to see a change in
the greater role women play in caring for their parents in old age.

On the one hand, it is evident that most of these girls *will* marry and
will have children. Under foreseeable labour market and ideological conditions they will also remain primarily responsible for housework and
childcare, regardless of their employment status. On the other hand,
these girls — and many others — are voicing their discontent with their
location in reproduction, the boys their satisfaction. Surface liberalization
of attitudes since the sixties together with the actual increase in (married)
women's labour force participation has also lent women more moral and
economic power to voice that discontent. These kinds of changes may
point towards both continuation of the trends to later marriage, childlessness and later childbearing and to increased marital conflict and divorce.
However, this can be interpreted as a process of polarization between the
sexes rather than as evidence of increasing homogeneity. The renegotia-
tion of the social division of labour between the sexes has yet to com-
mence in earnest; and only at a relatively superficial level is it possible to
say that women's and men's lives are becoming more similar.

Conclusions

Looking towards the future, it seems that polarization processes as a
consequence of the emergence of an underclass in the UK enjoy some
measure of empirical support. Additionally, there are as yet no serious
signs of a redistribution of work in either the production or the reproduction spheres. In this sense it is difficult to make an argument for assimilation of gender-specific divisions of labour and a corresponding significant
weakening of sex roles; a prognosis of *fundamental* social change in this
area in the foreseeable future is hardly justified. Finally, structural factors

suggest that youth as a social category will remain highly heterogeneous in character.

We can draw two major conclusions from these features. Firstly, framing conditions of social life in the FRG are indeed significantly different from those in the UK. The most important factors to consider here are, firstly, the two countries' differing *formal* youth transitions mechanisms (education–training–labour market; see chapter 8 by Helga Krüger in this volume) and, secondly, their diverging absolute and relative levels of affluence. Secondly, it is arguable that as a consequence of their different theoretical perspectives and value stances, analysts from the two cultures simply do not 'see' the character of their own and/or the others' social formation in wholly accurate ways. From the British point of view, West German youth as generally presented by West German researchers looks unbelievably homogeneous (but see chapter 13 by Auernheimer in this volume). Questions about which groups have been excluded, distorted and misrepresented cannot be repressed. From the West German vantage point, it looks as if the British are unable to part with their golden oldies of class struggle, not having noticed that contemporary youth has switched to CD video. They find the commitment admirable, but the validity dubious.

Leaving such debates to one side, we can identify points of contact and agreement. An increasing *regulation* and medium-term *extension* of the youth phase is evident in both cultures. The differences lie in the points of departure for these trends. In comparison with the FRG, British youth was, until recently, less subject to 'sociotechnicized' regulation; and the youth phase remains, on the whole, formally and culturally shorter in duration. If we were to adopt a more pessimistic version of the individualization thesis contained in critical modernization theory, we could find formulations which apply to both societies. The links of the sociocultural reproduction chain are only *seemingly* weakened by wider access to education/training qualifications and by stronger emphasis on quality of educational/task *and social* performance. Late/post modernist conceptualizations of social subjectivity dovetail well with the individualization thesis in this respect — as in, for example, Apple's (1982) concept of the possessive individual, 'a vision of oneself that lies at the ideological heart of corporate economies' (p. 261). He argues that the modes of technical control increasingly incorporated in school curricula are well-suited to the reproduction of this form of subjectivity, in which 'the mark of a good pupil is the possession and accumulation of vast quantities of skills in the service of technical interests' (ibid, p. 262). Cohen's (1984) critique of Britain's 'new vocationalism' offers an alternative formulation, one which points to the cultivation of a new form of social discipline based on self-improvement and image-management; systems of external regulation and negative santions are being replaced with invisible forms of social regulation and internal controls, into whose discipline young people must be trained (ibid, pp. 107 and 114). Such analyses direct us to new forms of standardization rather than to a simple destandardization of the youth phase.

The crisis in the distribution of work and employment is not receding. Young people are about to become rarer, but unemployment persists and underemployment is rising; secure, full-time employment with real perspective attached to it is also fairly rare, and it requires qualifications and experience. The future just over the horizon could equally as well turn youth into a tyrannized minority as into a pampered luxury commodity. Margaret Atwoods' feminist dystopia, *The Handmaid's Tale*, in which young women function as baby-machines for an aged population at risk of extinction, is not necessarily an implausible scenario. My intention is not to promote gloomy pessimism about the future, but rather to underline the fact that prognoses can reasonably take differing forms.

To return to the present: it is increasingly difficult clearly to hold apart the various theoretical perspectives which inform youth studies. In this sense, the efforts to produce more productive syntheses from former antitheses have met with some success. In the FRG these efforts have been undertaken more noticeably, perhaps because of a more self-consciously theorizing tradition in the social sciences in contrast with the greater pragmatism of British perspectives (despite the critical sociology of the seventies). Ultimately, I think it more important to ask where we want our theory to take us rather than where it derives from in the first place. In the UK, the clear trend is to hold onto theories of social and cultural reproduction as the anchoring thread, but to resist overdeterminism and overgeneralization and to ensure material conditions of social life never slip out of sight. It is precisely the recognition of far-reaching social divisions and fragmentation that places a questionmark over generalized theses of modernization and individualization processes.

The potential for social change rather than social reproduction does not ultimately rest upon making a wider range of opportunities, strategies and routes available to ever wider constituencies. The social construction of biography is inevitably linked with social position; the range of possibilities for action shift when individual or group position shift. The critical problem is empowerment for change which can function from existing social position, so that people do not have to face being torn away from their cultural and familial-personal contexts. This brutal choice was exactly that which was demanded of girls and of working-class children in the 1950s and 1960s, and which was equally demanded of the second-generation Commonwealth immigrant population in the 1970s and into the 1980s. Their structurally determined social disadvantage was to be rectified by individual social mobility through the educational meritocracy and by collective social mobility through increasing general affluence. The wounds consequent upon these policies (however well intentioned they in part were) are neither always minor nor do they automatically disappear, as recent commentaries and autobiographical writing show (see, for example, Carby, 1982b; Goodings, 1987; Heron, 1985; Ingham, 1981; McRobbie and McCabe, 1981). The seeds of transformation rest in those recurring critical moments when the contradictions young people face become explicit and are forcefully, painfully felt. It is in these moments of uncertainty and ambiguity that a window opens, that spaces for transformation become visible. Whether the chances they offer can be grasped productively is a complex question, but it is to the understanding and maximization of these opportunities that we should address ourselves.

Chapter 4

Persons in Their Own Right:
Children and Sociology in the UK

Diana Leonard

We have as yet only a poorly developed sociology of contemporary childhood in Britain i.e., a sociology of the social position of babies, infants and 3–11-year-olds and their relationships with adults and with other children. The situation in fact provides an interesting parallel with the sociology of women and gender relations before 1970 (Mathieu, 1977). Age, like sex, is one of the three fundamental variables constantly employed in empirical work in sociology and social psychology. But these three variables do not enjoy equally rigorous sociological definition, nor are their problematics equally systematized. One variable, class, has a long history and is now clearly recognized as a social category; but although information on sex and age is collected on all social surveys, these variables are not sociologically defined. They are seen as largely extra-socially determined, by physiological differences (as was class itself in the nineteenth century). That is to say, age relations continue to be treated as a set of groupings based on natural divisions, not as reciprocally related, opposed and socially defined and constituted categories. This situation continues unabated because most of the research on children which *does* exist, including most of the longitudinal studies conducted since 1945, have been produced by medical researchers and psychologists. An exception is the study of 700 children begun in 1958 by John and Elizabeth Newson at their Child Development Research Unit in Nottingham (cf. chapter 10 by Hood-Williams in this volume). Much of the available information on children is therefore concerned with the development of their bodies, intellects and personalities. Some of it is interesting to sociologists of childhood, both for its content and as texts 'locating' childhood, but unfortunately much which should be culturally and historically contextualized is in fact downright biologistic.

For sociologists existing work is, in addition, methodologically suspect, being based either on laboratory experimentation and observations in clinical surroundings, or on questionnaires or interviews with mothers alone. There are, of course, practical and ethical difficulties in interviewing children. For instance it is difficult for anyone, and particularly for men, to observe or to approach them and start talking to them in the street (though cf. Opie and Opie, 1969). Parents may be reluctant to allow observation or interviews in the home, and anyway the presence of an observer is likely to change a domestic routine; and particular interviewing skills are needed (cf. Rich, 1968). But it is nonetheless remarkable how rarely sociologists have interviewed children, even of 9, 10 or 11 years old, or observed them in ordinary everyday settings in Britain. The analysis in most of the medical and psychological studies of children is in terms of a conceptual unit of mother and child (and latterly also father and child) rather than the household or general situation in which the child lives. It uses attachment theory rather than a concern for family dynamics or the broader social networks around the developing child. In more sociological work, it is seldom children, but rather adults' relations with children — whom they control, or try to control, or to educate — which engages the researchers' interest. For example, in studies employing a life-cycle or life-course approach, there is seldom anything on the experience of childhood, but a lot on the experience of parenting. Children, or more specifically childcare, are seen as 'problems', and they are studied from the point of view of dominant group, as an issue of 'socialization' or 'control'. This is true whether the concern is maintaining the status quo or producing radical change. (cf. Statham (1986) talked to thirty parental couples committed to non-sexist childraising — but not to their children.)

> To use a very crude metaphor ... sociologists have been going about their study of children mainly like colonial administrators who might be expected to write scientifically objective reports of the local populace in order to increase their understanding of native culture, and who do so by ideologically formulating only those research problems that pertain to native behaviours coming under the regulation of colonial authority ... (Speier, 1976, p. 99)

There is, of course, some work which is useful to sociologists, even if it is not itself strictly sociological. For example, a few creative writers and photographers have tried to convey the 'intensity, variety and ingenuity of urban childhood', especially for boys (Ward, 1978); or to explore the world of toddlers and the discovery of sensations, movement and surroundings (Crowe, 1983). Some social psychologists have observed relationships within the home (for example, Richards, 1982; Dunn and Kenrick, 1982; Dunn, 1988) or talked to children about their feelings on their parents' divorce (Richards and Dyson, 1981). They have critiqued developmental psychology itself and its role in constituting age, gender and class through normalizing constructions of motherhood and 'the child' (see Riley, 1983; Steedman, Urwin and Walkerdine, 1985; Walkerdine and Lucey, 1989). The study of children's writing, writing for children, and the representation of children in literature constitute fields in themselves on which we can draw, together with work on children's speech (Martin *et al.*, 1976) and drawing. There is also a continuing concern with children's patterns of watching, or, as it is now more realistically seen, their active participation with TV and videos — and of course their schooling.

Following Aries' ambitious survey, *L'Enfant et la vie familiale dans l'ancien regime* (translated into English in 1962 as *Centuries of Childhood*) and Laslett's *The World We Have Lost* (1965, 2nd edn 1971), there has been a rapid development of excellent sociologically informed work on the history of childhood. Research has focused on the seventeenth, eighteenth and especially the nineteenth centuries, building up accounts of the history of age relations and examining, *inter alia*, mothering, childbirth, care of children in sickness, clothes, toys and pastimes, the regulation and socialization of children, education and religious preparation, the attention fathers pay to children in various social classes, and differences between the upbringing of sons and daughters. A particular focus has been the part played by various exclusions and specialized treatments in the constitution of 'the child', for example, by the law and social policy, via removal from employment and compulsory schooling, and children's relegation to separate parts of the house with specialized servants and activities. The history of childhood in the twentieth century is also starting to emerge via autobiography, oral history and general accounts. This material is itself being used in schools, where the social history of childhood has been added to the curriculum and undoubtedly engages children's interest. It is also used in popular sociology to support arguments that the situation of children could and should be changed. A notable instance of this is Jackson's account of *Childhood and Sexuality* (1982), which shows the cultural and historical relativism of the contemporary West's exclusion of children from the knowledge and practice of sex. She argues that adult anxieties do not protect children from sexual knowledge, nor do they preserve innocence. Rather they expose children (especially girls) to danger, teach them guilt, and create problems when 'sex education' has to be provided in schools. Work similarly arguing for children's rights has also been produced with a philosophical (Wringe, 1981) and jurisprudential (Freeman, 1983) perspective.

The first national conference on children's rights in England and Wales was held by the National Council for Civil Liberties (NCCL) in 1972 and a Children's Legal Centre was established in 1981 following the International Year of the Child. The Centre 'aims to promote recognition of children as individuals, participating fully in all decisions which affect their lives', and to this end produces briefing papers and reviews practice in such areas as children's rights when their parents separate; the restrictions placed on children in state care; corporal punishment; and children's rights when abuse is suspected. There are also related reflexive writings by lawyers and social workers on the civil and criminal law relating to children in England and Wales (for example, Geach and Szwed, 1983; Morris and Gillar, 1983; Hoggett, 1981); the assessment by social workers of children and their families; and the rights of the approximately 10,000 children in the care of local authorities and voluntary agencies. Children are a central concern of social administrators and those politically active around poverty and low pay. Rowntree recognized a 'cycle of poverty' at the turn of the century: the troughs families fall into when one adult has to leave the labour market to care for young or elderly dependents, and the burden of the costs of the dependents themselves (Rowntree, 1901). The pattern continues (see, for example, Rutter and Madge, 1976; Piachaud, 1981, 1982; Field, 1985). The result is a large minority of children growing up in poverty, and many children, an estimated 35 per cent of 11–12-year-olds, undertaking paid part-time employment, often illegally (Challis and Ellman, 1979; MacLennan, Fitz and Sullivan, 1985).

The increase in divorce rates since the war has increased concern for the welfare — psychological and economic — of children in 'one-parent-households'. An excellent government report (Finer, 1974) proposed changes in income and social support for all single parents, regardless of whether their situation was produced by 'illegitimacy', separation, divorce or death, but few changes have been implemented (Marsden, 1969; George and Wilding, 1972; Ferri, 1976; Wilkinson, 1981; Eekelaar and McLean, 1986). Although there is much concern about the effects of divorce on children, reliable information is sadly limited (Richards and Dyson, 1982). There are few studies of custody and access — only discussions illustrated with case materials, and people often use American material which may or not be applicable (cf. Murch, 1980). There is however a clear falling-off in children's contact with their non-custodial parent over time, especially if he (and it *is* generally the father) has new children with another partner. Some children, however, see more of their father after separation; and there is little or no correlation of behaviour before and after. We have even less research on the effects of step-parenting on children, and most of what there is is value-laden (Burgoyne and Clark, 1984). Those who investigate the development of children are usually wedded to a two-parent ideal and assume almost any step-parent is better than an 'absent role model'. Remarriage generally speeds the departure of the non-custodial parent, however, and seems to have a slightly negative effect on children. Certainly children seem to resist the change in their circumstances, given the number of popular books and articles on 'how to introduce your new partner'.

Work also remains to be done on drawing together material on children from existing work on the sociology of the family and local communities. Anthropologically influenced studies of particular communities (urban villages, small towns and rural areas) which were popular in Britain in the 1950s and 1960s have enjoyed a renaissance recently as a means of gaining insight into the effects of unemployment (Morris, 1984 and 1985). Children run in and out of these accounts and the texts still provide us with some of our best accounts of interrelations between households (i.e., neighbouring and kinship ties) and sub-cultural differences in child-rearing/socialization practices. But while a useful source, they are far from perfect. Again we find children as objects — for examples 'being baby sat' in a mutual interchange between neighbours — and we usually cannot distinguish which household members see which kin with what frequency, though we may hazard a guess that children see more of, or are in the houses of their grandparents, aunts and uncles, and certainly those of their cousins and neighbours, more than do/are adults. Some studies have made use of children's interaction or non-interaction (i.e., which children are allowed to play with which) as indicators of social boundaries (see, for example, Stacey, 1960). But it is much more common for researchers not to consider children and the links they build even when, for instance, discussing whether or not there is a 'decline of community' on working-class housing estates.

The sociology of the family has also seen a resurgence of interest and new work in the last fifteen years, but the development has been lop-sided. It has been almost exclusively concerned with gender: with marital relations and women's responsibility for childcare and the so-called 'community' care of the elderly, sick and disabled. While the tendency to interview only the wife when looking at marital relationships has been critiqued, the fact that only the mother/parent/caretaker/teacher is interviewed when looking at generational relations has passed largely unremarked. This is true even in areas where interviewing only parents is clearly likely to introduce bias, for example, the experience of parental remarriage, mothers' employment, the various forms of non-parental childcare, of fathers' involvement in childcare. Even in recent studies, children are not seen as social actors within the home and community. They are included in time-budget studies only as consumers of adults' time; and when researchers look at decision-making in households, children are beings *about* or *for* whom things are decided — always of course with their 'best interests' in mind. Nobody ever asks what domestic work children do: it is taken as given they do none or that what they do is negligible. Similarly their contributions to the household income is ignored. Even such welcome work as that of the Low Pay Unit on *Working Children* specifically excludes housework and babysitting, and does not tell us what the children's earnings are used for (cf. MacLennan, Fitz and Sullivan, 1985).

The influence of feminism in getting the internal structure and process of domestic and community relations back onto the research agenda is clear. Its emphasis on power, control, economics and social structures has been vital in areas which the dominant ideology (and many sociologists) present as voluntary and natural. But feminism has of course by and large concentrated this renaissance on *gender* relations. There are, however, important feminist writings — including some of the earliest writing in the second wave of feminism (notably by Millett, 1970; Delphy, 1970; and Firestone, 1972) — which not only present patriarchy as systematic oppression, but also as involving age as well as gender. (Firestone's chapter 'Down with childhood' still makes interesting reading). Christine Delphy's work is particularly important in this connection and can provide us with a starting point for a more strictly sociological, structural approach to the study of childhood. In *Close to Home* (1984), Delphy suggests that her work involves a joint concern for,

> firstly, the family in time: via the transmission of family property, i.e., with relations down the generations; and, secondly, the family in space: via women's oppression, i.e., with relations between spouses and between brothers and sisters.

She stresses the importance of the family as a non-market sector of the economy, underlining

> firstly, how much property changes hand through gifts and inheritance between family members, i.e., away from the market arena and under very difficult sets of relationships; and, secondly, how many goods and services continue to be produced in families.

Although much of what is produced within households is consumed within them, it is saleable: it *could* be sold. There is no difference of nature between household tasks and tasks done by waged labour; what differs are the relations of production within which familial work and waged work are performed.

The origins of Delphy's ideas lie in her research as a feminist rural sociologist. Studying farming in France from a woman's perspective clarified a number of important issues which, once recognized, could also be studied in non-farming and urban family households. Firstly, the agricultural sector spotlights the tie between occupational succession and inheritance. In farming virtually nobody becomes a farmer without inheriting land, or getting considerable parental help to purchase land. But farming also drew Delphy's attention to the fact that *the children within one family do not all inherit equally*, despite France's Napoleonic Code. In farming families, a farm is nearly always passed virtually intact to one son (usually the eldest, though the father can choose another as heir if he sees fit), supposedly to keep it as a viable unit. In some parts of France younger sons are helped as far as possible to establish themselves on new land or in occupations off the land; but in other parts, non-inheriting brothers stay at home, unmarried, and work for the brother who does inherit. Daughters never inherit land unless there are no sons. Instead they are given a dowry which is deemed to be of equal worth to what their brothers receive. However, it is different in kind and it does not allow them to exist autonomously. They need to marry. In other words, despite the presumption that all children in a family share the same class (or market) position, family farming shows they do not. This seems to be the case in other economic sectors as well. There is an ordinal and a gender hierarchy among inheritors, and the head of the household, the father, can exercise personal choice (preference) among children in the transmission of social, economic and cultural capital, inter vivos and on his death (see Delphy and Leonard, 1986).

Secondly, although in urban households most production for self-consumption is now done by the wife, on the peasant farms that existed in much of France until the 1960s, agricultural goods were produced not only by the farmer, but also by his wife *and by other relatives and his children*. This makes clear the duty of a wife and children to work for their household head without payment when he is able to use their labour, and to respect his authority. Such family workers are recognized and given a special title in the census (*aide familiale*) if they are adults, but working children are not enumerated. On this basis, Delphy has developed a theoretical formulation which stresses the structural *hierarchy* of family relations and the 'class' relations between genders and between generations. She has used the concept of a domestic mode of production to understand the relationship between husbands and wives, and also for the light it sheds on the conditions under which children and other relatives have escaped (some of) the obligation to do certain familial work — i.e., under which male adolescents and adults at least have gained the right to contract themselves (relatively freely) as waged workers.

Using class analysis to understand gender and generational relations is useful because it enables us to see the family, synchronically and diachronically, not in terms of individual choices or attitudes or roles, but as a social institution involving particular forms of labour relations. Shifts over time and differences and similarities between contexts (by class, region, gender), and the changing relationship between the family household and other institutions can then be looked at systematically. So too, and even more crucially because even more neglected, can the internal structure — the oppositions and oppressions — of the family-based household. The work I have been developing with Christine Delphy stresses mainly marital relations, but I should like to suggest here just a few of the questions such a structural approach raises about generational and sibling relationships (see also chapter 10 by Hood-Williams in this volume).

The Consequences of Smaller Family Size

The move over the last 100 years in all social classes towards having fewer children per married couple has tended to be considered mainly in relation to the effects it has had on women's health and their possibilities for labour market involvement. Fewer children mean mothers are not worn out by repeated pregnancies and will probably live longer; and there is now a period in wives' lives when they do not have responsibility for young children and can return to employment and supplement the family's income. The effects of smaller families are obviously much wider than this, however. The differential transmission of economic capital that Delphy noted among farm families in France was partly due to the form of property held (non-partible land), but also to the large average size of family. This meant that each child would inherit relatively little property if it were evenly divided. But if the form of property is different — say it consists of the largely cultural/educational capital of the professional middle-class sector — and if there are only two children in each family, then it may well be possible for the head of the family to make the necessary investment in one son to enable him to succeed to a position equal to or higher than that of his father, and for there still to be adequate capital to locate a second child at the same level. Further, if there are only girls in a family, as may well be the case if there are only one or two children, the same applies: one or both daughters can be the recipients of significant investments.

It is, however, an empirical question whether or to what extent parents (or grandparents) will spread their resources equally between children, or whether they will choose to concentrate them. We therefore need studies of the transmission of social, economic and cultural capital; and of the consequences of family size, sex ratio, and ordinal position in different socioeconomic groups. It is also worth reflecting that women's improved life expectancy and earlier child-bearing means that most will now live to see their grandchildren and great-grandchildren. Conversely, children will have many years of interaction with their grandparents and great-grandparents. However, in future generations, children are likely to have only one sibling and one aunt or uncle and few cousins. What are the consequences of these demographic changes going to be for children's experiences?

The Effects of the Father's Occupation

Our work on marriage has led us to stress the great variability of domestic life and particularly the organizing effect of the occupation (and personality) of the household head (i.e., usually the husband/father) on his family.

Studies of children have sometimes differentiated between their families in terms of socioeconomic groups (usually based on the census classification of the head of household's occupation, often then collapsed back into a simple distinction between 'middle' and 'working class'). By any criteria this is too crude. We stress, with Finch (1983), that in many occupations the wife (and children) are effectively married/tied to an occupation which affects most aspects of their lives. It determines not only their standard of living, but also their rhythms, patterns and place of living, and the tasks the wives and (maybe) children have to do. For example, the geographical location of their father's work may sometimes mean children live in an institutional setting — for example, on an army base, or in a foreign country (possibly moving frequently) if their father works for a multinational corporation. Their house may come with his job, as may their recreation facilities and social life, and his company may pay for their schooling. In such total institutional settings wives and children are subject to demands as to how they behave, and their status is defined vicariously — by their husband/father. If they have to move house frequently they may have constantly to make new friends and try 'to put down new roots'. If their father works from home or at home, children are even more affected. They may have to be quiet and behave nicely to visitors or accept their home being turned into the headquarters for a small business. Some fathers have jobs which colour their whole social personality — e.g., policemen, clergymen, and Members of Parliament, — and family members may find they have to be careful to whom they relate because of security and the importance of not establishing favouritism. Not only Caesar's wife, but also Caesar's children must be above suspicion. Some fathers are mentally 'at work' even when they are at home — and want peace and quiet; others want their wife and children to entertain them. Many are on shift-work or away from home for short or long periods of time. By the time all these occupations are added up, we are talking about the majority of children being influenced by their fathers' occupations.

Arguably mothers' employment also potentially structures children's lives. Certainly the general fact of whether or not a mother is employed, and whether full- or part-time, is what has attracted almost all sociologists' attention. But the effects on her children of the actual type of work a woman does has been virtually ignored. In practice we suspect a mother's job is not in fact likely to have much effect on members of her family (certainly it will have far less effect than the father's) since fewer 'women's jobs' have such marked repercussions, and also because it is required of a wife/mother that if she takes employment, she must ensure it has minimal effects on other family members. Paradoxically it is likely to be home-working, which is undertaken by women in order that they can remain at home to be available to their family, which is most likely to affect the family materially, since the house will be filled with sewing or other machines, raw materials and finished goods.

Children's Work

Wives frequently, but children probably less commonly, make a direct contribution to their husband/father's employment. Even quite young children can help in running a family business (for example, a market stall, shop, garage or a hotel). Quite a few children (see MacLennan, 1982) go out with their mother if she does cleaning or domestic work and some may help her (though possibly as many hinder her). Children certainly frequently act as 'back up workers' when parents work from home, taking phone messages, answering the door and pretending people are out if they do not want to be disturbed, serving coffee to visitors etc. And children have an important role in raising their father's social status by showing his normality (as a 'family man') and by undertaking appropriate activities in the community: dressing properly, being seen at appropriate venues doing the correct activities for their class and gender: 'proclaiming his good work through (their) own' (as Fowlkes (1980) says of US doctors' wives). Children also, girls more than boys, help with domestic work and with the care of other children. We lack any study, however, which can tell us just how much of what sorts of tasks they do from what ages. Studies of school absenteeism (Shaw, 1981) suggest it is not uncommon for young adolescents to stay at home to look after a sick family member or to let in tradesmen, and such duties may well start in pre-adolescence. Girls certainly do some baby-sitting from quite an early age. In terms of children's contributions to the household economy, we must also include, though we lack much evidence on, the paid work done by children (despite legal constraints on employment under 15 years). This may not produce much cash, but it does at least reduce the amounts parents have to find because their children provide their own pocket money (Wynn, 1972).

The 'work' required of most children today, however, is not that of contributing to their father's work, nor doing housework, nor undertaking paid work, but rather giving meaning to adults' lives. Most adults treat their home and the relationships and activities in it as central to their definition of self. Children are objectified as 'the reason' a father goes out to work and struggles to earn a living. Children prove their mother's femininity. Children provide a sense of immortality. Children must give their father and mother love, loyalty, obedience and moral support, hugs and kisses, and encouragement to take time off and relax. As Harris (1977) has commented, the increasing family-centredness of 'modern' families is in fact increasing *child*-centredness, which is sometimes suffocatingly restrictive for women *and* for children (see also Laing and Esterson, 1964; Laing, 1976). Like the 'idle middle-class wife' of the late nineteenth century, late twentieth century children exist to be enjoyed by adults and to appreciate the childhood that is being provided for them.

Differential Consumption

Delphy's theory also stresses that what is specific about the domestic mode is not only the relationships around work, but also the return dependents get for their work: their form of consumption. Wives and children do not get wages for their labour and obedience, they get maintenance and protection. They do not work for set hours at delimited tasks, they are on call and controlled twenty-four hours a day; and the upkeep that is provided for them is equally open-ended — it may be very good or very poor depending on the socioeconomic position of their household head and his personal willingness to pass goods on to them. Being maintained is very different from choosing what you want to buy with your own money in a market economy. It means children get what is deemed best for them, and they get very different things from adults — this being one of the ways in which childish status is marked out. The one area where we have good information on this is food (see Murcott, 1983; Charles and Kerr, 1987). Even what is supposedly children's free spending money, their 'pocket money', is controlled (see chapter 10 by Hood-Williams in this volume).

Children (like wives) resent this and do resist. Many altercations between children and parents occur about 'being bought' sweets or clothes or being taken to places they do not want to go to, or not allowed to go where they do want to go. If a child times things right (making a scene in the middle of the supermarket, or when its mother is busy or wants to chat to a friend on the phone, or when a pay-cheque has just been received), it may well be given an ice-cream or a new shirt or some other treat. But as other writers have shown (for example on adolescent males' use of the culture of masculinity or girls' use of feminine sexuality), this successful resistance is very two-edged because what the child wins merely reconfirms its childish location.

This view of family relations also leads us to ask about the meaning of 'leisure' for children. Leisure is a capitalist term: it is 'time which is not waged'. It is thus not applicable to married women or children. Children's work is continuous. They are never in control of their times and actions; they can be as constantly called upon to amuse their parents as any Victorian living-in domestic servant to perform a given task — or as summarily dismissed (to 'go and play' or to go to bed). Much of their lives is spend killing time and messing about.

Non-nuclear Families

Delphy's theory suggests we will understand family life best if we look at the changing work required of women and children (or to put it another way, if we focus upon the changing reasons for having a wife and children). How then does her approach explain the increased incidence of single parenthood and issues surrounding custody and 'care and control' after divorce?

Again I have to make the ritual call for further research, but there are among single parents (usually mothers) several distinct groups, of which I here identify just two. Firstly, there are women who have specifically chosen this course. They recognize the costs of marriage for women: the extra domestic work required; and that if women actually are among the minority who have high earnings, they are financially no better, possibly worse, off with a husband. Such women prefer to remain heads of their own household to ensure their hold on their children. Secondly, there are women who have become single parents involuntarily, by accidental pregnancy, desertion or divorce. They have often given up their pre-maternal market situation and have to rely on state benefits, help from kin, their own earnings, and a little child support from their former spouse. Clearly the situation of children in these two sorts of households is very different, in material standards and emotional stability, though they are often lumped together.

The point I want to make, however, is that Delphy's work suggests that in *either* case, husbands/fathers may continue to exercise rights to children, even when they do not live with and do not support the mother. 'Shared parenting', cohabitation and divorce do not constitute the end of the labour relationship of marriage, but rather its continuance in a different form (Delphy, 1976). Men may also (re)claim their children when they are older and need less physical care and attention. American work (Weitzman, 1985) has found that in the 1970s and early 1980s some men simply abandoned the children of one marriage if it ended, and had a new set with a new wife. This may have been an interim situation, following feminism's success in improving women's rights in marriages. Patriarchy may well be being 'reconstituted'. Men seem to be recouping feminism's own arguments: claiming equal (genetic) rights to children, and arguing that it is in the best interests of the children to maintain contact with two 'real' (biological) parents of opposite sex. Thus while for the first group of women identified above, it might seem that they are able to have children autonomously, in fact moves are afoot which will relocate them as much under the control of a man, with whom they do not live (via his access to their children), as has been the past experience of ex-married women.

Again, virtually all this work to date has looked at the changes from the *adult* perspective — at women's and men's concerns as they fight and continue to fight over money and access and custody. The experiences of *children* under these various different circumstances remain unexplored. One thing we can be sure of is that children of the same father, but resident in different households, do not share the same standard of living. The ones who live with him fare much better materially. Certainly the tensions of divided parenting are not being attentuated, and are not likely to be, given adult women's and men's changing reasons for, and mode of, having children.

Conclusion

This chapter began with the assertion that even in sociology, age is not treated as a social fact. Age relations are not socially defined, nor are the rules they follow, their codes and controls, formulated. Instead they are seen as, by and large, extra-socially determined and as the sum of individual children's (or elderly people's) activities, experiences and needs. (Or rather, in the case of children, their mothers' accounts of their activities, experiences and needs.) Childhood, youth and old age are not seen as defined in opposition to, by exclusion from 'adulthood'. Power relations between different age groups are therefore largely invisible because the relationships are seen as individual, complementary, and/or naturally based. Since this is very similar to the situation *vis-à-vis* the treatment of women and gender relations in sociology prior to 1970, it was suggested that feminist writing, which has developed the concept of patriarchy as a system of power relations, would form a useful resource for the sociology of childhood. The theoretical approach of the French feminist sociologist Christine Delphy to gender and generational relations within the family, focusing on changing work relations and economic hierarchy, was felt to be particularly fruitful. In this inevitably cursory account, I have suggested some of the insights Delphy's work offers into, for instance, the consequences (for younger sons and girls especially) of changes in family size and types of property, what men and women want from children (why they have them), differential consumption, and power relations in non-nuclear family situations. New empirical work, informed by this theoretical perspective, is now needed to enable a child-as-actor focus to develop within sociology.

Chapter 5

Growing Up in the 1980s: Changes in the Social Biography of Childhood in the FRG

Peter Büchner

Introduction

Sociological research into childhood, which would, for example, be comparable to the level of research into adolescence or the family, is only at its initial stages in West Germany. 'Sociological interest in children and childhood is still mainly influenced by the aspects concerning socialization theory. Childhood is interesting for its significance in the genesis of adulthood' (Kaufmann in Engelbert, 1986, p. 5). Childhood is seen as a transitional phase; only little attention is paid to childhood in its own right.

Since the German version of Ariès was published in the mid-1970s (the original in 1960), there has been a considerable upsurge in research into childhood, especially based on social history (for example, Weber-Kellermann, 1979b; Hardach-Pinke and Hardach, 1981; Schlumbohm, 1983). Nearly all the contributions in this field deal with the development of childhood. They describe the gradual process of acquisition of the status of childhood as a basic form of socialization and becoming socialized as well as childhood acting as an age-related part of life for shaping and training the new generation. Stimulated *inter alia* by the disappearance of childhood thesis (Postman, 1983), a new branch of West German research into childhood also deals with modern media and consumer childhood as an expression of changes in children's experiential worlds. These changes indicate an increasing approximation, perhaps a partial return to the characteristic features of *adult* life (for example, Bauer and Hengst, 1980; Hengst *et al.*, 1981; Hengst, 1985; Liegle, 1987).

Apart from individual, more or less detailed, studies about the life situation and the everyday lives of children (for example, Lang, 1985; Engelbert, 1986), contributions otherwise deal with specialized questions of research into childhood (for example, Doormann, 1979; Neumann, 1981; Specht and Weber, 1981; Zeiher, 1988). Usually, closely defined age divisions are important here: early childhood, the pre-school age group, primary school or late childhood or the transition to adolescence. A perspective directed towards childhood as a whole, as an important phase of the entire life course, is often not given sufficient attention. More often than not it is subordinated to the specialized approaches favoured by particular disciplines which deal with children and childhood: development psychology, education, psychanalysis, medicine, and so on.

Interdisciplinary approaches to analyzing childhood have emerged only in the last few years. These include, for example, a focus on 'Lebenswelt', i.e., socioecological approaches (Baacke, 1984), or work directed towards social policy for children (for example, Lüscher, 1979). Finally, since 1945 sociologists have attempted to investigate childhood from the point of view of changes in socialization conditions and of generational comparison (Preuss-Lausitz, 1983; Rolff and Zimmermann, 1985; Büchner, 1985; Jugendwerk, 1985; Fend, 1988).

Contemporary research into childhood in the FRG stands at the threshold of change. Honig (1988) refers to the erosion of a quasi presociological image of the 'nature of being a child'. Individual studies are increasingly considering the changing conditions under which children live and the changing social status of 'being a child'. These changes are interpreted in connection with individualization processes and their consequences for childhood in the family, in leisure, as a consumer or a subscriber to the media.

Parallel with the changing perspectives of youth research, there is also increased interest in children as *subjects* of the world they live in. This chapter takes up such perspectives by using the concept of the standardized biography ('*Normalbiographie*', Levy, 1977). I shall be describing noticeable and regular characteristics of the childhood life course in West Germany in the 1980s against the background of a transformation of children into adolescents. Just as recent writing (Bilden and Diezinger, 1988) has described male and female standard biographies as specific sequences of status role configurations, we can similarly specify historically specific configurations of the child life phase. Within this biographical perspective, the emphasis here is generally on the form of organization and recognizable ordering principles of the human life course, and especially on age-related life phases. Principally, it concerns the structural characteristics of current 'forms of childhood' (Fend, 1988), in terms of both their generation-specific realization as well as of their identity-giving effects.

However, what appears in generalized description to be a uniform course of development turns out to be in no way uniform on the ground.

On the contrary, it becomes an unsynchronized conflict-ridden and contradictory set of patterns (Zeiher, 1988). Thus, there are children and groups of children who, for example, are currently already absolving a 'modern' *Normalbiographie*, while others are enmeshed in considerable difficulties and resistances. Yet others (for example, many children of immigrants) are still growing up under traditional conditions. Nevertheless, a description of general tendencies is an important first step, even if general average findings for childhood can provide no more than a rough guide when referring to the childhood, for example, of factory workers' daughters or of sons of academics belonging to different age groups and living in different areas.

A description of changes in children's *Normalbiographie* further needs to take into account the continuities which still characterize childhood. Much of that which suggests change is in principle a reproduction of rules prescribed by society, or regularities expressed in age-specific behavioural patterns and expectations. Thus modern childhood remains located primarily in the family, despite changes in family structure and family life. The family still centrally shapes social lives. It remains the recognized form for parents and children to live together, even though the 'normal family' (especially in its restrictive form) is being gradually replaced by a whole host of family forms or other forms of living together like a family.

Modern childhood continues to be mainly (pre-)school childhood, that is to say it is part of the expected pattern of this life phase that 'growing' children have to complete a mass of development tasks as preparation for adulthood. Expectations presume that learning processes take place both inside and outside school. Finally, contemporary childhood continues to incorporate the concept of a 'leisured' childhood, increasingly differentiated out into consumer childhood, media childhood, and 'children's own' childhood (von Hentig, 1976).

The discussion which follows is a first step towards developing an understanding of the patterns of change in childhood *Normalbiographie*. Against the background of social structural changes, four selected aspects of the changing everyday and schooling lives of children are considered.

(i)   changes in 'growing up' in the family and relations between the generations;

(ii)   destandardization, biographization and individualization of the life course of children; shifting biographical points of orientation;

(iii)   changing space and time-related principles of orientation in children's *Normalbiographie*;

(iv)   the emergence of 'leisure careers' as illustrated by increased activities in sports clubs in children's day to day lives.

In conclusion, these changes in the childhood life phase will be discussed with reference to the role they play for processes of individualization and independence as these apply to children.

The Family and Intergenerational Relations

Childhood in the family remains important, but it takes place under very different conditions. For example, in West Germany there have been fewer and later marriages over the last twenty years, i.e., people are less likely to marry and marry later than formerly. The number of marriages has declined by a third between 1960 and 1982 (Grimm, 1985, p. 288). At the same time there is an increase in the number of divorces: 'We can expect 25 per cent of first-time marriages to be divorced again ... the willingness to remarry after divorce is also decreasing' (Langer, 1987, p. 165). A particularly important characteristic of modern family childhood is the fact that there is a marked decline in childbearing. More than half of current marriages are childless or have only one child, 35 per cent have two children, 10 per cent three children and only 3 per cent four or more children (*ibid*, p. 168).

Between 1970 and 1982 the proportion of two–parent families also dropped by 8 per cent, while that of single-parent families went up by 24 per cent to a total of 11 per cent of all families with children. Giesecke (1987, p. 10) speaks of a doubling over the same period of the proportion of all families with dependent children, and the tendency is still increasing. Additionally, 10 per cent of children born legitimately become 'divorce orphans' before they become of age; 6 per cent become real orphans through the death of one or both parents (Schwarz, 1984, p. 3). Apart from the rising proportion of cohabitation, childlessness and female employment, the trend to the one-child family is particularly important. Thus there is now a lesser likelihood that a child will grow up in a traditional complete family with siblings. One potential set of consequences might be termed as the loss of 'childlike' behaviour, a restriction of emotional relationships to those with parent(s) and decreasing opportunity for experiencing sibling relationships. 'Loneliness' of this kind can, under certain circumstances, have an effect on the child's ability to integrate or to make friends with children or with groups of children of the same age, resulting in a rising demand for the amount of social behaviour therapy (Grimm, 1985, p. 294). Clearly, under such conditions, the meaning of a 'family based childhood' within children's *Normalbiographie* must shift.

All this does not mean, however, that childhood is about to disappear as a life phase in its own right. The fundamental defining principle of childhood continues to be that of its *separation* from adulthood, as

Ariès so well described, even if in a somewhat modified form. Children today do become 'older' or go through the status passage from childhood to adolescence earlier: access to the adult world is available to them earlier. They may be also obliged to become self-dependent earlier insofar as parents and other adults find the consequences of childlike lack of self-dependence a nuisance or an inconvenience. This does not mean that children growing up at the moment reach maturity i.e., precociousness sooner. It is rather the case that fields of independence previously closed to children have now become available to them, allow them to act relatively freely outside school and relatively independently of the family as consumers, users of the media or leisure activities.

This accompanies a change in the relationship between the generations (Büchner, 1983; Fuchs and Zinnecker, 1985), which has an effect on the pattern of standard childhood biographies. The knowledge required for orientation, which is passed on in the family, competes at a relatively early stage with offers from outside the family. The stronger family influence regarding the biographical meaning of children's lives is, the more important the question of the effects of this 'detachment' on standard childhood biographies becomes. This is especially the case because the independence of children from parental care at an early biographical stage does not mean that children today grow up under less social control (Jugendwerk, 1985, p. 253). In fact, parents delegate areas of their socializing and educating competence to educational and other institutions. Parents are thus relieved of various duties in looking after and orientating their children, which also implies decreasing rights to watch over and sanction their children's activities.

These developments, which might be interpreted as a liberalization from parental upbringing, can equally be seen in terms of a new balance of social power and control. Effectively, they represent a redistribution of family and non-family spheres of influence on the course of children's lives (Büchner, 1985, p. 122ff). Since the seventies, children have had more room for manoeuvre, and this from an earlier age. The child's personality is now accorded more respect by the parents; authoritarian upbringing and the strict control of children's everyday lives are less common (Fuchs, 1983, p. 348f). Children have more freedom to make decisions about their own lives and they have greater possibilities for independence at an early stage. This is becoming a maxim of upbringing which is generally accepted and approved of, even if there may be slight differences according to the age, social status and education of the parent or guardian (Bargel, 1979).

The way parents (and other significant adults) and children interact with each other has become, in certain respects, more egalitarian; and this parallels a general trend towards an informalization of communication forms (Wouters, 1979). This means an easing of obligations, a certain degree of permissiveness of behaviour and a tendency to shift the balance of power in favour of children. Without fear of punishment, children can 'get away' with more, whereas parents and adults have to give more consideration to children's needs. However, a 'slackening of discipline' in patterns and styles of upbringing demands in its turn increased *self-discipline* (Elias would term this self-control). This requires 'biographical far-sightedness' at a relatively early age, if children wish to avoid losing status/prestige or competitive advantage. Children's increasing independence and expanding, novel play/activity opportunities both in the family and leisure time are not solely positive in their effects. We need to consider whether such changes in intergenerational relationships equally bring new and more subtle forms of social control in children's everyday lives.

The voluntary surrender (or loss) of responsibility and rights on the part of parents should be seen in connection with an increased reglementation of intra-family relationships between parents and children. Markers of such regulation include the orientation of laws on parental rights towards the principle of the *child's* welfare, supplemented by social legislation intended to support the family (income support, extended parental leave with state benefit, spouse and offspring maintenance payments, state guardianship provisions, etc.). Family policy is viewed ultimately in terms of helping and directing parents (or their substitutes) to provide the kind of socializing environment and 'product' socially required. In other words, the state has become the control agency for certain aspects of parent–child relationships.

Those activities and relationships which have been moved out of the family in no way *lack* supervision and control. Children are integrated into organized or institutionalized programmes of education or socialization, which might be termed 'modern leisure learning'. It is the ballet teacher, the sports trainer, the organizer of leisure activities and the social youth worker who fill the gaps that arise in upbringing and control. In addition, *impersonal* forms of social control based on situational requirements and bureaucratic regulations are possibly becoming much more significant. Such mechanisms are frequently not transparent to children, although they are affected by them in various ways; we need to study them more closely with reference to children's *Normalbiographie*.

Finally, there is the question of the pervasion of children's everyday life by media influences (for example, Bauer and Hengst, 1980; Hengst *et al.*, 1981). Without wishing to go into further detail here, such sources of information and orientation at least in part offer alternatives and potential challenges to parental guidance. If we can indeed argue that such developments contribute to an earlier acquisition of 'self'-consciousness by children, then it is plausible that parents, whether voluntarily or because they have little choice, are relinquishing traditional forms of authority relations.

The changes in intergenerational relations outlined here do not imply that the institutionalization of childhood as a special form of social organization is disintegrated, as suggested by Postman's thesis of the 'disappearance of childhood'. Rather a process of erosion in traditional life course patterns is taking place, one which centres on changing *relationships between* adulthood and childhood (or adolescence).

Destandardization, Biographization and Individualization

The way a generation lives is often described as being by and large biographically ordered. Programmes meant to run at a particular point on the age scale constitute a 'normal life course', in which biographical planning becomes an essential component of everyday life (Kohli, 1986a). This process of 'biographization of the life pattern' (Fuchs, 1983) has now encompassed the childhood phase. Social life courses become individual biographies.

The majority childhood *Normalbiographie* in contemporary West Germany is marked by changes in children's material living conditions and thus in socialization contexts, captured in the literature by the term *destandardization of the life course*, especially noticeable in the private sphere of family and gender relationships, partnerships and parenthood (Kohli, 1986b). Destandardization is accompanied by decreasing commitment/ attachment to the normative traditions of family life and leisure activities, and by a strengthened orientation towards values of self-realization as opposed to fulfilling obligations to others (Klages, 1984). Individualization processes thereby take root, offering new ordering perspectives for leading and planning one's life. The female *Normalbiographie* in particular is drifting away from the normative expectation of 'being there for others' towards claiming a piece of life for oneself (Beck-Gernsheim, 1983). Where mothers take this stance, daughters and sons cannot be other than in some way affected by that shift in orientation.

We can, with a degree of caution, suppose that the determining and orientating role of paid employment upon the course and style of people's lives has also changed — both for women and for men, if in different ways. Other sources and kinds of biographical orientation increasingly compete with 'work' in this sense (Kohli, 1986b). Thus, the biographical 'fixpoints' have shifted, and old familiar orientation points have lost their significance. The new dynamism in the childhood *Normalbiographie* stems from the fact that vital parts of the process of childhood socialization have becom detached from traditional social contexts and are controlled by 'market based opportunity structures (ibid).

Every child is increasingly expected to behave in an 'individualized' way, so that s/he will always be obliged to decide one way or another for a particular biographical variant. Children are thus expected to recognize and exploit these possibilities for choice; this implies that children must

somehow orient themselves to an *anticipated* life course. The more childhood in the family is eclipsed by influences and orientation patterns from
outside the family (school, leisure activities, media etc.), the more independent the opportunity (and drive) to making up one's own mind,
making one's own choice and taking one's own decision will become,
when deciding between alternative life courses or ways of life. This
development, described here as *biographization* of the life course, is one
element of a *destandardization* of the life course against the background of
plurality of forms and styles of life.

In this respect, the childhood *Normalbiographie* encompasses ever
greater areas of independence, which assume individuality and the ability
to plan, act and take decisions. Examples of such areas of independence
might include deciding individually what to buy, planning and managing
space and time, the selection and shaping of leisure 'careers', determining
media consumption patterns, displaying personal tastes, or choosing
appropriate modes of communication and social activities. School similarly requires the exercise of decision-making (for example, planning the
week's work, engaging in project-oriented learning, choosing options);
and schooling further presupposes an independence in establishing social
contacts. Thus, it would seem that on the whole there are fewer and
fewer compulsory components in the childhood *Normalbiographie*. In fact,
the structuring of age-stages over the life cycle as a whole is shifting, so
that, for example, there has been a marked narrowing of the status gap
between children, adolescents and adults. This is certainly connected with
the disintegration of clearly defined norms of orientation and behaviour
for particular age groups, so that it would be fair to say that childhood
and youth have gained a more autonomous position *vis-à-vis* other life
phases (Jugendwerk, 1985, p. 257ff). However, at the moment, we have
no appropriate empirical data for describing, in more detail, changes in
the life phase of childhood from a socially pre-determined status passage
to one marked by biographical independence.

Orientation Principles

Nevertheless, historically speaking, there are commonalities about childhood which are relevant for the *collective biography* of a generation. The
few, mainly ecologically-based, contributions to research on childhood in
this connection analyze children's shifting experiential worlds and corresponding changes in the way children acquire and experience space and
time (Becker *et al.*, 1984; Rabe-Kleberg and Zeiher, 1984; Berg-Laase *et
al.*, 1985; Harms *et al.*, 1985; Ledig *et al.*, 1987; Rauschenbach, 1988;
Zeiher, 1983 and 1988). Through their findings we can discern some of
the biographical pattern of contemporary childhood. Children's day-to-
day activities take place at spatially disparate locations making them more

dependent on transport and subject to stricter time discipline. The spaces in between rush past and are often perceived only superficially, with the result that a child's subjective map becomes a patchwork carpet consisting of islands of apparently unconnected space.

In contrast to the direction taken in some accounts, this group of studies tends to point to a greater division between child and adult worlds. So, for example, children are relegated to specially designated places for specialized activities because in the adult world they are considered as an irritation. It is not simply that children go to kindergarten and to schools, spending ever longer periods of time in education institutions as they grow up; the places 'for children' have multiplied — playgrounds, playschools, playgroups, formal and informal children's recreational and cultural programmes. All these social spaces have a specific purpose and are specialized for particular activities. Children tend to commute from one to the other, blowing their way through daily schedules — not only in school but also in extra-curricular activities, all of which entail going to specific places at specific times to do specific things. To absolve their schedules they require transportation, which usually involves depending upon adults to provide it. 'Taking possession' of a social space thus ensues under the protective accompaniment *and control* of adults. Road and traffic conditions force urban children away from playing in the street with the result that independent and unsupervised opportunities for social contacts are less available. Children's street world, formed relatively independently and composed of children from a variety of backgrounds and age-groups, is increasingly replaced by integration into various peer-group social sets, often chosen and supervised by parents for particular purposes and activities.

This breaking up, pre-structuring, specializing and organizing of spatial factors in the everyday life of a child has consequences. They come into contact with ever more people, and they do so in rapidly changing social situations, travelling across ever greater spaces increasingly frequently. Instead of having a few, more lasting, more manageable relationships (which are easier to cope with) children are now being confronted ever earlier with a large number of mainly brief, superficial and partial relationships. The frequent need to save time provokes, in addition, fragmented processes of learning and communication. These call norms of social behaviour into play which are generally applied to fleeting contexts — contexts are short-lasting and shallow and thus tend to be treated as 'disposable' relationships. A child no longer encounters another child as a whole person, but simply as the bearer of particular characteristics for a particular occasion, with the consequence that children may in fact spend considerable time together over a long period, yet never really get to know each other properly.

Participation in leisure activities becomes a matter of strict time discipline once the logistics of 'getting there' requires transport. Children must acquire early a competence for detailed planning of times, dates and arranging these with other people. Concomitantly, time spent waiting has to be bridged, spontaneous motives or sudden ideas are subordinated to the time schedule. A 'leisure timetable', held rather like an appointments diary, is essential if a child wants to take advantage of the activities and opportunities on offer and scattered around in space and time. The *pace* at which children (should) acquire skills and competences related to out-of-school leisure and sports activities is also increasingly redetermined and regulated by the specification of age-related norms of achievement. Just as these kinds of regulation construct children's school careers, they similarly construct children's *leisure* careers. The acceleration of the tempo of life that they thereby experience results in the feeling of *having no time* — a feeling which arises at ever earlier ages and which is experienced particularly by urban and by middle-class children. It is necessary to budget time exactly in order to participate as widely as possible in the range of leisure activities available; a great deal of self-control, flexibility and planning are required to coordinate time available and time required. In order to do 'everything at the right time' it becomes necessary to adopt adult concepts of time: this would corroborate the proposition that contemporary childhood is but a brief phase of life.

Preuss-Lausitz (1987) points out an important but little researched aspect of modern childhood in this connection: the discontinuities, contradictions and ambivalence which result from apparently increasing discrepancies between different fields of learning experience and the learning programmes they offer. So, for example, someone who is able, at a relatively early age, to make autonomous decisions about free time, personal purchases, pocket money, choice of friends or (later) initiating sexual relationships, will find it difficult to adopt the role of an immature schoolchild and to submit to the strictly ordered everyday routine of school life. When children display their unwillingness to accept these structures, teachers are inclined to refer to their cheekiness, insubordination — and perhaps suggest that they are socially disturbed.

Leisure Careers

It is 'failure' at school which has attracted the bulk of research attention, but failure to produce results in out-of-school activities may well have grown into a serious problem for children over the 1980s. Gaining status via educational achievement has lost some of its attraction in recent years: to become an 'educated person' is no longer an élite, but rather a universal goal. Using *leisure* activities as a new field for competition in this respect appears to have gained currency. The foundation of success in sport, music and performance/media must be laid earlier in life — just as young children are exposed to risk of failure as a consequence of entering the competition. Once again, decisions to 'go for gold' must be made very early in life; those children who take on the ambition to reach the top find their leisure appointments diary correspondingly packed.

The underlying philosophy which accompanies the provision of musical, artistic and sports activities positions these as neutral practices with manifold possibilities to develop character and physical training. Bourdieu accurately highlights the ideological underpinnings at work in the case of sport, in which classed subjects seek and acquire 'correct' perspectives on the body. To this extent, both active and passive participation in sport have a very different significance for different people and groups.

> Where for one person, visible athletic muscles are most important, others look more for elegance, gracefulness and beauty; where one person is concerned with health, others are looking for mental equilibrium etc. In other words: the class-specific division of sports practices is not only based on the distribution of the necessary means to cover their financial and cultural costs; at the same time they show a different perception and evaluation of the individual practices and their short and long term advantages. (Bourdieu, 1985, p. 586)

Cycling, ballgames and swimming are long-established leisure-sport activities for children, both with each other and with their parents. In West Germany, sport has traditionally held a favoured position in pupils' subject preferences, and it continues to do so (Aster and Kuckartz, 1988). At the same time, for the under-14s age group both boys' *and* girls' participation in organized sports clubs has risen dramatically since the mid-seventies. The trend for girls, especially those under 6 years of age, is very marked (Sack, 1980).

Children's distribution across the range of sports activities offered by clubs has also become more *differentiated*. The most popular remain, for the boys, football, for the girls, gymnastics; but *relatively* speaking these are less popular than they used to be. The same holds for handball, light athletics and swimming, whereas table tennis, tennis, judo, skiing and riding are growth areas. In the fifties, 90 per cent of the sports club child members were actively involved in three to seven different sports; in the eighties, 90 per cent of such children participate in eight to eleven different kinds of activities (ibid). The trends towards increased childhood involvement in sports applies both to urban and rural communities, though class differences remain. Middle-and upper-class children are overrepresented in nearly every kind of sport with the exception of football (ibid).

The rapid development of competitive sport and the efforts made by sports clubs to expand membership amongst children and young people, then to draw them into highly competitive, selective and systematic training programmes is quite remarkable. The recognized 'breed' of 'gym grannies' illustrates the servicing and supervisory functions allocated to, or taken on by, family members in this high powered context. Just why it is that sports clubs have become so attractive to children is, as yet, unclear. Sack (ibid) suggests that three factors are involved: firstly, the increasing value placed on competitiveness *per se* inside and outside school; secondly, the 'compression' of childhood has led to sports clubs and their activities taking over the social space of former 'streetlife' in children's worlds and cultures; thirdly, children have come to *identify* with successful competitive sports personalities, a process encouraged by intensified practices of talent scouting.

Sack's arguments are plausible, but ultimately unsatisfactory in comparison with the distinctive approach supplied by Bourdieu, which illustrates more clearly how the field of out-of-school learning has developed, alongside school, as a *decisive* competitive field for cultural and social capital. What we are observing is an aspect of a largely *individualized* form, of the acquisition of habitus (type of disposition) through leisure careers, which can only be indirectly influenced by the family of origin.

It may well be that choices between sports clubs are made largely in accordance with a logic of distinction drawn from family biography or the desire to set oneself 'apart'. Once established, however, a child's 'sports career' encourages exactly those kinds of trends towards autonomy and independence that are fostered in children's leisure time activities in general. The sports trainer, for example, takes on a recognized authority position, one which has direct biographical relevance for the child concerned. The values and norms encountered in other spheres of action might thereby find support — but equally disqualification and negation. Which values and norms ultimately gain the upper hand depends on the comprehensiveness and intensity of significance attached to the field.

Outlook

The most prominent changing feature of children's *Normalbiographie* is probably their earlier acquisition of independence across an ever wider range of fields, a trend connected with the individualization of life situations, life styles and thus life courses. Close family ties and the direct control of children's everyday life through the parental home, are being replaced by children's activities *outside* the family and by an increased orientation towards peer groups. What the shifting effects of the various socialization agencies (family, school, leisure, activities, media etc.) are likely to be is unknown, but certainly intergenerational relations have changed both in fact and in consciousness. The result has been an increase in 'self' confidence for more and younger children, especially since adults no longer consistently or universally insist on traditional authority relations with their children.

Whether relative independence from parents equally means autonomy in the sense of enlightenment is another question. Achieving a form of autonomy free from parental control largely takes place on the consumer market; in other words, under framing conditions defined beyond the familial sphere. Childhood autonomy needs to be explored within the context of the structure of dependency in which it paradoxically develops. Hence the 'emancipation' of children's *Normalbiographie* is highly ambivalent and contradictory in nature. An earlier (if partial) release from immediate parental control, access to material and cultural resources independent of parental influence, and an early formed desire for autonomy *can* overburden. This is particularly likely to be the case where children have had insufficient opportunity to exercise preferences, choices and decision-making options in low risk contexts.

These potential problems surface in the statistics on rates of social disturbance or psychological imbalance amongst children, which for the FRG suggest one child in five to display such symptoms. Only children in particular are vulnerable in this respect, a consequence of their lesser opportunities for contact with children around their own age. Official social work agencies register rising rates of disturbance and imbalance, together with increasing numbers of children seeking assistance with school-related problems. The question of the effects of high rates of television and video viewing together with the popularity of computer games has begun to attract considerable attention too (cf. *Frankfurter Rundschau*, 10 February 1988). We might then rather speak of children's *helplessness-in-independence*, left to themselves but themselves unable to deal with the uncontrollable tides of everyday life.

Nevertheless, this independence or *individualization* of childhood is in keeping with the times. Rauschenbach defines independence-autonomy as a kind of 'turning point' containing both opportunities and dangers for the *Normalbiographie* of childhood. On the one hand, it holds the promise of hope of a 'new person' as a desired goal as expressed through the playgroup movement or discussion about alternative independent schools.

> Non-interference from above, by teachers and parents becomes an educational principle, which should facilitate the potential for becoming 'different'. Fundamentally, if children regulate themselves, they can develop a 'social capital' which allows the mutual recognition of differing needs and personal activities. The aim of self-regulation is the creation of a common spirit which facilitates individual freedom. (Rauschenbach, 1988, p. 5ff)

A child who is encouraged to be independent-autonomous but who is given no experiences and resources to cope with this, i.e., s/he has escaped from direct adult control and can do what s/he wants, is not automatically self-dependent in this sense. To avoid confronting the constraints enjoined by becoming an adult effectively means an un-reflected acceptance of the social frameworks of action. Where this dilemma remains unacknowledged, biographical patterns founded upon indepen-dence-autonomy and individualization hold no more than the *possibility* for change: such concepts promise freedom, but they cannot deliver it. In this context, freedom runs into the danger of a normative definition as a freedom only of, and for, the strong.

Chapter 6

Schooling and Economic Life in the UK

Phillip Brown

Introduction

In the last decade there have been major changes in the way young people make the transition from school. In the 1950s and 1960s sociologists were primarily concerned with the transition from 'school to work' based on the assumption that the vast majority of school-leavers would find employment. Since the late 1970s this transition is achieved by a minority of school-leavers in many parts of the UK, whilst the majority now enter government-sponsored Youth Training Schemes (YTS).[1]

The extent of these changes is registered in table 6.1 which shows that in 1975 over 60 per cent of 16-year-olds in England and Wales left school and found employment. But by 1986 only 19 per cent found work and 45 per cent of 16-year-olds remained in full-time education.[2] Over a quarter of all 16-year-olds are now on a YTS and this proportion is likely to increase because school-leavers who refuse a YTS will no longer be able to claim financial support from the state until they are 18 years of age. Although the projected decline in the number of school-leavers, which will result in a third fewer young people looking for work by the mid-1990s, should to some extent, alleviate the competition for jobs which is currently experienced in making the transition into the labour market.[3]

Table 6.1 Educational and Economic Activities of 16-year-olds

	1975	1986
Full-time education	37	45
Government schemes (YTS)	—	26
Unemployed	2	10
In employment	61	19

The purpose of this chapter is to consider the *educational* impact of this 'economic thunder', especially on pupil responses to school. The changing relationship between education and the labour market, coupled with a significant shift towards the political Right in the UK, has had a profound impact on the educational system (Brown, 1989 and 1990). Along with other Western capitalist democracies, the 'products' of schooling have been defined as defective in terms of the stated 'needs' of employers. The official debate about youth unemployment has focused on the problems believed to be rooted in the school rather than the labour market. As a consequence, the government has opted for 'vocational' solutions. This 'new vocationalism' (Bates *et al.*, 1984; Ranson *et al.*, 1986) has involved an attempt to make compulsory schooling of more direct relevance to the future economic roles of pupils. However, in the UK it can be argued that vocational education has been aimed at the working class, and has left the overtly academic curriculum of the middle class unaltered (Brown, 1987; Chitty 1987). In the OECD report *Education in Modern Society* (1985) it was noted that:

> The essentially moral — and certainly ambitious — objective that each child should be educated to the limitations of his or her ability appears to have survived the economic thunder. (p. 11)

However, in the UK the attack on the comprehensive school for failing to meet the needs of industry has been part of a broader debate about the relative merits of selective versus comprehensive education; and a state monopoly of education versus a privatized system organized on the principles of the free-market. The Thatcher government has already introduced the Education Reform Act which includes the centralized control of the curriculum and provision to break up local state systems of comprehensive education, and an increase in the use of private schools (see Simon, 1988).

The specific nature and consequences of what I have called the 'ideology of parentocracy' — that is, where the education a child receives must conform to the wealth and wishes of parents, rather than the abilities and efforts of pupils in open competition — cannot be detailed in this chapter, but it will have an important impact on the future organization and experience of schooling in the UK (Brown, 1990).

With respect to pupil responses to school, it is the massive increase in youth unemployment over the last decade which is having a more immediate impact. As Watts (1978) has argued, although unemployment is not an educational problem, it is a problem *for* education. It is a problem for education because the majority of pupils in secondary schools adopt *instrumental* attitudes to school (Fuller, 1983; Brown, 1987). Therefore one would expect unemployment to threaten the foundations of pupil compliance.

An important part of this chapter will therefore involve an examination of the nature of pupil responses to school, and the consequences of unemployment. I will argue that there are variations in working class educational experiences which need to be explained in order to understand the impact of economic restructuring and unemployment. It will also be suggested that these variations in pupil responses cannot be interpreted solely in *structural* or *cultural* terms, which have dominated sociological explanations of working class responses. Pupil responses must be studied in terms of an interplay between institutional and cultural processes (Abrams, 1982).

In the conclusion I examine the consequences of social, economic and educational change in the way pupils will experience their schooling in the future. Obviously, any account of the consequences of such changes remain tentative, but it will be suggested that recent changes occurring outside of the school have resulted in cultural and generational discontinuity between working class children and their parents. The occupational and educational ambitions which parents have for their children, and the stock of cultural knowledge which parents previously passed on to their children, reflect past processes rather than the present experiences of large numbers of working class youth. Moreover, in many parts of the UK, the division between the rough and the respectable working class is now based on a division between the employed and the unemployed rather than a division between those in skilled (and apprenticed) jobs as opposed to semi- and unskilled employment.

It will also be suggested that there is a broad social class difference in educational responses to recent economic change, and that recent educational reforms in the UK will intensify the classroom crisis in many working class neighbourhoods, and reinforce (if not extend) existing educational and social inequalities. Hence, divisions on the bases of social class, gender and race remain of central importance to understanding schooling and the transition into the labour market. The individualization thesis adopted by Beck (see chapter 9 in this volume by Jones and Wallace) must therefore be questioned in the context of the UK.

Explaining Working Class Responses to School

In Britain the relationship between education and social class has been a central problem within the sociology of education. The continuing class differences in educational achievement has, at least until recently (Brown, 1988), perpetuated the search for causes and explanations of how working class pupils respond to their schooling given that most will enter mundane jobs offering little opportunity for career advancement. It is possibly this preoccupation which helps us to understand the extremely narrow focus of much of the research concerned with pupil experiences of schooling in the UK.

Explanations of pupil responses have been dominated by accounts of the working class, white male, anti-school sub-culture (Hargreaves, 1979; Fuller, 1983). Hammersley and Turner (1980) note that there are two plausible reasons for the relative absence of studies of other pupils' responses. The first is already noted, due to the overwhelming concern in the sociology of education since 1945 with the explanations of failure at school, and particularly the failure of working class pupils. The second is due to the fact that researchers have tuned into teacher preoccupations with problems of classroom control (p. 29).

A third reason why the male anti-school sub-culture has continued to receive so much attention, is due to the publication of Willis' (1977) book *Learning to Labour* which has ascribed considerable political significance to the school resisters, because their resistance to school has been interpreted (in my opinion incorrectly), as a rejection of capitalism, and therefore a potential source of social and educational change (Arnot and Whitty, 1982; Hargreaves, 1982).

This preoccupation with the deviant male pupil, has meant that there are few studies of other working class responses, because it has been assumed that if pupils do not reject the school then they must conform to it. Moreover, with few exceptions the educational responses of middle class youth and their transition into the labour market has been ignored (see Wakeford, 1969; Walford, 1986; Aggleton, 1987). The assumption that all pupils who do not reject the school must inevitably conform to it, has correctly been challenged by a number of symbolic interactionists (Woods, 1983; Hammersley and Turner, 1980; Turner, 1983). However, the problem with the interactionist accounts is that by focussing on the process of meaning construction within the school as an interactional context, they have failed to advance our understanding of why pupils respond to the school in the way they do, and why these responses are rarely arbitrary, but patterned, particularly on the basis of social class and gender.

Indeed, the major strength of the bi-polar model of a pro- and anti-school response — as elaborated by Hargreaves (1967), Lacey (1970) and Ball (1981), on the one hand, and Willis (1977) and Corrigan (1979) on the other — is that despite obvious limitations they do offer an explanation of why pupils develop the responses they do.

The problem with what sociologists in the UK have told us about the way working class pupils respond to the school, however, is not confined to its descriptive plausibility, but also to its conceptual power. On the basis of a study I conducted of 'ordinary kids' in industrial South Wales, it was not only untenable to describe working class responses in terms of a bi-polar model, but conceptually it seemed evident that when you take seriously variations in working class responses, it becomes apparent that the educational system does not simply 'fail' pupils from a working class background, nor do these pupils simply 'fail themselves' either individually or collectively.

Working class educational behaviour and attainment is best understood as an interplay between class culture understood as a set of resources which give rise to different ways of being in school and becoming adult among working class youth on the one hand, and the organization and selection processes of the school on the other. It is this interrelationship which holds the key to explaining the patterning and variations in working class responses to school. It is therefore necessary to reject as one-sided, any account which is based on either the process of *educational* or *cultural* differentiation.

Explanations based on the process of educational differentiation (which have dominated the sociology of education), view the school as a sifting and sorting mechanism which, given existing inequalities in the selection process, ensures that pupils from middle and working class backgrounds arrive at educational and occupational destinations appropriate to their class membership. The development of pro- and anti-school subcultures, among pupils who share a similar social background is also seen to result from the way pupils are channelled into different streams within the school, and treated differently by teachers depending upon their position in the scholastic hierarchy. Therefore the polarization of pupil subcultures is regarded to be the direct result of the hierarchical ordering of pupils which the adolescent understands to represent a corresponding hierarchy of social worth. Within such a regime Hargreaves (1967) argues that pupils in the lower streams experience failure and rejection, for which the anti-school subculture offers compensation:

> When the school system is viewed in the setting of societal values, the upper stream members are 'successful' and their efforts and values are rewarded by the status they derive. The low stream boys are 'failures'; they are status deprived both in school and in society; their efforts meet with little success. Their problem of adjustment is solved by rejection of societal and teacher values, for which are substituted a set of peer group values, and status derived from conformity to a reversal of societal and teacher values. (p. 176)

Explanations based on the process of educational differentiation, which come in both the Marxist and non-Marxist variety, have also described the development of occupational identities in much the same way. As a consequence of the schools' sifting, sorting and labelling processes pupils develop educational and occupational aspirations which correspond to their location in the academic order and projected location in the labour market. Therefore, the school not only ensures that working class pupils will be the least-qualified school leavers but also that by the time they leave school they have adapted preferences and expectations to a life in working class jobs:

> The educational system helps integrate youth into the economic system . . . through a structural correspondence between its social relations and those of production. The structure of social relations in education not only inures the student to the discipline of the work place, but develops the types of personal demeanour, modes of self-presentation, self-image, and social-class identification which are the crucial ingredients of job adequacy. (Bowles and Gintis 1976, p. 131)

Alternatively, there are a number of writers who have challenged this orthodoxy, and have attempted to explain working class educational and labour market experiences in terms of class cultural differences in attitudes and aspirations. Explanations couched in terms of a process of cultural differentiation correctly emphasize cultural differences in the demand for education and in the definition of desirable occupational goals. For example, in *Learning to Labour* Willis argues that the difficult thing to explain about how working class kids get working class jobs is not how the school allocates working class pupils to the lower bands, but why these pupils voluntarily 'fail' themselves. Rather than attempt to explain educational failure in terms of the available means to succeed within the school, Willis views middle and working class pupils as already culturally distinct. What happens in the school is simply an expression of cultural differences originating outside it. Working class pupils do not evaluate their relationship with the school in terms of what the school might offer given their location in the academic order, but in terms of the consequence of academic success for being a working class adult as understood in their 'parent' culture (Hall *et al.*, 1976). It is the class cultural definition of a future in manual labour offering little intrinsic reward, he argues, which leads to the basic exchanges on offer within the school to be rejected. Despite recognizing class culture as important for understanding pupil responses to school and the transition into the labour market, a major difficulty with cultural explanations such as Willis' is how to explain why large numbers of working class pupils do not develop an anti-school sub-culture. The difficulty results from a characterization of middle and working class pupils as culturally distinct, and the assumption that the development of pro- and anti-school sub-cultures is a manifestation of these cultural differences. This leads Willis to understand the counter-school sub-culture as the normal working class response to the school. And it is because the counter-school culture is assumed to be the normal working class response that he is led to lump together other responses as conformist, and to an explanation of the working class conformists (ear'oles) in terms of the school's success in ideologically incorporating these pupils into bourgeois modes of thought. However, the range of working class responses cannot be explained simply in terms of working class culture because pupil responses will, at least in part, reflect a selection from that culture, unless we regress to a form of explanation which relies on differences in working class family 'types' (Carter, 1966; Ashton and Field, 1976) or, like Willis, condemn the majority of working class pupils to the status of ideological dupes as the price for celebrating 'the lads' as cultural heroes.

Indeed, not all working class pupils do fail academically. Some do go on to higher education and into the professions. Moreover, even among those who do not escape the working class, there are major differences in response to the school and labour market (Ashton and Field, 1976; Jenkins, 1983). The fact that a large proportion of pupils from a working class background may 'make an effort' in school whilst at the same time not harbour ambitions beyond those of their neighbours, or conform to the dictates of teachers, has remained largely beyond sociological comprehension. However, if we are to adequately understand the impact of unemployment on the school, it is necessary to recognize that certain forms of pupil compliance are as much an authentic working class response to the school, as is one which leads to its rejection.

A further weakness of sociological accounts of working class experiences of schooling has been, at least until recently, the absence of studies which have examined the interrelationship between gender and social class. In the UK a plethora of recent studies have shown how girls are disadvantaged in the educational process. They have been shown to be channelled into low status subject areas; find themselves disadvantaged in the labour market because they have poor or inappropriate qualifications; and find themselves subject to employer discrimination. The vast majority of the literature concerned with gender divisions in the school has also found that girls tend to have a more favourable attitude to school; are willing to remain in full-time education beyond the compulsory school leaving age; and have as strong a commitment to finding a job when they leave school as do boys. But as Davies (1984) has noted, although girls appeared more compliant in general, when difficult, it is the girls rather than the boys who present more problems to teachers (p. 56).

There is evidence of a bi-polar model among female pupils, although this may not lead to the development of a conspicuous anti-school subculture, because they are guided by a code of femininity (Woods, 1983; Ball, 1981; Llewellyn, 1980). Nevertheless the study of female responses to school has challenged the belief that if pupils 'make an effort' in school they must be conformist. Lees (1986), for example, found that some of the girls in her study were pro-learning but not pro-school, which she argued was the result of the sexist attitudes of teachers and male pupils. On the issue of value orientations towards education it has usually been assumed that girls are less instrumental in their orientations to school than boys. This was certainly found to be the case in one of the early studies

Figure 6.1   Value Orientations Towards Education

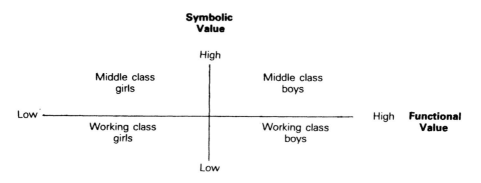

which examined the relationship between social class and gender (King, 1971).

King distinguished between the 'symbolic value' of education where it was valued as an indicator of social status, and the 'functional value', in which it was valued as a means of finding desired employment. On the basis of the four-fold typology shown in figure 6.1, King concluded that girls from both a middle class and a working class background, were less instrumental in their attitudes to school than boys. More recent evidence, however, leads to the conclusion that *instrumental* responses to school are no longer the preserve of boys, and this may well reflect the increasing involvement of women in the labour market, and the increasing import-ance of occupational as opposed to domestic identity (of wife and mother) (Gaskell, 1987; Lees 1986). Fuller (1983) has found, for example, that both Afro-Caribbean and Asian girls had instrumental attitudes:

> They had an instrumental orientation to education, believing that it could offer them something useful (paper qualifications) in their longer term efforts to obtain a measure of control over their lives. So long as it was providing those opportunities they were pre-pared to conform minimally within the classroom and maximally in terms of doing the work that was set. (p. 177)

The problem with a lot of the research concerning pupil responses to school and the transition into the labour market is that it has so far failed to show the interrelationship between social class and gender. The argu-ment I want to develop here is that, despite important differences in the way male and female pupils experience their schooling, in terms of their relationships with teachers, the subjects they study, etc., there are impor-tant *similarities* in the way girls and boys from different social back-grounds respond to the school, particularly in the nature of their *instrumental* attitudes to school (see also Gaskell, 1987).

The Middleport Study

The Middleport study of schooling and unemployment was based on data collected from three co-educational comprehensive schools, two in working class catchment areas, and the third in a middle class area.[4] The conclusion of this study was that pupil responses to school were closely related to future occupational aspirations, and were primarily *instrumental*. In other words, their reasons for 'making an effort' in school depended upon the school's perceived value as a distributor of credentials which would open doors to desired occupations. Yet in the Middleport study although the dominant response to school was of an instrumental nature, regardless of social class background or gender, it was equally clear that the dominant form of instrumentalism was different among working and middle class pupils. Among the middle class pupils we found a 'normative instrumental' orientation. This type of instrumentalism was 'normative' because the pursuit of qualifications was accompanied by a degree of intrinsic interest in some of the academic elements of the school curriculum. For them what was learnt at school, even if it did not directly relate to their occupational interests, was viewed as a necessary prelude to the acquisition of knowledge which was both 'required' and 'desired'. It is this characteristic of their future employment which acted to bring these pupils closer to the normative aspects of the formal culture of the school.

Among the working class pupils an 'alienated instrumental' orientation was the dominant response. Their instrumentalism can be regarded as 'alienated' because their involvement in the formal context of schooling was fairly limited. They did not identify with the school's perceived aims, with what teachers 'stand for', or the majority of what was taught in classroom lessons. The only elements of interest and perceived 'relevance' that did exist for them were on the practical rather than the academic side of the curriculum, which were assigned a lower priority and status by the vast majority of teachers:

Jane: Well, I suppose maths in some ways, but all this Pythagoras and all that jazz, I don't think that's worth it, you know. I used to be alright in maths when I used to work. I used to do loads of things then, count loads of votes up, but all the rest then, I think it's dull. As long as you can count and take away and divide and times, you know.

Mark: History, with history now, say somebody wants to be a motor mechanic say, I can't see where history comes into it, you know, I can't really see what history has got to do with school, you know ... with learnin', 'cos history is ... it ... deals with the past.

These 'ordinary' working class pupils 'made an effort' because they believed that modest levels of endeavour and attainment (usually leading to practical rather than academic qualifications) would help them 'get on' in working class terms (see below). Hence, these pupils were less attuned to the formal culture of the school since the types of employment they aspired to were perceived to be 'practically' based. It was this character-istic of their future employment which acted to alienate these pupils from much of which was taught in school, and led them to question the overly academic curriculum which paid scant attention to the individual's ability to *do* the job. The alienated instrumentalism of the ordinary kids also helps us to understand why these pupils have had little reason to stay in full-time education beyond the compulsory school-leaving age. Their occupational aspirations, at least until recently, have largely been met without the need for academic success.

The Impact of Unemployment

The collapse of job opportunities for school-leavers in the early 1980s has had a serious impact on pupil responses to school. This is particularly true of those pupils with an instrumental orientation. Nevertheless, it would appear that unemployment is affecting working and middle class re-sponses in different ways. Among middle class pupils whose instrumental orientation is likely to be 'normative', unemployment appeared to have led them to attach an even greater instrumental importance to school work. Getting qualifications had become more, rather than less, impor-tant as more and more school-leavers chased fewer jobs. Access to higher education is also perceived to have become more competitive, therefore getting the best possible examination results appeared to be the best insurance policy for the future, no matter what:

> *Jane*: It's hard enough to get a job as it is, there's no point in not
> getting qualifications, because you think you're not goin' to get
> a job. You got to, um try hard ... there's so much competi-
> tion you've just got to do the best you can, you have got a
> chance then ... to get a job or go to university.

The impact of unemployment on working class pupils, who were more likely to adopt an alienated instrumental orientation, has proved to be far more worrying for the school. Whereas they were previously willing to 'make an effort' in order to 'get on' in working class terms, they have increasingly questioned the school's value and purpose, as the jobs many of them want have all but vanished. Moreover, because the academic curriculum held little interest or relevance for the ordinary kids, teachers have found it difficult to encourage pupils to work in school for intrinsic reasons:

> *Amy*: All the teachers are the same, they say 'oh you should get
> this, you could pass in this', but they're no good to you, when

you're leaving. I don't see the point in havin' 'em ... people these days have got qualifications but they still haven't got jobs.

The teachers I spoke to in Middleport also acknowledged that most of what is taught in comprehensive schools has always been irrelevant to the future lives of working-class school-leavers. However, despite considerable bouts of boredom, low levels of academic endeavour and attainment exhibited by the ordinary kids, and a sense of futility among many of the school staff, teachers were able and willing to justify what they were doing on the grounds that modest levels of academic achievement appeared to provide access to the sorts of jobs their pupils wanted. This rationale for a far from satisfactory situation can no longer be sustained, and the realization of this fact is seriously affecting teachers' morale, and forcing them to find new ways of justifying their day-to-day practices both to themselves and to their pupils (Brown, 1987). The conclusion of the Middleport study cannot, however, be read as offering evidence of the total collapse of working class compliance in the school. Their instrumentalism was not solely based on a rational model of opportunity-cost. Their willingness of 'making an effort' also had a moral dimension, which provided them with a sense of dignity and self-respect. Although a discussion of this argument takes us beyond the scope of this chapter, it does need to be noted that considerable peer-group pressure was exerted among the ordinary kids not to give up completely, because a refusal to 'make an effort' was the basis of their condemnation of the Rems (non-examination pupils).

Towards a Conceptual Model

What this study clearly illustrates is the inadequacy of bi-polar models of pro- and anti-school working class responses, because it ignores the alienated instrumentalism of 'ordinary' working class pupils as they approach the end of compulsory schooling.[5] It is also important not to lose sight of the fact that some working class pupils do develop 'normative instrumental' attitudes, and in a small minority of cases a 'normative' orientation, which involved a response to school as an end in itself rather than as a means to obtaining certification. Figure 6.2 presents a typology of working class responses to school.

This typology is intended to show the relationship between pupil orientations to the formal culture of the school, the way in which these different orientations are associated with different ways of 'being' a working class pupil within the informal pupil culture, and finally the interrelationship between pupil and social identities which I will examine in terms of pupil Frames of Reference (FORs).[6]

Figure 6.2   Working Class Responses to School

Orientation to school	Alienated	Alienated instrumental	Normative/ normative instrumental
Location in the pupil culture	Rems	Ordinary kids	Swots
Frame of reference (FOR)	Getting in	Getting on	Getting out

The reason for introducing the notion of pupil FORs is to enable a conceptual link to be made between pupil identity and wider meaning structures which are class specific. FORs are class specific because they represent the 'typical' ways in which working-class pupils from Middleport construct and assign meaning to different ways of being in school and becoming adult. Therefore, although the moral careers of pupils are lived by individuals they are at the same time the typical destinies of members of collectivities (Abrams, 1982, p. 282). Thinking in terms of FORs therefore provides a conceptual link between pupil and social identity. It enables us to examine variations in working class responses to school without losing sight of the fact that the way working class pupils behave in school is the result of an interplay between the class cultural resources which are deployed in school, and internal school processes. It is also useful because it conveys the idea that FORs are not only constructed on the basis of past experience, but also include a projection into the future which provides the individual with a sense of continuity, predictability and meaning during a time of considerable uncertainty as they seek to make the transition from childhood to adulthood. During the final stages of schooling it is occupational identity which lies at the heart of the individual's lifeline between childhood and adulthood. This is not to suggest that all school-leavers have a clear idea of what job they want, but they are aware of the sort of jobs they would like and which they have a chance of getting.

The existence of different FORs among working class youth registers the fact that they are knowledgeable agents who have their own theories about life and their particular place in society. Pupil FORs are creatively constructed, reproduced and transformed, drawing upon the raw materials of class culture. This culture is the historical product of the past educational and labour market experiences of working-class people. Therefore, the rapid increase in youth unemployment during the time these pupils were in the secondary school has serious consequences for becoming adult and for the collective understanding of what it means to be a working-class pupil.

What figure 6.2 shows is that there are three ways of 'being' in school (Rems, Swots and Ordinary Kids) among these pupils, regardless of gender, although this should in no way be interpreted that gender differences within the school are unimportant. With respect to pupil

FORs, girls and boys will interpret the process of becoming an adult in different ways, and this obviously includes the development of an occupational identity which in most cases, centres around different kinds of jobs. What are significantly similar, however, are the cultural limits of pupil educational and occupational ambitions.

The term Rem is taken from the term 'remedial'. However, it is important to note that although the term remedial is used with reference to non-examination pupils, it has important moral connotations. It is not that the Rems are believed to be 'thick', but rather that they are unwilling to 'make an effort'. It was the members of the conspicuous male anti-school sub-culture who were most likely to be referred to as Rems. The Swots are alternatively those pupils located in the upper bands of the school and who were identified as spending all their time working and never having a laugh or getting into trouble with teachers. In the two working class schools included in the research, to be studying for 'O' levels (academic qualifications) was almost by definition to be a Swot. The Ordinary Kids stand somewhere between the Rems and Swots. They are defined with reference to what they are not (Rems or Swots), rather than for what they are, 'ordinary' or 'average'. These different ways of *being* in school and the orientations to school life which this involved, are explicable in terms of the way these pupils made sense of their educational experiences when related to the culturally defined ways in which it was possible to become a working class adult. These working class FORs which can be characterized in terms of Getting In, Getting On or Getting Out of the working class — are the historical product of the shared social and educational experiences of working class people, which are imbued with social significance and convey varying degrees of social status. At the heart of these social experiences are the economic activities of adults living in the locality. It is therefore hardly surprising that occupational identity has had an important impact on the demand for education, and that this demand has been limited as a consequence of class inequalities (Brown, 1987, p. 171).

The Rems rejection of the school as boring, irrelevant and frequently repressive is based upon a FOR which can be characterized in terms of 'get into' the culture proper: away from a world of school kids and into the world of working class adults and employment at the earliest possible opportunity. The Swots are more willing to accept the demands of school life and 'swot' for examinations. Their FOR is characterized in terms of a belief that by arming themselves with enough qualifications to compete for middle class jobs they can 'get out' of their class of origin. Yet as we have already seen, the majority of working class pupils neither simply accept nor reject the school, but comply with it despite the fact that much of the academic curriculum is irrelevant to their present and future lives. At the heart of the Ordinary Kids' response to school is a FOR which can be characterized in terms of 'getting on' within the working class, although this FOR has been seriously affected by the collapse of job opportunities for school leavers in the early 1980s.

This model may help us to explain one of the reasons why working class pupils have not pursued an academic career and why so many of them have deserted full-time education at the first hurdle. Given the social and historical context of the post-war period, within working class neighbourhoods such as those found in Middleport, academic achievement was never necessary for the vast majority of working class pupils to realize their childhood ambitions and maintain a sense of personal dignity and respect. However, this has not, and does not, preclude some working class pupils developing a FOR in terms of 'getting out', which places a premium on school success. It neither rules out the contention that the school has an important impact on which pupils develop which FOR. The FORs exhibited by particular pupils are not simply the result of early childhood socialization. The educational system does play a part in reinforcing or transforming pupil FORs. There is a loose fit between family background and pupil 'frames of reference' because of the interaction between the 'institutional context and the processes of class cultural production' (Hogan, 1982, p. 61). A recognition of the school's role in framing the life chances of working class youth is important because it avoids the tendency for 'cultural' accounts to drift into forms of voluntaristic explanations, which underplay the significance of the school's ability to determine the life chances of pupils, whether or not large numbers of working class children were to be convinced of the value of academic success. It ignores the way in which the school is structured and organized and the differential power relations which pupils from a disadvantaged background confront.

It is in terms of the school's selection processes that we can understand why the school has the potential to transform the FORs of particular pupils, and why it has failed to offer much of a challenge to the educational and social identities of working class children in general. The Middleport study supports the view that, in order to win pupil compliance, teachers do try to convince all pupils that 'swotting' is worthwhile, and that if they work hard they can achieve a better future than that which confronts their school friends. However, 'swotting' has a social and moral significance which means that it incurs social costs, such as social stigma and isolation from childhood friends. Swotting is not, therefore, a viable option for the majority of working class pupils (given its irrelevance to their present and future lives), *unless* opportunities are seen to exist for educational and social advancement (and even then they may be rejected). It is this interrelationship between class culture and school structure which provides the key to understanding intra-class variations in the demand for education. It also helps us to understand why the structure of educational opportunities and content of schooling has an important impact on working class educational behaviour and why youth unemployment and the process of deindustrialization in working class neighbourhoods is likely to have a major impact on working class FORs.

Middle Class Responses to School

Before considering the implications of contemporary economic and social change on the educational experiences of working class youth in Britain, I want to briefly outline a tentative model of middle class orientations and FORs. This is shown in figure 6.3:

Figure 6.3   Middle Class Responses to School

Orientations to school	Alienated/ alienated instrumental	Normative instrumental	Normative/ normative instrumental
Location in pupil Culture	Rems	Ordinary kids	Swots
Frames of Reference	Falling out	Getting in	Getting on

What is of interest here is that the working class ordinary kids would be the Rems in the middle class school, because they will be unable to reproduce the labour market position of their family, as they are unlikely to obtain the academic credentials necessary to take the academic route into further and higher education. In other words, they confront the possibility of downward social mobility (see Jones, 1987), of 'falling out' of their class of origin. The ordinary kids in the middle class school clearly have an eye for 'getting in' to the middle classes and are prepared to work for academic qualifications. The Swots in such a school are those who are highly motivated to get to the top, or who are strongly oriented to the pursuit of knowledge as an end in itself. They are seen to be willing to make extraordinary efforts to 'get on' in middle class terms, and are viewed by other middle class pupils as never having any fun, or as never going out at nights because they spend all their spare time doing homework.

Conclusion

In this chapter I have argued that high rates of youth unemployment have had an important impact on pupil responses to school and their preparation for entering the labour market. In the UK the research evidence leads to the conclusion that few pupils from a working class background view the school as a way of 'getting out' of their class of origin. Nevertheless, the majority have been willing to make an effort in school despite their scepticism concerning the value of becoming 'educated' as it is defined by teachers. This opposition and sense of alienation from the school has intensified as a result of high levels of youth unemployment. Growing numbers of ordinary working class pupils feel that they have less of a stake in school and society. They are being stripped of a sense of dignity and respect because the occupations which form an element to social identity and to becoming adult in a respectable fashion have disappeared, and so has one of the major reasons for bothering to make an effort in school. The increase in working class alienation from school is associated with a sense of fatalism and powerlessness, which is likely to result in a growing sense of entrapment and social disorganization within working class neighbourhoods, rather than to their emancipation.

The discussion about pupil educational experiences and FORs indicates that if the school has its part to play in alleviating such problems, the educational system must be organized so as to expand the educational opportunities of the working class, not to restrict them. This is crucial not only because some working class parents and pupils may view the school as the only way out of the deindustrial rut, poverty, and a life on the dole, but because the motivational patterns of working class pupils are based on the interrelationship between identities and institutions. As we have seen pupil understandings of being in school are closely connected to class cultural understandings of becoming a working class adult. They will not, therefore, easily give up an understanding which serves to define who they are, and to maintain a sense of social dignity unless there are genuine opportunities to make a *new* future.

This reluctance to alter their way of seeing the world and their future within it, is not based on an ignorance of alternatives, as some people have supposed (Hampson, 1980). When the ordinary kids discuss school and adulthood they are not expressing attitudes based on an ignorance of alternatives, they are expressing collective knowledge of ways of being a working class pupil and adult. Their FORs are grounded on the material practices of working class people, transmitted from generation to generation, and are the basis for establishing personal dignity, social identity and social status in a class society. Having said all this, it is also true to say that the ways in which the ordinary kids understand their futures are based upon past processes rather than present structures. Many of the skilled manual jobs available, especially to males, have disappeared. Moreover, the mass redundancies which were also part of the shake-out of labour and process of economic restructuring, meant that a significant minority of their fathers and mothers also have some direct experience of unemployment. In such circumstances parents are less likely to have access to employers and contacts who could put a 'good word in' for their son or daughter (Harris *et al.*, 1987; Ashton *et al.*, 1989).

The way in which working class parents and pupils are now making sense of the role of the school and their future employment is an issue which requires urgent study. However, it does appear that the cultural resources available to working–class children in the 1980s may equip them to cope with the prospects of a livelihood which many of them will no longer be able to attain.

Moreover, does this signal the decline of class culture as a formative element of educational and occupational identity? Ulrich Beck (1987) has noted that:

> ... as a result of shifts in the standard of living, subcultural class identities have dissipated, class distinctions based on 'status' have lost their traditional support, and *processes for the 'diversification' and individualization of life styles and ways of life* have been set in motion. As a result, the hierarchical model of social class and strata has increasingly been subverted. It no longer corresponds to the realities. (p. 341)

In the UK there has also been considerable speculation about the social implications of economic and social change in the 1970s and 1980s. Newby *et al.* (1985) hypothesized that 'the recession has been associated not with the emergence of class struggle and class politics, but with a retreat from class politics into a privatized world within the home' (p. 95; see also Lukes, 1984).[7]

However, when Marshall *et al.* (1988) subjected this hypothesis to the empirical test, using a national sample, they concluded:

> Our analysis suggests that modern Britain is a society shaped predominantly by class rather than other forms of social cleavage, no matter whether the phenomena under scrutiny are structural or cultural in nature. (p. 183)

This is not to deny the importance of social and economic divisions within the working class. Indeed, the divisions which have been typically based on the distinction between the 'rough' in semi- and unskilled jobs, and the 'respectable' in skilled occupations, has become more complex but no less prevalent (Wallace 1987; Jones, 1987), and some are having to cope with the 'new social condition of unemployment' (Willis, 1986; Coffield *et al.*, 1986). There are also a number of commentators in the UK who have recently argued that the divisions between working class households are becoming increasingly polarized (see Pahl, 1988).

In the context of the UK it is therefore necessary to question Beck's notion of 'individualization' which assumes that social class is no longer a significant determinant of educational and labour market experiences. The 1980s has been a decade when class differences have been reinforced both objectively and subjectively. Not only are the rich getting richer and the poor getting poorer, but the class competition for educational cer-tification is also increasing, as the middle classes become increasingly dependent on educational achievement as a way of reproducing their class privilege. The impact of unemployment has further intensified this competition, and there are clear signs that the middle classes are beginning to invest more heavily in private education.

The government's response to the intensification of middle-class demands for 'education' has been an increased willingness to allow the rapid expansion of private educational establishments in response to market forces, whereas the new vocationalism is being used to reform the education of the working classes to meet the 'needs' of industry.

The extent to which the vocationalization of working class education will succeed in leading the ordinary kids to continue to make an effort remains unclear. However, the combination of inequalitarian educational policies and the economic circumstances confronting working class parents and children, is likely to increase class conflict over education and generate increasing problems of classroom control.

Notes

1 The Youth Training Scheme is a government-sponsored two-year programme of work experience, offering some off-the-job training.
2 When students complete their eleven years of compulsory education from ages 5 to 16, some opt for a college of further education rather than remaining in the sixth form (for 16–18-year-olds), because of the range of courses on offer or because in a college of education they feel that they are treated more like adults.
3 This should not obscure the fact that there are significant regional differences in individual chances of leaving school and finding a job (see Ashton *et al.*, 1982).
4 451 questionnaires were completed by 16-year-old pupils from the three schools. The information gathered from these questionnaires was used to identify the range of pupil response to schooling and their occupational aspirations and expectations. I also observed classroom lessons and participated in informal lunch-time activities in the youth-wing by working in the school 'tuck-shop'.
5 While there is a vast literature on the concept of class and its use in social research, and much debate about its meaning and heuristic value, there is universal agreement that class refers to the economic aspect of inequality. Moreover, regardless of how it is defined theoretically, when it is used in social and educational research occupation is taken as an indicator. In this study in Middleport, South Wales, the two comprehensive schools which provide the major source of data are both in working–class neighbourhoods, where the majority of employed fathers are in skilled and semi-skilled manual occupations; it is by virtue of these occupations that they can be treated as part of the working class. Having identified the class location of most of the respondents of this study, in this somewhat crude manner, it is possible to explore different aspects of the categroy thus defined, and these aspects need not necessarily be economic. The term 'social class' (Marshall, 1950) is frequently used in the British literature to refer to hierarchically ranked cultural groupings. Rosser and Harris (1965) suggest in their study of family life and social change in South Wales that it is probably more fruitful to think of social classes primarily as broad cultural groupings which cannot be reduced to distinctions between occupational categories, because there are also important regional factors to be taken into account (Massey, 1985).
Another reason why it is more fruitful to understand occupational categories

in terms of broad cultural groupings is that snapshots of occupational categories ignore the fact that the working-class neighbourhoods of Middleport have their own history which provides a fund of knowledge and experience about what it means to be a working-class pupil or to be unemployed in a given lcoality. This historical dimension of social class is crucial. As Thompson (1977) has expressed it, 'to understand class we must see it as a social and cultural formation, arising from processes which can only be studied historically' (p. 12). Therefore, the attitudes, values and conduct of working-class pupils and school-leavers in Middleport are not wholly invented *de novo* by them; 'they draw upon a fund of experience built into their lives outside the school and built up historically within working-class communities in general' (Giddens, 1986, p. 299).

6   In the search for an approach which links class location and educational experience in a way which is sensitive to variations in working-class responses to school, Bourdieu's notion of habitus (1986) appears to have some explanatory potential. However, although the concept of habitus has the potential for demonstrating the interrelationship between class location and educational experience, Bourdieu and Passeron's (1977) concern to demonstrate that the educational system functions as a key institution in advanced capitalist societies for the reproduction of social inequalities leads to a naive structural account of working-class educational experiences. Moreover, there are at least two further reasons why a different conceptual schema is needed. Firstly, when the idea of habitus is related to concrete situations, it becomes difficult to unravel what the concept is being used to describe or explain. Swartz (1981) notes that 'habitus' presents a number of conceptual and empirical ambiguities and that its conceptual versatility, which permits the movements between different levels of abstraction, 'frequently renders ambiguous just what the concept actually designates empirically' (p. 346). Secondly, the problem for Bourdieu, which he shares with Willis, is how to explain variations in working-class orientations to school and employment. The way the working-class habitus (or culture?) is understood by Bourdieu represents an extreme form of social and occupational closure. Jenkins (1982) has correctly noted that Bourdieu's understanding of the working-class habitus relies on

> an almost lumpen model of the working class which ignores that class's internal differentiation and stratification and underestimates the importance of the *possibility* of mobility limited in scale and scope, in the legitimation of patterned domination.

7   I am grateful to Professor Ray Pahl for directing my attention to this debate.

Chapter 7

Caught between Homogenization and Disintegration: Changes in the Life-phase 'Youth' in West Germany since 1945

Heinz-Hermann Krüger

In this chapter I shall attempt to trace the changes in adolescence in the FRG from the post-war period to the present. In view of the length of this period of history, I shall emphasize a comparison between the immediate post-war period and the 1950s with the current situation. The first section empirically describes trends and changes in adolescence and adolescent biographies on the basis of representative surveys, statistics and qualitative youth studies. This material, which points to the conclusion that there have been structural changes in adolescence over the period considered, is then interpreted in the light of critical modernization theories.

Historical Review

As a result of the confusion of the war, we — my parents, my sister and I — had to leave our home town, Dortmund, and ended up in Christianseck in Wittgenstein after being evacuated twice, first to Hermsdorf (Sudetenland) and then to Langenbeck in the Black Forest. We arrived there at the beginning of 1943 in the middle of the winter. On 12 March 1945 our flat in Dortmund was destroyed during a heavy air raid. In May, when the war was over, my mother made sure we could go back to Dortmund. Through 'connections' — without which you could not get anywhere to live in those days — we were promised a flat in Dortmund. We packed our things and turned up at the front door with a removal van: the previous day, another family had moved in. We were able to stay with my aunt, it was dreadfully cramped — our furniture was all stored with neighbours — from August 1945 until February 1946. During this time, I did not go to school, I was nearly eight and already had eight months of real school time behind me. (Essay by Wolfram Weiss, Gymnasium Dortmund, 4 June 1956)

This extract from a sixth-former's essay in 1956 is an example of how the war and its follow-on effects adversely affected the plans of the whole population, presumably not just in Germany, often sending them into complete disarray. This could be seen in many different ways: children were evacuated during the war; afterwards they had to help rebuild their homes or procure food; pupils began their schooling late; some of those sitting their 'A' levels (*Abitur*) had already been soldiers and prisoners of war; people were getting married at uncharacteristic ages. In contrast, the 1950s were marked by a strong impulse towards 'normalization'. This applied not only to the objective living-conditions of adolescents — for example, the severe unemployment of the early 1950s had been replaced by full employment at the close of the 1950s. It was felt equally strongly that social biographies, especially those of young people, should be brought back into balance. State youth care protection agencies (*Jugendschutzverbände*) and powerfully moralizing social preachers warned against the consequences of an 'abnormal' adolescent biography. Restrictive youth protection legislation attempted to counter the signs of disintegration of adolescent biographies caused by the effects of the war.

If we leave official state policies and legislation directed at youth to one side, what actual terms did the adolescent biography actually take in the 1950s? The 1950s are a decade which can still be regarded as belonging to the classical 'adolescent epoch'. In other words, the concept of youth as a moratorium, as an educational province, and as an active stage of development — as described in theories of adolescence stretching from Rousseau through Stern to Spranger, right through from the mid-eighteenth century to the mid-twentieth century — remained a reality, certainly for a small number of middle-class, male adolescents (cf. Zinneker, 1985a, p. 34). As an illustration of the fact that only a very limited number of young people in the 1950s enjoyed an extended adolescence through an extension of their formal education, we might note that in 1951, only 4 per cent of the male and only 2.7 per cent of the female school-leavers' cohort sat the *Abitur*. The proportions for the 1957 cohort (7.4 per cent male, 3.8 per cent female) had not appreciably increased (Bartram and Krüger, 1985, p. 85). Working-class children were at a particular disadvantage in the school system during the 1950s. They had only minimal chances of getting as far as the *Abitur* averaging 4 per cent of the annual cohort over the decade (Fröhner *et al.*, 1965, p. 61). The problems facing working-class children attending grammar school (*Gymnasium*) at that time is illustrated in this extract from another pupil essay:

> I first thought about going to grammar school in the fourth year at primary school; although my parents are working-class, they were prepared to foot the costs. This was the start of a different world for me. My fellow pupils said: 'You're sitting next to the sons of factory owners and doctors now.' As I was the only one from our school to take the entrance exam — nearly everyone in our primary school was working class — I was always on my own during the exam breaks, while the others all played together ... Something else bothered me more. What did I have to do so nobody from my class would find out where I came from? I tried and tried to find an answer; I didn't want to ask anybody home, because I wanted to avoid friendship right from the start. That didn't mean that I wanted to pretend to be a 'rich boy', I just felt I had to protect myself. (Essay by Karl Siepmann, Gymnasium Gronau, 2 June 1956)

While Karl's biographical reminiscences deal with being at school, thematicizing the strategies of a working-class adolescent for surviving at Gymnasium during the 1950s, his peer Erich's fictitious reflections on the everyday life of a sixth-former (*Primaner*) highlight a rather different perspective:

> Human life is divided into several sections. There is childhood, adolescence, then you are the prime of your life, you learn a profession and start a family. This is the most mature and the richest time for a human being. The life and times of a sixth-former form the link between adolescence and learning a profession for that class of people dedicated to the humanistic disciplines. (Essay by Erich Weisshaupt, Gymnasium Dortmund, 4 June 1956)

In Erich's critical thoughts on the life course, it is clear that he regards being a sixth-former as a special biographical status, simultaneously an intermediate stage and a link between adolescence and adulthood. By implication, the point is raised that in the 1950s' social reality there were *other* adolescents, those who did not possess this special sixth-former status, they but passed through an adolescent stage which was then immediately succeeded by adulthood. For the vast majority of the adolescent generation of the 1950s, their biography was marked by a brief adolescence. Figure 7.1, based on data from the *adult* survey of the 10th Shell adolescent study (Fischer, Fuchs and Zinneker, 1985a) illustrates this point. It shows the typical ages at which more than half of those interviewed experienced particular biographical events, differenti-

Figure 7.1

Source: Fischer, Fuchs and Zinneker (1985) Bd. V, pp. 169–72; Bonfadelli u.a. (1986) p. 37

ated by sex. Thus in the 1950s, most adolescents left school aged between 14 and 15, had their first sexual contact when they were about 18, finished vocational training at about the same age, moved out of the parental home between 22 and 23, and got married between one and two years later. So most young people would pass through the various stages of adolescence in the socially accepted order: first you finished school and training, then when you started work, you had your first sexual contact, then when you finished your training you left home and soon afterwards you got married. Three features were typical of the stages of the female 'standard biography' (*Normalbiographie*) in the 1950s: firstly, formal vocational leading to a recognized qualification (*Berufsausbildung*) was by no means usual for girls in the 1950s. The Shell study found that a quarter of those women aged between 45–49 and almost half those aged between 50–54 had not, on their account, completed any such training (Fuchs, 1985, p. 210). Secondly, on average, women got married two years earlier than men (at 22). Thirdly, it was clear for most girls and women in the 1950s that they would give up paid work when their first child was born, with no expectation that they would return to employment later. A statement from a girl at a further education college in 1956 on the subject 'How do you envisage equal rights for men and women?' provides a good example of contemporary gender ideology:

> We've got a profession and a female human being does just as much as a man !!!!! So we're entitled to the same pay!!!!! However, if a woman's married, has got children, her husband's job is paid well, and she still goes out to work, then she should pay so much tax that it's not worth her while to work any more. A woman belongs in the kitchen and to her children. That's the way God, or if you prefer, nature has planned things, so that women are maternally-minded and gentle. Can you imagine a household where the father does the mother's job and the mother goes to work? (Essay by Dagmar Riemann, Essen Further Education College, 4 June 1956).

Most adolescents in the 1950s left elementary school (*Volksschule*) at the age of 14/15 after the then compulsory eight years of formal education. They then started work, usually on a 48–hour-week, with only very few leisure activities available for their limited free time. It is hardly surprising, that apart from the few *Gymnasium* pupils or members of sub-cultures like teddy boys or *Exis*, most members of this generation have not evolved a conceptual understanding of 'adolescence' in reflecting upon their own lives (Zinneker, 1985a, p. 35; Krüger, 1985, p. 8). In the memories of many, adolescence collapses into a tacked-on appendage between the end of childhood and the beginning of adulthood.

Now, apart from the external changes which of course you go through, we all grew up pretty quickly, what with having to start work when we were 15, 8 hours a day.... We were in at the deep end, too; and there were more children, the same age as me like, 14 or 15, when I started at the factory. And then I was, so to speak, actually already grown up. (A 43-year-old man with a Volkschule education, quoted in Fuchs, 1988, p. 3)

Current Changes in the Adolescent Phase

If we compare the current social construction of the adolescent phase with the stages of adolescent biography in the 1950s, major structural changes are exposed. These changes might be defined by the terms homogenization and disintegration. The driving force behind the homogenization of the adolescent phase was to a large extent the reform in education of the 1960s and 1970s. The extension of compulsory schooling, the wider acquisition of school-leaving qualifications and finally educational and training schemes as a cosmetic solution to youth unemployment have all led to a marked extension of education as part of individual life history. For most people in the 1950s, schooling was completed at 14 or 15 years of age. In the 1980s most young people leave the educational system at 16 and 17-years-old, but a considerable proportion of 18-year-olds are still in full-time education (cf. Baethge, Voskamp and Schomburg, 1983). This means that the length of time spent at school has been extended by two to three years in comparison with the 1950s. It also means that the overwhelming majority of young people nowadays do not depart from the education system in the early stages of adolescence. In fact, school and adolescence are now parallel life events (cf. Hurrelmann *et al.*, 1985).

This extension of the amount of one's life spent in education has been accompanied by considerable changes in the distribution of pupils throughout the different kinds of schools. Whereas in 1952, 79 per cent of seventh-grade (i.e., aged 14) pupils attended elementary and secondary modern school (*Volksschule/Hauptschule*), 6 per cent technical school

(*Realschule*) and 13 per cent grammar school (*Gymnasium*), in the school year 1982/83 only 39 per cent were at a *Hauptschule* and the remainder were equally divided between the *Realschule* and the *Gymnasium*, with 7 per cent at some form of special school (Hurrelmann *et al.*, 1988). It has been especially girls who have profited from this expansion. In the early 1960s, girls were still clearly underrepresented at the *Gymnasium*, but by the 1980s they had overtaken boys both at the *Gymnasium* and at the *Realschule* (Faulstich-Wieland *et al.*, 1984, p. 120). Educational opportunity for working-class children has also improved to some extent. Pupils of working-class origin now comprise 10 per cent of *Gymnasium* pupils, and have thus doubled their representation since the 1950s; nevertheless class-based educational inequalities remain strong (Rodax and Spitz, 1982). Parallel to the statistical rise in girls' educational participation and achievement levels, their orientations to employment and their projected life plans changed too. Today, paid work is a taken-for-granted component of the female *Normalbiographie*. The proportion of those aged 20–29 who are employed (rather than at home and engaged in domestic duties) has risen considerably between the 1950s and the 1980s; over the same period men in their twenties have become less likely to be paid work than they formerly were (Fuchs, 1983, p. 344). Moreover, unlike the 1950s generation, it is usual practice for girls of the 1980s generation to complete a *Berufsausbildung*, in spite of the considerable difficulties faced by 1980s youth as a consequence of economic recession and high unemployment. In contrast, young men in the 1980s, unlike those of the 1950s, express interest in family-oriented life aims almost as frequently as do girls (Zinneker, 1987, p. 317).

The 'schooling' of youth (*Verschulung*) and a decreasing gender-differentiation in life-plans are two indicators of homogenization processes. Further indicators lie in the expansion of the amount of time young people have at their disposal together with an increase in youth-oriented leisure activities and opportunities during the 1980s. Eighties youth is marked by a differentiated spectrum of leisure interests, preferences and activities, ranging from travelling through music to literary involvement (such as writing poetry). This spectrum was not available to adolescents in the 1950s, neither from an objective nor a subjective point of view (Zinnecker, 1985a, p. 38). Moreover, the significance of informal peer contacts for young people has increased, the spectrum of a leisure-oriented public has expanded, and the cultural availability of lifestyles covers a much broader range.

We can describe the structural changes in the youth phase in terms of homogenization processes, but at the same time contrary processes of destructuring (*Entstrukturierung*) can be detected (Olk, 1988). This term describes the phase of transition of adulthood as dissolving into a disconnected sequence of partial transitions, as shown in figure 7.2. Based on the results of the *adolescent* survey conducted as part of the 10th Shell

Figure 7.2

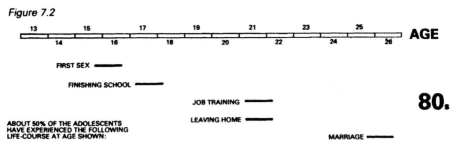

Source: Fischer, Fuchs, Zinneker (1985) Bd. V, pp. 169–72; Bonfadelli u.a. (1986) p. 37

study (Fischer, Fuchs and Zinneker, 1985a), it shows the typical ages at which the respondents had experienced various life events, as did Figure 7.1 (p. 107) for the adult sample. If we compare the data in the two figures, it is immediately apparent that the majority of adolescents in the 1980s attend school for two to three years longer than those of the 1950s did, but they have their first sexual contact two years earlier, finish vocational training about three years later, leave home about a year earlier, but get married three years later (Bonfadelli *et al.*, 1986, p. 37). Still more interesting than this cross-sectional comparison is, however, a comparative analysis of the chronological ordering of the life events. Most adolescents of the 1950s experienced the various life events in their 'proper' order — first they left school, then they took up an active sexual life, they did not leave home until several years after completing job training, shortly after which they got married. In contrast, for young people today the pacing of pathways through the adolescent biography is marked by increasing inconsistencies and tensions. For example, first sexual contacts take place while they are still at school, so that unlike for fifties teenagers, there is a chronological overlap of schooling and the onset of active sexuality. Marriage and children no longer follow hard on the heels of leaving home; instead, a new intermediate biographical stage of living alone and independently has developed (cf. also Gaiser and Müller, 1987, p. 10).

This disintegration and stretching out of transitions to adulthood becomes clearer if we look more closely at two central transitional life events — marriage and entry into employment — and add some further data to the picture. A destandardization of the family cycle is particularly noticeable. Since the mid-1970s, the average age at marriage has begun to rise once more, reversing a long-established trend (Jaide, 1988, pp. 50–51). Furthermore the *distribution* of age at marriage has opened out, and the number of single people aged 20–29 has risen tremendously over this same period (Fuchs, 1983; Rosenmayr, 1986). It has also become evident that there is a greater distribution of the age at which people enter employment together with a tendency to start work later in life. In 1960, 4.3 per cent of those aged 19–26 attended university or polytechnic; by 1985, 18.2 per cent (Bertram, 1987b, p. 138). But the increasing numbers of higher education students in the FRG is not the only reason for these changes. The critical reason lies in a weakening of the transition into employment which has set in since the mid 1970s, and which especially affects young people aged 20–25. The absolute numbers unemployed in this age group are high: 171,620 in 1975, rising to almost half a million by 1985; but expressed in percentage terms, rates of unemployment are also *much higher for this age group than for all other age groups* (*ibid*). This development show quite clearly that for at least a section of today's adolescents it is becoming increasingly difficult to make the transition into the employment system. At the same time this voluntary release or involuntary exclusion from employment means, for more and more young people, an extension of economic dependence and dependence through to a later stage in their lives. On the other hand, independently-constructed entry into social and cultural life (leisure, the media, consumerism, sexuality, etc.) takes place ever earlier, with the result that the clear differences between the age-stages of childhood, adolescence and adulthood are losing significance. Hence, the life course as a whole is becoming increasingly undifferentiated, and adolescence is marked by a destructuring of forms of behaviour and orientation patterns formerly specific to that phase of life (Kohli, 1985; Olk, 1988).

What are the effects of these objectively demonstrable processes of destructuring and disintegration on the ways in which young people today make sense of themselves within their biographies? In an ongoing research project we have used narrative interviews with 18-year-olds to explore this question. We have found that normative concepts either of chronological age or of socially constructed age-stages no longer play any significant role in young people's reconstructions of their biographies. Even where such concepts *were* thematized by the respondents they often appeared independently of the life phases assumed by life-course research. For example, Michael reports on fighting with other boys 'during his youth' — which he locates in what researchers would call childhood: 'Yes and well, it went on for two years, they just kept hitting me, really, until I hit back. Earlier, I can't remember, in my youth, *when I was seven*, I didn't fight much' (interview with Michael Klein, 3/10–3/17 my emphasis).

In their biographical reminiscences members of the 1950s adolescent generation who were interviewed in the Shell survey often regretted a non-existent or very truncated adolescence (Fuchs, 1983, p. 3), thus hinting by implication that they still do not have a clear idea about the order in which major life phases occur. In contrast, the young people we interviewed used these concepts very much at will. In other words concepts of life phases are losing their function of chronological marking and orientation. To put it another way, our data might be showing that the processes of destandardization and destructuring described and discussed in the youth research literature are finding their expression in the thematics of biography as voiced by young people themselves (Krüger, Ecarius and von Wensierski, 1988, p. 54).

Social Change and the Youth Phase: A Commentary

The arguments proposing homogenization and destructuring which dominate current theoretical debate amongst those interested in the study of adolescence (Fuchs, 1985; Hornstein, 1985b; Krüger, 1988a; Olk, 1988), or even those proposing an outright dissolution of the adolescent phase (von Trotha, 1982), are by no means new. In fact, Schelsky's (1957) standard work on fifties adolescence based its arguments, too, on the hypothesis that a levelling of class- and gender-specific forms of adolescent behaviour together with an alignment of social age roles was under way — changes which would have far-reaching effects. Schelsky's levelling-alignment hypothesis was not, in fact, an appropriate description for the realities of adolescent biographies and transitions in the 1950s. The Shell survey material discussed earlier demonstrates clearly the class- and gender-differentiated youth phase characteristic of that era. My own research into the emergence of an interational-commercial 'mass' youth culture in the West Germany of the fifties similarly points up the inadequacies of Schelsky's propositions in relation to that period (Krüger, 1985). However, in view of the currently demonstrable trends towards homogenization, Schelsky's hypotheses do seem to be acquiring a new currency.

Youth theorists would certainly and justifiably doubt the validity of a hypothesis proposing the levelling-out of class-differentiated adolescence. Zinneker (1986 and 1987), for example, follows Bourdieu (1982a) and attempts to place ideological concepts of adolescence and changes in the youth phase within the framework of social class groupings. I favour a different theoretical approach in my analyses of the connection between social change and the youth phase; in my view, Bourdieu's theory of the social reproduction of a full employment society pays adequate attention neither to social class mobility and assimilationist trends nor to the dissolution of class-cultural identities. Nor are gender divisions thematized adequately. Finally, Bourdieu's theory does not contain a well-developed understanding of subjectivity, so that it is not in a position to deal sufficiently with the dialectics of social and individual change processes. I find it both more productive and more plausible to interpret the structural changes in the youth phase which we are currently observing in the light of critical modernization theory formulated by Habermas (1982), Offe (1983) and, in particular, Beck (1986). In these analyses, attention is drawn to the ambivalent consequences of welfare–state–led modernization in post-war capitalist West Germany. This modernization process did not fundamentally affect capitalist structures of reproduction and inequality; and it has led, especially since the end of the 1960s, to a generalization of social risks and ecological danger. It has equally led to the emergence of new social inequalities, prompted by a labour market fractionalization marked by an expanding secondary employment sector in which under-employment, multiple and casualized job contracts and 'flexible' use of labour are characteristic. Further, modernization has entailed a questioning of gender-based role and task ascription, which has been accompanied by the polarization of gender relations and interpersonal conflict. In much the same manner, class-cultural communities have dispersed and dissolved, paralleled by processes of socio-cultural emancipation from traditional ways of life. The consequences of all these changes are far-reaching, for everyone. People increasingly find themselves confronted with the necessity to take their lives, in social terms, into their own hands. They are faced with an unsettling and hazardous injunction for 'flexible response' in all areas of their lives, and they can no longer rely on intersubjectively mediated cultural support systems to help them cope effectively.

It is sets of simultaneous oppositions which define this social diagnosis of contemporary life: old and new forms of social inequality; increasingly androgynous life patterns and the polarization of gender relations; life is a highly-individualized racetrack which offers a variety of scenarios for negotiating one's course, but against a background scenery of high accident risk, frequent obstacles, and precariously-balanced solution options.

The dialectics of old and new social inequalities can be seen operating in the education system and in the transition to employment. We noted earlier that working-class children have doubled their representation in the *Gymnasium* population from 5 per cent to 10 per cent; there is also a discernible increase in the number who successfully complete the *Realschule*. But when we consider that 50 per cent of all 13–14-year-old children of civil servants attended the *Gymnasium* and only 20 per cent the *Realschule*, it becomes clear that in spite of the reforms that have taken place since the 1960s, school has remained *the* institution where old social inequalities are reproduced (Helsper, 1988, p. 258). *New* social inequalities become evident if we consider the level of education of young unemployed people who were aged under 25 years in 1982. Seventy-four per cent of them had attended the *Hauptschule*, and two-thirds of *Hauptschule* pupils are, in turn, of working–class origin. Nevertheless, 16.7 per cent of the young unemployed had been to the *Realschule*, 6.1 per cent had attended the *Gymnasium* (Klemm and Koch, 1984, pp. 128–30). The dialectics of gender relations, in which the closing of old gaps meets with new forms of discrimination against women, and in which proclamations of equality clash with conventional practices, can be illustrated by looking at current patterns of education and training and at gender-specific life plans. In terms of formal educational achievement, including higher school qualification levels, girls have now outpaced boys by a small margin. However, between 1973–1983 there was a decline in the proportion of those holding an *Abitur* who went on to higher education; this decline was sharper for girls (from 90 per cent to 53 per cent) than it was for boys (90 per cent to 70 per cent) (Bauer and Budde, 1984, p. 84). It is also the case that the proportion of young women entering the labour market without any form of vocational training behind them dropped from 30.5 per cent in 1961 in 10.4 per cent in 1981. On the other hand, at around 35 per cent, the percentage of girls among all vocational trainees in the 'dual system' has not changed over this period (cf. chapter 8 by Helga Krüger in this volume). Girls continue to enter those occupations which are most heavily-dominated by women in much the same proportions as was the case in the fifties: shop assistant, hairdresser, clerk and doctor's receptionist (Faulstich-Wieland *et al.*, 1984, pp. 121–30). In other words, the recently acquired achievement bonus in girls' favour does not bring them a corresponding reward in terms of participation in higher education and vocational training or on the labour market. The alignment of the life plans of boys and girls which has been claimed by some studies turns out to be but superficial if examined more closely. Job *and* family have become equally important in the life plans of *both* boys and girls. However, it remains both typical and expected in the eyes of a majority of boys and girls that, after the birth of the first child, the wife gives up her job for a few years and takes on primary responsibility for childrearing, not the husband (Seidenspinner and Burger, 1982, p. 13). In other words, there is no basis for either the expectation or the reality of gender equality when it comes to the division of labour between spouses. The contradictory effects of a shift towards individualization as a general phenomenon throughout society are reflected in the destructuring and individualization of the adolescent life phase. Overlapping status transitions in adolescence and the differentiation and pluralization of life concepts and cultural lifestyles have expanded the available spectrum of individual biographical options and choices. Fuchs (1983), for example, inteprets individualization in this rather positive way — but there is at the least another side to the coin. Individualization can equally well lead to status insecurity and psychosocial problems for young people, given the instabilities now characteristic of family life, schooling and on the labour market. There is clear evidence of the fact that structural changes in the adolescent phase can lead to symptoms of psychological and social stress among adolescents in a recent representative survey carried out by Hurrelmann *et al.* (1988). However, our own qualitative study also shows the seriously disruptive effects on both lifeplans and general orientations that can follow from these changes and instabilities. We found that the unpredictability of education-employment transitions and the multiple dissolution tendencies observable in the conventional nuclear family had negative effects of these kinds. Equally the traditionalism of the social world of the school has given way to a sharper and colder schooling environment where only achievement, competition and getting ahead count, which is just as problematic in young people's experience (Krüger, Ecarius and von Wensierski, 1988 p. 53).

In sum, we can say that in West Germany since the 1950s, as a result of the extension of schooling, of the increase in leisure activities and cultural life-styles, of late entry into the employment system and of later marriage, the adolescent phase is now more homogeneous in character and is longer than it was formerly. In this sense, we have the objective prerequisites for the psychosocial moratorium described by Erikson (1974): a phase in which young people are protected for a while from the obligations and ties of adulthood, and as a time of searching for the experimenting with social identity. But from the biographical perspectives of the adolescents we interviewed, youth looks more like a psychosocial laboratory, a phase of stress and *obligatory* individualization. And so we are left with the apparent paradox that what we had classically come to understand as 'adolescence' has, in the West German context, been gradually transformed not only into a more homogeneous phenomenon and experience but also seems to be dissolving before our very eyes.

Chapter 8

The Shifting Sands of a Social Contract: Young People in the Transition Between School and Work

Helga Krüger

Transition Studies and Youth Research

Over the eighties a new kind of youth research has been emerging in West Germany. 'Youth' as a social identity has come to be seen not only as an expression of the *standardization* of the life course, but also as encompassing its own internal 'life course agenda'. This approach thus emphasizes the demands and opportunities of individual biography, as these arise from the social structuring and cultural contextualization of the transition between childhood and adulthood. It considers the coping strategies employed by young people during transition processes; and it is also concerned to register socially structured changes in the forms taken by those processes and the institutionalized contexts in which these take place. Such contexts transport, break and transform cultural patterns, but equally point to the social structural basis of the shifting options with which young people are confronted in moving towards adult status. It is the 'typical' young person's experience of transition which is central to this approach, rather than the spectacular youth (sub)cultural forms and styles which dominate not only media images but also youth research itself.

Within this general approach we can distinguish two different empirical styles of research. Firstly, there are those studies which, on the basis of retrospective qualititative or quantitative cross–sectional designs, trace developments and changes in the ways young people think about paid work and life as a whole (the Shell Jegendwerk studies, 1981 and 1985; Seidenspinner and Burger, 1982; Allerbeck and Hoag, 1985; Baethge *et al.*, 1988; Zoll *et al.*, 1988). Secondly, there are longitudinal studies, which trace processes of development and of orientation. These see 'youth' as a complex set of branched pathways, where the routes available and adopted have consequences for how young people may come to terms with their situation and experience (IAB, 1980; Diezinger *et al.*, 1983; Heinz *et al.*, 1985; Friebel, 1983; Herget, Schöngen and Westhoff, 1987). Labelled explicitly in the literature as 'transition research', both their singularly German quality and the fact that only now are they beginning to attract wider notice require some explanation.

West German youth is, relatively speaking, subject to a much more traditionally established, standardized, institutionally regulated and hence socially legitimated transition system between schooling and paid work. This transition system determines the routes taken by particular groups, acting rather as the 'bones of the life course corset' (cf. Beck and Brater, 1977). It consists of a highly complex and differentiated vocational training system, which, from the beginning of this century, has developed alongside the traditional grammar school track. The hierarchical structure of vocational training, which is related to the wage rates system, corresponds to the hierarchically structured labour force. However, it is, of course, during the youth phase that routes into the labour market are determined, i.e., at what educational and qualification level a person will enter the labour force. Recurring 'selection cycles' mean that the majority of young people face these sorting/allocation mechanisms at periods ranging from between one to three years.

Existing social patterns tend to attract little research attention when they seem to throw up few obvious problems for those implicated or for other aspects of social structure and processes. Youth and structural unemployment over the eighties have, however, made it difficult for people to develop a planned life perspective founded on the expectation of secure, life-long employment. As such, this has contibuted to a destandardization of the life course. This raises the important question of how far contemporary youth continues to orientate itself towards paid work and work relations within the conventional labour market. Those studies which have focused upon youth (sub)cultures and styles appear to signal just such a shift in value orientations, of a general rather than specific to class, gender and national-cultural cleavages. The privileges of adult status have been made partially accessible to young people, through, for example, rising standards of living, changing consumer patterns, a more liberal approach to sexual expression and relationships, and the expansion of leisure opportunities and activities aimed specifically at youth. Young people's perspectives and activity patterns, seen from this angle, would support the contention that they are distancing themselves from paid employment as a 'central life interest' and that they are no longer as predisposed to engage in instrumental-rational planning in order to secure it.

In the West German context, studies and analyses of youth transitions have acquired a particular significance in the context of contemporary theoretical debates, which have focused upon Beck's (1983) individualization thesis and Bourdieu's theory of the reproduction of cultural capital (Bourdieu and Passeron, 1971; Bourdieu, 1983). Both perspectives have been applied to the situation of contemporary West German youth, notably by Zinneker (1986, and chapter 2 in this volume). As far as comparative youth studies are concerned, transitions research attracts increasing attention because it promises some insight for potential explanations of and solutions for the transitions crises and youth unrest that surfaced in European societies during the eighties (in some countries more than in others). There has been a growing tendency to cast admiring and wishful glances at West German arrangements, where an established, legitimated transitions system not only selects and allocates *but also protects* individuals as they move between schooling and employment, adolescence and adulthood. For let us be quite clear: the West German transitions system is a highly effective mechanism of social integration, one which has critical socio-political significance within consensual understandings of the social contract between the state, employers and workers.

The basic principles upon which the West German transitions system rests are not always readily apparent to outsiders, which sometimes leads to misinterpretations when considering how that system might offer potential solutions for other national contexts. Thus I want now briefly to explain what these principles are, before turning to an account of the findings of recent transitions studies.

Youth as a Dual Process of Education and Formation

The multiple educational/training routes which comprise the transition system constitute, both in fact and in terms of consciousness, groups of young people who have differing future prospects. Figure 8.1 shows, in simplified terms, how these future life chances are distributed for the educational/training system (using 1980 as the benchmark).

Even in simplified form, the diagram reveals just how complex that system is. To appreciate the implications for young people's futures of the decisions made and the routes taken, we need to link employment sectors and levels with their corresponding entry qualifications. The secret of the integrative force of the West German transitions system, whose nature people from other countries find so difficult to understand, lies in the *principle of correspondence* between educational *certificates* and *formal levels* of gainful employment. The list which follows (on p. 120) accordingly gives an overview of the hierarchical structure of the employment system:

Figure 8.1   The educational system in the Federal Republic

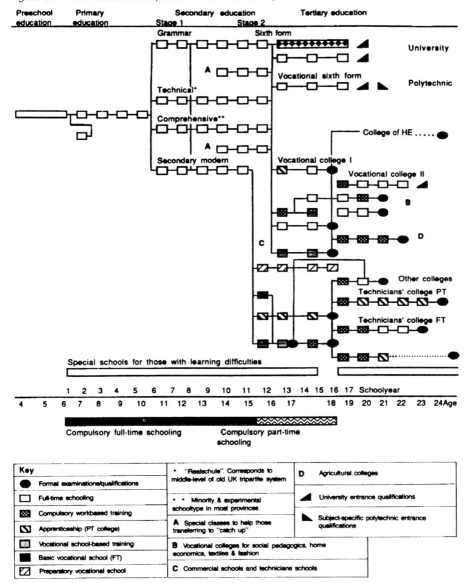

Source: J.H.Knoll Erwachsenenbildung und berufliche Weiterbildung in der Bundesrepublik
Deutschland, Grafenau, 1980, pp. 14–5 (transl. LAC)

Entry qualification level required	Occupational positions thus accessed
university degree (Magister, Staatsexamen, Doktorgrad) professional scientist, top management,	= academic level: e.g., teacher, doctor, professional scientist, top management, lawyer, apothecary; and the senior civil service
polytechnic degree	= polytechnic level: e.g., engineer, social worker, middle management, personal secretary; upper intermediate civil service
technical college graduate	= master craftsman level: e.g., master artisan (painter, motor mechanic, etc.), secretary, technician, nursery teacher; intermediate civil service
vocational training certificate	= skilled worker level: e.g., electrician, hairdresser, sales assistant, typist, office worker, receptionist, child care worker, medical/dental assistant; lower civil service
no vocational education/training	= unskilled/semi-skilled levels: e.g., office and administrative assistants, assembly line workers, roadworkers, cleaners

Each of these five levels can be accessed *only* through the possession of formal educational/vocational qualifications (or the lack of such in the case of the lowest level). This correspondence principle is rooted historically in the merging of two separate systems of regulation, each of which controlled access to and exercise of particular occupations and forms of employment, and which have been taken over into the modern industrial and service economies' occupational hierarchy. The first system was that developed through the artisan and craft guilds, producing the three-fold *vocational* qualification hierarchy of unqualified assistant/apprentice, journeyman and master craftsman. Today, these levels correspond to those of unskilled/semi-skilled worker, skilled worker, and those possessing intermediate level specialist qualificationas. The second system was that developed within bureaucratic administration organization for the four levels of the civil service (lower, intermediate, upper intermediate and senior), each of which is attached to corresponding levels of *educational* qualification. The firm structuration of educational/vocational qualification from the level of the unskilled worker to that of the university graduate established itself in the *private* sector as well as in the public sector. It strongly regulates the boundaries of movement in both directions; even in company-internal training and promotion systems, the principle operates that individuals cannot progress beyond the ceiling of the occupational level for which they are formally qualified through their educational achievement and/or vocational training. The legal basis for this classificatory and regulatory system is the formal wage rates system, which takes its cue from the level of educational qualification achieved by an individual *in the first instance*. The possession of formal certification at a particular level gives individuals the legal right to a specified corresponding wage, given that they find employment in the occupation for which they have been educated and trained (cf. Krüger, 1986; Schlüter, 1986; Drechsel *et al.*, 1988).

Formal certification is thus of enormous significance for an inevitable and inescapable standardization of the life-course. In the FRG, it would be virtually impossible for the infamous dishwasher to become a millionaire (unless s/he won the pools). Becoming self-employed or founding one's own business depends quite concretely upon the formal qualifications possessed, which must correspond at least to the level of the master craftsman. Our *unqualified* dishwasher would have no recourse but to recycle her/himself through the educational/training system first. Insuperable barriers similarly exist between the academic occupational level (whether self-employed or not, whether in the private or public sector) and all the rest, which remain impermeable throughout the course of a working life. However, the distinction between non-manual and manual work, which has been so significant in the UK and the USA as a consequence of the core distinction made between unskilled/semi-skilled and skilled work, is not clearly marked in the FRG setting. The effects of the barriers created by the correspondence principle are especially noticeable for women. Opportunities for upward occupational and career mobility subsequent to entering the labour force are so highly constrained, whereas acquiring the formal certification and training needed to enter at a higher level has been more difficult for women to secure (for a variety of reasons, including life-cycle patterns).

The task areas subsumed under the five levels are, of course, labelled as occupations; and their corresponding educational/vocational qualifications must reflect the contents and skill requirements of these tasks areas. Therefore, the direction taken by the requisite courses of study/training each correspond to a prescribed 'occupational specification' (*Berufsbild*), whose parameters are agreed through legally binding negotiations between employers and employee representatives (such as the trades unions). Those without the relevant qualifications may only be employed in those task areas which are *not* regulated by an occupational specification, and which are therefore *not* anchored in the qualifications hierarchy of the educational/training system. It is no coincidence that the community and social care employment sector is one that falls outside the regulatory system; it is predominantly staffed by women.

The high level of unemployment of recent years (which has especially affected young people trying to gain access to the labour market) may have prompted an interest in transitions research, but it has in no way unseated the existing mechanisms, whether in principle or in practice. (The real challenge here will come as a consequence of EC economic integration after 1992 and the increased inter-nation labour force mobility which will follow in its wake.) The difficulties over the eighties have, however, produced a rising insecurity in individuals' expectations about what will happen to them in the transition between schooling and the labour market. The labour market no longer has the capacity to absorb all those who are qualified, at whatever level. Young people are now noticeably unnerved about the immanent operating logic of the system (cf. Heinz *et al.*, 1985). What had been seen as a firm foundation for transitions now appears rather to comprise shifting sand; this is a fundamental change in framing conditions for West German youth, and must be seen as of some considerable significance for youth research.

Youth Transitions as a Dual Process of Individualization and Standardization

Two-thirds of today's youth cohorts secure an intermediate level secondary leaving certificate (*Realschulabschluß* or *mittlere Reife*, approximately equivalent to five GCSEs), either directly or through building upon their foundation level certificate (*Hauptschulabschluß*) in the post-16 vocational education/training system. It has been girls especially who have attempted to improve their educational qualifications in this way; the intermediate level certificate is rapidly becoming defined as the minimum acceptable and marketable standard of qualification (cf. Rolff and Zimmermann, 1985). At the same time, an ever higher proportion of those who secure a higher level secondary leaving certificate (*Abitur*, equivalent to 'A' levels for university entrance) choose to complete a vocational education/ training course before going on to higher education at university or polytechnic. Graduate employment prospects have deteriorated in recent years, so that 18+ school-leavers look to a vocational qualification not only as a potential fallback but also in the hope that it will give them an extra advantage on the graduate labour market. Once again, twice as many young women as young men from this group adopt this strategy. Friebel (1988a), summarizing these trends, notes that at the beginning of the seventies 80 per cent of vocational trainees (effectively, apprentices) held a foundation level leaving certificate. Almost all of the remaining 20 per cent had attained an intermediate certificate. Trainees entering with the *Abitur* were very much the exception, because at that time over 90 per cent of this group went on to university/polytechnic study. But by the mid-eighties the proportion of vocational trainees with only a foundation level leaving certificate had almost halved, whereas the representation of those holding an *Abitur* had risen to 13 per cent overall (and in the industrial-commercial sector to 17 per cent).

These figures point to the increased competition for access to vocational education/training places *within* employment levels, especially for occupations with buoyant job prospects. As a result, young people try to secure a 'market advantage' over their peers. In the first instance this may mean taking full-time school-based vocational education courses in the hope that these will help them to get a good apprenticeship in the 'dual' sector of the transitions system (where on-the-job training is combined with part-time or day release college study arrangements). However, those with an intermediate level leaving certificate (who already have a qualification advantage over *Hauptschüler*) will accept a good apprenticeship if this is offered, rather than continuing in full-time school-based vocational education (cf. Mertens and Parmentier, 1982; Stegmann, 1987). Those who complete an apprenticeship but are then unable to find a job are inclined to embark upon a new apprenticeship for a different occupation or take full-time vocational education courses to improve their qualifications. (It has become standard practice to take on more apprentices than can be offered jobs subsequently. Employers can receive subsidies for trainees, who also provide low-cost labour.) We can see from these patterns how the transitions system is overloaded with predetermined routes for certification and progression which branch off at every step along the way. In addition, the dual sector now attracts the full range of school qualification levels — which was formerly not the case. These circumstances have resulted in an extension of the youth phase of the life-cycle. Youth unemployment may have contributed to this extension, but it is more particularly a consequence of a qualifications accumulation process, which itself results from attempts to minimize risk in a context where the opportunity to shape a satisfactory future is highly constrained.

Years spent in education	Type of qualification attained	Age of labour market entry
9	Foundation level leaving certificate (*Hauptschulabschluß*) and no subsequent vocational education/training	16
12	Foundation level leaving certificate plus apprenticeship (*Lehre*)	19
10	Intermediate level leaving certificate (*Realschulabschluß*) and no subsequent vocational/educational training	17
13	Intermediate level leaving certificate plus apprenticeship	20
13	Higher level leaving certificate (*Abitur*) and no subsequent vocational/educational training or higher education study	20
16	Higher level leaving certificate plus apprenticeship	23
18	Higher level leaving certificate plus university or vocational polytechnic degree(s)	25+
21	Higher level leaving certificate plus apprenticeship plus university or vocational polytechnic degree(s)	28+

Friebel (1983) has argued that age classifications in contemporary West Germany still provide adequate definitional markers for 'youth' as a social category. This applies not only in the sense that transition into the labour market marks *the close of* the youth phase, but equally in that the various lengths of possible educational participation mark stages of progression *through* youth. Friebel demonstrates this with a descriptive table of the youth transitions plan (reproduced on page 123). It shows that length of educational participation ranges from nine to twenty-one years, and that length of time spent in the transitions system stretches across three to twelve years. The shorter the time spent in the general educational system, the more extended are the possibilities for time spent in the transitions system and the more frequent intermediate confrontations with the apprenticeship market and the labour market become. This chronological perspective on the youth phase nevertheless continues to mask the fact that the various educational/training participation categories also imply differing 'option logics' in relation to employment prospects. As decisions between alternative courses of action, these option logics do not, however, arise at the same age or with similar frequency for all young people. What are the implications of these differences in subjective terms?

Blossfeld's (1985) cohort study, which compared people born between 1929–31, 1939–41 and 1949–51, was able to confirm empirically the view that initial labour market placement is crucial for determining the course of employment biographies. Youth transitions studies indicate that young people are aware of this fact, but that they see it more as an individual problem rather than as a matter of collective destiny for all young people. They experience the problem of transition as an insistent catalogue of multiple demands and requirements. Passage into the tripartite secondary schooling system itself constitutes the first decisive turning point, one which determines which sets of routes through the transitions system are available for selection. Using figure 8.1 (p. 119) as a guide, we can see that those who transfer to the *Gymnasium* (grammar school) at 11+ can pursue their education over the next nine years in relative peace and quiet. They are placed on a route which leads directly (or, if punctuated with an apprenticeship, indirectly) towards higher education — as long as they can achieve at the level required in the interim. Those who transfer to the *Realschule* (the middle level secondary school) can look to their prospective leaving qualification advantage over *Hauptschüler* (secondary modern school pupils) as a transitions cushion. But for this last group, transition from primary to secondary schooling marks the first turning point in their *employment* biographies as well as in their educational histories. It sends an unavoidable signal for the direction of their future existence. Representing the views of his peers, one of the 14-year-olds in our study (Heinz *et al.* (1985)) remarked that

Well, secondary modern school isn't exactly the best, is it? ...
And when an employer sees that on your application ... it
doesn't matter if you've got top grades, you've had it — the
word 'secondary modern' is enough. If you've been to the *Realschule* it doesn't matter much if a few of your grades are low —
you'll get taken on anyway.

Secondary modern pupils early learn to be very realistic about their
future chances. Our study (*ibid*) followed both 14-year-old *Hauptschüler*
through to the age of 17+ (i.e., a year after they had left school) and a
separate group of young people as they made their ways through different sorts of post-16 vocational education/training. On the basis of the
findings, we can draw the following conclusions about the development
of employment/occupational orientations for this category of young
people:

1　The search for information about vocational education/training
　　options from neighbours, relatives, friends and family members
　　begins early — three years before leaving school, i.e., at age 13+.
2　At this age, pupils already begin to discard occupational prefer-
　　ences related to personal interests and inclinations in favour of a
　　realistic assessment of what is open to them, given the school
　　type they attend and their views of their abilities.
3　Secondary modern school pupils are overwhelmingly drawn
　　from working class and routine non-manual family backgrounds.
　　All the young people we studied wanted to reach a higher level of
　　formal educational qualification than that demanded by their
　　parents' current employment level. They rejected the idea of
　　getting unskilled or semi-skilled employment in order to earn
　　'good money' as quickly as possible; this does not promise an
　　acceptable future, in their view.
4　Level for level, both girls and boys aspired to a broad spectrum
　　of vocational education/training routes, but they assessed their
　　chances of successful transition into the labour market from the
　　various routes available very differently.
5　As they approached the end of their school careers and became
　　more intensely involved in the search for an apprenticeship, they
　　threw any remaining personal occupational preferences complete-
　　ly overboard. They simply wanted *any* apprenticeship they could
　　get for the employment level at which they could presently aim,
　　i.e., skilled workers, since this first placement would act as the
　　basis for their future employment career.
6　Young people's motivation and determination to secure the qual-
　　ification attached to the route pursued varies directly with their
　　assessment of its value on the labour market. If that route seems

to offer a formal certificate with little currency value, young people of both sexes judge it to have no purposeful educational or training function at all.

7   When they consider their own positioning in the transitions system in relation to those with more favourable prospects, young people conclude that their (poorer) *ability* to achieve explains why they have not done better than they have. When they consider their positioning in relation to those with less favourable prospects, however, they conclude that they have been *lucky* to have ended up where they are. Structural constraints thus appear as obstacles which can be overcome by effort and achievement rather than as the cut-off mechanisms which ensure reproduction of social inequalities in the distribution of cultural capital.

Thus, competitive jockeying for position on the labour market begins very, very early. In our study, direct transfer from secondary modern school to apprenticeship took place only for 35 per cent of the boys and 28 per cent of the girls. This means that *only for a minority* did the competitive process provisionally then end. Those who do not succeed in securing an apprenticeship on leaving school can, of course, attempt to improve their educational qualifications or take up a full-time school-based vocational training course. They know full well, however, that these routes are really the first *interruptions* in the construction of an employment biography. Similarly, since apprenticeships with large and successful firms are more likely to result in finding permanent employment in the occupation concerned, those who have only managed to secure an apprenticeship in a small firm know their future job chances are considerably poorer to start with — but are still better than for those who have not found an apprenticeship at all. In like fashion, those young people who have attended the *Realschule* know that they are more favourably positioned to transfer directly to an apprenticeship, but also that this advantage is bought at the cost of entering the transitions game a year later (since they leave school at 17 rather than 16). They will also, of course, complete their apprenticeships a year later (at 20 rather than at 19).

Young people certainly make use of the diversion routes and holding manoeuvres available within the vocational education/training system. They do so not only in order to improve their labour market chances, but also to secure financial support. Only those who have been previously employed are entitled to unemployment benefit, but apprenticeships or other forms of training do not count as employment. State-run and employer-provided vocational education/training provision are both subsidized through the public purse, so that trainees all receive some form of pay or allowance (at widely varying levels). Courses which do not provide a marketable qualification unsurprisingly suffer a much higher drop-out rate. Young women are particularly willing to climb onto and stay in this transitions carousel. They do at least as well as boys at school and in trianing, but the sex-segregated labour market places them much less favourably than it does boys, and so they are more inclined to think that improving their qualifications will improve their chances. It then appears that consciousness of the link between 'education' and 'the market' is the basic general pattern for coping with the conditions set by the youth transitions systems.

Both *Hauptschule* and *Realschule* pupils must begin to construct their own biographies at an early age. The routes upon which they find themselves are initially defined through their educational achievement, which is the formal basis of their placement in the tripartite secondary schooling system. This framing definition then provides the context in which responsibility for positioning and subsequent decisions is placed firmly within the self. At every stage in the process, individuals are called to account for that which they have, or have not, achieved. All transition biographies are in some sense individual, of course, but their shapes are prefigured and framed by the structures of the possible and the actual. So, for example, our study shows very clearly that girls do not end up in stereotypical education, training and employment sectors because of gender socialization in the family, but rather because of their realistic evaluation of the labour market's opportunity structure. They are obliged to accept the implications of these conditions if they want to secure vocational training and employment career prospects of some kind. *Retrospectively*, though, both young women and young men claim that what they actually did and are doing conforms to what they had wanted and planned for their futures. In other words, they style their histories to look like planned consistency, which we might term as a process of *biographical construction* in which objective and subjective option logics are linked with each other. This process forms a basis for the development of new perspectives, turning structural dispositions into active patterns of action which centrally incorporate both material and personal independence. Those whose hopes are repeatedly dashed, however, become less willing to discuss the difficulties and complexities of the balancing act required of them as they negotiate the transitions carousel. Whether in closed schedule or open ended interview contexts, such young people were inclined to be evasive or to mask their responses.

In point of fact, occupational interests and preferences are shaped by the conditions of the labour market but are understood within the ideology of free choice and decisionmaking. Everyday, school, and vocational guidance language speaks unreflectively in terms of fulfilling occupational choices and preferences — and this is the kernel of the problem which faces young people. Freedom of decision is understood within the context of *ability* to take decisions, is operationalized as such in theories of occupational choice, and is practised as such in vocational guidance testing schedules. This set of meanings and practices veils the fact that 'vocational maturity' (and 'immaturity') is determined through the exigencies of the training and labour markets — not through clear markers of personal failings or bad decision-making on the part of those involved. Young people, however, retain dominant understandings of transition processes and outcomes regardless of their actual experiences. Their interpretations reflect their powerlessness over against the structurally composed dilemma between occupational choice as an individual response to labour market demands and as a personally free decision. Since they still have to be able to function in this situation, young people must draw on patterns of meaning which are anchored in a biographical reference system. These enable retrospective interpretation in terms of individual responsibility. Labour market conditions are now reworked into a process of gradual personal realization of 'what I always wanted' — a perspective essential to developing a positive stance towards the opportunities which are actually made available. Interestingly, young people are not generally conscious that their decisions are also anchored in gender-specific terms. They attempt to interpret their experiences in the transitions system as 'gender neutral' for as long as possible. For girls, this means that gender-linked barriers are seen only in terms of (potential) obstacles that can be overcome by their own efforts, and not in terms of structural constraints.

Young People's Orientations to Work

West German studies of youth (sub)cultures and styles plainly suggest that the patterns of behaviour of young people from different social and cultural milieux have become more similar. Youth transitions studies, on the other hand, do not support the view that young people's values have changed as far as gainful employment is concerned. On the contrary, the more precisely groups of young people are specified according to their social, cultural and familial origins, the more clearly can we see the natures of their orientations to work. These two sets of findings require us to look more closely at the relationship between the reproduction of material social inequality through the transitions system and the convergence of lifestyle in leisure and private life.

The persistence of the reproduction of social inequality is patently evident from the distribution of pupils by social class origin within the tripartite secondary schooling system. Following comprehensive primary schooling, about 30 per cent of pupils attend the *Gymnasium*, 40 per cent the *Realschule*, and 30 per cent the *Hauptschule*. Given a 10 per cent degree of tolerance, however, the *Hauptschule* is populated by 'lower' class children, the *Realschule* by 'middle' class children, and the *Gymnasium* by 'upper' class children, regardless of the particular stratification classification system used to allocate the pupils. About 12 per cent of working class children ultimately find their way to university via the *Gymnasium*. The educational system thus returns children, by and large, back to the milieux from which they came. In between, however, the transitions system forces young people, and most insistently those from lower class backgrounds, to insert a recognition of achievement, effort, self-responsibility and equality of opportunity into their social learning experiences. They encounter these 'lessons' early and repeatedly, at frequent intervals. Their 'cultural capital' is expressed in terms of individual learning strategies — which lead them, for instance, to improve their qualifications: almost half eventually manage to secure the *mittlere Reife*. But they do not 'see through' those lessons as part of a structurally imposed compulsory curriculum. The competitive rounds of elimination in the dual sector of the vocational education/training system jumble together young people from different social backgrounds and with varying educational qualifications. Their day-to-day interaction produces patterns of acculturation which are spurred on through the leisure and consumer industries and which are expressed through superficial homogeneities of lifestyle. The class-specific *cultural* empire of the apprenticeship thus outwardly disintegrates, whilst still remaining the mechanism of social reproduction of class position for lower class youth.

In like manner, the questioning or rejection of work as a central life-value remains a matter of style rather than substance. Neither Baethge (1988) nor Zoll (1988) could support the view that paid work had lost meaning for the young people they studied. On the contrary, in their search for personal identity, employment and occupation were at least as important to half of Baethge's respondents as were other areas of life. Neither had paid work declined to minor significance for the other half, who had identified leisure, private or family life as at the centre of their life-concept (*ibid*, p. 134). Diezinger *et al.* (1983), in a longitudinal study of unemployed young women from lower and middle class backgrounds, equally found that orientations to work and to vocational education did not disappear, despite the rising resignation that they felt as time passed and their attempts to find training and employment were repeatedly disappointed. What was striking, under the circumstances, was rather their continued ability actively and independently to shape some form of life-concept. It seems possible that the 'changing values' discussion in the youth studies field rests upon a misinterpretation of research findings arising from the tendency of many studies to direct their vision away from structural conditions. As Baethge (1985) has pointed out, it is precisely in leisure and private life that the potential to affix individual meaning is greatest; activities may be identical on the surface, but they can be invested with quite different meanings for the person thus occupied (for example, visiting a disco).

Perhaps the divergent findings are a question of research design and method. Cross-sectional studies fix and freeze the momentary context of action, biographical age-stage, and the thematic/situative framing of the data collection technique. They therefore mask the inner dynamics of forms of expression in other segments of action and existence. Neither can they readily take into account that sharply differing biographies may underlny observed similarities in patterns of behaviour at a particular point in time. In other words, the homogeneity which appears to characterize age-cohorts is but a *static* homogeneity — a construct and artefact of research design. There is, however, also a danger of false generalization from the particular, when the analysis of individual biography is not placed within its structural context. Such contextualization cannot restrict itself to the school/classroom situation alone; similar educational positioning covers a spectrum of meaning in the biographies of young people with varying qualifications and future perspectives. Additionally, the timing of data collection itself is of enormous importance. The transition system's turning points place markers for the construction and reconstruction of biographical continuity. The point at which information is sought in relation to these markers determines the shape of the story told, a story which then continues to change its shape as the transitions process unfolds. The story at any one point is no more a reliable guide to understanding and explaining individual biographies any more than is a cross-sectional survey. Both are likely to result in false generalizations.

A similar set of problems arises from open-ended data collection methods, in which respondents are encouraged to tell their story in the way they choose. As noted earlier, as efforts to establish an employment future are disappointed, the willingness to voice one's 'failures' and fears that one will never succeed declines. Thus, where young people do not speak about these concerns, we should neither conclude that they do not actually have them nor that they do not place much value on work. It is only through active researcher probing and intervention on these topics that the disappointments and fears become visible (cf. Heinz, 1988).

The Comparison of National and International Contexts

High rates of youth unemployment or fractured, delayed transitions between education and employment have not been peculiar to the FRG over the eighties. Nor is it the case that the discovery of youth as a significant sector of the market for leisure, consumer goods and lifestyle images is restricted to West Germany. The fact that young people in the FRG continue to put great effort into establishing a secure employment biography underlines that passage into adulthood — via the socially structured transitions system between school and the labour market — remains of fundamental significance despite the loss of a guaranteed outcome. Two factors seem to converge here. Firstly, the *disillusionments* built into the transitions system itself *creep up on people* very gradually, since there are numerous possibilities for looping, repeating, diversions and (apparent) qualification upgrading along the way. Every missed opportunity represents itself as but a missed opportunity to gain access to a higher rung rather than to employment per se. Having missed one opportunity automatically means gaining access to a new opportunity to enter the labour market lower down the ladder. Downgrading takes place gradually and every step contains promise as well as disappointment. The educational sorting and filtering to which young people early become acclimatized is also interpreted as having employment relevance, so that confrontation with the labour market is introduced over a lengthy biographical phase, during which decisions and turning points do not appear to have an irrevocable character.

Secondly, this structural principle is reinforced by normative principles which offer explanations for missed opportunities and thus offer ways of coming to terms with disappointments and compromises. Young people are utterly convinced that both the chances and the obstacles they meet in the transitions system are a consequence of their *own* efforts and achievements. This perspective is socially grounded in the expectation and demand that individuals are themselves responsible for the patterns and outcomes of their entry into employment.

Since the introduction of comprehensivization Britain has, in formal terms, a state schooling system which is much more egalitarian than that of the FRG. It has been theories of social reproduction and the concept of the cultural code that have dominated explanations for the persistence of social inequalities of educational opportunity and outcome. In France, it is the concept of cultural capital and theories of its transmission which have been used to account for intergenerational continuities of class membership. Traditionally, France has operated a competitive educational system which is highly selective and elitist at its upper echelons. Youth research in the FRG, however, seems to have attached itself to the thesis of modernization of the social structure through individualization processes which bring a convergence of formerly class or gender specific differences amongst young people. Studies have identified changing organizational forms, peer group relations and patterns of leisure and consumer behaviour as the empirical witnesses for this perspective. But if we look directly at the West German transitions system, we see quite clearly that regardless of individual effort at school and in the vocational education/training sector, social inequalities persist — young people continue to inherit their positionings and destinations from their family backgrounds. At the same time, it is true that each constellation of patterns of behaviour, educational motivation, coping strategies and gradual accession to actual labour market opportunities produces its own story, beyond the dimensions of class and status. An individualized programme of social learning does, in this sense, emerge through the stabilising and determining patterns of a belief in equality of opportunity and individual achievement. Reintegration into the milieu of origin still takes place, but it does so through an individualization which is in fact a process of alienation. The motto 'every man for himself' (sic) underpins the pressure towards an early onset of individualization and biographization — at least, in what room is left for manoeuvre once the constraints/opportunities of gender and class have left their marks. The evidence is that this perspective on life offers an adequate enough long term motivational basis. New collectivities are indeed accreted around leisure culture and experimentation with youth styles, but the shifting collectivities assembled in the transitions system have quite different implications. Behind the collective term 'youth phase', processes of structural *differentiation* take their course.

However, the findings of phenomenological and interactionist youth research do challenge us to inspect how disappointments and disillusionment in the transitions system are connected with the construction and consolidation of gender-specific identities and cultural patterns. Our study (Heinz *et al.*, 1985) showed girls to be much more resilient than boys in coming to terms with the structures of opportunity and disillusionment. Young women focus much more energy on building up their own employment biography, despite the fact that their actual chances of reward for their efforts are much lower. They do not take refuge in an orientation towards housewifery and motherhood, although the opportunity to do so is still offered within the transitions system itself. From the range of full-time school or college based vocational education/ training courses available, many still contain significant curriculum components around the traditional female tasks of nursing, nutrition and childcare. Girls taking such courses do not evaluate these components any differently than they do others, i.e., they judge them accordingly to their labour market currency value. Girls continue, of course, to experience a double socialization process which prepares them for second class status in both the family and on the labour market. Nevertheless, that process appears to offer some potential for resistance; the cultural capital girls thus acquire contains elements of counter-definition as well as of reproduction.

For boys, on the other hand, dislocation and fracture in the process of constructing an employment biography appears to produce a tendency to clutch at the symbols of masculinity available in the leisure and consumer fields as a substitute source of identity and status. Patterns of resistance do not seem to develop in other spheres of life, perhaps because male socialization is more unidimensional in character. Male gender and occupational roles *converge* onto a future role as the breadwinner. It would appear that for young men, normative expectations instilled from early childhood socialization onwards are more powerful than are the realities of life, so that escape into the 'masculinity' offered through the worlds of leisure and consumer images is a more acceptable alternative.

Comparative research could be of considerable significance for exploring the relationships between the cultural and structural dimensions of social change in gender roles and adult status. However, comparisons between young people and the youth phase in West Germany and Great Britain are destined to produce distortion and misunderstanding where they do not take into account the very real differences between the two countries in the structures and mechanisms of transition. In this discussion, I have attempted to show just how these operate in the FRG, and to explore what their consequences are for the attitudes and behaviour of youth as a heterogeneous social group.

Chapter 9

Beyond Individualization:
What Sort of Social Change?

Gill Jones and Claire Wallace

There is no such thing as society; there are only individual men and women and there are families. (Margaret Thatcher, 1987)

In this chapter we will consider two significant paradigms which have informed youth studies in recent years: the idea of 'individualization' from West Germany and that of social reproduction from Great Britain. Using empirical data and drawing on recent research we then consider an alternative hypothesis, which proposes that increased structural diversity, far from reflecting freedom of choice and 'individualization', instead represents new outward forms of the traditional patterns of inequality. These inequalities are rooted in capitalist and patriarchal social structures.

Individualization Theory

Beck (1987) has argued that in wealthy Western industrialized societies, but especially in West Germany, class divisions and traditional collective solidarities have been breaking down since 1945. He suggests that the loss of class solidarity and the traditional support networks of the family and the community have led to an increased emphasis on the individual private world. There are, however, contradictory tendencies and when the individual is under threat from bureaucracies, 'new sociocultural commonalities' could emerge, based on the interests, ambitions and commitments of individuals rather than on class identity. These processes of change are still under way and patterns of social inequality persist, obscuring from view the changing social meaning of inequality. Nevertheless,

> . . . subcultural class identities have dissipated, class distinctions based on 'status' have lost their traditional support, and *processes for the 'diversification' and 'individualization' of life styles and ways of life* have been set in motion. As a result, the hierarchical model of

social classes and strata has increasingly been subverted. It no longer corresponds to the realities. (*ibid*, p. 341)

Beck argues that the process of individualization is no longer restricted to the bourgeoisie. In all sectors of society people are demanding more control over their own lives despite the increased risk that may result from the loss of traditional forms of group support. Risks are therefore more shared. Educational and labour market institutions stress individual success and encourage competitiveness. The pressure of competition means that people become isolated among their peers and must take responsibility for themselves. Life thus becomes a 'biographical project'.

Youth is a crucial moment in this biographical project (Bertram, 1985; Hartmann, 1987). Olk (1986 and 1988) argues that the twentieth century has brought an increasing *standardization* of youth as an age-phase reaching its peak the 1950s and 60s. Since then however, a process of 'individualization and diversification of life situations and life styles' (Olk, 1988, p. 129) has taken root: youth has become increasingly *destandardized*.

Firstly, in terms of work, there is a tendency to remain longer in the education and training system and become more comprehensively trained due, so Olk argues, to an increasing need for technical competence in the labour market. Pathways into work have become more extended and complex (*ibid*). Young people's career paths have become less structured with the increasing diversification of the youth labour market, and are more likely to be the outcome of individual choice (Heinz, 1987). According to Beck (1987), while education leads to increased career opportunity (or at least to protection from downward mobility), it is the labour market which is the principal cause of individualization, through competition and occupational and geographic mobility.

Trends in the transition into work have been accompanied by changes in attitude: some surveys suggest that young men are increasingly likely to judge work according to whether they think it is worthwhile, rather than to adopt a blind allegiance to the work ethic; at the same time they are less work-centred in their life goals (Jugendwerk der deutschen Shell, 1981 and 1985). Young women, on the other hand, no longer perceive family-building as their only goal, but may be more likely to seek fulfilment in the labour market (Seidenspinner and Burger, 1982). Research in Britain by Burnhill and McPherson (1984) suggests, however, that this finding may apply mainly to more educated women.

Leisure styles are becoming as important as work in terms of individual life goals (Baethge, 1985). The mass market has increased the choices available to individuals. Hence leisure too has become individualized. Young people are able to seek their own pursuits regardless of parental direction. Hartmann (1987) argues that technology and housing developments mean that they have more choice: they can afford to buy their own leisure and have their own rooms in which to pursue these choices. They can thus develop unique cultural styles and adult authority is decreased.

Finally, it is argued that the family life cycle is becoming increasingly destandardized in all Western countries. Increasing divorce, cohabitation and extra-marital childrearing, along with the tendency for more young people to set up independent households prior to marriage, mean (it is suggested) that there is more diversity, and thence choice, of family forms. The relationship between young people and their parents is also changing.The increased emphasis on individual rights has been reflected in legislative changes (Hermanns, 1987) which define children's rights as distinct from those of their parents, women's rights as distinct from those of men.Parents have less control over their children: for example, the parents of young people who were questioned during recent riots in Stockholm often did not know where their children were at the time (Hartmann, 1987). On a more general level, Beck (1987) has argued that competition in the labour market has led to the breakdown of traditional relationships such as community or family ties, and a trend towards relationships based instead on shared interests. According to this theory, there is therefore likely to be even greater strain on family relationships once young people enter the labour market.

Whilst there is some evidence of structural change, the individualization thesis also depends upon interpretation of changing values. The Shell surveys of young people in West Germany, for example, provide some of the evidence for the theory and were in part the result of a moral panic about youth in the wake of terrorism, rising unemployment, the peace movement and the success of der Grünen (Hübner-Funk, 1985). The findings were held to show that young people in Germany were becoming increasingly disaffected and inclined to pursue their own individualized creative values rather than unquestionningly accept external authority (in contrast with young people in the fifties). Hartmann's (1987) 'optimistic' version of individualization for example, argues that individualization leads to more choice and autonomy. This echoes the idea of competitive individualism put forward by the New Right in Britain and the United States. In the 'pessimistic' variant it is associated with increasing risk of downward mobility, uncertainty and stress (Heinz *et al.*, 1985).

The individualization thesis can seem reminiscent of 'middle American individualism', described by Gans (1988) and identified 150 years ago by De Tocqueville. There is, however, a major difference: Gans and the New Right are prescribing an *ideology* of individualism, while Beck is describing what he sees as a real social process. This perhaps illustrates the extent to which the presentation of individualization may depend on the national context. The degree of uncertainty introduced into an otherwise highly structured German system in recent years contrasts with the unstructured and relatively open system of labour market allocation which has existed for some time in the USA and also, until very recently, in Britain.

A number of problems arise with the individualization thesis, particularly insofar as it has been applied to youth studies. Firstly, youth is seen here as a unitary concept, whereas it seems to us that many of the findings are group specific. Some affluent and middle class young people, with expanding career opportunities and extended education, may be in a position to choose between competing alternatives. For others, mainly those of working class origin, there may be less choice and more risk, with declining labour market opportunities and lower incomes. Risks may be concealed by institutional structures; in Britain, the Youth Training Scheme obscures the issue of youth unemployment and presents a largely false image of opportunity for young workers. Paths to adulthood, far from being individualized, can still be predicted from social class origins to a great extent in both Britain and West Germany.

The thesis fits the position of young men more than that of young women, whose autonomy may be restricted by lower wages, more parental control and sexual labelling (Lees, 1986). Furthermore, race and ethnicity receive little attention in this model, despite the fact that in both Britain and West Germany the relatively secure position of young white workers is partly based on the fact that members of ethnic minority groups suffer the main risk of unemployment.

Baethge (1985) argues that whereas Erikson's concept of youth as a moratorium, a period of experimentation, could be applied only to middle class youth at the time, it can now be applied to youth more universally since all young people are becoming like the middle class. In our view this is erroneous. Individualization theory (in its more optimistic forms a modern variant of embourgeoisement theory) cannot be applied to young people in general, ignoring as it does inequalities of opportunity resulting from the continued stratification of our society by social class, gender and ethnicity.

Social Reproduction Theory

In Britain, by contrast, theories of social and cultural reproduction have helped to provide an explanation of the way in which an alienating and oppressive power structure is able to reproduce itself in each generation. Theories have been developed mainly from the work of Marxist scholars (Althusser, 1971; Bowles and Gintis, 1976; Bourdieu and Passeron, 1977; Willis, 1977). In Britain, the empirical focus has been on working class youth, and social reproduction theories provide an alternative explanation to that emanating from Germany. We can also look at this approach in terms of work, leisure and family.

The reproduction of work roles takes place through socialization by the education system, the family and the peer group (Willis, 1977; Corrigan, 1979). While many young people are able successfully to adapt to the school system, for some, particularly educational non-achievers, both the experience of state schooling and later experience of working class jobs are oppressive and alienating. Some, therefore, adopt a 'creative response' by forming a working class anti-school sub-culture which validates, and eventually helps them to adapt to, dead-end and powerless jobs (Willis, 1977). The emphasis in social reproduction theory has been on the reproduction of the working class, rather than on the middle class or on prospects for upward mobility among those who are disadvantaged within the education system and the labour market.

Again class has been emphasized in the study of youth sub-cultures, which are described as a response to a class problematic and a way of coming to terms with class positions (Hall and Jefferson, 1976; Mungham and Pearson, 1976).

Research in this area has neglected the family and the position of young women. More recently, feminists have examined the way in which familial expectations structure girls' ambitions and experience (Griffin, 1985; Sharpe, 1976; McRobbie and Garber, 1976). It is argued that the reproduction of the family is an outcome of patriarchal structures which serve to oppress young women and benefit capitalism. The family is seen as a crucial agent of social reproduction because it provides the main context for the construction and reinforcement of gender identities. However, just as studies of youth sub-cultures focused on men, so studies of family expectations and household formation in youth have tended to be restricted to women. Attempts to produce gender-symmetrical studies of men and women in terms of both their labour market behaviour and their domestic responsibilities are lacking.

Social reproduction theory has been subject to considerable criticism. First, it has been argued that the model is too static. It does not, for example, take into account changing social conditions, such as changes in the labour market and rising unemployment. Some have argued, too, that the idea of age as a category has been dismissed too readily (Smith, 1981). In failing to incorporate an age perspective, social reproduction theory neglects the processes of transition to adulthood which are inherent to youth. Secondly, though the approach sought to reintroduce social class into the study of youth, there were problems with its mode of class analysis: it focused too exclusively on male working class youth, ignoring middle class youth and women, and thus failed to locate young people in the context of wider social structures (Jones, 1987). It has been argued that the concept of class has been reified and its importance assumed rather than demonstrated (Connell, 1983; Marsland, 1987); that divisions within classes have been neglected (Jenkins, 1983; Wallace, 1987); and that other dimensions of social stratification such as gender and ethnicity have been underemphasized (MacDonald, 1980; McRobbie, 1980; Cohen, 1988). Finally, it is argued that there has been too much emphasis upon spectacular and rebellious young people at the expense of 'ordinary' ones (Jenkins, 1983; Brown, 1988).

Towards an Alternative Explanation

Neither German individualization theory nor British approaches to social reproduction have in our view been able to provide an adequate explanation of the position of young people in modern society. A class analysis needs to take account of the power relations in society (Jenkins, 1983, cf Willis, 1977) and to consider the position of both middle class and working class young people; a gender analysis should take account of men as well as women. Both need to consider the temporary nature of youth through the study of the construction of age transitions and also its generational perspective through age relations. Despite Mannheim's (1927) writing on 'generation-units' within the generation it did not indicate the nature of relationships between them and there has been no successful further elaboration of these ideas which can combine the age/ generation perspective with one which concerns itself with the causes and nature of inequalities in youth (Jones, 1988a).

No adequate framework therefore existed for understanding patterns of diversity within youth, and the perspective of the life-course intro-duced in recent years, demands a further reevaluation. We suggest that a framework is still needed. As Bertaux (1981) pointed out, it is the context of social relations between individuals with differing life histories which brings biography into the realms of sociology.

How can we pull together these different issues? It is not an easy task to locate the study of the individual life course within a framework of the social structure, which comprises complex social relationships and is subject to historical change. Individualization theories describe 'collective life histories' (following Mannheim's 'generation units'?) accepting that pathways are not infinite but suggesting that the patterns are determined by individual ambition and motivation. In our view these patterns are socially rather than individually constructed; they reflect class cultures and the relationship between the different patterns reflects the class relations of a capitalist society.

Our research has led us independently to a similar conclusion — that patterns of transition in Britain show *not* increasing individualization *but instead* continuity the basic class structure and reproduction of class patterns. Because of this continuity, social class, gender and ethnicity still crucially determine the destinies and the values of young people. We are going to show this empirically, focusing mainly on class and gender issues because of the nature of our data, firstly taking a closer look at individual biography in its social context and then by considering recent change.

Individual Biography and Social Structure

The empirical research reported first is part of a study of stratification in youth, which is described more fully elsewhere (Jones, 1987 and 1988b) and draws on data from the National Child Development Study (NCDS), supplemented with data from the General Household Survey (GHS). The NCDS is a cohort study of all the people born in Britain during one week in March 1958. Its fourth sweep in 1981 contained 12,537 respondents aged 23 years and provides current and retrospective data since the previous sweep when the cohort was aged 16 years (Shepherd, 1985). In order to learn about young people beyond the age of 23, we turn to the GHS. This is an annual British survey of individuals in households and, unlike the NCDS, is a cross-sectional data set, providing a picture of age transitions only through age comparisons (OPCS, 1981 and 1982). A sample of 12,036 people aged 16–29 was obtained by combining the GHS data for 1979 and 1980.

Class Histories

Individual class histories represent the interface between biography and social structure. They raise issues about social class as an individual construction and class as a collectivity. They highlight the problems of examining individual transitions in the context of social change. In order to study class careers in youth, one has to face head on all the specific problems of defining class in youth (see Jones, 1987), but it is only by doing so that any understanding of the position of young people in the social structure can be obtained.

Young people in work show greater mobility, both occupational and social, than older workers. On entering the labour market, some young people embark on work careers (either long-term middle class or short-term working class careers, according to Ashton and Field's 1976 typology) which may take them into new positions in the class structure. Over time their social class position may therefore change, both in terms of the occupational class of their first jobs and in relation to their class of origin. Though some young workers are in dead-end careerless jobs of the kind described by Willis (1977) and Ashton and Field (1976), for many the pathways of their class careers are as extended and complex as the pathways into work referred to by Olk (1988) and Heinz (1987). Figure 9.1 indicates male intergenerational movement from class of origin and intragenerational movement between the class of first job and current occupational class at 23 years.

Figure 9.1   *Mobility routes from class of origin — males*

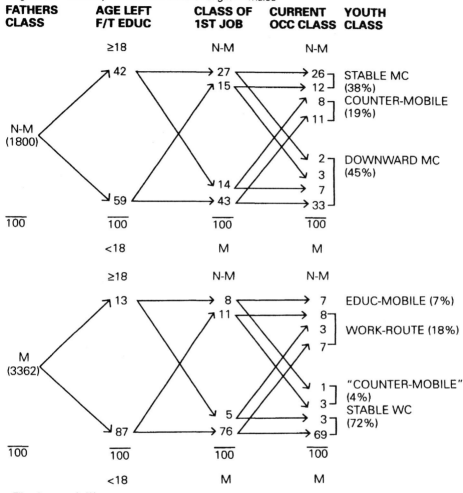

FATHERS CLASS | **AGE LEFT F/T EDUC** | **CLASS OF 1ST JOB** | **CURRENT OCC CLASS** | **YOUTH CLASS**

File: Longmob (9)
Source: NCDS
Key: **F/T** – Further/Technical; **OCC** – Occupational; **MC** – Middle Class; **WC** – Working Class

Such social mobility in youth could reflect freedom of movement in the class structure. Such an interpretation would fit Beck's (1987 p. 351) point that social class groups have lost their independent identities, so that the idea of social mobility pales into insignificance. What light can figure 9.1 shed on the issue?

Firstly, there *is* a lot of movement between class positions in youth. Individualization theorists could suggest this to be indicative of the contemporary meaninglessness of social mobility. Movement between class positions occurs both frequently and fairly randomly. These data do not, however, show intergenerational mobility as of that order: by the age of 23 years, 76 per cent of sons of working class fathers are in working class jobs and 57 per cent of sons of middle class fathers are in middle class jobs.[1]

Neither is the movement between classes random — on the contrary, there was significant counter-mobility in these data. Nineteen per cent of middle class sons regain their class of origin by the age of 23; it is likely that this proportion will increase as the years pass, so that the sons of the 45 per cent currently downwardly mobile will regain their class of origin (Jones, 1987). Counter-mobility is structural, not a random form of mobility; it is a basic mechanism of social reproduction of the middle class. Furthermore, there are clear indications that the family of origin may provide active help during the process of counter-mobility (Jones, 1986), contrary to Beck's (1987) suggestion that in order to survive, people have to sever old connections and take charge of their own lives (p. 344).

Finally, Beck (*ibid*) argues that education is primarily a protection against downward mobility, rather than a means of upward mobility. The data in figure 9.1 show that education appears to protect the middle class from downward intergenerational mobility (and figure 9.2 shows that this is even more the case among women). Yet equally, upward mobility from working class origins and counter-mobility among middle class sons is most common among those who have been longer in education. In times of recession, we could argue that upward mobility via education rather than work-based routes becomes relatively even more dominant than these data already indicate.

Figure 9.2 shows the same general pattern of class reproduction for women. Closer examination indicates that among women, class positions prior to marriage are more likely to be determined by educational achievement than by subsequent upward work-life mobility.[2] In consequence, women tend to show greater intragenerational stability in their early class careers.

Class reproduction is not straightforward and individual work-life mobility should not therefore be cited as evidence of fluidity or a gradual breaking down of the class structure, but rather as a mechanism for its continued stability. The concept of individual choice has limited value — the nature of the choice and the ability to choose at all may be determined by class and gender. In contrast to individualization theorists, we argue that individual ambition and motivation may be restricted by structural opportunity and constraint. There is nothing new in this argument — Roberts drew it to our attention during a similar academic debate in 1968.

The 'youth class' groups empirically identified in this study can be specified more clearly:

Figure 9.2 *Mobility routes from class of origin — women without children (See Jones (1987) for explanation of manual and non-manual classes for women)*

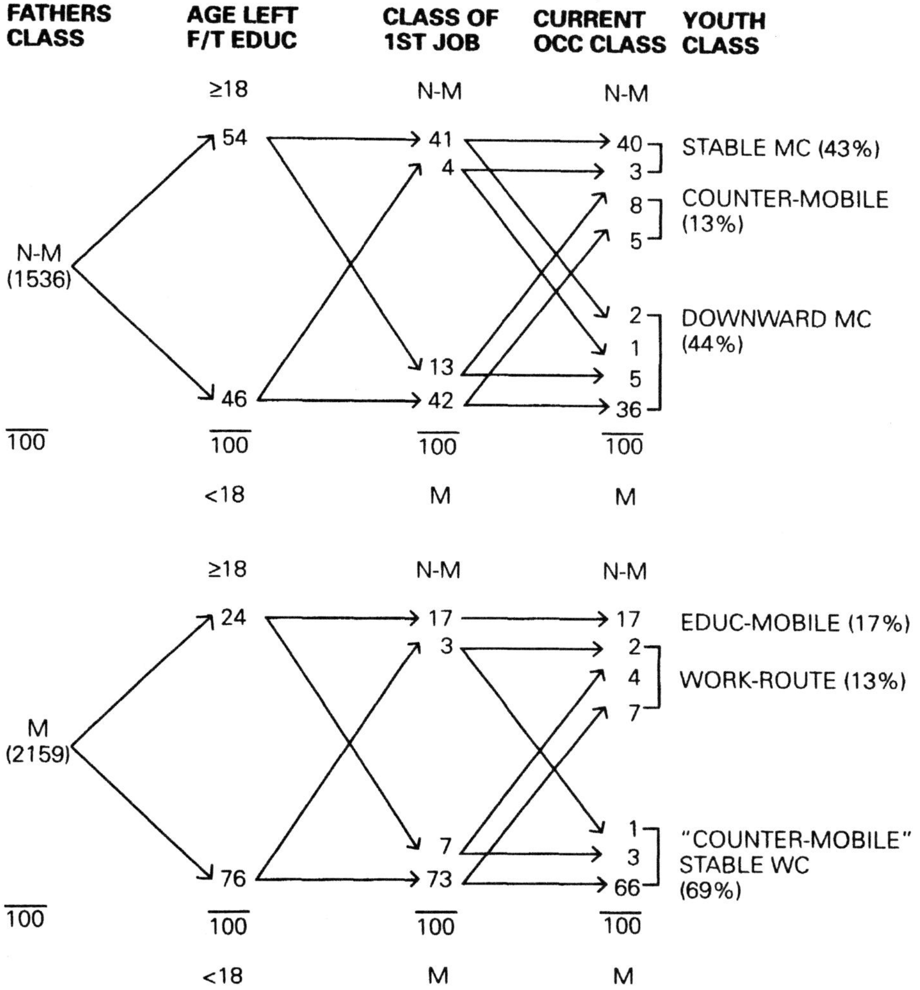

FATHERS CLASS	AGE LEFT F/T EDUC	CLASS OF 1ST JOB	CURRENT OCC CLASS	YOUTH CLASS

File: CARMOB (9)
Source: NCDS
Key: **F/T** – Further/Technical; **OCC** – Occupational; **MC** – Middle Class; **WC** – Working Class

Stable Middle Class — comprising those of middle class backgrounds who appear to move directly into non-manual work (reflecting the effect of class origins and education);

Education-Mobile Working Class — those of working class backgrounds who achieve upward mobility into non-manual work through full-time education;

Counter-Mobile Middle Class — those of middle class backgrounds who enter manual work (or, in the case of women, low-grade non-manual work), and later retrieve their class positions through work mobility, or a combination of work and education routes;

Work-Route Working Class — those from working class families who achieve upward mobility, through work rather than full-time education routes;

Downwardly-Mobile Middle Class — middle class early education-leavers who enter manual work, some of whom will become counter-mobile in time, while some will remain downwardly mobile;

Stable Working Class — those from working class backgrounds who are early school-leavers, move into manual work and are unlikely to be upwardly mobile.

A current study of social stratification in youth would need to expand on these categories. In particular, the stable working class should perhaps be divided according to attachment over time to the labour market in order to understand variation within the working class, as Wallace's study (discussed below) suggests. The above groupings disting-uish between current occupational class groupings according to longitu-dinal class careers.

The Effect of Class Careers on Voting Behaviour

Beck's central argument is that the social meaning of inequality is chang-ing and subcultural class identities have dissipated. Voting behaviour has traditionally been seen as an outcome of class identity. If class identity has dissipated, then there should be no patterns in voting according to past or current social class, and if, as Beck suggests, mobility lacks significance, voting should not vary according to the patterns of social mobility.

Table 9.1 is an analysis of voting behaviour and illustrates that, contrary to the above hypothesis, voting is one of the ways in which class pathways are clearly reflected in attitude and behaviour. The NCDS cohort was asked in 1981 for which party they had voted in the 1979 General Election. Table 9.2 shows that voting behaviour is closely associ-ated with class of origin, which therefore dominates among the indepen-dent variables comprising the typology. The table shows, nevertheless, that voting varies considerably by class pathway. The two extremes of voting behaviour are displayed by the stable middle class, 47 per cent of males and 45 per cent of females voting Conservative, and the stable working class, with only 14 per cent of males and 19 per cent of females voting Conservative. The mobile groups fall between these two ex-tremes. The effect of class of origin can be seen throughout. For example, although the counter-mobile middle class and the work-route mobile of working class origin achieved mobility in similar ways and are currently

Table 9.1   Party Voted for in 1979 General Election (at 21 YRS) by Youth Class and Sex (%)

Party Voted for	Stable MC	Counter-Mobile	Down-ward MC	Educ-Mobile	Work-Mobile	Stable WC	All
Men							
Conservative	47	39	31	31	28	14	24
Labour	21	20	23	32	29	39	32
Liberal	12	14	9	14	10	6	8
Other	2	2	3	4	2	3	3
Did not Vote	18	24	33	20	30	39	33
All (=100%)	(617)	(321)	(779)	(222)	(595)	(2543)	(5077)
Women without children							
Conservative	45	40	40	35	26	19	.30
Labour	17	15	16	28	28	34	25
Liberal	13	10	14	12	9	7	10
Other	2	4	1	2	1	3	2
Did not Vote	23	33	26	24	33	35	30
All (=100%)	(582)	(200)	(673)	(335)	(278)	(1519)	(3623)

Source: NCDS

Table 9.2   *Educational and economic activities of 16-year-olds in Britain* (%)

	1976	1986
In full-time education	40	45
In employment (outside YTS)*	53	15
On YTS/YOP	0	27
Unemployed	7	12
	100	99
Total 16-year-olds (=100%)	(821,000)	(860,000)

Derived from Table 39, *Social Trends* 18, 1988, HMSO.
* Includes in 1976 the unregistered unemployed and those who were neither employed nor seeking work (for example because of domestic responsibilities) and in 1986 those who were seeking work but not claiming benefit and those neither employed nor seeking work.

in non-manual work, their voting behaviour is very different: 39 per cent of counter-mobile men and 40 per cent of counter-mobile women voted Conservative, compared with 28 per cent of work-mobile men and 26 per cent of work-mobile women. It is not just current occupational class which is relevant to the analysis, therefore. A longitudinal class typology increases our understanding of the association between class and voting behaviour; and it is instructive to distinguish mobile groups within current occupational classes.

We have shown that overall patterns of social inequality remain relatively stable between generations and that there are outward measurable signs reflecting these inequalities. Voting is one example, but young people also follow different paths to adulthood, and these patterns of transition too derive from class and gender inequalities.

Family Formation

The longitudinal class typology provides a conceptual framework for a class analysis of transitions to adulthood in work, housing and family formation. The findings we present in figure 9.3 show a broad general picture of these transitions, broken down into the median ages at which young people reached the 'milestones' of leaving school, starting work, leaving home, getting married or cohabiting, and having children, according to their sex and class. It should be emphasized that each of these transitions is complex and there is no 'normal' progress from one state to another. Adulthood may not necessarily depend on passing these milestones, or on passing them in any particular order.

The data in figure 9.3 show clearly the variation in the median ages at which transition milestones are passed by different social groups. There are broadly two sets of transitions, those related to employment and those related to family formation. Regardless of the age at which the first set of transitions is passed, there is a fairly constant time relationship between the two sets of transitions across all youth class groups, but with considerable variation according to gender. The median time gap is around seven years for men and four years for women. The suggestion here is that whatever the nature of class careers, the spacing between entering work and family building does not vary; thus early school-leavers become marriage partners and parents before college leavers. Overall, men tend to spend longer in the labour market than women before beginning to form families. This may be because they have more to gain by doing so. These data vividly illustrate the different structuring of transition milestones according to gender. In general, adulthood begins earlier for women.

Social class nevertheless still structures the paths to adulthood. The age of leaving education and entering the labour force is class related. and so therefore is the starting point for the transitions to adulthood. Family formation transitions typically comprise three stages: setting up an independent home, forming a partnership and having children. Figure 9.3 shows how the stable middle class may space these stages over several years, perhaps for career considerations, or because they want to save towards a home, while the stable working class, in contrast, compress them into a considerably shorter space of time. In consequence, the period of youth begins earlier and is less gradual and protracted for the

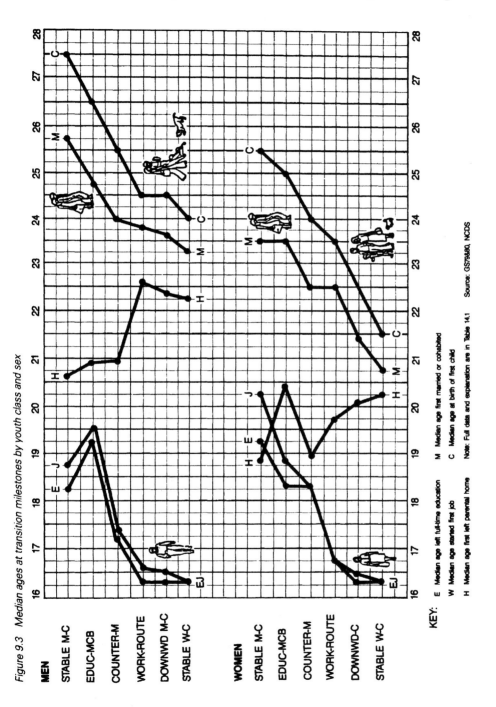

Figure 9.3 Median ages at transition milestones by youth class and sex

working class than for the middle class. The data show that in Britain in around 1980, delayed marriage and child-bearing were only common among more educated women (cf. also Seidenspinner and Burger, 1982).

The need for a longitudinal approach to social class, and for the concept of class to be more finely tuned to the circumstances of young people, is highlighted in a longitudinal study conducted by Wallace (1987) between 1979 and 1984. In this study, 153 16-year-olds were initially contacted, and it was likewise found that the way in which young people made family and housing transitions was constructed by the nature of their entry into the labour market. However, by 1984 it was evident that social class affected the likelihood of sample members being unemployed, and within the broadly working class school-leavers a subsection had been unemployed for significant lengths of time. Their opportunities and life-styles were significantly different from those who had been mainly employed. One third of the eighty-four interviewed in 1984 had been out of work for at least a year.

It was evident from these interviews that it was not so much their position at any point in time which was important, as the *cumulative biographical experience* which served to advantage or disadvantage them and to affect both their objective position and their subjective perceptions of their position. For example, whilst in general most of the sample disapproved of starting a family whilst being unemployed, in practice many of them had done so, but they were more likely to be cohabiting, or living with their partners in their parents' home, than to have left home, married and established an independent household in a 'conventional' way. Only those with regular jobs were able to marry and buy their own homes and this depended mostly upon their partners also having jobs.

Over a period of five years there was an increasing divergence between the mainly employed and the mainly unemployed in terms of their ownership of consumer goods, the peer groups to which they belonged and the way they spent their time. Denied access to commercial leisure, the unemployed increasingly associated with other unemployed and became isolated. Time came to have a different meaning for them. Young women became more absorbed into domestic life in the parental home. In this way a subcategory of non-workers was evolving for whom 'individualization' would have an entirely different meaning.

Both studies discussed here show the extent to which beliefs and transitions in youth are structured by class and gender. We stress, however, the importance of problematizing the concept of social class and re-conceiving it in a way which is appropriate for the study of young people. It is only then that the continuity of class structures and the structural inqualities resulting from them can be perceived.

Recent Change in Britain: Is There Evidence of Individualization?

It is possible, of course, that circumstances have recently changed to such an extent in Britain that individualization theory can now be applied. In this final section of this chapter, we shall consider this possibility.

First, the extension of periods of education and training is observable in Britain, too, as discussed by Brown in this volume. The introduction of the Youth Training Scheme in 1983 has contributed very significantly towards this trend. Whereas half of all 16-year-olds were in employment in 1976 the majority now continue in post-16 education or training (though among the latter there will be some employees). Furthermore, increasing credentialism means that 89 per cent of school-leavers had some form of qualification in 1980/81, compared with only 27 per cent in 1961/62. During the final years at school, lessons in 'life skills' encourage young people to equip themselves with the 'profiles' which will allow them to compete effectively in the labour market. The problems of structural unemployment are thus individualized: if a young person cannot get a job it is because they were inadequately prepared, rather than because there is no job available. This is reflected in the commonly-expressed view that some people are out of work because they do not want to work.

Consumerism is more widespread. It is evident that many people seek to define their status group according to their consumer styles rather than the status of their jobs. Consumer items may symbolize major life transitions — in terms of status, a motorbike, a stereo and the accoutrements of a home are outwardly as important as job status, although the cash or credit facilities for buying such things depends on employment income. Consumerism can be seen as a badge of achievement, stressing the individual nature of success.

Within the young middle class, rising incomes for graduates bring more career and consumer choice. Those in highly paid jobs are able to capitalize on the recent rise in house prices to increase their wealth; they can see their success in terms of individual effort (Wallace, 1987). The term 'yuppie' has become a by-word for the high-spending, trend-following (and stereotypically Porsche-driving) young adult consumer. Such flamboyant success is, however, mainly associated with men. Gender inequalities in earnings and opportunities persist in the middle class too, increasing as women take on domestic responsibilities (Dex, 1985).

The successful working class may similarly see their success in terms of individual effort:

> I mean, the government ain't giving me any money, or anything like that. I mean, it's purely because we done it, see we could have sat down and said 'Things will come along, things'll come

along', but then you don't get what you want do you? (Wallace, 1987, p. 136 quote from respondent)

There is, nevertheless, an increasing divergence between these, and the less fortunate. The 16+ school-leaver transition *has* become increasingly standardized: rather than being left to fend for themselves in the labour market, young people are now more likely to receive a small allowance, lower than a wage, while on a training scheme. The various routes within this interstitial 16–18 period may determine their later fortunes. What is evident is that this whole period is subject to increasing outside intervention. Control has been removed from the young and put in the hands of professional guidance experts, teachers and intermediaries in the labour market, such as the managing agents who run YTS. Under these circumstances, therefore, increased diversity cannot represent increased choice. Young people have instead increasingly been turned from young workers and 'affluent consumers' into wageless dependents of the state or their families.

In the long run, unemployment proves an effective labour discipline. Young people resign themselves to the opportunities available, as numerous studies have shown (for example, Roberts, 1968; Heinz, 1987).

Wallace (1987) found that between 1979 and 1984, 44 per cent of 109 school-leavers (interviewed in 1980) on the Isle of Sheppey had taken jobs which were of lower status than they had hoped for. Many of these leavers were forced into unskilled factory work when they had hoped to find skill-training of some kind. Some pursued an alternative strategy, taking jobs which might provide good 'informal' work experience, but this was not always successful. Five years later, roughly half of the 84 traced were still in jobs which were worse than they had originally hoped for in 1979. As one young man put it:

Oh, it's lousy pay. Well they can hire whoever they like, can't they? They can kick you out and they know they can get someone off the dole queue, so they don't have to pay much do they? They can find anyone, can't they? It's so simple so they can keep the prices down. It's as simple as that. You can't earn no more. (Wallace, 1987, p. 128 quote from respondent)

Current training schemes, some have argued, assist in the general pattern of socialization by lowering some young people's expectations and moulding them to fit low paid, unskilled jobs (Buswell, 1986). Training schemes may also act as a form of social control, aimed at containing and restraining the young unemployed (Benn and Fairly, 1986; Finn, 1987).

There are, therefore, new mechanisms of social reproduction: YTS too creates forms of stratification. There is widespread cynicism about the scheme: many school-leavers enter YTS only because there is no alternative. In a study by Parsons (1988) young people ranked a job as first preference, training second, further education third and unemployment, not surprisingly, in last place in their hierarchy of choices. The expansion of opportunities held to have taken place for school-leavers is thus not perceived by them as such. Their choices have not been broadened merely channelled. YTS caters mainly for working class youth — the bottom 40 per cent of the school population. Even if trainees successfully complete the scheme, even the more optimistic estimates suggest that a third are likely to find themselves unemployed afterwards.

Within YTS itself, there are divisions between 'good' and 'bad' schemes and between 'premium-funded' places (for the more rebellious, so-called 'low ability' and 'problem' youth) and 'basic' places for the rest. The success of YTS depends on the local labour market context, and there is variation between labour markets (Raffe, 1988b). This kind of stratification is largely outside the control of the individual school-leaver who is allocated a particular place on the scheme by professional guidance experts. In most cases, trainees do not know that they have been labelled 'premiums'. Therefore, it could be said that the YTS system reproduces social divisions in a more structured way than the open labour market system of allocation which is now complements.

It might be argued that young people have a 'choice' as to which occupational sector to enter on the YTS, but this overlooks issues of occupational segregation by gender and race. In this sense, YTS replicates the segregation practices of the labour market. Despite the professed policy of equal opportunites, young women are clustered into schemes leading to traditionally female areas of employment. Even where they enter non-traditional occupations, they are likely to be engaged in more 'feminine' tasks — for example, cleaning the car in the car maintenance classes (Cockburn, 1988). Ethnic divisions are reproduced in the new training schemes in response to pressure from employers and racist assumptions prevail both inside and outside the schemes (Wrench, 1986). Young people from ethnic minorities are likely to find themselves in the 'premium' place schemes which tend not to lead to full-time jobs.

In terms of leisure styles, it is evident that wage-earning 'affluent teenage consumers' such as those seen in the 1950s and 60s no longer exist. Training and education allowances are far lower than wages, and the abolition in 1988 of supplementary benefit for those under 18 means that they get no alternative income. For the declining numbers who find jobs (15 per cent of 16-year-olds in 1986) relative wages have fallen (see Wallace, 1988). Hence, young people's consumption patterns depend upon what they can earn from part time jobs and the extent to which parents can subsidize their pursuits. Where this is the case, they are able to continue to participate in teenage consumer patterns, but in families suffering from multiple unemployment this is unlikely to be so. (Payne [1987] has shown that the young unemployed are likely to come from families where other members are unemployed).

Young people in Britain today may have less money and less control over their finances. Nevertheless, they are drawn into consumer markets at younger and younger ages, encouraged to use credit and have high expectations of obtaining consumption items (Hutson and Jenkins, 1987). This places increased pressure on them, especially if they are unemployed.

These trends mean that young people are increasingly expected to turn to their parents for support. Furthermore, recent legislative changes, such as raising to 25 years the age of eligibility for full rates of state benefit, ensure that the period of young people's dependence is extended. The intention appears to be to locate the social and moral control of young people in their relationship with their parents (Abbott and Wallace, 1988). Girls in particular are likely to be absorbed back into the parental home in times of rising unemployment; the same has been found for young Asians (Brah, 1986; Wallace, 1987). This means that relations with parents become crucial (Hutson and Jenkins, 1987) and the position of young people in the household economy also becomes important. The extent to which children can turn to their parents for financial support is however related both to income and to differing class, regional and ethnic practices. Legislation cannot overcome these differences. In low income families, teenagers' contributions form part of the family budget, as they have done for decades. In more affluent families the financial aid may run the other way — with parents supporting their children. For some young people who have left home to search for work, or because family relationships have broken down, there may be no parental support at all. Some find themselves both unemployed and homeless.

There have been changes in the patterns of family formation. The decreasing dominance of the concept of the 'nuclear family' is evident in Britain too. Nearly all the couples in the Wallace (1987) study, for example, cohabited prior to or instead of getting married and a number had children outside marriage without feeling that this was particularly stigmatizing.

Unemployment appears, however, to be affecting patterns of household and family formation. Experience of unemployment both leads to a postponement of traditional working class marriage and home building and to the substantial dependence of the new household upon the home of origin (Fagin and Little, 1984; Wallace, 1987). Overall, a more protracted and protected youth may be an emerging response to recent social, economic and legislative trends. Government policies seeking to increase parental control and thus (it is argued) to reduce juvenile crime are based on middle class ideologies of family life. They fail to take into account the socioeconomic structure:

The origins of crime lie deep in society: in families where parents do not support or control their children, in schools where discipline is poor; and in the wider world where violence is glamourised and traditional values are under attack. (*Conservative Party Manifesto*, 1987, p. 55)

While middle class families may have the resources to provide a home and subsidize the income of their young, many, particularly working class, families need young people to assume adult responsibilities at an earlier age. One outcome of current policies may be an extension of *working class* youth according to the models of transition to adulthood currently prevalent among the middle class. For young people who lack financial resources, this will represent not embourgeoisement, but a hollow sham of middle class practices.

Conclusion

Problems with the 'young' are often produced as evidence of social change. The concern about 'counter-culture' in the 1960s, for example, was followed by research which revealed the basic conformity of young people, and showed that far from reflecting a generation war, youth culture was sub-cultural in form, rooted in the class cultures of adults. Perhaps that same debate is being reenacted in Germany at present.

Those arguing for increasing 'individualization' have pointed to consumer choices, labour market diversity and uncertainty and to changing family patterns. Whilst acknowledging many of these changes, we would want to emphasize the importance of continuity in social reproduction. Neither risks nor opportunities are evenly distributed. Longstanding forms of class and gender inequalities are being reproduced in new ways. The importance of age as an allocating mechanism and dimension of stratification may be increasing. But new divisions are also being created among young people themselves, between the employed and unemployed, or between trainees on different types of training programmes. These new divisions warrant further consideration.

We began this chapter by quoting Margaret Thatcher, but we reject her view of the social world. Individuals, whether in families or not, live in a society which is complex and unequal. Neither political nor sociological theories can fruitfully ignore the ways in which this social context continually impinges upon individual lives. Our focus must therefore take in all that lies beyond the individual.

Acknowledgments

We are grateful to OPCS for the use of the General Household Survey, to the NCDS User Support Group at City University for the use of the National Child Development Study and to the ESRC Data Archive for providing both data sets. Our thanks also go to Andrew McPherson, David Raffe and Ray Pahl for their helpful comments on an earlier draft this chapter.

Notes

1 In the class schema used here, shop assistants are classified as manual workers.
2 The class schema has been dichotomised on different lines to take account of the different occupational structure for women. Those in junior non-manual work (Class 3) have been divided into those with longer in education (18 and over) and those who left full-time education before the age of 18; the more educated have been grouped with the higher non-manual classes (1, 2) and the less educated with the manual classes (4, 5, 6). This allows a dichotomy which is more meaningful for women than the usual manual/non-manual divide. It means, however, that by definition, women in Class 3 'Manual' (on the basis of their lower educational level) cannot become upwardly mobile into Class 3 Non-manual, but all class movement which can be identified among men (from Class 4 to Class 3, or from Class 3 to Class 2, for example) whether through work or education routes, can still be identified among women.

Chapter 10

Patriarchy for Children: On the Stability of Power Relations in Children's Lives

John Hood-Williams

The thesis of this chapter stands against writers who suggest the disappearance of childhood (Postman, 1982; Sommerville, 1982) in a post-industrial, deindustrial or, perhaps, a post-modern world. It is often claimed that the restructuring of the capitalist economy in Western Europe has brought a radically new capitalism. This new society has many analysts and many descriptions. It has, for example, been termed disorganized capitalism (Lash and Urry, 1987; Offe, 1985). The major themes explored in the plethora of writings on the new society (some well-known examples are Gorz, 1982; Lukes, 1984; Hobsbawm, 1989) include the radical reduction in the size of the traditional manufacturing sector, which has, in turn, reduced the size of the traditional male industrial working class; the growth of the service sector and of outwork in smaller factories and of part-time women workers; changes in patterns of ownership and control; the internationalization of production and of mass communication which constrains the autonomy of nation states and heightens the sense of the 'simultaneity' of events (the 'global village'); the modern difficulty of relating social, cultural and political life to traditional class relations which we can see in the emergence of the Women's Movement, the Green Party, anti-racist groups and so on; the growth of concern with the person, with privatism and with forms of radical individualism which, although they have a potential for anti-authoritarianism, have been effectively woven into the politics of the New Right in Britain since 1979 (see chapter 14 by Brake in this volume).

One of the issues raised by these writings is their effects on the family and kinship system, which is the home both of our conceptions of childhood and the most significant social relationships within which children are imbricated from birth (Lasch, 1977; Seabrook, 1982). In fact, it is rather interesting that analysts have confidently announced a new society on the basis of discussions of class, paid work and politics whilst, for the most part, steadfastly ignoring the character, or changes in the character, of the kinship system. Our question is then: has the kinship system, and in particular childhood, also entered some new modern phase? Much contemporary writing on the family and kinship stresses change, breakdown and reorganization. Attention is paid to divorce, remarriage, single parenting, illegitimacy, cohabitation, reductions in family size, and so on. Contemporary debates over the family and kinship are ordered around a concern over family and community *breakdown* (Leonard and Hood-Williams, 1988) and a separate school of social scientists stresses that kin relations, like capital itself, have also been radically disorganized (Barrett and McIntosh, 1982).

Few writers, even in the field of family and kinship, pay much attention to childhood and parent-child relations, but the logic of these wider discussions points towards notions of radically new childhoods in a changed world. My argument will be that such a notion is unwarranted. Sociologists, like other consumers, love the 'new', and although there is an exciting quality to much of the writing that suggests the emergence of a new form of capitalist organization, much of its drama derives from a misreading of history (Kumar, 1986) and a fascination with the deterministic powers of new technologies. Industrializing societies were never actually societies dominated by a massive urban working class employed in large factories. That was a fiction of Engels, Dickens and Mrs Gaskell. Sociologists (Murray, 1988) are fascinated by new high technological forms of assembly line production (in, for example, car plants) but the assembly line has never been typical of capitalist production in general. The most recent evidence suggests that older conceptions of class solidarities retain an importance that undermines these accounts of the demise of class (Marshall *et al.*, 1988). With respect to kinship the fashionable announcements of the end of traditional arrangements is somewhat premature, as some are beginning to assert (Chester et al., 1981; and see chapter 4 by Leonard in this volume, for a detailed discussion of this issue).

My argument here is that, whilst we may not ignore changes within the wider economy and recent cultural and political developments, a central characteristic of child relations is that they have remained remarkably traditional. Childhood today remains a firmly exclusionary status. Children, I shall argue, remain subject to authority relations which are aptly invoked by reference to Weber's notion of 'patriarchal authority'. The old concerns over obedience and respect, often translated into a new language, remain — even if they have been complemented by an interest in children as companions as well as subordinates. Legal changes have not markedly altered the postion of children as non-legal subjects (Fitz, 1981a). For example, the role of children in such matters as divorce is that of property to be fought over, despite the legal fictions of 'the best interests of the child', which in practice turn out to have rather more to do with adult gender struggles (Brophy and Smart, 1981; Weitzman, 1985; Smart, 1984). The disciplines of social science, when not ignoring children, continue to render the child as the incompetent other (Skolnick, 1974). Even the recent moral panic in England over the sexual abuse of children in Cleveland ended by affirming the rights of *parents* and criticizing the interference of doctors and social workers (Feminist Review, 1988).

One major difficulty in writing about children is that we have hardly begun to problematize the character of adult/child relations (see chapter 4 by Leonard in this volume; Ambert, 1986) but have tended to take for granted and to naturalize the obvious divisions of age. The readiness to accept childhood as a social construct since as long ago as Aries (1962) has not been translated into sociological analysis. We are at a very early stage in learning how to think about these social relations, let alone how to research them. This means that we have to write at a far higher level of generality than we would like. We need a theory of adult–child relations within the kinship system that recognizes the interrelationships between age and gender relations, which draws our attention to the key structural features of childhood and, in particular, which recognizes differential distributions of power, resources and rewards along the dimension of age. Such a basic structural analysis foregrounds historical continuities without ignoring modern mediations in these relationships. But the final judgment as to whether it is right to stress change or continuity cannot, unfortunately, be made since we know far too little about the daily lives of children outside school.

Weber and Patriarchal Authority

The structural characteristics of modern child relations within the family might best be thought of by reference to Weber's remarks on traditional authority and in particular to his comments on patriarchal authority. Weber is not widely thought of as a theorist of the family, but early writings by feminist social historians and sociologists used his work to analyze marital and gender relationships (Davidoff, L'Esperance and Newby, 1977; Bell and Newby, 1976; Davidoff, 1983). More recently reference has also been made by feminists (Barrett, 1980) as well as by Weberian scholars; a revival of this aspect of Weber's work seems in progress (Collins, 1986). Of continuing relevance, in my view, is his description of the central features of patriarchal authority. They continue to apply to key features, not only of husband/wife relations but also of parent/child relations which have not been 'rationalized' within developed industrial capitalist societies.

In Weber's account authority is part of a wider interest in forms of domination which is one of the central features of social life. 'Without exception every sphere of social action is profoundly influenced by dominancy' (Weber, 1968, p. 941). What he means by dominancy (outside market relations) is 'the probability that a command with a specific content will be obeyed by a given group of persons' (p. 212). Domination is identical to 'authoritarian power of command' (p. 946). Traditional authority, of which the most important kind is patriarchal authority, relies for its legitimacy on its appeal to tradition. It is based on 'personal loyalty'; it is not owed to specified rules but to a person. Contrawise 'when resistance occurs it is directed at the master not against the system as such'. Patriarchal authority is not rational but is personal and based on whims, tradition and custom; it is exercised by a human subject as a person; it is 'an immediate relation of command and obedience' (p. 227 and 1006–8).

All this need not necessarily deny the deeply affectual dimension to parent–child relations, any more than it does in marital relations. Indeed one of the tasks of some modern childhoods is to be companionable, to be fun, to be loved and loving as well as to meet the more traditional requirements to respect, honour and, above all, to obey. Nor are children simply objects of patriarchal authority; on the contrary, drawing attention to key structural features makes clear the deep personal investment in these relationships and reference to the character of controls similarly draws attention to those key areas of resistance and struggle. Yet few accounts recognize these issues around the differential distribution of power and control in family relationships.

A stress on the divisions of power within families faces the contradiction that families may also properly be regarded as resources against a frequently heartless world. On behalf of the working class and black communities writers have sought to defend the character of family and kinship systems since, in these cases, they provide a bulwark against class and racial oppression (Humphries, 1977; Carby, 1982b). There are difficult issues here, especially since it is undoubtedly the case that dominant accounts of the kinship systems of these groups have focussed on their deficiences (hence we are taught to regard child abuse as a purely working class phenomenon when it is not; we have all heard of the arranged marriages of Asian communities whilst missing the considerable structuring of the 'free' marriages of the West and so on). There are contradictions and contradictory experiences for black girls who may, on the one hand, find themselves subject to quite considerable working demands as carers of younger siblings or as home workers whilst also deriving considerable support from their families in the face of white racism. Nevertheless, an account that sought to describe the daily lives of modern children could not ignore child abuse in ethnic communities, for example, on the grounds that such communities are the victims of rasicm. Neither should one resort to 'leftist' explanations that seek to explain child abuse among the working class in terms of the development of commodity relations (Seabrook, 1982).

Wives and Children

Weber's account of authority relations remains a starting point for analysis of even modern childhoods. However, Weber's account is certainly very loosely constructed when it comes to the question of what kinds of social relationships support such forms of authority. We need to conceptualize the character of modern family relations themselves. This means conceptualizing patriarchy more precisely. The restrictive definition that I want to work with here is what I would call *family patriarchy*. Family patriarchy is constituted by two sets of interrelated and contradictory relationships: firstly, those between the sexes, which we may call *marital patriarchy*; secondly, those between parents and children, which we may call *age patriarchy*. Family patriarchy is a *complex*, whose principles have been usefully analyzed in some detail by Delphy and Leonard (1990). Central to their account, which focuses upon gender relations, is the recognition of the continuing necessity to study family relationships as *economic* relationships.

Family patriarchy is composed of long-term relationships of personal dependency in which family dependants (wives and children) are supported by, and subject to, (typically male) heads of households. Built into these relationships are clear imbalances in the distribution of power, resources, work and rewards. The dependency of family relationships is not the dependency of the wage since families are, distinctively, places within which the common currency of money, of profit, of loss, of 'rational' economic exchange, is out of place. Indeed it is supposed to be characteristic of the modern family that it is no longer a site of economic activity. This is classically expressed as the movement of the family from a unit of production to a unit of consumption. Delphy and Leonard (*ibid*) have performed a service in showing us how inapt such modern conceptions are and more recently, with a less critical eye, Ray Pahl has suggested something similar (Pahl, 1984).

The legacy of this writing, which provides an important stimulus both to problematizing the concept of childhood and to focussing empirical studies, is to turn our attention to hidden aspects of family life. A new agenda of concerns emerges which presumes the existence of antagonistic relations within families and which focuses our attention onto the differential distributions of power, work, violence, and rewards. All this is at some distance from analyses which study children through concerns around play, pedagogy, development or even mass media and mass markets. We can take up some examples of relevant issues from this approach and try to show the payoffs that derive from it.

Children, Wives, Work and Money

Given that the concept of family patriarchy is a useful way of proceeding, we need to specify in which ways the dependencies of children parallel those of wives, and in which ways they are different. It may still be argued that wives are an economic 'investment' for husbands, largely for the labour they provide; it is hard to suggest that this is widely the case for Western children. Indeed, we might say that the development of modern childhood itself marks the movement of children from productive contributors to domestic economies to objects of more or less conspicuous consumption. Historians of the developing split between the public world of work and the private world of a new bourgeois family form from 1750 in England have been sensitive to the removal of wives from the public world of commerce, politics and from what came exclusively to be known as 'work' (Davidoff and Hall, 1987), but what happened to wives in this period also happened to their children, who were indeed part of the justification for the move. An important, if not central, part of the new interior lives of the Victorian bourgeoisie was precisely the nursery, with its new, special products-special toys, books and clothes. And of course, at the heart of this new culture lay a new status for children.

Few people today in the Western world have children for profit or for their economic contribution to domestic economies; the costs are high and the long-term reward uncertain. Whether this has anything to do with the reductions in the numbers of children in such societies over this century would not be easy to demonstrate. Nevertheless, it remains extremely difficult to define and identify what is to count as 'work', especially within modern family relationships, which are predicated upon notions of love, duty, service, obligation and tradition. Such difficulties are doubtless no historical accident since they effectively hide the contributions of women, wives and, I suggest, children. For example, the popular conceptions of 'reproduction' (McIntosh, 1978; Beechey, 1978; Dalla Costa, 1972) assume that children are 'reproduced' in schools and homes by adults — but this suggests that reproduction is simply something that happens *to* children; it ignores the extent to which children, especially in schools, are actively engaged in the work of 'reproducing' themselves.

I would endorse the argument that children's work is both important and ignored. Daughters, in particular, may share with wives the tasks of providing considerable amounts of domestic labour — including child care and even sexual servicing within families. Some rural or ethnic groups may particularly utilize the labour of their children. For example, over 40 per cent of West Indian families with dependent children are headed by a lone mother, and yet we also know that the involvement of such women in waged work is higher than for white mothers. Squaring this circle apparently means the use of public and private child care and may involve the work of older daughters too (Driver, 1982; Ballard, 1982; Barrow, 1982). On the other hand, much of the work of modern children may be the work of display, companionship; the intermittent work of the object of desire. It is *affectual* work. Children are required to *be* and especially to 'be good'. Like much of the Western economy it seems that many children have shifted into the service sector.

Western children are legally excluded from paid work; we have few studies of their relationship to money. The money that children receive is 'pocket money'. We know something of the *level* of pocket money that children receive. In the UK the Walls ice cream company commissions an annual survey from Gallup on this topic (see also McGrath, 1973), but we know little about the *concept* of pocket money.

Pocket money is literally money 'for the pocket'; the name implies that not only is money passed to the child but that control over how that money is to be spent is also passed over. The best account we have of pocket money (Newson and Newson, 1976) quite properly runs on from a discussion of the money children are paid for the sexually divided family work that they perform. It is very difficult to tease out the relationships between money paid for work and money paid simply because of the status 'child'. Money is paid to children regularly, irregularly, because a task was just performed or because some tasks are typically expected to be performed, as savings and with and without strings. As one travels down the occupational scale the amount of money regularly given rises. However as the Newsons (*ibid*) point out, since background material supports are greater for middle class children these differences may not add up to much. If working class children have to spend their money on items that may be readily available and 'free' within middle class homes then the apparent advantage of working children is arguably eradicated. Middle class children get their money rather more regularly (as does the head of their household) but much of the money they do get comes with strings (McGrath, 1973). Their parents try hard to get them to spend the money in ways approved by the parents. Various incentive schemes operate: for example, if the child buys a book rather than, say, a toy, half of the cost of the book is met by the parent. Working class children experience fewer controls of this kind; in this sense their money is more clearly pocket money. Some parents report that pocket money 'was really meant to be wages'; some seemed to give money in order to be able to 'fine' children; many think that, in theory, children should not be paid for work. Money is thus variously regarded as a punitive device or a pedagogic device. In my view the complexities and unease about money derive from the general feeling of its inappropriate place in personal family relationships — a feeling that children should not try to bargain for, or calculate, the value of their errand; parents on the other hand, should not calculate the value of the supports they provide.

The Newsons detected a desire to overindulge children, especially among working class parents. This acted partly to compensate for what they saw as their own more materially difficult childhoods. More recently Seabrook (1982) has complained of the 'shower of desirable things' descending upon children which have become the modern substitutes for their 'real' needs. But his analysis of the extent to which the market has opened up private family relations and commodified them is an illustration of the kind of writing to which I am objecting (cf. Beck, 1987; Lasch, 1977). Children's familial dependencies have precisely *not* been substituted by some new relationship to the market. A brief analysis of just one of the market-provided 'desirable things' demonstrates just this: children's toys.

It will never be possible to understand the meanings and significance of children's toys if they are not set within the context of the relationships of family dependency; it is erroneous to treat children simply as consumers in commodity markets. In the first place toys do not reach children in the commodity form; the vast majority of toys reach children as *gifts*. Indeed, 60 per cent of the annual US toy market comes to children in the form of a *Christmas gift*. We know from anthropological work (Mauss, 1970) that gifts are a very special form of exchange which require their own reciprocities. Gifts are not typically given 'freely'. Some return is expected. Gifts are also not entirely the product of the rather more 'free' choices of consumers in the commodity markets. Children are economic dependants: their access to such markets is always importantly mediated by familial dependency.

In the second place, we might consider the social functions of toys. Some toys contribute to the 'solitarization' (Sutton-Smith, 1986) of the child, in that their function is to make the child responsible for the management of its own behaviour (as in 'run along and play with your new toy'). Other toys are intended to function as family ideologies, i.e., they function to build family unities by creating a shared activity (as in board games). We could consider other aspects; however, the point is that the consumption of toys cannot be understood merely in terms of the 'commodification' of family life, and neither may it be understood simply in terms of its cognitive uses (as in psychological accounts). Toys may only be understood in the context of the family relationships, including those of economic dependency, that I have sketched out here.

The Controls of Age Patriarchy

Children's insertion within relations of economic family dependency is associated with particular forms of social control which impact upon the daily life of children in such a way as to make nonsense of claims that the status of childhood is 'disappearing'. If we had to name one central principle that underlies the condition of children, we could well choose obedience which, in essence, simply states that children should obey their parents — in whatever way demanded. This principle seems remarkably resilient, even if it is masked by more complex deployments such as the notion that children should not only obey but should want to do so. Within the demand for generalized compliance specific controls seem to operate, reminding us more of the accounts of feudal relations or of the relations of rural farm workers (Newby, 1977) than of post-modern reconstructions. What appears distinctive about these controls over the child's life is their reference to space, body and the child's time. We can profitably discuss each of these issues in turn.

Obedience

The application of the obedience principle is various both in terms of what parents think it is important for their children to obey them in, how long they allow for compliance, their degree of concern as to how the children should feel about it, the extent of the delight they take in their children actually being contrary and so on. In a mid-sixties study, numbers of mothers and some fathers of 7-year-olds were both exasperated and partly delighted in the obduracy of their children (Newson and Newson, 1976). Children are clearly not supposed to be the centres of their own determination. These issued are discussed more fully below, but despite this delight, and despite small numbers of primarily boy children (who even at age 7 seemed quite beyond the controls of their parents), the Newsons' accounts are striking for the taken-for-granted quality of this principle. To be a child seems commonly to be an 'immediate' relationship of command and obedience; notwithstanding the variety in the exercise of command and the forms of compliance.

Over the twenty years that have passed since the Newsons conducted these studies, it has been argued that the principles of social control operating essentially in the school have undergone some changes. Bernstein (1977) in particular discusses changes in forms of pedagogy which suggest that new principles of social control and new principles of social integration have resulted from the influence of new middle class groups. Bernstein analyzed a new type of pre-school/infant pedagogy which he called 'invisible pedagogy' (crudely captured by reference to the 'progressive educational movement') for which English primary schools acquired an international reputation from the late 1960s onwards. The term 'invisible pedagogy' refers not to any sudden new change in the distribution of power with respect to the basic features that regulate pedagogic relationships in the school or in the home, but rather to a shift to rules which are implicit or diffuse from the point of view of the child. In a related, though theoretically less sophisticated, manner, the Newsons have examined the extent to which contemporary forms of child rearing are 'child centred', i.e., incorporating parental 'recognition of the child's status as an individual with rights and feelings that are worthy of respect' (Newson and Newson, 1976, p. 287). In their view, child-centredness is 'not be equated with permissiveness or indulgence' but rather, 'child centred parents voluntarily relinquish the authoritarian stance and instead deliberately concede to the child the right to exercise choice and autonomy' (pp. 286–92). It is the contradiction at the heart of the concept of child-centredness which is of note here. Children are to be treated *as if* they were independent, *as if* they were individuals with a right to choice and autonomy. The old conformities to parental will remain. Indeed, how could they not, given that the structural relations between parents and children are unchanged. Children remain dependent subjects even if attempts may be made to mask that dependency.

Nevertheless, the emergence of the concept of child-centredness does suggest some change in the *modality* of age patriarchal control, change which may be class specific. Harris (1983) suggests that the new ideologies of child-centredness have indeed undermined the powers of parents over children. When this is coupled with the idea that parents are responsible for the kind of children they produce, we have a situation in which far greater power is extended to children over parents. Children have 'the power to determine the self and social esteem of the parent', parental controls are now exercised with anxiety, and we have 'the sort of emotional dependence in the *parent* conventionally associated with children' (*ibid*, p. 245). Developments of this kind may well provide opportunities for different forms of resistance for children, but they do not upset conventional power relations or the material dependency of children (as Harris recognizes). Nevertheless there is nothing new in the idea that parents are responsible for the children they rear; historians have traced this belief back to at least the sixteenth century (Pollock, 1983).

Walkerdine and Lucey (1989) have also recently suggested ways in which daughters regulate the behaviour of their mothers. More precisely, they have produced an excellent discursive analysis of the effects of the 'progressive' pedagogies that so interested Bernstein. They show some of the ways in which constructions of the middle class mother as a pedagogue and of the mother–daughter relation as 'rational' and 'reasonable' constrains such mothers whilst pathologizing working class mothering. However, they perhaps over emphasize the regulative powers that the discourse offers to children. Their analysis rested on a group of 4-year-old girls; at times, we are persuaded to forget the ease with which age dependencies empower adults in such a relationship. For example, the constraints of the construction of a 'good mother' may be readily momentarily sidestepped when physical force (or violence) confirms a small child's dependency.

Space

Children's lives are highly localized and spatially restricted. Children need to be within sight, or within particular distances, or inside the house within a particular room or rooms, and so on. Confinement — to an area, to the house, to a room or in a bed — is part of the everyday parameters of childhood as well as a disciplinary mechanism. Tidiness is the arrangement of things in space according to certain rules; children, like their things, have to be tidy. We know that these rules are sexually specific — girls are subject to more restriction than are boys. The logic of many of these restrictions is that they are intended to protect children. However, just as feminists have pointed to the irony of women needing the company of a man to protect them from other men (however unreliable this protection turns out to be), so children need protection from particular adults to protect them from strange ones (again often rather unreliable protection given the levels of abuse within the home by familiar men). The geographical restrictions on children and the long list of places where they may not or cannot go (either through legal bars or through the adult-centred architecture of public life) effectively extend into a restriction over those who are their principal carers — women.

The car and the telephone mean that (for those parents who have access to them) the geography of the child's life is extended. There are clear class differences in the Newsons (*ibid*) evidence here: supervision is extended by these media over greater localities, especially for parents who live in areas they regard as unsuitable sources of friendships for their children. This has implications for parents, too, since such supervision may be time-consuming (see chapter 5 by Büchner in this volume).

The Body

Childhood seems remarkable for the degree of intervention onto the body of the child. Children's deportment, posture, movement, nudity, appearance (their whole 'look' including clothes, hair, etc.), the requirement to be touched, lifted, kissed and to kiss, etc., are subject to degrees of intervention and control unparallelled outside family life. Marked concern over, and attempts to control, the appearance of children are coupled with this intervention, although the extent and nature of this concern and control varies in practice. Children's appearance, like that of wives, reflects the honour of the patriarch and is subject to regulation for that reason. The sustained interest in style associated with youth may have rather more to do with the resistance to this regulation than is commonly recognized in accounts of youth culture.

Family relations then are not only personal ('particularistic' in Parsonian terms) but, it seems to me, specially corporal. These relations both prescribe and proscribe sexual relations between members (Leonard and Speakman, 1986), in a context where physical relationships unmatched in other social relations clearly exist. Co-residence brings an immediate and quotidian quality of social relations into play, including the quality of physical proximity. These relations are, arguably, the very *home of physicality*; not only of touching, hugging, etc., but also of physical force and physical violence (Macleod and Saraga, 1988; Dobash and Dobash, 1980). It is not the grim obduracy of the division of labour which has a special relationship to familial systems of control but (the threat of) physical force or violence. This latter aspect of family relations is qualitatively different from the rational disciplinary controls of bureaucratic authority. Disciplinary procedures which confront children are still importantly those which operate on their bodies. 'Smacking' (the Newsons' term) is apparently a no less common experience for very young English children today than it was in the late 1950s. How far we are justified in drawing parallels between physical controls over children and physical controls over wives is difficult to assess, not least because of the contradictory location of wives in family patriarchy where wives have authority in age relations but are dependent in marital relations.

Time

It is not only quotidian controls over the daily rhythms of the child's day (which in part derive from rhythms outside the family itself) but equally controls over the principles of the child's own progression through childhood itself which are central to childhood and its struggles. Bernstein's (1977) concept of 'framing' describes something similiar to this within the pedagogic relationship in schools, but we could usefully adopt it for considering parent–child relations in families. Accounts of childhood indicate the child's own age to be crucial both in the ordering of daily life, and in struggles over that ordering (Aries, 1962; Gillis, 1980). Parent–child relationships operate on the basis that childhood is essentially a continuously transitional status. The child is always present as its future in the here and now; what is done now is done in part for the future. In other words childhood is a career — an arguably banal characterization, but one which has not been consciously applied to the conceptualization of childhood any more than it has been widely used in understanding many other social relationships, including marriage.

At a broader level, the importance of this precise measure of the unfolding in time of the age of the child is connected to what has been called the modern (post-1850) 'chronologicalization' of time reflected in the strict age cohorts of the school system (Gillis, 1980). Children are always at or between stages, always developing and always negotiating the new freedoms that may come with the new age (Holte, 1964). Childhood is not only a continuous transition of ages and stages in the writings of psychologists but also in daily struggles with parents for different treatment. The ontology of children seems firmly linked to their age, and since their age is always changing this produces a transitional being. Many of the intergenerational struggles between children and their parents may be regarded as struggles over the rates of transition from one age stage to the next. These rates have normative values; hence, a child strategy is always to refer to where in the transitions their friends are, or sibs were at that age. The adult responses, with notions like 'precocious' are equally normative, since one cannot logically be in front of, or behind, one's own development (Riley, 1983).

Parents are inclined to express this transitional journey on which children find themselves in terms of the acquisition of personhood. Certainly pre-adolescent children are not intended to constitute centres of their own determination, to be centred persons, to be independent of their parents (and their rules), nor to have the last word or 'answer back'. The term for children who adopt personhood earlier than they 'should' is cheekiness, a term of disapproval referring to a linguistic style adopted by children in interaction with adults. Speier (1976), for example, has described children's restricted conversational rights in the school setting, whereas the Newsons' (1976) data is replete with similar observations for the home environment. Children of all ages may be termed 'cheeky', but parents increasingly tolerate cheekiness as their children get older — it acts as an indicator for emerging personhood (cf. Newson and Newson, unpublished manuscript, where personhood was understood as becoming a 'gaffer'). Being an adult means being your own boss — at least for men — whereas children, non-persons, are not their own boss at all. The parents in the Newsons' studies looked forward to their children becoming persons; some delighted in the early obduracy that signalled this transition, describing their children as having definite personalities.

Personhood is sexed, however. The problems some mothers have in managing the behaviour of their sons derives partly from the contradictions between appropriate masculine and appropriate child behaviour. Boys must be boys, i.e., masculine — but they are equally young, a social condition which is closer to femininity. There has been little discussion of the extent to which available forms of masculinity are defined through their contrast to age specific definitions of appropriate attitudes and behaviour. Whilst there has been considerable discussion of the binary nature of masculine-feminine distinctions, a consideration of the interrelationships between masculine: feminine and childlike: youth is underdeveloped (but cf. Walkerdine, 1983, for an opposing account). Many of the examples Postman (1982) gives to demonstrate the 'dissolution' of childhood into adulthood are examples of gender continuities, in which childlike characteristics, for example, (sexual) innocence, are linked with feminine characteristics.

The systematic age-grading practised in the school system together with understandings of child development drawn from psychology (viz. Piaget, 1953; Werner, 1957) importantly prompt the kind of transitional and developmental model of childhood described here. Mothers' own accounts of 'childhood' — not only middle class mothers' — accord with this model (cf. Brannen, 1989). Its application implies a common sense of childrearing in which the meaning and significance of parental action is future-oriented — today's punishment will produce a better person tomorrow, as it were. There is little evidence that this powerfully appealing common-sense notion has any effect whatsoever on subsequent events (Clarke and Clarke, 1976). The Newsons, too, after over thirty years of substained research, are unable to point to any clear-cut relationships between child-rearing climates and ontological outcomes. In other words, the evidence does not fit a metaphor of child development in which a snowball rolling down a hill accretes a final form larger than but influenced by its initial shape. A more appropriate metaphor might be that of a strip of film, joined and continuous, but capable of carrying within it a sequence of different images.

The kind of chronologized time embodied in schooling's age-graded structure is one dimension of the way time and childhood are related; another is institutionalized time within kinship structures, which are not age-graded in the same ways. British studies (Child Health and Education Study, 1970; National Child Development Study, 1958) have tended not to pick up this aspect of kinship structure, a consequence of taking the individual child rather then children-within-families as the unit of analysis. Time-orderings in kinship structures move beyond chronological age-relations to encompass ordinal position, sex/ordinal location, patterns of inheritance practices (cf. Delphy and Leonard, 1980; Fitz and Hood-Williams, 1982).

Controls over children's time, space and bodies are obviously interrelated: how far a child may move at what times of day; what a child may wear in particular contexts, etc. Another example might be the rules which govern the spatial arrangement of items, i.e., the rules of tidiness, which are time-specific: the kitchen may be the playroom until it is teatime. Although I have tried to formalize the principal areas of control to which children are subject, I would also, following Weber, wish to stress the arbitrary and whimsical nature of age patriarchy. There is considerable variability in what counts as appropriate behaviour for a child, and in what does not so count; there is considerable variability in the disciplinary mechanisms employed by parents. Nevertheless this variability is distinctly secondary to the general principle of obedience. What children have to obey is but the background: the 'what' is what parents tell them to do. When parents are asked why they hit their children, the largest response category comprises those answers difficult to classify clearly, i.e., the punishment has not been meted out for specific actions, but rather for general disobedience or defiance — the child's specific action is immaterial (Newson and Newson, 1976).

Parenting is very much a personal affair, which means that disciplinary procedures vary widely too: tailored to fit the individual child, to differentiate between children, to produce the most effective result, or matched to a child's particular dislikes, etc. Parents, like managers everywhere, use measures they think will work and which they are able to use — hence the incidence of parental corporal punishment declines sharply around 11+ (*ibid*). Parents are inclined to regard hitting older children as undignified, but they also consider it to be decreasingly tenable from the physical strength standpoint — children are more able to escape or defend themselves.

A New Kinship System?

Arguments proposing that significant, even dramatic, changes in modern Western family and kinship systems have taken place in the recent past constitute a challenge to the thesis presented here: that childhood remains a firmly exclusionary status, one which is created from traditional forms of authority and from relationships best described as domestic, rather than capitalized, modes of production. Whilst it is untenable to argue that nothing has changed since the sixties, I contend that changes which have taken place — especially the demographic shifts — have been misunderstood (cf. Hood-Williams, 1984). Despite the observable changes, there is little evidence for an imminent and radical reorganization of family life, and this includes children's lives.

A typical list of recent changes refers to increases in divorce, declining numbers of first marriages, increases in cohabitation, growth in the number of single parents, declines in the birth rate, and general increases in the variety and diversity of family forms. Both British (Seabrook, 1982) and American (Lasch, 1977) writers have interpreted these as radical changes in traditional familial relationships; for the FRG, Beck (1987) sees the trends as evidence of rising 'individualization'. Lasch, with bitter irony, savagely criticizes the notion of 'non-binding commitment' — an increasingly apt description, he suggests, of modern personal relations.

Beck (1987) argues that 'individuals are now compelled to make themselves the centre of their own life plans and conduct' (p. 342). Additionally socialist feminists in Britain have suggested that although traditional images of family life retain a powerful *ideological* significance they now have little relationship to the *actual* organization of domestic life (Barrett and McIntosh, 1982). But the changes may be understood in a rather different light — one in which important continuities emerge.

These issues are directly addressed by Leonard (see chapter 4 in this volume; cf. also Leonard and Hood-Williams, 1988; Chester et al., 1987) but we might note at once that list of family change can be countered by a list of family continuity. Divorce for example, whilst generating a considerable noise of crisis, is actually still rather low: in 1987 just 1.3 per cent of all UK married couples, and 0.86 per cent (1986) of those in the FRG, divorced. Further, divorce rates are matched by remarriage rates; divorce itself may be regarded not as the termination of marriage but, for those with children, as the continuation of 'marriage' in another form (Delphy, 1984). This second list, however, is no firmer a base for arguing that nothing has changed than was the first list for the opposing thesis. We can certainly find evidence of new features of modern childhoods (see chapter 5 by Büchner in this volume); we have considered changes in the obedience principle. Additionally, the stress on the personal character of family relations needs to consider the changing character of father/child relations, a relationship increasingly better characterized as universalistic. Children, like wives, are becoming increasingly *substitutable*, at least in some areas of North America and Western Europe, where divorce leads to rapid decline in the contact between children and fathers (Weitzman, 1985). This pattern must be set against contemporary struggles by some British men's groups (such as 'Families Need Fathers' and 'The Campaign for Justice in Divorce') to increase the number of custody awards to fathers.

No doubt the perception that modern kinship patterns continue to retain durable characteristics of the gemeinschaft requires further study, especially with respect to children. We need to think through the consequences of what have been called 'neo-conventional' accounts of the family for the everyday lives of children. To resist arguments proposing the demise of the significance of familial relations in the actual organization of domestic life (Barrett and McIntosh, 1982) is not to end by saying nothing has changed. Furthermore, to discover evidence for the continuance of traditional forms is in no way to celebrate their durability. If we want to problematize the concept of childhood we need to begin with a conception of patriarchal authority that even today maintains childhood as a firmly exclusionary status; we need to take serious account of the cross cuttings between age and gender; we need an agenda that is much more sensitive to questions of power and control; we need to recognize children as active, if excluded, subjects and not as the incompetent objects of adult policies; we need to see children as social relationships in which our very understanding of childhood is constructed out of our notions of adulthood. In all of this we have hardly begun.

Chapter 11

Illusory Equality: The Discipline-based Anticipatory Socialization of University Students

Steffani Engler

Introduction

The research discussed here forms part of an ongoing project about West German university students and biography; in *youth* studies, this group has not often been considered. University students have tended to be viewed from the perspective of the sociology of education or of work and occupations. However, it can be argued that with the extension of the youth phase and the social, cultural and economic positioning of those in their twenties, university students fall under the concerns of youth researchers (cf. chapter 2 by Zinneker in this volume).

In 1960 4.3 per cent of 19–26-year-olds were at university; in 1985, the proportion had risen to 18.2 per cent. Between 1960 and 1985 the number of university students rose from almost 250,000 to 1.3 million; by 1988 numbers had risen still further to 1.5 million. Currently, approximately 17 per cent of the student body in any one year have just begun their studies (cf. Bertram, 1987b, p. 138; Statistisches Bundesamt, 1987, p. 65; and dpa reports). In 1968, 7 per cent of the relevant age-cohort had secured university entry qualifications (*Abitur*) by the time they left school; now, the proportion has reached 28 per cent. Of those qualified, 55 per cent of the young women and 71 per cent of the young men intend to go to university (cf. Der Spiegel N.47, 1988, p. 84; Statistisches Bundesamt, 1987, p. 64). These figures mean that increasing numbers of young people are moving through the status passage of university studies. In this discussion we shall not consider the narrower question of the status passage from school to university. National Service (in the armed forces or in community care) or a voluntary social service year frequently come inbetween. In recent years, increasing numbers of young people with an *Abitur* complete an apprenticeship before embarking on university studies (cf. chapter 8 by Helga Krüger in this volume).

The wider question of the status passage *through* university studies, the process of anticipatory socialization into university, has been rather neglected until now. The first section of this chapter gives an overview of what we do know about this from the literature. In the second section, I shall present some examples of anticipatory socialization processes from our own data. Specifically, comparisons will be made between electrical engineering, education and law students in order to illustrate how different these processes are according to subject discipline. The discussion closes with a consideration of how processes of anticipatory socialization can be theoretically understood within the context of social reproduction. Here, Bourdieu's (1982a) concepts of habitus and social space are used as key analytic tools.

An Overview of the Literature and its Perspectives

Youth Research and the Concept of Status Passage

As noted above, youth research has, until now, paid little attention to university students and the socialization processes they experience. Yet over the eighties there has been considerable discussion about the extension and destructuring of the youth phase. Writers have mooted a change or accretion of personal and social development 'tasks' for those in their twenties, an individualization of youth biographies, or indeed the end of adolescence altogether (Fuchs, 1983; Hurrelmann *et al.*, 1985; von Trotha, 1982). The concept of status passage receives some recognition in these debates insofar as youth surveys have uncovered changes between the 1950s and the 1980s in the timing and sequencing of characteristic life events (cf. Fuchs, 1985; Jugendwerk der Deutschen Shell, 1981, 1985; Zinneker, 1981 and 1985b; and chapter 7 by Heinz-Hermann Krüger in this volume).

The interpretation of these changes in the literature varies, but it is noticeable that current youth research perspectives are locked into a certain tension. On the one hand, the youth phase is viewed as a long-term status passage in which preparation for adulthood is the central focus. On the other hand, youth is accorded its own raison d'etre as a phase in the life cycle. The term 'status passage' is also employed in different ways. Olk (1986), for example writes of a 'disintegration of the firmly structured status passage of youth' (p. 45). In his analysis, the youth phase is interpreted as a life-cycle status passage to adulthood. Fuchs (1983) also sees youth definitively as 'a time of preparation for adulthood', and suggests that 'the status passage of youth is beginning to look like a youth biography' (p. 342). However, Hurrelmann and Heit-meyer (1988) discuss the youth phase as covering a wide range of status passages, whose natures, timing and relationships to each other are changing (pp. 61–2). Where movements through status passages turn into an uncoordinated sequence, the degree of independence and autonomy of action accorded to an individual can vary sharply between the different status passage fields. Despite the differences between these various accounts, the end of the youth phase is consistently placed at the point where individuals enter the world of production, i.e., employment. Discussion of university studies as a *transition* phase between youth and adulthood has been, however, neglected.

Fundamentally, the theoretical analyses available in the literature are inadequate in two ways. Firstly, status passage is not understood as a *process*. Secondly, the *reproduction of structured gender and class inequalities* through the changing constitution of the youth phase is largely ignored. Hence, for example, Fuchs (1985) refers to statistics on educational participation by sex in support of the (widely held) thesis that youth has become less gender-specific in nature (and will continue to move in this direction). Quite apart from the limits of statistical data in this respect, more differentiated analysis of the figures does not readily support such a view (cf. Faulstich-Wieland *et al.*, 1984). Mechanisms of social and cultural reproduction are more complex than this in the first place; but in any event, structural changes in the ways individuals subjectively come to terms with constraints and possibilities have not been contextualized within theories of reproduction and change. If we are to explain anticipatory socialization processes at university in these terms, then we require a set of concepts which can grasp the issues at hand. Zinneker's (1986) use of habitus and social space effectively recodes the disparate conceptual frameworks found in contemporary youth research in terms of class-linked interests, and as such, takes a first step in that direction.

Higher Education Research

Whilst youth research neglects university students, higher education research does not consider changes in the youth phase. Nevertheless, research in this field covers a very broad spectrum of questions — Schneider (1985) located 276 separate studies on university students and their studies which had been conducted since 1985. Of particular interest here are those surveys which provide data about why and under what conditions (qualified) school-leavers decide to go to university rather than take up employment, and to study one subject rather than another. (In principle, all those with an *Abitur* have a right to take up university study, and to do so at the university and in the subject of their choice. In practice, access to the most popular subjects — such as medicine, psychology, and currently business studies — is regulated by quotas and by *Abitur* grades, because the universities do not have the capacity to absorb everyone).

Socially structured inequalities in higher education participation rates remain. As in the UK, the FRG bases empirical stratification analysis upon an occupational status hierarchy. The most commonly used simple classification system does not exactly correspond to British categories, but rather to distinctions between groups of employees according to legally defined contractual conditions of work. *Arbeiter* corresponds approximately to skilled workers and below; *Angestellte* to all levels of private sector employment from routine non-manual upwards; *Beamte* are civil servants — of all levels. The two latter categories do not, then, clearly distinguish between social class or status levels, though patterns of inequality still show up. Relative to the distribution of these three groups across the labour force, civil servants' children are heavily overrepresented amongst university students, the children of *Angestellten* are somewhat less overrepresented — and those from *Arbeiter* families are very heavily underrepresented. The proportion of university students from this last group, effectively from the core of the working class, has risen four-fold since 1952 (then 4 per cent, now 16 per cent), but 46 per cent of the labour force are *Arbeiter* (cf. BMBW, 1986, p. 101; Schnitzler, 1983, p. 30ff; Statistisches Bundesamt, 1987, p. 84). A number of studies have explored the ways in which social background factors structure not only the decision to go to university, but also the choice of degree subject and attitudes towards university life (see, for example, Giesen *et al.*, 1981; Lewin and Schacher, 1981; Peisert, 1984; Peisert *et al.*, 1981). The difficulty with these studies for our purposes is that they are primarily quantitative in character, based on representative questionnaire surveys. By their very nature, they cannot address the dimensions of action and process essential to status passage and socialization analysis (cf. Frieberts-häuser, 1988).

In the case of gender-based inequalities, general rates of participation in higher education have shown considerable improvement: in 1950, women were but 20 per cent of university students, by the early eighties 40 per cent (Schnitzler, 1983, p. 25). Their distribution across degree subjects and levels remains imbalanced. Recent feminist-oriented studies have brought women students in from the periphery of research attention, investigating experiences and problems of university life from a gender-specific perspective (see, for example, Bock *et al.*, 1983; Erlemann, 1983; Gerok, 1985; Hoppe, 1985; Limbach, 1986; Richter, 1984; Scholl, 1985; Weigel, 1986). However, the characteristic open-ended thematic interview used in these studies also has its limitations. The information elicited is of a purely subjective nature, focused on the self and offering a view of the world exclusively through the eyes of an individual. Those structures and processes which do not find their way into consciousness cannot surface through this method, something of particular importance in the case of exploring gender inequalities, where many aspects of patriarchal relations remain partially or wholly unrecognized by the subject (cf. Ecarius, 1988).

Anticipatory Socialization Processes in Subject-specific Cultures

Research into the professional and community cultures attached to degree subjects and their university departments is a fairly new departure, arising from a dissatisfaction with existing perspectives on socialization in higher education contexts (cf. for example, Huber, 1980; Liebau, 1982; Portele, 1985). The concept of habitus plays a significant role in its analyses, in that the formation of habitus comprises the central, 'if latent, outcome of higher education socialization processes' (Huber *et al.*, 1983, p. 144). In other words, habitus is used to describe and express the *result* of anticipatory socialization processes.

In the first instance, the task has been to demonstrate whether indeed different university disciplines may be described as 'cultures', and if so, what their characteristics are. Is there such a thing as a 'discipline habitus'? Do those studying different subjects display different patterns of consciousness, behaviour and values? It would appear, from the research available, that we *can* speak in these terms; the discipline habitus is acquired through everyday discursive practices in university life. What Bourdieu describes as class habitus finds its analogy in the university world as discipline habitus. Research into education and social inequality generally stops at university entrance, as if selection processes ceased at that juncture. The study of subject-specific cultures, on the other hand, has been able to deconstruct the ideological illusion that all students are equal and equivalent. Much work remains to be done. Analyses of subject-specific cultures have not, to date, paid adequate attention to the question of their relative autonomy (cf. Liebau and Huber, 1985, p. 337). Neither have they seriously considered the articulation of such cultures with gender relations. Moreover, there is the matter of whether a concept which was developed in the context of explaining the reproduction of *class structure* can simply be transferred across to the analysis of the production and reproduction of subject-specific *university cultures*.

Our study is based on ethnographic methods, in order to catch *both* the processual quality of status passage and socialization *and* the active participation of individuals in these processes. The concept of initiation rites frames our analytic perspective, but in this case we see students as very much engaged in initiating themselves — they choose which initiation routes they will pass through and they decide when they belong to the initiated, i.e., when they see themselves as members of a subject-specific culture (cf. here Ecarius, 1988, p. 113ff; Popp, 1969, p. 11).

Distinctive Dispositions: Socialization into University Life

In order to help new students adjust to university life, the 'old hands' organize orientation sessions on a departmental basis. What these sessions cover and how long they continue varies enormously; as does the extent to which lecturers are involved and cooperate with the students concerned.

So, for example, in the Education Department part of the orientation programme includes a 'breakfast party', which takes place in a common room for departmental student use. The common room has a cosy atmosphere, equipped with a range of domestic furniture and equipment. The facility was set up by the students themselves, and it well represents the departmental culture. The more 'senior' students take on the responsibility for buying in the breakfast food stocks, which are of a particular kind: Third World coffee, wholemeal bread, varieties of cheese, fresh milk and butter, honey from the health food shop, and even some cold meats. In preparation for the orientation event, students rearrange the furniture to make room for the breakfast tables, and ensure there are enough chairs for everyone. The welcoming atmosphere does its job, encouraging people to chat with each other in pairs. The food selection itself offers immediate conversational topics, ranging from healthy eating to current political debates. About forty first-year students turned up to the breakfast we observed, of which about two-thirds were women. There had been a loose arrangement to meet at 9 a.m., and there was no sense of a formal close to the session. In fact, this one lasted until about 11.30 a.m., and the atmosphere was reminiscent of a rather large commune.

The Department of Electrical Engineering also puts on a breakfast for incoming students, but the character of the event is very different. To begin with, it is scheduled to take place in formal university space — rather like a lecture room. The arrangement of the (official) furniture is not changed in preparation for the event. Again, the 'senior' students arrange for the food, so that the new students have only to come equipped with a cup and a knife — but there are no plates provided, the idea is to use the table top instead. The bread rolls are ordered from and are delivered by a large bakery; two 20-litre Thermos flasks of coffee are bought from the Students' Union. The rest of the food is purchased from the supermarket: margarine, jam, chocolate spread and long-life milk. The atmosphere at the breakfast we observed was rather like that of a canteen, reminiscent of the coffee break at a large company. It had been scheduled for an hour, beginning at 8.30 a.m. The event did begin punctually, but the approximately 100 new students who came along did not participate in the last-minute preparations like setting the tables. There are very few women students present. Neither did much conversation get going; after about twenty minutes the first people started drifting away to stand around in the corridor waiting for the next orientation event to get under way.

The senior students in the Law Department do not invite incoming students to breakfast. They neither make use of official university accommodation, nor do they attempt to change the character and atmosphere of university space. Instead, they arrange for an evening in a local pub — but not a 'student dive', rather a 'respectable' hostelry frequented by non-university people. It is scheduled to begin at a given time, but there is no specified end to the event. At the meeting we observed, about 100 people came, equally split by sex. Tables had been reserved in advance, and these were then pushed together so that larger groups could form. The relaxed social atmosphere with beer and wine (or orange juice) was reminiscent of a rather large group of pub regulars, and it seemed that important social contacts were being made. There was much anecdotal storytelling about schooldays and toasts were drunk to a successful time at university.

That these three settings differ is evident. But how can they be explained theoretically? What links do such activities and experiences have with processes of social reproduction?

Status Passage as an Interface in Processes of Social Reproduction

The senior students in each of the three departments discussed above were active shapers of the processes of initiation to which incoming students were exposed. They had chosen the setting in which orientation meetings took place: the room, the food, the organizational arrangements, the scheduling, and so on. In doing so, they were indicating to the new students what it means to be a member of their department, their subject-specific culture. The differences are symbolized by the use of china: paper cups, for example; or by the choice of breakfast over against an evening in the pub. The senior students represent a discipline habitus, one which they have acquired through the same kinds of socialization processes they are now exercising in relation to new students (cf. Bourdieu and Passeron, 1971, p. 56). In this sense, the process of self-initiation is prestructured.In our view, these surface differences in style and taste have a deeper social meaning and function than we might initially suppose.

The concept of habitus serves as an explanatory principle between structure and practice, between the conditions of life and lifestyle (cf. Bourdieu, 1982b, p. 277). Habitus exists in the individual as a classification system 'made real': it is the structuring product (*opus operatium*) of a structuring structure (*modus operandi*). Habitus forms the schemes of perception, thought and judgment through which situations, actions and objects are recognized, intepreted and evaluated. At the surface level, habitus is expressed through lifestyle and taste.

In his earlier writing, Bourdieu defined habitus as the generative grammar of patterns of behaviour (1974, p. 150), but in more recent accounts he has distanced himself from such Chomskian terminology, which is too redolent of deterministic rules for human action. Social life does not comprise rule-following, and habitus is not a set of rules in practice (Bourdieu, 1987, p. 99 and 1988, p. 165). It is more a question of filtering out the *social logic* of human action — that which is intuitively grasped by the quality of 'social sense'. Whilst habitus is to be understood as a durable and transferable system of dispositions, i.e., *both* a structured *and* a structurating structure, this should not be equated with the impossibility of change or with mechanistic processes of social reproduction. On the contrary, a new habitus can be acquired, rather like the Pygmalion model: Bourdieu himself used the example of working-class girls taking a training course as hostesses. In his words (1982a) they come out as different people, having learned to walk, sit, laugh, smile, speak, dress and make themselves up completely differently (p. 328−9). Habitus, as a matrix for perception, thought and action, incorporates and synthesizes all past experience, but is open to all future influences. In this sense, it implies the potential for constant change and transformation. Bourdieu's version of social and cultural reproduction is not, therefore, about denying the possibilities for individual choice and freedom of action. Rather, it is based on the view that the kinds of choices available, or the given room for manoeuvre, are made possible and conditioned by the structured social contexts in which people find themselves. Transferred to the higher education context, this means that first-year students arrive at university already equipped with a 'habitus of origin', which has been structured in the specific social context in which they have grown up Anticipatory socialization processes now begin systematically to remodel the habitus of origin into the discipline habitus, according to the subject-specific culture to which the incoming student is exposed and inducted into.

Analytically, the concept of habitus allows us to see the outcomes of such socialization processes empirically. University study is a transition stage, in which individuals participate in at least four cultural contexts — their culture of origin, student culture in general, their subject-specific culture, and their future occupational culture (Huber *et al.*, 1983, p. 160). These four cultural contexts structure and are structured by the student way of life and by the relevant discipline habitus. Students entering the Department of Education experience an induction programme, here in the shape of a breakfast party, which points the way towards a very different 'field' than that suggested by the electrical engineers' breakfast. But it would be mistaken to regard subject-specific cultures as insular in nature, as disconnected from the wider social order. Relative autonomy means precisely what it says: disciplines are systematically linked with social power hierarchies and therefore with structured social conflicts, so that they cannot be understood in isolation from their relations with the outside world (Liebau and Huber, 1985, p. 337). It is at this point that we must move beyond habitus to consider the concept of social space, for questions of disposition, lifestyle and taste must be connected with actual life situations, with real social positionings.

Social Space

Bourdieu's central research question concerns the reproduction of social power in class societies; he is concerned to identify the systematic ways in which social classes are reproduced and reproduce themselves. In this connection, he is interested in understanding the nature of habitus as a *structured* structure (rather than as a structuring and structured structure at one and the same time, as we discussed in the previous section). In order to grasp this *aspect of habitus more fully, Bourdieu adopts the heuristic construct of 'social space', which is understood as a spatial network of relationships (see figure 11.1, p. 181).

The construction of this space incorporates a new version of class theory and an extension of the term capital. Bourdieu (1983) distinguishes between economic, cultural and social capital, each of which functions (in differing ways) as a source of power and resources in the competition for social position. In the relational network shown in figure 11.1, economic and cultural capital take on the key roles. The novel aspect of this approach is its inclusion of a horizontal axis, which expresses *the kind of* capital held by a group (or an individual) in terms of the relative weighting between economic and cultural capital. The vertical axis expresses *how much* capital is available to a group (or an individual). There is constant competition over the acquisition and relative value of these varieties of capital; groups and individuals are interested in revaluing the 'currency' they hold over against that of others. In the final instance everyone wants to improve their position in the relational network.

Subject-specific Cultures in Social Space

How are the three subject–specific student cultures we have discussed here positioned within the social space represented by Bourdieu's relational network? Given the various kinds of factors which define and influence the material, social and cultural circumstances of student life, we can

Figure 11.1   Social positions (by occupation) in the social space of capital ownership (after Bourdieu)

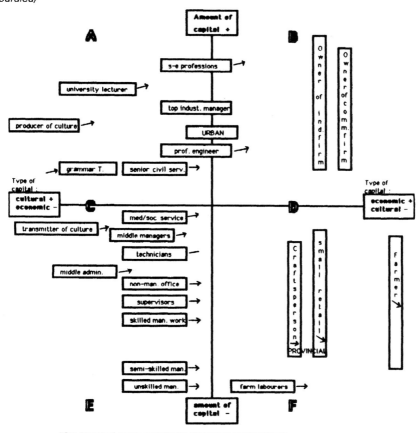

Source: Bourdieu, 1982a, pl. 212f, modified by Zinneker, 1986, p. 101.

position students *in general* as shown in figure 11.2 (p. 182). In other words, university students are placed at the extreme left-hand side of the horizontal axis. They have plenty of cultural capital, but little economic capital. Students are also placed around the centre point of the vertical axis, with a weighting towards the lower half of the network space. This means that they have about average or slightly below average amounts of capital resources.

Because social space is a relational network, the spatial patterns repeat themselves at greater levels of magnification. In other words,

Figure 11.2 Social space of capital ownership: Magnification of the field of subject-specific student culture.

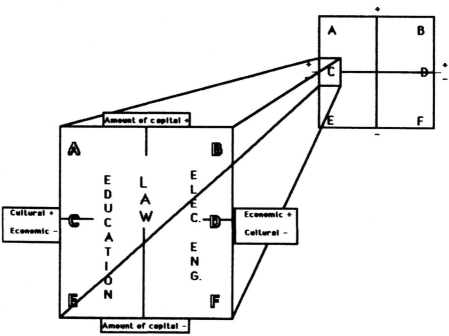

when looking at a particular sector of social space filled with, in this case, university students and their culture, the relations between types and amounts of capital resources reappear in similar form. (This does not mean, of course, that wider social relations are simply repeated in a microcosm, rather that the *principles* of those relations are repeated.) Figure 11.2 therefore extracts the field of student culture from the larger social space and positions the subject–specific cultures discussed in this chapter within the magnified field.

The positionings shown in figure 11.2 are provisional, and serve a heuristic purpose. The important point is that subject-specific cultures can now be placed in the context of social reproduction processes. We suggest that the discipline habitus parallels occupational cultures linked with the study of a particular subject. In the Department of Electrical Engineering, the orientation breakfast is integrated into a predetermined and fixed time and activity schedule for the day. University study is thus defined as work and its purpose is to gain credentials. The breakfast takes on the character of a workbreak, and its organizational principle appears to be the optimal use of time. The world of the professional engineer is also characterized by a strict division between work and leisure time. This division is already suggested by the nature of the orientation breakfast, where its only function seems to be that of satisfying bodily needs for sustenance.

In contrast, the Department of Education breakfast party practises a more generous, almost profligate, use of time. Careful attention is paid to fostering social relationships, and it is up to individuals to make the best use of their time as they see fit. The teaching and social welfare occupations connected with this area of university study are especially concerned with human relations, individual personality and personal development. Dealing with people and their social problems cannot be governed by time schedules; on the contrary, it is time which is invested in people, which can then appear as a 'waste of time' from the outside.

But in the Department of Law's pub culture, time is divided into the working day and free time in the evening, which can be used to exchange information and keep up social contacts. Studying and leisure are separated in time and in space. Lawyers must consider their actions at work in the light of legislation and the social order. They cannot consider individuals as human personalities, but must see them as social objects in relation to the law. Professional competence requires specialized factual knowledge and an ability to weigh up social power relationships as these impinge upon the legal sphere. Pubs are highly appropriate places for relaxed conversational exchange of information and opinion. Professional casework takes place during the day, informal discussion about it in the evening.

The different understandings and use of time across the three subject-specific cultures discussed here are but one aspect of the differentiation of student lifestyle. Whatever aspects we choose to consider, such differentiation forms part of the socialized acquisition of attributes of distinction and inequality; and these attributes are linked with occupational status positions. As part of our project, Apel (1989) has investigated the question of whether predispositions for socially unequal positions become habitualized during the course of university studies. In other words: does the acquisition of a discipline habitus incorporate aspects of induction into an (anticipated) social-occupational habitus?

A comparison between law and education students' everyday cultural practices found that the latter were more concerned with individuality and creativity, spending a large part of their free time in educational-cultural activities. Law students were much more likely to make a clear distinction between their studies and their leisure time, with a clearer orientation towards their future professional lives and the adult world in general. It seems quite evident that from earliest student days processes of socialization into distinctive subject-specific habituses take place which symbolically represent (anticipated and actual) positionings in the spatial network of social power relations. It becomes plausible to suggest that socialization into university culture exerts an influence which reaches far beyond student life; excising the social logic of these processes within the framework of social reproduction is the task with which we are now faced.

Chapter 12

Youth, Race and Language in Contemporary Britain: Deconstructing Ethnicity?

Roger Hewitt

Despite economic migration being primarily a young person's pastime, curiously the first numerically significant waves of migrants from the Commonwealth to the UK were a little too early to have registered with the sociology of youth.[1] Migration from the Caribbean began seriously in the early 1950s and continued in substantial numbers only until the early 1960s. Other migrant workers from the Punjab, Gujarat and Silhet, in modern Pakistan, India and Bangladesh, primarily established themselves from the mid-1950s until the mid-1970s. There were, of course, other migrants — East African Sikhs, Hindus and Muslims — who came as political refugees and who were by no means all especially young, but the migrant population was a young population — single men without families, couples yet without children — transforming their qwn transition from education to unemployment into a migration from their countries of origin to a Britain eager to fill the posts available in the then expanding metropolitian economy.

It was not, of course, that these migrants were not written about by sociologists — naturally they were — but that they did not constitute part of the definition of 'youth'. They were part of other definitions — of 'race', of 'ethnicity', of 'migrant labour' — where they became established within what Paul Gilroy has called the 'victim/problem' discursive couplet (Gilroy, 1987), and it was only later that the connections were made between the second generation of black British people of Caribbean and Asian origin as 'problem' and youth as 'problem'.

The sociology of youth with reference to race has many missing parts of this kind. Indeed, it is a strangely limited narrative. It has been confined almost entirely to but two themes: the first is that of white working class racism and its relationship to youth unemployment; the other is that of black youth in the throws of a putative 'crisis' of economic and cultural identity. There is no doubt that the racism of white adolescents from the 1950s until the present has presented a problem of

serious and sometimes tragic dimensions. There have also been periods —
for example, from the late 1970s until the early 1980s — when political
groups and parties of the far right, such as the National Front and the
British Movement, have succeeded in linking explicitly neo-Nazi prop-
aganda and political practices with sections of white working-class youth
through cultural engineering — hijacking skinhead style from its niche
within 'two-tone' youth culture and transforming it into a major signifier
of racist politics (Hewitt, 1986, p. 30). This continues to be a resource for
establishing a starkly limited but, for some, resonant emblem of white
working class ethnicity (Hebdige, 1981) amongst small but destructive
pockets in urban areas.

It is also true that something very significant happened to Afro-
Caribbean youth in the 1970s. Most especially significant was the numerical growth of the black teenage population, for the 1970s witnessed the
emergence into adolescence of the children of those who had come to
Britain from the Caribbean in the 1950s to make a new way of life and
create families of their own. There were, therefore, perhaps good reasons
why black youth should have been noticed and to some extent researched
for the first time. They had made their appearance as a significant part of
the urban landscape, had grown up and into prominence so that by 1981
approximately 50 per cent of the black British population was under 20
years of age (CRE, 1980, p. 82).

The distinctive culture which black British youth of Caribbean
parentage forged during the 1970s was severely regarded as constituting a
rebellious protest against dominant white values; against the economic
pragmatism of their own parents; against economic disadvantage; against
police discrimination and racism (Pryce, 1979; Garrison, 1979; Troyna
and Cashmore, 1982). It was consistently conceived in negative, reactive
terms. Despite its characterization as a movement concerned with forging
an identity drawing on Caribbean (and especially Jamaican) roots, involving a Rastafarian rejection of the white 'Babylon', and/or the embracing
of the meretricious stylistics of Kingstonian street culture, it was, above
all else, seen as a defensive reaction and far less, if at all, as the evolution
of a new urban British culture in its own right. For these reasons, whole
pathologies of black youth were mapped in terms of the extent to which
black youth culture was embraced (Troyna, 1979). Those who embraced
it most were deemed to have 'rejected white society', and were attempting to live out the 'contradictory injunction' productive of an identity
crisis amongst young blacks with personal, social and political repercussions.

These, then, have been the two major themes of race and youth
within the sociology of youth, often linked inevitably by the explanatory
power of 'unemployment' — the putative disaffection of black youth tied
to the unmistakably high levels of black youth unemployment; and white
adolescent racism seen as an almost inevitable consequence of competing

against black youth within the labour market, against a backdrop of massive general youth unemployment. ('Unemployment', has, at times, been asked to do excessive overtime in the service of explanation.)

In fact, purely *sociological* studies of white adolescent racism were surprisingly few, studies in social psychology tending to address this issue (and, indeed, questions of youth and ethnicity/race in general) more sustainedly (Cochrane and Billig, 1984; Milner, 1983; Davey, 1983). This, I suspect, had much to do with a sociological romanticism concerning white male working-class youth which seems to have disfigured both gender and race research amongst the young. Certainly the almost embarrassed awkwardness of references to the racism of young white working-class males in some accounts (Pearson, 1976; Hebdige, 1979, p. 58) would seem to suggest that this is the case. However, one apparently politically acceptable relationship of white to black (male) youth, and one which seemed to occur at several removes from racism, was the relationship forged within sub-cultural stylistics — a relationship first indicated by Phil Cohen (1972) and later explored and expanded upon by Dick Hebdige (1976 and 1979).

Hebdige's work was important in successfully sidestepping the dominant themes of race and youth research. In concentrating on cultural relations he drew attention to the possibility of more than the antagonistic polarities which were being established right across the spectrum of discursive production. He offered a reading of the stylistic appropriation and transformation of black culture that was grounded, importantly, in the culture of black young men as it had been developed in Jamaica and transposed to the UK at a relatively early stage — the 1960s/early 1970s — an embellished portrait of an historical moment prior to the development of the distinctly black British youth cultures of the later seventies and after. (For a critique of Hebdige's approach, however, see Cohen, 1980, pp. ix–xviii.) In this almost archaeological endeavour there were few signposts and it is not surprising that interpretation and reconstruction played a rather more dominant part than, say, ethnographic techniques. However, it must be said that in focusing on sub-cultural style itself and on a very narrow sector of British youth, the broader social effects and dynamics of multiracial urban life amongst the mainstream young remained beyond vision. Hebdige's book *Subcultures: The Meaning of Style* was published in 1979, but in important ways the opening of the new decade of the 1980s marked a new phase in both the political and cultural development of black youth and of black and white youth together in urban contexts. In March 1980 the Commission for Racial Equality published a report called *Youth in Multi-Racial Society: The Urgent Need for New Policies*. It was apocryphally sub-titled 'The fire next time' after James Baldwin's celebrated essay. It warned that unless a range of policy initiatives were taken there was little that could prevent 'serious strife in the eighties' (CRE, 1980 p. 74). Within months of its publication serious rioting occurred in the St. Paul's district of Bristol, followed in 1981 by further serious rioting in Brixton, South London. Both riots were sparked by 'poor relations' between the police and young blacks. These events seemed but the fructification of the complex of social and political issues surrounding black youth which had come to be articulated with increasing regularity during the latter half of the previous decade. Yet one of the most surprising features of these riots was the very high proportion of *white* youth also actively involved (something that was also true of the riots occurring in several English cities in 1985) a feature quite inexplicable either in terms of the 'great divide' theories of race and youth sociology and social psychology, or in terms of the sub-cultural account offered by Hebdige. Why were white youth involved side by side with young blacks if racism was supposed to divide them? Could it be that the 'unemployment', once wheeled out to explain youth racism, might also be pressed into service again to explain black and white youth together, unified in their opposition to a common oppression? These events seriously called into doubt the usefulness of most of what had been written about youth and race — except, perhaps, the disaffection of black youth — up to that point. The picture was clearly far more complex than had been allowed.

This was not the only respect in which the move into the 1980s signalled important changes. The profile of Afro-Caribbean youth culture itself took a less politically 'readable' turn in moving away from Rastafarian themes and embracing the glossier urban street styles of New York breakdancing, and hip hop, blending North American, Caribbean and urban British images and cultural trajectories into something that was less monothematically revolutionary and which emphasized its own expressive effervescence far more than any set of conditions against which it might be said to be posed — a movement, indeed, away from any implication of mere 'defensive response' and towards the elaboration of an indigenous, vigorous black youth culture in its own right and for its own autochthonous reasons (Gilroy, 1987; Back, 1988).

A further transformation took place in the case of Asian youth following the move into the eighties. This occurred on a number of levels. Until 1981 the popular image of Asian youth was of passivity and quiescence, even in the face of the most extreme forms of racism. The picture was by no means justified, Asian youth had been organizing in self-defence against neo-Fascist groups in the East End of London and in other English towns and cities throughout the latter 1970s. However, in 1981, the popular image was radically altered following wide media coverage of an attempt by large numbers of skinhead youth to hold a provocative concert in Southall, an area of West London famous for the size of its Asian population. For the first time in (white) public consciousness, Asian youth took part in a massively visible repulsion of the racist abuse and attacks handed out to shopkeepers and others by neo-Fascist skinheads on the streets of Southall. A formidable confrontation occurred following which the pub where the concert was to be held remained but a charred ruin. This event was part of a particularly gendered form of self-assertion amongst Asian youth and this kind of development — the elaboration of organized physical resistance to racist attacks and abuse — has also been accompanied by other less political developments involving street machismo, territoriality and violence within the Asian youth community. These developments have not gone unnoticed by Afro-Caribbean and white youth, neither have they remained unqualified by the political action of Asian young women (Bains, 1988).

At another level, important developments have also been observed with respect to the social mobility of young Asian women. Within the Sikh community, for example, it has been reported that because of the dramatic entry of women into the labour market over the past decade, coupled with the realization of the importance of academic credentials to free women from the kinds of unskilled factory jobs older women had been forced to accept, there has emerged an intense interest in higher education for women. This has had a strong impact on familial sponsorship of girls' education and recent studies show that Indian females in Britain are taking their 'A' levels in considerable numbers and out-performing their male counterparts (Gibson and Bhachu, 1988). Whilst the Asian community has always had a strong entrepreneurial and professional tradition, the ascription of minority status is being not so much simply *challenged* as ignored and rendered an irrelevance by many Asian young people — including young women. The transformations taking place within the traditional community matrix of kinship, religious practice and custom are apparently no mere replacement of Asian with Western values but the establishment of economic and cultural initiatives often within the traditional ideological framework. The young people caught up in this process are forging a distinctively British Asian, not South Asian or East African, set of practices (Bhachu, 1988).

At the level of popular culture, the same distinctively British Asian stamp has been apparent in the development of Bhangra music and its following. This has been a truly national phenomena, with Bhangra music — itself initially a form Punjabi folk music associated with harvest — being transformed and blended with numerous other muscial influences and especially those of Western rock. The promotion of Bhangra music through recording and concerts — including the afternoon concerts which are attended by many young Asian people at a time of day when their parents either do not object or cannot detect — has clearly been helped by the entrepreneurial flare apparent within the community, but there is no doubt that Bhangra has also resonated with a new mood amongst British Asian youth. Indeed the developments within the Asian British youth communities have been amongst the most significant and dramatic of all the developments in British youth culture in the eighties.

My own research interest has been concerned with part of the process of cultural hybridization alluded to above in connection with Asian youth and Bhangra and the neighbourhood contexts providing the grounds for the appearance of so many young whites in the 'black' riots of the eighties. If is, no doubt, one of the most common cultural processes yet it too is especially difficult to write about and describe because, in a sense, it is about a process of popular or folk deconstruction where the very terms themselves needed to describe and account for the 'hybrid' forms evaporate and become unreal once their relation to other terms have been conceptually undermined. In particular I have been concerned with the processes through which white working-class adolescents in London and elsewhere have come to use, to varying degrees of skill, the Creole language of Afro-Caribbean youth. This means that I have addressed questions of interracial friendship between black and white young people, the immediate social contexts, networks and ideological terrains within which these occurred, modes of processing racism within the peer group, as well as the forms of cultural exchange taking place across racial lines even at the most subtle and phonemic level. The work has been situated at the 'ethnography of speaking' end of the sociolinguistic disciplinary spectrum.

I do not intend to describe or even refer in much detail to this work — those who are interested will find it referenced here. Rather, I would like to indicate a number of themes and issues which have emerged from this work and which have also been echoed in recent work by other researchers. These are themes which, it seems to me, raise new issues that cluster around this previously invisible phenomenon — the truly multiracial face of urban Britain as it has been developed by young people themselves.

I would like to start by saying something about the language of Afro-Caribbean youth. The creoles spoken by the older generations who were born and raised in the Caribbean are internally differentiated, depending on place of origin and class location. These include the English-based creoles of Jamaica, Barbados, Guyana etc., and the French-based creoles such as those of Dominica and St Lucia. Regardless of parental origins, however, the use of a creole largely derived from Jamaica has established itself as the creole primarily used amongst Afro-Caribbean youth born and raised in the UK, a consequence of both the numerical dominance of early immigrants from Jamaica and of the importance of Jamaica as a source of popular culture amongst the young. This creole, variously referred to as British Jamaican, British Black English (Sutcliffe, 1982), British Youth Caribbean Creole (Brandt, 1984), or, specifically with regard to the capital, London Jamaican Creole, has established itself as something of a prestige youth language amongst young blacks and its prestige has also spread to other non-Afro-Caribbean youth in certain urban contexts (Hewitt, 1986). (Here I will simply refer to it as 'Creole'.)

It is not the only or primary mode of communication amongst young blacks, all of whom employ one of the regional varieties of British English for most communicative purposes and many of whom speak little or no Creole at all. In London the speech of young working-class blacks is London English, or 'Cockney' as it is still sometimes called (Sebba, 1987). Rather, Creole exists as a second linguistic resource which is switched to on certain occasions, triggered by certain interactive contexts, by certain topic shifts and in relation to specific interlocutors. Skills with Creole vary greatly and numerous factors, including social class, gender, neighbourhood demography and individual involvement with black youth culture are influential here.

The analysis of code-switching practices is at a fairly rudimentary stage. However, there is considerable evidence that, as well as in other contexts, switches from London English into Creole frequently occur in interactions where power is contested in some way, Creole availing itself especially of connotations of 'street authority' within the black adolescent peer group and beyond. These kinds of switches, articulated around internal peer social relations are, however, also capable of extension to relations with those outside the peer group. In particular, with respect to the politics of Creole use, these strategic moves are also a feature of switches where conflicts with those in authority occur or are enacted in narrative — conflicts, for example, with the police, with teachers, youth workers, employers, social security officers and so on. In other words, a common peer group discursive structure is reutilized in interactions that open on to social structure. As it is usually whites who occupy these institutional positions it is not surprising that switches to Creole frequently occur as an immediate resource for resistance to the mundane face of racial domination. Most importantly, this resource for political challenge is available even to youngsters with minimal fluency in Creole and ʌ limited range of Creole-utilizing discursive strategies (Hewitt, 1989).

The picture of code-switching practices is considerably confused, however, when the specific local English of young blacks which provides the alternate code is examined, for the English of many black youngsters also itself displays evidence of Creole influence beyond those stretches that might plainly be treated as switches. Lexical and grammatical forms often enter from Creole sources, although which forms, where they appear and how frequently varies greatly from speaker to speaker (Hewitt, 1989; Sebba, 1987; Sutcliffe, 1984). Furthermore, in the many urban areas where black and white were born and grew up together, attending the same schools and occupying the same recreational spaces, one linguistic consequence is that both Cockney and Creole have come to have an impact on the speech of black and white alike. Indeed there has developed in many inner city areas a form of 'community English', or multiracial vernacular which, while containing Creole forms and idioms, is not regarded as charged with any symbolic meanings relating to race and ethnicity and is in no way related to boundary-maintaining practices. Rather it is, if anything, a site within which ethnicity is deconstructed, dismantled and reassembled into a new ethnically *mixed* 'community English'. The degree of Creole influence on the specific local vernacular is often higher in the case of young black speakers but the situation is highly fluid and open to much local variation. There is, therefore, a two-way movement evident in the language use of black London adolescents in which a de-ethnicized, racially mixed local language is creatively being established alongside a strategic, contextually variable use of Creole (and other markers of ethnicity) often employed as markers of *race* in the context of daily anti-racist struggle. (The above account is a condensed version of arguments in Hewitt, 1989.)

The emergence of a multiracial vernacular has clearly come about through something more penetrating and process-related than the term 'culture contact' is able to capture, and the details of its emergence are really only intelligible when adolescent interracial *friendships* are examined. Interracial friendship amongst adolescents is extremely common in inner city areas in the UK but has been seriously neglected within the sociology of youth and race. Indeed, it has so far only been addressed systematically as a result of a sociolinguistic interest in the emergent languages of urban youth. Neither is it, despite common beliefs to the contrary, restricted to relations between white and Afro-Caribbean youth. Important work on the multiracial peer group in areas where adolescents of South Asian and East African parentage are numerically significant is showing how a local vernacular can emerge displaying items and idioms drawn from Punjabi as well as Creole and white urban vernaculars, each specialized in certain ways in multiracial peer group usage (Rampton, 1987a). Furthermore, there is also evidence that some white youngsters have even acquired a fluency in peer group Punjabi (*ibid*) just as have some whites acquired a fluency in Creole (Hewitt, 1982 and 1986). Again strategic uses of socially marked varieties have been observed amongst young Asians including the deliberate exploitation of images of Asian linguistic incompetence through the employment of a feigned Indian English 'foreigner talk' subverting and redeploying long-established stereotypes of the 'babu' familiar from the days of the British Raj (Rampton, 1987b). Thus the two-way movement noted above with regard to Creole and the multiracial vernacular may also be glimpsed here. Here, indeed, we may see again a process of deconstructing ethnic boundaries on the one hand, yet on the other utilizing constructions of ethnicity as an instrument not of any circumscribed communal/ethnic struggle, but as a strategy in quotidian anti-racist engagements.

What appears to be emerging is a de facto, multiracial adolescent culture founded on processes of friendship and close interaction in which racism is not ignored but dealt with in part through cultural practices. If I may be allowed to make a distinction between 'ethnicity-in-itself' as the lived texture of specific cultural forms and 'ethnicity-for-itself' as the strategic use of cultural symbols and practices within specific political arenas, it is as though an unstressed, non-symbolic *mixed* urban ethnicity is emerging amongst urban youth in certain areas, whilst specific ethnic elements within that complex are drawn upon for well-defined political purposes in specific contexts. Furthermore, while *encoded* forms of non-racism and anti-racism seem to be preferred by the white youth participating in those cultures (Hewitt, 1986), there is also persistent evidence of explicitly articulated anti-racist political commitments amongst white youth too, stemming perhaps from a close knowledge of the forms of racism to which their minority friends are exposed. Here, at least, we may begin to have some ethnographic handle on those 'black' riots in which whites also figured so prominently in the early and mid-1980s.

In apparent - confirmation of the evidence generated by these sociolinguistic/friendship studies, recent work conducted at the Birmingham Centre for Contemporary Cultural Studies by Jones (1988b) has addressed other important aspects of the relationships between black youth and culture and white youth. This work, too, emphasizes the previously neglected dimension of interracial friendships and tackles the historical trajectory of the relationship black culture — especially black musical culture — has had with mainstream white youth. Distancing himself from Hebdige's subcultural analysis, he addresses, rather, the unrecorded yet profound influence black culture has had beyond the ambit of spectacular youth cultures. Like the sociolinguistic work in this field, Jones does not ignore the issue of white adolescent racism, but .situates it as one important element within a complex field of cross-racial affinities, transformations and encounters that are currently taking place in multiracial inner city areas — in this case not London or Bedford but Birmingham and the West Midlands generally.

His book contains a detailed historical account of the musical culture of Jamaica and of its transposition to the UK, together with a close ethnographic study of its impact on white youth as mediated both through the commercial media and through local peer group affiliations and neighbourhood networks. The very close similarity between the experience of interracial friendship and the proximity of interpersonal and group allegiances found in my work and that revealed in Jones' study is a most striking feature of the book and seems to suggest that what has been observed is more than a regional phenomenon (compare, especially, Jones, 1988b, pp. 177–202 and Hewitt, 1982 and 1986). Furthermore, Jones similarly maps the emergence of an articulated notion of local community that included black and white inhabitants and was enshrined in local ideologies of interracial 'cooperation, mutuality and reciprocity' (Jones, 1988, p. 212) which flow from and reinforce the broader cultural and the more directional political practices.

The book is partially structured around the question of what kinds of meaning are emerging as attached to the concept of nation and national identities, as ethnicities previously regarded as alien become not merely discrete parts of British society but integrally woven into its fabric. Part of his answer is captured in a quotation from one of his white informants deeply involved in and committed to his own multiracial neighbourhood:

> Its like, I love this place ... there's no place like home ... Balsal Heath is the centre of the melting pot, man, 'cos all I ever see when I go out is half-Arab, half-Pakistani, half-Jamaican, half-Scottish, half-Irish, I know 'cos I am! [half-Scottish-Irish] ... Who am I ... Tell me? Who do I belong to? They criticize me, the good old England. Alright then, where do I belong? ... you know, I was brought up with blacks, Pakistanis, Africans, Asians, everything, you name it ... Who do I belong to? I'm just a broad person. The earth is mine. You know, we was not born in England, we was not born in Jamaica ... we was born *here*, man. It's our right! That's the way I see it ... That's the way I deal with it. (*ibid*, p. 240)

One important aspect of these new forms of self-definition — and anti-definition — is the wedge it appears to drive between culture/ ethnicity and nationalistic consciousness, for as the above quotation seems to suggest, once narrowly-defined notions of a tightly homogeneous culture are eroded, a major prop in the appeal to nationalistic sentiment is also removed.[2]

The same movement towards new cultural formations amongst the young has also been noted by Gilroy and Lawrence (1988) who write:

> Young people in the heart of the cities ... in many significant respects share a culture. It is assembled from many different elements, and incorporates recognisable fragments from previous struggles and traditions of resistance. In many areas the culture and politics of working-class youth exhibits a seamless and organic fusion of Black and White sensibilities. (p. 141)

They are right to warn, however, of the fragility of these initiatives when they remind readers that:

> There can be little doubt that the nationalistic fervour generated in the South Atlantic [the Falklands war] cements the notion of a racially exclusive and biologically-based national culture in opposition to experience of Black-defined pluralism at the two-tone grassroots of the inner city. (*ibid*)

Here we have a major theoretical, as well as practical, issue in the description of race and youth in the UK in the late 1980s. On the one hand a consciousness of 'grassroots' developments among young people and their processing of racism which Jones (1988b) expresses as follows:

> Young people are already actively involved in producing their own anti-racist solutions, regardless of political initiatives from above. For in the identities, cultural forms and social arrangements evolved by the young themselves out of their engagement with the black community lies an implicit rebuttal of racism and nationalism more potent than any multicultural ideology or stilted local government initiative. (p. 236)

On the other hand it is essential to include a consciousness of the ever-present potential in racist and nationalistic discourses through which these new multi-racial patterns of ideology and behaviour thread their way. Indeed, the question has to be asked: what is the force of Jones' use of 'implicit' here when applied to something as remarkable as a 'rebuttal of racism and nationalism'? It is easy to allow optimism to run ahead of the facts.

It seems to me that some of the linguistic practices described in the earlier part of this chapter may prove helpful in developing a model that captures some of the subtleties and apparent contradictions of the situation. Especially useful may be an awareness of the existence of local multiracial vernaculars (which mirror the *de facto* multiracial adolescent cultures more widely), set against the strategic switching to codes that are drawn from symbolic resources tied to specific political constituencies and idealizations of those constituencies. For here, if we treat movements either into socially charged symbolic acts, or into explicit political action as similar in some ways to the sociolinguistic form of code-switching to symbolically marked forms, then the evocation of not only ethnicities but also class fractions and gender may be treated as switches, and as political steering devices that are capable of transforming, or more delicately qualifying and augmenting the immediate social meaning of group and individual interaction. And just as innumerable subtle shifts occur in linguistic code-switching between the mixed code and the specialized code, so we might perceive a similar subtlety in the shifting between what is politically *stressed* (explicit) and the 'implicit' (possibly unconscious) terrain of quotidian social existence. Indeed, the relationship between local multiracial cultures and racist practices is only in fact 'contradictory' if the former is treated as something capable of being somehow *in itself and to its members* 'implicit' (rather than that 'implication' existing largely for the commentator alone).

Thus the movements within local multiracial cultures may display, under certain conditions, a range of 'switches' (some of them fleeting and momentary) in ideological practice — whites, for example, invoking the semiotics of unicultural community closure and the symbols of white working class identity, Afro–Caribbeans drawing on the storehouse of roots and other resistance symbolisms, women constructing marked challenges to patriarchal structures (including through an exploitation of their own class and ethnic resources) etc. — in each case for temporary, strategic political purposes, and then moving back into the unstressed and usually unexamined codes which may or may not be 'implicitly' political in their own right. By no means will all such ideological code-switches be resistive or, indeed, revolutionary. Like the shifts into the racist discourses of community closure that muddy the waters of the new multiracialism, many may be just the opposite. Nevertheless, with respect to race at least, the *ground* has shifted and we must now approach what the *figures* do in new ways.

Notes

1   I would like to acknowledge the support of the ESRC who funded the research project on which this chapter is based: Language Use in the Multiracial Adolescent Peer Group, award no. C00232390.
2   It is interesting to note that the projected erosion of a fixed and unified 'national culture' for anti-racist and anti-nationalistic reasons, also has implications for *all* claims relating to ethnic integrity and rights based on the matching of political and cultural/ethnic domains. It is a logical problem at least as old as Herder's vigorous anti-racism formed alongside his libertarian ethnicism and anti-statist politics. Interestingly, Herder would appear to be both the founder of European anti-racist thought *and* of modern cultural studies, although to the best of my knowledge this has never been acknowledged, at least not in the UK.

Chapter 13

How 'Black' are the German Turks? Ethnicity, marginality and Inter-ethnic Relations for Young People of Turksih Origin in the FRG

Georg Auernheimer

Introduction

The life situation of second generation Turkish immigrant guestworkers has some unmistakable parallels with the situation of black youth in the UK: high unemployment and an unfavourable labour market position, partial ghettoization in areas with substandard accommodation, and subject to a multifaceted racism in everyday life. In this sense Turkish guestworkers are without doubt the 'visible minority' in the FRG. At the same time, we can identify clear specificities in relation both to living conditions and cultural background and resources in the way young people deal individually and collectively with their situation. So, for example, the nature of West Germany's immigration laws leave young Turkish people in a position of basic uncertainty over their future: *rights* to permanent residence are not legally enshrined. Alternatively, we might examine the nature of available cultural traditions and to what extent these resist transformation and synthesis with new cultural elements.

Here it would seem that young Turkish people are in a less favourable position than those, for example, of Caribbean origins in the UK. Through parents, relatives, the West German Turkish community and/or a childhood spent in part growing up in Turkey they are usually versed in elements of a rural culture interspersed with a host of modern elements. It is not only distance to so-called western culture that restricts their room to manoeuvre and to find their own identity (as is frequently popularly assumed), but rather the gap between their traditions and the proletarian urban way of life. Given its character, sociohistorically speaking, as an ethnic melting pot, Caribbean culture may offer more favourable background resources to its members. Cast in terms of language, it would appear that in an urban situation Creole offers a better opportunity for self-determination within the dominant white British culture (Hewitt, 1986 and chapter 12, this volume). Young Turkish people, in contrast, have to choose between using German or reverting to Turkish, whereby they are often fluent in neither and resort to using mixtures of the two — which is not the equivalent of a creole. The 'helplessness' of young Turkish people contrasts here with the prouder self-determination of young black people in Britain. Yet albeit modest, there are signs of the search for a new identity within the second generation German Turkish community. Helplessness in the face of discrimination helps to explain why there is a strong 'isolationist' tendency in their patterns of social relations, i.e., socially young Turkish people converse largely with each other. It is in this point that they differ from the second generations of other guestworker nationalities (cf. Esser *et al.*, 1986).

Where the terms *cultural identity* or *ethnicity* are used here, it is with an awarness that they do not refer to something static, but rather to the historical process of individualization. Whilst bearing in mind Cohen's (1988) warning not to make a fetish of the inexorable images and myths of ethnicity, it remains the case that the validity of the cultural conflict hypothesis has frequently and repeatedly been called into question (cf. Auernheimer, 1988; Bukarow and Llaryora, 1988; Czock, 1988; Hamburger, 1986; Twenhöfel 1984). An alternative and *processual* understanding of ethnicity is founded on the view that people actively struggle with the actual conditions of their lives, using the cultural resources available to both to evaluate their social condition and as a yardstick for their actions. Hence, the form and quality of their struggles can be traced back to the character and availability of those cultural resources. *Both* conditions of life *and* available cultural resources (whether as cultural traditions or as their transformation in the new context) determine ways of life and the potential for social action. Young Turkish people in the FRG face specific problems in relation to these issues; this specificity arises from their socio-structural and cultural locations; and therefore we require a particular consideration of their situation. The analysis which follows also demonstrates why it is necessary, in comparing their situation with other ethnic-racial minorities, to take both dimensions — the socio-structural and the cultural — into account.

The repertoire of symbolic meanings (i.e., means of communication and representation) which a social group has at its disposal constitutes its *culture*. This repertoire is actively created by the members of that group in interrogation with its traditions, and is used in developing a sense of identity and security as well as in shaping social action. Cultural meaning systems exist in relative autonomy and, in historical process, in a dialectical relationship to the course of material life, i.e., to the mode of production and class position. Changing ways of life may lead to changes in dominant cultural themes (cf. Greverus, 1971) and to the transformation of cultural meanings, although these transformations can be of very different natures (cf. Lipp, 1979).

Empirically speaking, we still know little either about the everyday culture of working class youth of Turkish origin, or about the forms of racism with which they are confronted. Many studies using the individual–biographical approach are available, but hardly any ethnographies of groups. In the FRG, writing about racism (*Ausländerfeindlichkeit*; direct translation: xenophobia) tends towards the moralist rather than the analytic. It is also of some interest and significance that a division of labour exists between those specializing in youth research and those concerned with ethnic/race divisions (*Migrantenforschung*; direct translation: migrant research). The large-scale youth surveys of recent years have virtually ignored young people from ethnic minority groups. There are signs of impending change here, but it remains accurate to say that ethnic–racial divisions have not been incorporated into West German theory and research about youth and young people's lives.

Young Turkish People in the FRG: Biography and Way of Life

The historical patterns of guestworker migration to the FRG have resulted in a strong proportional increase over the 1980s in the numbers of young people of Turkish origin growing up or born in West Germany. The statistics include, of course, considerable numbers of children who followed their parents at a later stage, or who have 'commuted' over the years between the two countries (cf. Esser *et al.*, 1986, pp. 74ff: Mühlfeld *et al.*, 1987, p. 3). Labour migration from Turkey to the FRG reached its peak in the early 1970s, the first guestworkers having been hired at the beginning of the 1960s. At that time the typical, and male, migrant worker came alone, without accompanying family members. These moved to West Germany to live only much later — many during the 1970s, some as late as the 1980s — because in the first instance the guestworkers themselves had assumed and hoped to return to Turkey before very long. It was only very gradually that they gave up this orientation towards return.

Although there has been considerable debate over the significance of the age at which migration occurs for the process of cultural identity formation in childhood and adolescence, it is clear that length of residence has to be taken into consideration in order to acquire a meaningful and accurate picture of the social worlds in which Turkish–origin adolescents live. Those who joined their families as teenagers and who now work as miners in the Ruhr presumably have a different relationship with their socio–cultural environment than do those of their peers who have either wholly grown up or who at least attended school in the FRG. We do know, for example, that their social networks are smaller (Esser *et al.*,

1986, p. 509). In fact, 86 per cent of Turkish-origin youth aged 15–24 in 1985 had attended school in West Germany for some period; nevertheless 14 per cent had never done so — disproportionately young women (Mehrländer, 1986, p. 47). Perhaps we should recall here that we are not dealing with small absolute numbers: 1.4 million Turkish citizens were registered as resident in the FRG in 1985, of whom about half were under 25 years of age. To place these figures in perspective, in the mid-eighties the population of the FRG was approximately 61 million, and the proportion of those residents holding foreign citizenship was around 7.5 per cent. Within this group, Yugoslavians, Italians and Greeks, and to a lesser extent the Spanish and the Portugese, comprise significant and classic guestworker categories; but by far the largest sub-group are from Turkey, constituting about 30 per cent of the foreign population. West Berlin has, at around 13 per cent, the highest proportion of foreign residents; Schleswig-Holstein, with about 3.5 per cent, the lowest. The guestworker communities are concentrated in those regions and cities with a classic industrial production base, for example, Hamburg and Nordrhein-Westfalen (NRW), and in those regions with healthy economies and hence high demand for labour, for example, Baden-Württemberg's urban-metropolitan areas.

The ethnicization of social difference in the FRG is no less marked than in France and in the UK: life perspectives and plans are heavily constrained by the insecurity surrounding rights of residence, by educational underachievement, by severe labour market disadvantage, by residential and community ghettoization, and by institutionalized processes of discrimination. The situation of minority youth is not identical in all states; so, for example, in West Berlin and in NRW the provincial governments have improved the legal position of second-generation migrants by disconnecting their status to reside in the FRG from that of their parents. Nevertheless, their fundamental legal position as foreigners, subject to legislation, remains qualitatively different from indigenous youth unless they change their formal citizenship. As yet, the children of guestworkers do not possess a *right* to West German citizenship, even should they decide to make an application (although there is currently a measure of political initiative to introduce such a right, along with the introduction of local election voting rights for certain categories of foreigners).

In terms of formal educational achievement, Turkish children on average secure fewer and lower-level school qualifications than either their West German peers or working-class children from other minority groups. The secondary educational system in the FRG is largely tripartite in character; in 1985, almost 80 per cent of 12–15-year-olds of Turkish origin attended secondary moderns (*Hauptschule*), and of these 40 per cent found themselves in classes with a high proportion of non-indigenous pupils (Klemm, 1987; Esser *et al.*, 1986). We are speaking, then, of an effectively segregated school system. Only 2.6 per cent of those aged

15–24-years-old attended a grammar school (*Gymnasium*), and they were underrepresented in major further education institutions — 3.4 per cent had attended a technical college (*Fachschule*), 22.3 per cent a vocational training college (*Berufsschule*). The credentials inflation at secondary school qualification level which has accompanied the competitive youth labour market of recent years has displaced minority youth into a still more disadvantageous position. In Mehrländer's (1986) survey, almost 61 per cent of Turkish young people aged 15–24-years-old said they had been unable to obtain an employer-based apprenticeship (*Ausbildungsstelle*). On these kinds of figures, rates of intergenerational upward mobility are unlikely to be significant, so that the second generation will, at best, largely step into their parents' shoes in the labour market — and 72 per cent of Turkish adults in the FRG are unskilled or semi-skilled workers (Mehrländer, 1983 and 1986). Given that rates of unemployment are estimated to be extremely high among young people of Turkish origin, in many cases their propects have deteriorated in comparison with those of the first generation guestworkers.

Almost half the West German Turkish family population have found themselves marginalised into low-quality residential environments: typically they live in old housing with poor amenities or in high-rise buildings built as part of slum-clearance programs; and in neighbourhoods with underdeveloped community and transport infrastructures, in proximity to industry and with high levels of pollution. At least 40 per cent and possibly more live in neighbourhoods populated largely by non-Germans; a significant proportion of these neighbourhoods are additionally ethnically highly homogeneous (Esser *et al.*, 1986; Mehrländer, 1986).

Specific Patterns and Problems of Cultural Orientation

We now need to ask what cultural resources, both contents and practices, are available to young Turkish people living in the FRG; resources which, in the light of their social and material disadvantage, are of assistance to them in their search for identity and membership during the youth phase. Three kinds of problems arise: the culture of origin loses meaning; family strategies dominate individual lifeplans (familism); individuals acquire a marginal identity and positioning in relation to both cultures of reference. In West Germany, Turkish youth shares the first two problems with young people from other ethnic backgrounds, whereas they experience particular conflicts in relation to the third as a consequence of their positioning within racist discourse.

The Disintegration of Traditional Cultural Meanings

Cultural norms and values, as — in Leontjew's (1982) terms — ideal forms of social experience, correspond with specific social practices. Where social practices shift, so must cultural ideals change accordingly, if they are to serve any useful orienting purpose. Historical change and social migration produce tension between social practices and cultural ideals which for the individual implies the experience of conflict. Second generation migrants in particular are prone to experience the culture of origin as *making no sense* for their lives. One possible solution is the tacit personal redefinition of cultural traditions; but frequently problems of sense-making and indentity formation are the consequence. Such problems are intensified by the collision between the promotion and expectation of an individualist subjectivity in conformity with dominant Western bourgeois forms of socialization and the collectivist subjectivity fostered and demanded with pre-bourgeois social and cultural formations.

Clearly minority ethnic communities modify their cultural traditions: in this case rural farming elements remain but are dominated by an urban proletarian cultural form, even though the time perspectives contingent upon the historical migration process retain their significance. Minority culture and ways of life are decisively formed through the partially transfigured remembered images of the mother country (*Heimat*) and in the dream of return; manifold contradictions are the consequence. So, for example, whilst husband-fathers in becoming guestworkers may have set certain traditional cultural norms and values to one side in leaving their families alone for many years, they equally invoke elements of those traditions in their relationships with and actions towards their wives and children. Certainly Mühlfeld *et al.* (1987) concluded from a study of the life plans of second generation Turkish guestworkers that the wage labourer identity is both biographically focal and dominates the specific features of a Turkish upbringing; Esser *et al.'s* (1986) study of cultural modernization processes among Turkish and Yugoslavian guestworkers similarly found the host context to play the decisive role, marked generational differences notwithstanding.

The 'senselessness' of traditional norms and values is reflected in young people's own accounts. Figen, in 1982 a 16-year-old girl who had lived in West Germany since she was 4 years old, wrote in a letter to youth workers that 'I couldn't any longer carry on playing the role of a Turkish girl, just there for sex and babies. I was dead against the idea of being a sex object. I resisted the image of the routinely subservient woman.' Of the three detectable kinds of response to this 'senselessness', Figen's strong, explicit and almost provocative rejection is the least common. Much more frequent is the denial of conflict and the repression of culturally 'deviant' needs; Henn and Werkmann (1985) describe interviewing a very young married woman, who at first projected herself as very happy until her underlying deep depression burst through. The third, and partially successful, response comprises the redefinition of traditional cultural norms to permit a co-existence with a modern self-identity. In this case, for example, a Turkish student continues to subscribe to the norm of premarital sexual abstinence, but on the grounds of mutual respect between the future spouses rather than that of maintaining family honour. Beyond this categorization of response, it is difficult to assess how far conflicts related to cultural alienation take pathogenic forms.

The disturbing strangeness of traditional culture for second generation migrants often impresses itself through visiting their family's village; Straube (1987) provides an account of a young Turkish woman's experience:

> I found the fact that the village women discussed everything between themselves difficult — it was strange for me. So I simply didn't speak at all . . . They kept asking me why I hadn't yet had a baby. I said 'My husband hasn't got a job, and we want to enjoy life a bit before we have children.' That made them think I didn't want children at all. I didn't give a damn what they thought of me. Then I said that we wanted to wait. After all, people in Turkey don't all have children straight away either. Well, at the beginning I felt really strange — but then I got used to it, to the fact that village people talk about everything. (p. 270)

This account illustrates how distantly removed from her family's culture of origin this young woman had become as a consequence of living in a modern industrial society based on wage labour. Firstly, she had internalized its norms of privacy and intimacy, thus finding the directness and open familiarity of traditional female social groups unsettling. Secondly, she countered the persistent questioning about starting a family with values to which the new way of life exacts espousal — the individual pursuit of happiness and an expectation that life is planned autonomously and rationally. For this young woman, traditional norms and values have become senseless and incomprehensible; equally, the view that starting a family is better left until employment and income are secure is an absurd principle in the traditional rural context.

It is especially in these accounts of visits to Turkey that Mühlfeld *et al.'s* (1987, pp. 152–4) interview study points to greater or lesser degrees of alienation from the traditional culture of origin. For example, the social control of behaviour exercised in Turkish villages is an irksome experience. Young men find it remarkable that young women in Turkey 'immediately want to get serious' and 'immediately think of marriage'. The norms of modern achievement-oriented society have been internalized: traditional life is evaluated against these, rather than in its own terms, so that the visitors comment 'the people have no aim in life, they live fatalistically'. In the eyes of some, poverty and lack of success are judged as self-inflicted. In other words, visits 'home' are partially seen from the perspective of the modern Western tourist.

Traditional life contexts may be experienced as a closed book, the confrontation with its norms utterly irritating to young people; again, Straube (1987, p. 332) provides us with a grotesque account from a 15-year-old Turkish boy living in the FRG but already married to a girl in a Turkish village:

> I still feel like an adolescent. Just because I am married doesn't mean I have to be a man. Until I was 14 I was allowed to go to the playground. Now I am only allowed out of the house for a few hours at a time because I go around with my friends and go to the cinema, and my father doesn't like it. I think it's stupid that I'm married, and I don't have any real friends anymore. The girls laugh at me and make jokes because I'm married ... At the moment I'm not allowed out. My father didn't want to me to go out, and I didn't like that at all — after all, I *am* married! I asked him why he didn't want me to go out, and he just said 'Because'. I told him I'd go out as soon as he had left the house, but he didn't believe me. So when I really did, he beat me. Then I ran away for two days, sleeping on the street. He forbids me everything, even though I'm married! Yet he said himself that for him, a boy who is married is a man. I don't like it one little bit when he orders me around. He could ask me what *I* want for once.

Heßler and Rilling (1987, p.109) similarly report from their work with Turkish juvenile delinquent boys in West Berlin that, paradoxically, they insist upon their grown-up status at the same time as substantiating their continuing status as children by begging their fathers to recognize them as grown-up.

The emptiness of traditional cultural meanings for young people leads to personal alienation from parents and relatives, simply because cultural meaning systems are no longer shared. Figen wrote in her letter (see above, p. 202) that 'I no longer got on well with my mother, as I had done in the past. It seemed as if we were worlds apart'. Feelings of alienation are often reinforced by parents' and relatives' attempts to maximise control of young people's activities, a principle drawn from traditional cultures which do not operate through internalization (Elias, 1977; Schiffauer, 1987). The young people themselves repeatedly discover that their lives cannot, in reality, be controlled by external interventions of this kind; they develop expectations to act independently and to plan their own lives. They prefer self-control, arguing that they are able to respond appropriately to situational demands and normative expectations. In other words, a universalistic orientation replaces traditional particularistic morality, so that it is no longer external rule conformity but rather internal posture that counts. Yakut *et al.* (1986, pp. 91 and 95), in interpreting Emine's apparent acceptance of traditional male avoidance rules, point to the way in which she relies on her own convictions when the situation requires contravention of those same rules — when she needs a lift home, she does not refuse to be driven by a male without other company. Their data show how accusations of inconsistencies typical in rural moral conventions serve to justify young people's impressions of traditional culture as founded on ridiculous double standards: 'That's why we're not allowed to do anything ... The family honour would be sullied if we went into a cafe. What rubbish! They let me smoke and drink beer. But it's forbidden to go into a cafe ... [Laughs] ... Isn't that just stupid?' Young people, especially girls, frequently complain bitterly that their parents and relatives do not trust them; these feelings are explained by the desire for moral autonomy and self-control fostered in their 'post-conventional' social environment. Müller-Spude *et al.* (1985) cite an extract from a group interview with young Turkish women attending a vocational training college:

> And then [my father] said why he wasn't going to send me to college.... Because he was afraid [what would happen] with the boys who are here! ... He didn't trust me! That was terrible for me. I kept asking myself what I'd done [wrong]. I went to school, got good marks, saw to all the housework all on my own, looked after the children. How did he come to think such a thing? (p. 235)

However, Mühlfeld *et al.* (1987, p. 132) reached the conclusion that young Turkish people seldom fundamentally oppose the normative perspectives and concrete expectations of their parents. They are more inclined to agree with the principles, for example, in relation to family honour, but to problematize the extent of the practical restrictions to which they are subject. Esser *et al.*'s (1986, p. 512) Duisburg Turkish working class family case studies turned up no evidence of manifest generational conflict. Even Heßler and Rilling's (1987, p. 107) Berlin study found no evidence for polarization in favour of or against their families on the part of the juvenile delinquents, though this does not mean that parents reacted uniformly to their sons' behaviour — in some cases, fathers overtly dissociated themselves from their delinquent offspring. On the contrary, they found these boys' cultural orientations to be both multiply and ambivalently patterned.

Families and Individuals

A traditionalist family orientation is, on the one hand, still very strongly present for second generation Turkish adolescents, not least because the family offers shelter and protection in insecure and difficult life situations. On the other hand, familism obstructs the development of that individualized autonomy structurally arising from modern socialization, so that an individual construction of life-plan — especially for girls — is subordinated to the family strategy. It is here essential to contextualize such questions firmly within the institutionalized patterns of social disadvantage to which these young people are subject, if we are to avoid deflecting inequalities onto the pseudo-explanatory shoulders of ethnically-specific 'mentalities'.

Familism inevitably demands that individual life-plans are waived altogether or at least incorporated within the logic of the kingroup's collective perspective for its future. The transitional social formations from which most migrant workers have come no longer display intact traditionalism either; but in its original form, familism does not in essence demand individual sacrifice for the simple reason that individualism does not develop in the first place. Familism is expressed in a range of apparent trivialities, so, for example, in the observation that many family members — especially women — do not have rights to an independent personal budget; to divide resources within families in this way would be met with incomprehension. Heßler and Rilling (*ibid*, p. 105) note that it is fathers and elder sons in guestworker families who are most likely to have (sometimes generous amounts of) 'pocket-money' at their disposal. As a rule, all wage-earners are expected to contribute at least the major part of their income to the household purse. Bielefeld *et al.* (1982, p. 27) report that a family often holds a joint bank account to which the male adolescents have formal access, although they are unlikely to draw on it without their parents' permission. The entire family economy is based on joint ventures such as the purchase of a house or of land in their country of origin. Money is thus family property (cf. Esser *et al.*, 1986, p. 511). These apparent trivialities indicate not only a different way of life, but also imply consequences for the way young people plan their lives and futures: in the case of long-term conflict with parents, they cannot easily take recourse in moving out to live independently because they have no personal savings to finance this (quite apart from internal cultural barriers to such ideas).

Familism means that critical decisions which irrevocably affect the course of each person's life fall within the competence of the husband-father alone, perhaps together with his eldest son or with his wife. Others, especially children and even more so daughters, may not be consulted at all. Individual autonomy is sharply constrained in the question of marriage partners, again, especially in the case of daughters; occupational choices may also, though less frequently, be directed in line with family joint ventures, such as setting up a small business 'back home'. Yakut *et al.* (1986, pp. 120 and 135) underline that occupational choice is a *family* affair rather than a matter of individual ability or preference, but neither is it something which the family *discusses* as such — family communication structures do not facilitate discursive problem solution. Adolescents may hold divergent views from their parents in the matter of their occupational destination, but current labour market conditions for minority youth make a fiction of choice in the first place. Arranged marriage is a different question, however, causing considerable conflict for young people; it massively contravenes their modernist views. Contrary to popular cliché, even in rural Turkey it is seldom that a marriage is arranged wholly without the consent of the parties concerned (Mertens, 1977, p. 67; Schiffauer, 1987, p. 201). It would be utterly exceptional in guestworker families, despite the widely differential degree of participation accorded to young people in such decisions. Nevertheless, the modern Western understanding of 'free choice' wholly in the hands of individuals themselves seldom finds favour — marriage is properly a family affair.

Yet, despite variations in orientations, young people continue to regard the family strategy as significant for their future plans, where as a matter of course they incorporate their fathers'/parents' projects, for example, working in the shops and businesses already bought or planned; especially for girls, returning to Turkey with their parents; and even staying behind in the FRG to work after parents have returned (cf. Mühlfeld *et al.*, 1987, pp. 183–5).

Marginality

The concept of marginality was developed to describe the experiences of US immigrants as being positioned on the peripheries of, or between, two cultures; in its original formulation, it placed the locus of marginality within the individual. Subsequently, emphasis has shifted to analyzing the features of marginal situations and the ways in which people respond to them (cf. Heckmann, 1981). Boos-Nünning (1986) concludes that second-generation Turkish adolescents in West Germany face a currently insoluble reference group problem (p.140). Where they privilege the validity of their own individual perspectives, they find themselves rejected by their minority community and subject to pressures to conform to indigenous German culture and society. Those who are prepared to conform in this way run into problems with their families, but cannot count on being truly accepted into German society either. Problems of self-identity, social positioning and uncertainties surrounding one's actions result. Conflicting normative expectations of behaviour can be eased through compartmentalization and separation of action contexts, but those who are subject to ethnic-racial stereotyping, prejudice, discrimination, and rejection inevitably experience anxiety and loss of self-esteem *unless* — and this is decisive — the minority (sub)culture offers a source of positive identification and self-confidence. Those young people of Turkish origin who have spent most or all of their lives in the FRG can no longer make any positive sense of their families' generally rural farming cultural tradition; they therefore have little alternative, as a heavily discriminated minority, but to choose between a strong commitment to ethnicity through traditionalism and an embarrassing, ambivalent denial of their ethnic heritage leading to self-reproach and self-doubt. In this context, Mühlfeld *et al.* (1986, p. 101ff; and 1987, pp. 157–68) remark upon their tendency to adopt the xenophobic opinions of many Germans, for example, that there are too many Turks in the FRG, which explains the racism to which they are subject; they see the answer to their problems as lying in becoming inconspicuous. The essential marginality of their situation becomes evident to them when they find themselves disparagingly identified as *almanci* ('German-Turks') on their visits to Turkey. They are thus viewed negatively by members of both the host culture and the culture of origin.

Two obvious and widespread practices in response to marginality have already been mentioned: striving for inconspicuousness or invisibility; and withdrawal into ethnic traditionalism, which can take on a distinctly regressive character. Both responses can be invoked, according to situational requirements, by the same individuals. An as yet small proportion of young people are actively engaged in creating a new cultural tradition by combining a conscious, positive commitment to their ethnic and cultural origins with an openness to the socio-cultural context of which they are now a part. These are typically educationally successful young people who hold markedly modernist orientation patterns, and who make sense of their situation in political terms; they exemplify the *processual* nature of ethnicity. Alternatively, young people might attempt cultural assimilation by identification with the FRG and with Germans, although this stance involves considerable self-deception given the extent of their exclusion. In fact, Esser *et al.* (1986) report that, with few exceptions, young people of Turkish origin in the FRG do see themselves as explicitly Turkish; self-definition as cosmopolitan constitutes a potential solution to their dilemma (Auernheimer, 1988, p. 147ff).

Leisure and Peer groups

Some have taken the view that, in the difficult process of cultural re-orientation, what has been termed by Heckmann (1981) as the ethno-specific 'colony' takes on important social functions for members of minority communities. This may hold in some instances and to varying degrees; but it seems not to be the case for second generation youth of Turkish or other ethnic origin the FRG. Gade's (1983) study of minority community associations (*Ausländervereine*) in Frankfurt identified a certain turgidity in their activities and atmosphere; they were unattractive to young people. These associations were founded by first generation migrant workers, who continue to dominate their leadership. Where they retain a strong emphasis towards the country and culture of origin, second generation youth finds little support in its search for orientation and identity (Lopez-Blasco, 1983; Öker and Önal, 1986). It has been the minority group *political* rather than cultural associations which have begun to recognize and respond to these problems.

The 1980s have seen the emergence of a creative avantgarde amongst second generation migrant youth, where the mingling of elements is directed towards developing autonomous cultural forms. Characteristically, music constitutes a focal expression of such developments. There is now an established oriental rock, or Saz-Jazz-Rock, 'scene' especially evident in Berlin and NRW; its style can be described as a synthesis of Turkish-oriental and Euro-American musical ingredients. However, those who are creatively involved in the 'scene' are few, and the enthusiastic response of the audience amongst minority youth is not, of itself, a remedy for their situation. Many young people are simply overtaxed and see no future for themselves; all too often this leads to non-productive escapism. Drug addiction is atypical for young people of Turkish origin, but addiction to gambling is characteristic. Gambling here means playing the slot machines in the amusement arcades patronized largely by young people, the numbers of which have increased dramatically in recent years, especially in urban localities with high guestworker populations.

Popular media reports over the 1980s have posited the formation of youth subcultures specific to second generation minority communities, primarily but not wholly ethnically homogeneous in character. We have very little research as such in this area. The importance of intra-ethnic networks and of social meeting points where groups of young men talk and play *tavla* among themselves has been noted both for the Turkish and Yugoslavian communities (Bielefeld *et al.*, 1982; Stüwe, 1982). The peer-group is of enormous significance for young men of Turkish origin; its cultural antecedents lie in the social functions of the Turkish cafe and in the traditional patterns of social interaction in Turkish villages and the *Gecekondu* quarters (Kleff, 1985, p. 214ff; Stüwe, *ibid*). In this sense, the style of minority youth subcultures draws on traditionalism. In contrast, Lutz *et al.*'s (1983) ethnographic account of the *Chikagos* multinational but non-German dominated rocker-type youth gang in Frankfurt indicates alternative sources of cultural style. However, the research base for useful comparisons between different minority youth subcultures remains inadequate.

The leisure activities of young men of Turkish origin include sport, especially football, as an important element — in NRW alone, 161 'foreign' football teams were registered in the provincial sport association

(*Landessportbund*) in 1980. Since the 1960s 'foreign' teams have organized their own trophy competitions, although in recent years they have increasingly preferred to compete within the inidigenous local and provincial leagues (in which they are very successful). A good many sports associations were founded on the initiative of particular guestworker communities but have in varying degrees developed multiethnic/ multinational identities; nevertheless the majority of their members come from minority groups, which the German-dominated provincial sports associations under which they are registered find undesirable — and have attempted to stem with restrictive practices and general disapproval (Abel, 1984; Kilchenstein, 1987). Abel's (*ibid*) survey of guestworkers' leisure activities found 40 per cent of the men, but only 16 per cent of the women, to hold membership in a sports-oriented club or association. Whereas sport is clearly the most popular activity for the men, women prefer family-orientated pursuits (knitting, listening to music, watching television) and dancing/folkloristic activities, although only 12 per cent said they had no interest at all in sport. Both religious-cultural factors regulating women's social lives and class-cultural factors specifying approporiate male sporting preferences operate to shape leisure activities.

Social networks are predominantly intra-ethnic in character; contacts with the indigenous German population occur through sport (and are therefore largely restricted to men) rather than in other contexts. It has recently been estimated that 65 per cent of the second generation Turkish community belong to *wholly Turkish* social networks, in sharp contrast to the highly ethnically-mixed networks of the Yugoslavian community (Esser, 1988; Esser *et al.*, 1986). The data suggest that in urban localities where an ethnically homogeneous minority community forms a high proportion of the population, youth peer-groups tend similarly towards ethnic homogeneity. Hewitt (1986) does not find similar patterns for London, but remarks on the importance of local social milieu for the patterns which emerge. There is indeed some indication that social relationships between German and Turkish youth develop well in those ethnically highly-mixed areas where, for example, church and trade union organizations are positively influential within an established working-class cultural tradition. On the whole, however, the indications are that second generation Turkish youth does not mix with other groups, whether of indigenous German or of other minority ethnic origin.

Certainly those who came to the FRG as adolescents are heavily reliant upon their own families and ethnic community for their social relationships (Esser *et al.*, 1986). The results of self-report surveys such as Mühlberg's (1987), in which two-fifths of Turkish teenagers claim to have close friendships with German peers, are in this respect probably unreliable, if only because of culturally-based differences in the understanding of the term friendship. Language preference, if not also competence, in any case constitutes a barrier — three-quarters of the interviews in Mühlberg's study, for example, were conducted in Turkish. It is likely that when these young people speak of having an international circle of friends, they mean a group of various ethnic national backgrounds which does not frequently include indigenous Germans. Lutz *et al.'s* (1983) ethnographic study of working-class German and minority ethnic group cliques and subcultural environments in a youth club revealed quite dramatically the physical and social distancing between those of Turkish origin and other young people. There is considerable scope here for further field research.

Conclusions

We might conclude that the material and social position of young people of Turkish origin living in the FRG is comparable to that of black youth in the UK, but that in contrast they have access to fewer cultural resources for positive self-assertion. We do not find evidence, not even in strongly 'Turkish' localities, of a specifically Turkish youth (sub)culture which is able to take up, on even a neighbourhood level, something approximating to a hegemonial stance which would include influencing the perspectives of other groups of young people. We can point to the modest and sporadically present beginnings of autonomous cultural forms (oriental rock music) and confidence-boosting activities (Turkish football teams; folklore as cultural celebration) which, in time, might act as powerful positive symbols of creativity and collective identity beyond the small groups of active participants; and whose attraction for the indigenous community might function as a source of more positive images of the Turkish population. It is dangerously easy to overrate the significance and the potential, particularly under the weight of the ideology of assimilation-integration which continues overwhelmingly to dominate political and social debate. In other words, this ideology and its corresponding policies have hardly been subject to critical questioning in the FRG, as the current storm of general fury over the suggestion that West Germany (should recognize that it) is a *multicultural* society shows only too well. The research community, too, has oriented itself to questions which reflect dominant policy frameworks and social perspectives towards the minority ethnic-racial groups; the neglect of gender divisions is similarly painfully evident in the research that has been conducted. Therefore, the social, political and research discourses are at a different stage of development than is the case in the UK.

It is highly unlikely that ethnic-racial divisions amongst youth will lose their strength and significance in the foreseeable future, regardless of what progressive opinion may hope for. It is possible that an ethno-specific youth subculture could develop, which at the end of the day is effectively class-specific in nature, in that social class inequalities are increasingly superimposed by ethnic-racial divisions. In particular localities, such a subculture might acquire a strongly Turkish character; it is plausible that working-class youth of Turkish origin will articulate a separate and distinctive cultural form. Whether and how it is possible to provide support for such processes of emancipation without patronizingly treading on their toes is a question we have not markedly begun to address.

Chapter 14

Changing Leisure and Cultural Patterns Among British Youth

Michael Brake

Introduction

The current situation concerning changing leisure and cultural patterns in childhood and youth in the United Kingdom has to be seen in the overall changing context of British society, and in its historical antecedents. Major recent changes include the increase in unemployment, which has greatly affected youth; to a lesser extent the spread and consequent 'moral panic' of AIDS, and its effect on sexual life; and the introduction since 1979 of policies and legislation specific to youth, as part of the Conservative government's law and order platform. There has been a concentration in particular on public order issues, taking the form, firstly, of controlling trade union activity in public — particularly pickets and demonstrations, and, secondly, of the safety of public space, especially the streets and areas of public interaction — such as football terraces.

This aspect of public policy and legislation operates at the level of production and maintenance of hegemony in British society. The current government is committed to defeating organized trade unions, in defence of its free market and monetarist position. It is also concerned with controlling the possibility of further urban unrest, such as that seen in both 1981 and 1985. This unrest has constituted uprisings by youth against heavy police surveillance and new forms of policing in working class areas (and especially those with large black communities).

The first section of this chapter traces the trends in youth culture research from the 1960s to the 1980s. At the present time, sociological research on young people is not embedded in the context of youth culture and youth sub-cultures, but has been redirected into studying *either* problems generated by policy and legislative decisions, *or* groups seen as particularly problematic or delinquent. The focus is *either* on the inner city sections of youth, in a situation compounded by massive youth unemployment, *or* on groups which have come to (inter)national attention. This often revolves around societal response to those factions of youth perceived by the media as social problems, and around whom a 'moral panic' has developed. Those involved are heroin abusers and football hooligans, but evidence equally points to the accelerating teenage alcohol problem and the increased use of knives in assaults among young people. The government has tried to play down the involvement of inner city unemployed youth in crime, by claiming (with little empirical evidence), that there has been a vast increase in crime in small towns and rural areas among lower middle class, employed youth, involving theft and petty fraud. As crime of all levels has increased, the government has attempted to individualize crime, firmly resisting any suggestion that it is a response to such structural problems as unemployment, poverty and homelessness among young people.

Historical Aspects of the Sociology of Youth Culture, Youth Sub-cultures and Adolescence

In the post-war period, first American and then British literature was concerned with youth culture and sub-cultures. An interest developed out of the urban sociology tradition of the pre-war Chicago school, into the study of teenage delinquency and life styles, focusing on drug use, violence and theft among mid and early teenage males involved in neighbourhood gangs. Sociologists interested themselves in the connections between working class urban life and the development of youth cultures, an interest which generationally addressed broader social problems experienced by social classes, especially the working classes and those factions which came from immigrant or ethnic cultures. This literature belonged within a liberal tradition, arguing for more investment in youth leisure in the inner city and for better educational/occupational opportunity structures. This 'Chicago ecological' research often involved the social defence of the respectable population of the city. It was a mixture of *both* a genuine attempt to democratize education and opportunities for the children of working class, immigrant and ethnic groups, *and* an attempt to assimilate them into the great 'American melting pot'. It was also a reflection of fears, and often displaced envy, of young urban teenagers. Structural functionalist theorists (for example, Elkin and Westley; Parsons; and indeed Coleman), were interested in how adolescent rebellion could be harnessed into formal career structures, and in how it related to a period of independence, a moratorium essential in preparing young people for entry into the adult world. Coleman seriously suggested a sort of Olympic Games not focusing on sport, that central feature of American high school culture, but on academic success, where the clever kids and not the 'jocks' (athletes) got the status and the girls. (This was obviously, a pre-Seoul model of the Olympic Games, where athletes ignored drugs.) The interest, then, of this sociological approach lay not merely in rebellion and order, but in the labour discipline necessary for a young work force, whether intellectual or manual, and in the reproduction of ideological formations for maintaining the social relations of production necessary to American capital.

The 1960s marked an ascendancy of alternative theoretical positions. The symbolic interactionist perspective of the neo-Chicago school, and particularly Becker's influence, interested researchers in the world of the deviant, in making heard the voices on the margins. It was also the time when deviants themselves became involved in sociological research. These never thinkers reversed that positivist approach which argued that criminality generated laws into the proposal that laws generated deviancy, and that societal reaction generated secondary deviance into a moral career. Methodologically phenomenology and ethnography moved onto centre stage. Matza's greatly underestimated *Becoming Deviant* (1969) challenged positivist criminal statistics by a method which looked at the social careeer of the deviant, and the meaning system constructed by the social actor. Matza (1964) asked us to appreciate the subject involved in delinquency, rather than to compose prediction studies casting the deviant as object. This developed an understanding of the existential position of the subject in the social context of the world of facticity, within which the subject interacted.

In Britain an interest developed in the social structure and sub-cultures of downtown neighbourhoods which were found to be quite different from their American counterparts. Violent gangs (outside perhaps Glasgow) were unknown; gangs tended to be street corner social groups, whose delinquent behaviour had to be seen in the context of the attempt to have a good time amidst deprivation and poverty. An important British work was Stan Cohen's analysis of the societal reaction to sub-cultures where he brilliantly combined a social analysis of judicial process with the deconstruction of mass media reaction and stereotyping. The subject of this was an ethnographic account of interactions within the youth cultural phenomenon of 'Mods' and 'Rockers'.

Deviancy theory, drawing on the work of (for example) Lemert and Becker, moved to a radical analysis of youth culture which reflected and analyzed wider issues in sociological practice. Ethnomethodology, ethnography, social reality, cultural practice and reproduction, ideology and consciousness all became part of deviancy theory. A neo-Marxist 'new criminology' was suggested, (Taylor *et al.*, 1973), in turn eventually replaced by the 'new realism'. Much of the British work came from the National Deviancy Symposia, and the CCCS. Here symbolic interactionism ethnography, the appreciation of the subject, became interwoven into both Marxist and Althusserian socialism. The CCCS used an amalgamation of structuralist thought, in particular the work of Althusser and Levi Strauss, ethnographic phenomenology and semiotics, interwoven with a cultural analysis of mass media, which linked up — often brilliantly — the current issues of the day and their representation in popular culture. Taking Gramsci's interpretation of the state, they examined civil society to unpick youth subculture's struggle for cultural space. Reading the text of youth cultural style, and using the work of Lacan, Derrida, Kristeva, Deleuze and other post-structuralist French theorists, they maintained the centrality of Marx's dynamic of class struggle to situate youth cultures in a wider social context.

Hall *et al.*'s *Policing the Crisis* (1978), unpicked the post-war crisis not only in the economy, but also the crisis in legitimation of the British state. Young people inherited not only a location in the class structure, but also the culture of that class as mediated by neighbourhood, local economy and family. What youth cultures offered were 'imaginary' solutions to structural contradictions. It was then possible to 'read' the sub-cultural style as a text which articulated statements about the particular generational problems of specific class factions. Hall *et al.* (1976 and 1978) were to capture elegantly the meaning of sub-cultural resistance by tracing social anxieties about a post imperial Britain losing its place in the world and concern about social change and permissiveness in urban society. These anxieties and concerns became displaced, and projected onto urban youth, but particularly onto black youth. In this way the two significations of 'black' and 'young' became a metaphor for the folk devil threatening British society. It fed into fears and prejudice about young people, and upon Britain's open and institutionalized racism. Subsequent contributions (Pearson, 1983) to this 'new wave' underlined both the historical normality of panics about 'hooligans' and the interest of the negotiation of identity within groups locked out of more orthodox forms of development, i.e., that 'ordinary' majority, who were either completely uninvolved, or only partially and peripherally so in the more notorious youth cultures.

Late 1960s youth became a cause for concern via a rising disassociation from education and disaffection with traditional middle class career structures. Middle class as well as working class youth came to public attention (Brake, 1980). Student youth in particular either involved itself in romantic rurality or in direct political action. The reality of scarcity as a result of the recession was to put an end to all this, but it was of major political concern at the time. (Indeed Reagan was elected governor of California on a ticket to end the radicalism on Berkeley compus.)

Some time later Willis (1977) considered the positive and negative contradictory aspects of male working class youth cultures and their relationship to 'shop floor' culture at work. His lads (an anti-school sub-culture), were oppositional to the academically oriented boys (the 'earoles'), and developed a manual workerist, sexist and racist anti-authority sub-culture which corresponded accurately to the work culture of the factory floor they would inherit. This was not simply reproduced intergenerationally but, as a contradictory 'double articulation', managed to create a culture specific to this generation and to penetrate the ideo-logical mystification of the school, with its claims to egalitarianism and free choice and its credentialist emphasis. This very resistance contained the kernels of both class defeat and class power; as a culture it was both open and closed. It is his development of homology, of the connections between life style, leisure time, music and clothing, which formed the basis of his cultural analysis (see Willis, 1977 and 1978; Hebdige, 1979).

This work, the 'new wave' of sub-cultural theory, has been subject to criticism at two levels. Firstly it has been accused of romanticizing youth culture, and its use of post-structuralist and cultural analysis has been regarded with suspicion. Secondly it has been criticized within the same orientation by feminists for its emphasis on masculinity, work process, and marginalizing girls (See Chapter 3 by Chisholm in this volume).

A major criticism against most deviancy and sub-cultural sociology is that of its masculinist bias. Leonard (1980) and McRobbie (1980) have produced a feminist critique which points the lack of focus of sub-cultural studies on youthful social relations concerning the family. Patriarchal attitudes and structures have been unthinkingly reproduced, and girls have been treated as marginal, rather than structurally different. Deviance has been seen for young women in terms of their sexuality, whilst that of young men is in terms of their aggression. Girls are restrained at school by their reputation (Lees, 1986) and are disliked by boys if they are independent, and stigmatized if seen as sexually 'easy', or if seen as 'choosy'. In a London school where I carried out informal interviews recently, the girls showed a pattern of independence from males. They dressed in anti-feminine styles, with jeans, bowling jackets and construc-tion boots with long white male underpants (or sometimes boxer shorts), and went on 'girls' nights out' with their female friends where they insisted 'no boy would dare to intrude'. Their female friendships were very important and genuinely respected.

Youth culture as an area of research has now been replaced so that the interpretation of sub-cultural texts and style has given way to a more material analysis. British sociology is more concerned with youth policy, legislation, youth unemployment, and in the transition or 'broken apprenticeship' (now elongated), from education to work. The sociology of education has continued to focus on school sub-cultures, developing the theoretical debates generated by youth culture. It has also focused on those groups notably absent from youth culture, black youth and girls. There is no large scale research centrally studying youth culture at pre-sent. However, I will attempt, in the conclusion to this chapter, to speculatively read some of the youth cultural trends obtained from interviews with young people and from an analysis of the mass media.

Young People and the Thatcher Law and Order Campaign

Apart from the unemployment crisis the government's major concern has been that of law and order. In the much vaunted 'enterprise culture' under Thatcherism, millions of people are either unemployed or are living in poverty and desperation. With unemployment set at levels unthinkable a few years ago, with keenly felt regional differences between employed and unemployed people, we have seen a situation where the role and nature of policing have become of considerable importance. Law and order has been a major plank in the last three elections, and since the 1981 miners' strike, we have seen the emergence of highly political chief police officers. There have been major changes in legislation, especially since the street uprisings in 1981/82 and again in 1985, which almost exclusively involved young people, a large proportion of them black. This brings into our discussion of youth, leisure and youth culture the relationship between young people and the police, and some of the areas of focal concern for the government, the public and the police. The government has attempted to marginalize as social problems those groups which have appeared in the press as 'folk devils', and has argued that their existence has nothing to do with unemployment.

One example of this has been the concern with rising violent crime in small market towns and villages. Teenage drinking has contributed to this problem, and there is indeed evidence that children aged from 12 upwards have intensified alcohol consumption patterns. There has been concern over the use of knives, often carried by boys who have never been in trouble with the police before but who are frightened by the rumours of other local youths being 'tooled up' (carrying weapons). This behaviour can be traced to the emphasis on machismo, on violent masculinity prevalent in the mass market operating around the 'ninja' cult, developed from Eastern martial arts and weaponry, brandished with flourish in violent videos. The government has tended to profile the rural connection, because it suggests that it is youth in general, rather than unemployed inner city young people, who are violent or criminal and pointing out that there has been an increase in cheque and credit card fraud among youth. The implication, again, is that those involved are employed youth; in fact it merely indicates that it is now easier to obtain a credit card (your own or someone else's).

Heroin abuse has also been in the press; the research into inner city areas in fact suggests that heroin dealing of a minor nature appears in the run down areas of the inner city (Pearson, 1987; Parker *et al.*, 1988). It is the occupation of unemployed youth who have no time patterns in their lives, and Pearson argues that it in fact gives meaning and status to unemployed young people, it counteracts depression by organizing their day into meaningful segments of time — getting up, buying, dealing, and taking illegal drugs. Parker *et al.* (1988) found large numbers of youthful heroin users on certain run down housing estates, nearly always male and aged about 19. The pattern of heroin abuse has altered considerably. It still reflects (as always) friendship patterns, you take drugs with your friends, but the old 'junkie' sub-cultures are now replaced by provincial inner-city friendship networks. These groups are in no sense bohemian, or taking heroin as an act of rebellious commitment, but as an act of desperate escape from unemployment and poverty.

Outside of this group there seems little cause for concern. A recent national survey of school children finds that heroin and solvent abuse has been greatly exaggerated (Schools Health Education Unit, 1988). Only 2.6 per cent of pupils had used solvents, and less than 1 per cent used heroin. However, over a half had taken a painkiller in the last fortnight, and 15 per cent of first-year boys, and 52 per cent of fifth-year boys had drunk alcohol in the previous week. It is worth noting that another survey suggested that the average 15–17-year-old (i.e., an under age drinker) spent £10 per week on drink in 1988.

Football hooliganism is a British social problem which has reached the international headlines, with its sinister implications of far right wing youth groups involved in extreme nationalism. Territoriality is central to football hooliganism, and where drink is involved, violence occurs. This takes on an unpleasant nationalist aspect at international matches (encouraged in the war with Argentina). As football becomes more professional and commercial, and less involved with working class fans, its unrespectable elements infuse their bleak lives with its aggressive and macho values, flaunting a nationalism which is often equally present at Conservative party annual conferences.

Policing, Police Powers and Young People, with Particular Reference to Black Youth

We have seen considerable changes in British policing since the late 1960s. Routine policing has increasingly been organized around the imperatives of social surveillance, moving away from the traditional neighbourhood based policing, personified in Britian (and abroad) by the 'bobby on the beat'. The keeping of the peace, or the prevention of crime has been replaced by an intensive, technically efficient maintenance of public order. This has been referred to as 'firebrigade' or 'reactive' policing, with a priority on rapid response. There has at the same time been the development of specialized quasi-military police units (Special Patrol Groups and

Police Support Units) which are very often armed. They are used in the rapid dispersal of public order situations, from fights outside pubs, through incidents outside soccer stadia to preventing demonstrations or unoffical pop festivals and trespass.

Ever-present in the law and order debate is the spectre of Northern Ireland, which did much to fuel government support for police powers. The other key moments were the youth uprisings of 1981 and 1985, which reflected the deteriorating relations between black youth (and adults) and the police. Police powers in Britain have broadened considerably during the last few years, especially under the Police and Criminal Evidence Act (PACE) 1984, which has increased the powers of a policeman to stop and search adults and young people, and the Education Act 1986 (2) which obligates school governors to consider representations on curriculum matters from their local Chief of Police, and which instructs them both to liaise with the police and to report on this annually. The Public Order Act 1986 is aimed at preventing riot, affray, processions and assemblies. It was drawn up to prevent the annual hippy peace caravan to Stonehenge, and has since lead to violent confrontations at this event. The Criminal Justice Act 1982 introduced the 'short sharp shock' for young people, i.e., short sentences in detention regimes with very strict discipline. This was developed in response to the more controlling, anti-rehabilitative lobby in both the judiciary and Parliament. Both crimes and imprisonment have risen under the Tory governments, but the Labour party was not itself free from the politics of repression. 'One sign of success in the fight for law and order is that more people are in prison. (Mervyn Rees, former Labour Home Secretary). Yet these authoritarian regimes seem to have failed, in that whereas the inmates quite liked them, their effect on uniformed staff's morale was negative.

The effects of PACE in England have not yet been adequately analyzed; but in Scotland a year after the implementation of the Criminal Justice (Scotland) Act 1981, the numbers of people detained without charge had doubled to 438 per 100,000. Over half of these were under 20 years old. There are variations in the use of the powers of detention without trial, and these do not relate to actual local crime rates, but rather to police practice. Furthermore the police have extended their right to hold peopke without trial by holding people 'to help them with their enquiries'. A Home Office study in Britain has suggested that the use of stop and search laws in London and Liverpool has led to one third of males under 30 being stopped and searched by the police (Willis, 1983). Black youth, and younger rather than older youth, were more likely to have been stopped and searched. An arrest was made only in 5 per cent of the cases, so they are plainly exercises in police authority and surveillance. In Britain, policing by consent has moved towards policing by control, and youth is bearing the brunt. These findings have been confirmed both for Wolverhampton (Willis, 1988), and in London for black youth (Small, 1984). Black youth in particular was heavily involved in the street uprisings, and feels that the police and the media ignore racist attacks, arson, murder and harassment of black people, yet use saturation policing and sweeps (the sudden attack on a black community or neighbourhood), using as an excuse looking for drugs or stolen property (Gifford, 1986; Scarman, 1982). Black youth centres, usually also the political and legal advice centres in black communities, are seen as areas of conspiracy by the police but as defence bases by the black communities. Dislike and distrust of the police are attitudes generally held by young working class people. They dislike being moved on, or being told to break up a crowd which is doing nothing, and they dislike being 'lifted', that is, being taken to the police station for questioning. Generally, the more personal experience young people have of the police, the more negative their attitudes. These youthful experiences are intense and traumatic.

There is a long history of poor relations between black youth and the police, especially the London Metropolitan police. In the mid-1970s there was a not only a crisis in the economy, but also a crisis in the legitimation of the state, often responded to as a crisis in authority relations. Concern about Britain's fading international importance, and its internal social changes including its changing internal population, led to a resurgent nationalism, which led to the superimposing of two major folk devils, the 'unBritish' black immigrant, and youth, and a moral panic over 'mugging' (a form of robbery from the person). There was a composite stereotype of young 'mugger' black, and this in turn led to a mass media presentation of a relation between black youth and crime. This was at a time of massive increases in black youth unemployment. The black community also felt that it received insufficient police protection from racist attacks, and indeed only in February 1989 is this being taken seriously by the police. Black self defence groups were often criminalized (The Islington 18, Bradford United Black Youth League and the Newham 8 for example), and police concern increased after the inner city uprisings of 1980/81 and 1986. After the Bristol uprising of 1981, where the police were unable to enter part of Bristol city whilst black youth rioted, national computerized surveillance and police assembly systems were introduced. The riots of 1981 were a result both of intensive police raids on black communities and of the constant stop and search surveillance of black youth. The Scarman Report (1982) on the Brixton (London) riots by a law lord carefully spread the blame for the disorders, but did suggest the police bears some responsibility for the way they policed black youth. The police themselves considered this criticism, mild as it was, a betrayal, and for the first time in 1982, the London Metropolitan police revealed 'mugging' statistics which gave the ethnic origins of both assailant and victim. Mugging is only 3 per cent of London crime, but nevertheless the mass media responded characteristically ('London's streets of fear'; 'Britain's most brutal streets'). It is worth noting that a Home Office study of youth at the time of the riots in Birmingham found that for the 16–25 year-old age group, 41 per cent Afro–Caribbeans and 36 per cent whites had been stopped and searched during the previous year. Those involved tended to be young, unemployed and spending much of their leisure time on the streets (Field and Southgate, 1982). Since then there have been similar events in London in 1985.

One response has been to try and implement multi-agency policing, that is, the extension of youth surveillance from the police to the schools and social work agencies. The Education Act 1986 (2), as we have already seen, attempts to link schooling with policing; the aim is to forge good relations with black youth. It is argued that this is an attempt to police by ideology, using the school as a front line. The policy has been resisted by London teachers in particular, fearing that the police will use their new influence in the schools to obtain information on illegal activities, and that they cannot therefore consent to allowing the police into schools. This response has in turn increased right-wing political pressure on left-wing London boroughs, whose education authorities are already facing pressure because of their policy and educational programmes on anti-sexism, anti-racism and gay rights. Legislation is beginning to move into these areas too, most notably to date in the Local Government Act (1988), Clause 28 of which forbids schools' presentation of homosexuality as desirable, or of homosexual relationships as 'pretend family relationships'.

What Happened to Youth Culture? A Semiotic Muse

As I have indicated, there has been a move from an interest in youth culture as style, the semiotically inclined work of Paul Willis and Dick Hebdige, to an examination of the effects of a prospective worklessness or workfare future on the young. Style itself, that symbol of rebellion, that benchmark of the ritual of resistance, still exists, of course, created by young people, and worn as a sign of defiance. Black sub-cultures such as hip hop with its aggressive music, dance and style are still strong, reaffirming the positiveness of black identity in a white racist world.

If there is any theme which holds together the different elements of youth culture, it is 'street cred' (street credibility). But style has also been expropriated as a commodity by the bourgeoisie. The youth culture group receiving most media attention is that of the young upwardly mobile adult, the Yuppie. Acronyms abound covering those past their teenage years, for example Dinks (double income, no kids). All are related to Mrs Thatcher's 'enterprise culture', with its emphasis on success at any cost. In fact this group is not young, but it does attempt to purchase youthfulness through the acquisition of style. Style now marks off the street wise, the hip, and advertising suggests that the 40-year-old executive can purchase from the styleographers, together with his/her Filofax, a sense of being part of a hip in-group.

It is fruitful and indeed symbolic of the current style consumption to turn to the image of youth in current television advertisements. These nearly always focus on the individual. In particular favour among advertising videos is the lone male youth, wearing Levis (Levi 501s had their highest sales ever in 1988), emphasizing the individual — the cowboy, the rebel without a cause. We see an allegorical symbol used by capital to deal with both the terrains of the legitimate market and the hidden economy. The (perhaps unemployed) loner is transposed into the consumer. Armed only with 'street cred' s/he is making it in the dark empty urban streets, which are both symbolically and realistically dangerous. Males are foregrounded, nearly always with a reconstructed 1950s style, as part of his bricolage, he exudes individualism and independence, virtues favoured by Mrs Thatcher, rather than the innocent high school culture of yesteryear's 'Happy Days'. There is a celebrated Levi 501 advert which shows a handsome, elegant young man stripping down to his boxer shorts (no hip person wears jockeys now), and coolly washing all his clothers in the laundromat. He is above his surroundings.

The lager market is aimed at teenage drinkers, mostly illegal underage drinkers, and currently produces the most sophisticated, witty advertisements. One has cleverly culturally recoded the Levi 501 ad. The Levi 501 ad is rerun, with the addition of two older men, scruffily dressed, who watch our hero undress in the laundromat and comment, 'You can see he is not a Carling Black Label drinker, he doesn't wash his underpants'. Another lager ad shows a grainily-shot young busker (again 501s, and hair gel) playing a saxophone, trying to get close to his balding black sax hero. A can is thrown from the fridge, (life style point) the youth gets through commodity purchase. He is then seen on stage throwing full arm punches. As in the first ad, all you have to do is win. This in a society where a local neighbourhood can have four-fifths of its youth unemployed. Unemployed youth are ignored, they are losers, poor, perhaps with a mysterious whiff of violence, but not glamourous like the successful. We can trace the sax, grainy textures, and hair gel from the impact of magazines such as *The Face, i-D* and *Blitz,* or from television programmes such as *Network 7* or *Night Network.*

In 1980 *The Face* and *i-D* appeared and reacted against the alienation of punk, or the distance of black sub-cultural style, to bring the youthful and often alternative middle class back in. These magazines differ from the radical, parochial *City Limits* and *Time Out* to focus on style. Singers like Boy George and groups like Spandau Ballet emerged. There was a sense of belonging to a cool community, albeit often individualized, and of expropriating both black music and black soul. Basically this was a new form of cultural rebellion seen in Mods and rudies, without the violence or the crime. It was hip, cool and laid back, dictated by 'style bibles' and marketed by clothing shops. It allowed the values of the 40-year-old executive, looking elegant and being ambitious and successful, to be overlaid onto being stylish. It had strong adherents among middle class youth, who constructed minor sub-cultures within its London adherents. The clubs were very important, catering for those who wanted a hip environment within which to display imaginative wardrobes and dance steps. Among the clubs emerged the One Nighter clubs, which are clubs within clubs, where the premises are used for one night for a particular hip clientele. Entry is strictly controlled, the doormen excluding any stiffs (non in-group members). Styles range from careful reconstruction of the New Romantics, to the carefully mixed styles of deconstructed punk and reconstructed '30s.

The latest craze of 'house' or 'acid house' music has caused a considerable moral panic via adult misunderstanding of the phrase. Acid house parties have no formalized clothing, just casual jeans and trainers, with acid house T shirts (actually considered very passé by Acidcognoscenti). 'Acid house' comes from two phrases: firstly, from Frankie Knuckles' Chicago 'Warehouse' club where the music was first played in 1983; secondly, from Chicago musicians' slang, in which 'acid burning' means sampling, i.e. using someone else's song, lyric or record. However, ageing hippy parents assumed it to refer to LSD or lysergic acid, the psychedelic drug of the 1960s. Associated in this way following one notorious death with the drug 'Ecstasy' (a powerful stimulant) at a 'house' party, it led to a media moral panic; but in actuality overreacting police raids on 'house' one-nighters found no more drugs than in any other teenage meeting place. Consequently venues for 'acid house' are held secretly, the address being passed by word of mouth to avoid the police, and they range from aristocratic homes to derelict warehouses. Their clandestine settings and the threat of police raids add a sort of early Chicago speakeasy atmosphere, irresistible to rebellious youth.

Youth culture is now replaced by style, and is firmly part of the consumption process. Youth culture is now expropriated from the young, especially working class youth, and is consumed by the privileged élite amongst youth. It excuses anything in the name of style, racism, right-wing views, success, consumption, money making, and is based on exclusivity and envy. The consumers reflect the models, the media is the massage, the world is a market inhabited by the winners. The losers return to the job centre.

Conclusion

Youth then is sited today within a series of contradictions, responded to by society as sexual subjects, yet having to grow up sexually facing the dangers of AIDS. It is traditionally involved in production and consumption, yet this is precluded by unemployment which creates a broken cultural apprenticeship. It is caught up in, at best, sub-employment, in a world where the Yuppies are winners, and everyone else is a loser. The enterprise culture leaves youth to be marginalized, powerless and often criminalized in its response to what are basic structural problems. Unemployed youth is more anxious, worried about clothes, appearance and money, more likely to commit suicide and is less likely to spend time in relationships. Youth is located in the crumbling infrastructure of the inner city, and its inherited world has changed drastically. This is the context in which a sub-employed youth underclass struggles to survive, and to have fun.

Youth cultural formations may then attempt to solve these problems by escape into the junkie sub-culture where lack of active engagement is legitimated, and where the loss of what Marie Jahoda called time structures is refound only in the world of dealing. The identity and status given by work is sought elsewhere, perhaps abstracted to territoriality expressed by a football team, or abstracted to nationhood and its accompanying mythical reactionary articulation of supremacy. For black youth the importation of plethora, of anti-colonial struggle brought home, means their lives can be given meaning by being part of the war made on racism, no matter how ill targeted. Working class girls caught up in patriarchal reproduction may escape through the traditional avenue of pregnancy, which at least means if they have to perform unpaid domestic labour, it is for themselves and their own children. What is clear is that class is still the predominant social formation, shaping people's lives, albeit overlaid by gender and race. However, let us also remember that most youth remains optimistic, energetic, can be seen having a good time, strutting their stuff, dancing wildly, laughing loudly, doing nothing with great verve. They manage to survive whatever the adults do.

Chapter 15

West German Youth Cultures at the Close of the Eighties

Wilfried Ferchhoff

Youth (sub)cultures appear and express themselves in many different ways. They cannot always be clearly defined and distinguished from each other. The enthusiasm of the observer and commentator can lead to unjustified mystification of youth cultural forms, whether in terms of their cultural autonomy, their 'inevitability' under given life circumstances, or of their potential for resistance against existing power structures. With these points in mind, I shall attempt to describe and explain some of the features of contemporary youth (sub)cultures in the FRG.

In the first part of the discussion, I shall describe how the youth phase has changed in the decades since 1945, placing these changes within the context of the 'destandardization and destructuring' thesis (cf. Chapter 7 by Krüger in this volume). We can see from the varied life practices of contemporary adolescents that economic, social and cultural conditions in the family, at school, at work and in the peer-group are interwoven in precarious, conflictual ways. The second section (drawing on Baacke and Ferchhoff, 1988) presents and attempts to justify the proposition that the term 'sub-culture' is drifting away from the term 'youth culture'. The reasons for this lie in young people's intense participation in mass culture and the culture 'industry'. Moral and social ties to (sub)cultural life contexts are subject to persistent erosion, caught between the simultaneous trends towards individualization, homogeneity, and pluralization of life conditions and life styles. In conclusion, I offer a descriptive typology of contemporary youth culture, drawing on the findings of recent research. In my view, we must take leave of the notion that 'youth' can be defined and understood in a uniform, generalized manner. Not only has the clearly delineated status of 'youth' dissolved, but the trends towards differentiation and pluralization are self-evident (cf. Ferchhoff, 1985). The aim of this contribution, then, is to do justice to the empirically substantiated differentiations within youth culture(s).

Changes in Youth and the Youth Phase

Through to the 1960s, working for a living was something familiar and central to the lives and experiences of almost all young people who did not come from affluent backgrounds. Today, paid employment has been replaced by the tasks of school-based cognitive learning. Young people find themselves in institutionalized education and training environments for a much longer period, extended at *both* ends of the childhood and youth phases. The status of youth has become increasingly equated with the status of pupil or student; and most young people are 'better educated' than are their parents (cf. Chapter 2 by Zinneker, in this volume).

This shift in experience away from paid work in production towards unpaid learning work does not mean young people reject the 'work ethic' or work-related life values. It is rather that a shift of emphasis has taken place, away from work seen in terms of 'material reproduction' and towards work seen in terms of its meaningfulness and of personal involvement (cf. Baethge, 1985 and 1988). Baethge *et al.* (1988, p. 41ff) suggest that paid work remains significant for young people in six ways: to gain economic independence from parents or from the state; as an ordering structure for everyday life, which brings a sense of security; as that 'elixir' which gives meaning to life; to realize experientially one's potential and personal autonomy; to provide for a secure material and social future; and as the medium for acquiring social position and status.

The socially constructed meaning of adolescence formerly implied that young people were expected to forgo experiences, postpone the fulfilment of their desires, and exert considerable effort to achieve appropriate goals. In other words, young people were expected to defer gratification and to adopt a certain asceticism. Young people today are less disposed to submit to such expectations, given both generally changing values and specific difficulties of orientation to the future and education-work transitions. For at least a section of contemporary youth, adolescence is no longer primarily a phase of transition between childhood and adulthood, no longer simply a form of preparation for the future. It is equally an independent phase of the life cycle, to be experienced and enjoyed for its own sake and in the here and now, strongly influenced by consumerism, market forces, the media and fashion (Hornstein, 1985a). Many young people today are consciously oriented towards immediacy — they need to be able to keep their options open, to respond flexibly in the face of uncertainty, unpredictability, and diffuseness. The structuration of young people's everyday lives in this way suits the youth consumer market rather well. Its products, both material and symbolic, are 'image-intensive and highly seductive, swiftmoving and ephemeral, demanding no real personal commitment and suffused with contrasts' (Böhnisch, 1988, p. 150).

The older generation no longer functions for the younger as a model for desirable (or even possible) ways of life. Neither are adults the sole fount of wisdom and guidance for young people. In these senses, the generation gap has narrowed. Adults and young people can engage in similar leisure activities; school and employment roles are similarly structured, evoking similar socialization and learning experiences and invoking similar survival strategies. Both groups influence each other when it comes to matters of style and taste. In the consumer market and in leisure activities, it is young people who are increasingly the trendsetters (cf. Scherer, 1988, p. 199).

Within the family, including in the working-classes, both spousal and parent-child relationships have become more egalitarian. There has been a shift away from the hierarchically structured, authoritarian household towards family living arrangements based on partnership and negotiation, i.e., family relationships have become more liberal and informal in nature (cf. Krüger, 1988c, p. 218). Parallel to this trend, the sharp distinction between gender worlds, roles and identities is receding in all age groups, and especially in the case of young people.

Parents are in any case no longer in the position to 'protect' their children from 'harmful influences', a traditional aspect of educated middle class parenting values, because alternative values and behaviours cannot be screened out. Liberalization of moral and sexual taboos for all age groups have increasingly emancipated young people from deferral of sexual experience and from the strictures of their guardians in these respects. Such changes mark and further accelerate earlier detachment from the parental home, despite the fact that the family circle as a haven of intimacy, emotionality and privacy is enjoying something of a renaissance (see here Jaide, 1988, p. 217). Yet whilst young people may be further removed from parental guidance and control in terms of values and patterns of behaviour, they are increasingly financially dependent upon their parents for longer periods of time.

Patterns of upbringing are now directed towards self-determination and personal autonomy, so that young people are placed in the position of determining their own biographies with fewer supports to lean on in the process. The consequence of being offered choices is that one is obliged to make a choice — and to accept the responsibility for one's decisions. In other words, pluralization and individualization may bring greater opportunities for self-determination, but at the cost of the security and stability lent by community and tradition. Individualization processes may be interpreted as bringing a new quality to young people's lives, but, more importantly, that new quality places *infinite demands* upon the individual in the context of *finite personal resources*. In this situation, the risks of failure multiply, collective solidarities weaken, and pressures to conformity rise (cf. Bilden and Diezinger, 1984, p. 191).

Many of the changes discussed can be viewed from the perspective of shifts in forms and sources of social control. In the case of young people, there has been a double shift: firstly, from the field of production to the field of culture and, secondly, from the intimate environment of family, local community and church to the public environment of the consumer and service economy. There seems little doubt that the consumer market for young people has enormously expanded and differentiated — and that young people's purchasing power has grown alongside this. It is hardly coincidental that current (adult) debates about 'youth' focus on the merits or otherwise of discos, video shops, amusement arcades, etc. Large sections of youth appear to have quietly emigrated to these various locations, many of which render them publicly invisible. At the same time, the range of opportunities available on the leisure and consumer markets does provide young people with some room for autonomous manoeuvre, some space for self-socialization. In historical terms, West German youth has access to more advantages than former generations: they travel a lot, they run their own vehicles, they have their own rooms at home, they can select from a range of clothes, music and artefacts of style to create their own personal expression, they are presented with a plethora of organized and informal sports, cultural activities and youth clubs, they enjoy considerable freedom of sexual expression.

It is youth style, primarily expressed through music and fashion, which now appears to be the medium through which personal identity is sought and found, rather than membership of an established community or milieu. But elements of style have no fixed form or stability — quite the reverse, they can be combined, modified, taken up and discarded almost at will. It seems to be exactly this ephemeral quality of forms of identification offered through the media that accounts for the attractiveness of media culture with young people living in a highly individualized society. The question that remains is whether such (transitory) 'imaginary communities' can and do substitute for the real communities and groups of traditional social and cultural organization. Can they function as 'home' in the same way as the family or the neighbourhood did? Certainly, however, we cannot assume that the increasing pluralism of youth cultural style and their associated group settings leads to a liberal acceptance of that which is different from oneself. On the contrary, the differentiation and diffusiveness of young cultures defined through style may bring an intensification of insider/outsider boundaries. Egocentric and ethnocentric group behaviour, sometimes explicitly aggressive in its exclusion of alternative forms of cultural expression, is not unusual.

From Youth Sub-culture to Youth Culture

The term 'sub-culture' was coined and has been traditionally used to refer to cultural segments and groups both different from and somehow inferior to dominant and 'high' culture. By definition, sub-cultures are

dependent upon dominant cultural segments and groups for their existence, i.e. they are defined in terms of their *'difference from'* and are *tolerated
by* the larger cultural context. To speak of youth sub-cultures in these
polarizing terms no longer fits the empirical facts.

The concept of sub-culture further implies that societies and cultures
are made up of segments which can be precisely differentiated from each
other. Yet the traditional distinctions made between 'authentic' youth
cultures created 'from below' by young people themselves and 'imported'
youth cultures brought in 'from above' by the commercial culture industry no longer seem clear. Transitional and mixed forms of 'common
culture' abound; a plurality of styles are plied through the media. These
forces act to diversify youth culture beyond the bounds of emancipatory,
oppositional and social protest. They also rob established dominant and
high culture of its blanket legitimacy to evaluate divergent cultural forms
in its own terms; the structures and consistencies of disparities are sof-
tened. In this context, to speak of sub-culture seems inappropriate. Where
all young people are involved in and influenced by some form of youth
culture, does it make much sense to label some — or even all — such
expressions as sub-cultural?

The youth cultural studies tradition in the UK brought a materialist
and structuralist conceptualization of culture to bear on those forms of
cultural expression which give birth to classed and historically specific
ways of life, in which a group's social and material experience is then
founded (cf. for example, Clarke *et al.*, 1979, p. 41). The studies of
adolescent sub-cultures in this tradition assume that individual sub-
cultures can be precisely located in class terms. They therefore stand in a
close relationship to structures of social and economic inequality and to
political power structures.

However, the class structures of advanced modern societies, and the
class cultures associated with it, are very much obscured from view. The
term youth culture (as opposed to sub-culture) recognizes this fact. It
speaks to the universe of synthetically produced images and meanings,
which are intended to represent classless individuals and their corresponding patterns of behaviour. Youth sub-cultures find themselves routinely
confronted with these images and meanings of 'youth culture.' Their
members reject some aspects, adopt others, reshape yet others, and then
through their own aesthetic practice they involuntarily return those images and meanings to the market. The 'industrial producers' of youth
culture live off the reversal of this process: they pick off sub-cultural style
elements and insert them into their image palette, and then distribute
them through the media and product aesthetics. In this way, distinctive
sub-cultural style is generalized to youth culture as a whole. The majority
of young people are consumers of youth *cultural* lifestyle images and
meanings; only seldom do they explicitly participate in *sub-cultural* style
(cf. Mehler, 1986, p. 307).

In Britain, the concentration of CCCS research interest upon 'authentic' and class-specific youth sub-cultural style resulted in the exclusion of large sections of contemporary youth from its analyses. It could not register the tentative exploration of, and experimentation with, youth cultural styles which is characteristic for so many young people. Further, where the focus centred on the relationships between youth sub-cultures and their class-specific 'parent' cultures, CCCS studies underestimated the significance of the commercial distortion and admixture of youth subcultures. The erosion of traditional community milieux and the influence of the classless meaning matrices supplied through the culture industry have reached a stage where it is probably no longer accurate to speak of the 'authenticity' of youth sub-cultural practices. It now seems difficult to make clear distinctions between such 'authentic' expressions and their commercialized imitations, particularly in the light of the destructuring of the youth phase itself and the overall destandardization of the life-course. Processes of social reproduction now integrate *both* the material *and* the cultural; it is more relevant to think in terms of internationally disseminated variations of styles and lifestyle groupings, within which differentiated forms of self-realization, independence, self-assertion *and* dependence can exist underneath similar surface images and expressions.

At all events, the situation in the FRG is not analagous to the picture drawn for the UK. West German youth sub-cultures and youth styles do not (any longer) clearly correspond to cultures specific to class, milieu or status group origin and membership. Rather, it is secondary, incorporated and commercialized styles which dominate the picture, whose origins can be detected only through residual elements (such as gesture and slang). It is thus doubtful whether a case could be made for cultural hegemony nor for the structural polarizations of the class relations that accompany this. An interesting point in this connection is the fact that in the past, identifiable youth sub-cultures were very much 'of their time' — the teddy boys were definitively a forties/fifties phenomenon, the mods and rockers were embedded in the sixties. In their original form, they cannot be torn out of their historical specificities. The recycling of these sub-cultures of the past as contemporary style elements points to both hedonist and pluralist aspects of present-day youth cultures. It is as if contemporary youth cultures are a form of playing games with asserting individuality, in which the underscoring of cultural *expression* denotes a reaction to the emphasis on *discourse* which remained the medium of distinction until the early eighties.

Of course, there are youth sub-cultures which are relatively autonomous, including economically, and which are engaged in building up alternative networks. But it would be inaccurate to generalize from these cultural forms; it is more appropriate to speak of a 'bounded independence' of cultural systems. This implies that the concept of the cultural is not restricted to the level of superstructure, but is rather to be seen in terms of habitus. The ways in which one secures a living and the political views one holds can now be seen in terms of cultural habitus — a consequence of the enormous significance lent to cultural forms of expression by the media and the consumer market. Perhaps making life culture aesthetic, creating aesthetically structured living environments, is a culturally productive response in a world which erodes traditions and dissolves ties. The very transience which comes with that response brings risks, but perhaps such risks are unavoidable in the world we have come to know.

Contemporary Youth Cultures — A Typological Sketch

The five-fold typology presented here is based partly on a reading of the available literature and partly on my own research findings. It is very much a provisional sketch, and does not pretend to be either exhaustive or definitive, but is intended to give something of the topographical flavour of the West German youth cultures scene at the present time.

New Age Mysticism

I have placed into a first category those numerous forms of social withdrawal which include not only drug sub-cultures but also religious and quasi-religious sects and groups. They all represent a neo-romanticist longing for cosmic harmony, seeking salvation in a rather narcissistic introspection. This wave of psycho-religion or occult mysticism promises substitute worlds of shelter, happiness, harmony and salvation in the midst of depravity. Since the great gods of progress and power seem unstoppable by means of political opposition, the only apparent solution is that of turning inwards, striving for a personal transformation which brings harmony between the self, nature and the cosmos. The experiences made on this journey of self-discovery are rather like an inner celebration of mass. Movements of this kind, especially where sect-like groups and organizations play a role, tend to demand rigid inner controls which 'reassemble' and extinguish individual ego; and they rely heavily on 'prophets' to show the way forward. Essentially, such movements are a reaction to a world experienced as hollow, utilitarian, and technocratic; they offer young people a means to deal with crises of identity.

There are, however, other routes to developing alternative social and creative competences, represented by the counterculture or 'progressive' youth cultures (cf. Brand *et al.*, 1986; Lenz, 1988; Michel, 1986). Those young people who choose this variety of youth culture tend to be rather better educated (and older) than average; they are likely to come from the 'new middle class'. i.e., where parents are employed in professional service occupations. In these progressive circles, value is placed on anti-consumerism, the 'simple life', and a 'moralist economics', combined with survival strategies based on impoverishment and stepping beyond the bounds of social hierarchies. Individuals are expected to engage in permanent reflexivity, to behave 'authentically' and spontaneously, and to consider the grander questions of the purpose of life. Cohabitation and communal living within the framework of sexual equality is characteristic, as is sociopolitical engagement on behalf of peace, environmental issues, human survival, a caring society, participative democracy, and self-actualization in all areas of life.

Whilst members of this group are critical of the alienation and destruction ensuing from technological, military and bureaucratic modernization processes, it is not the case that all fractions are opposed to technological progress in itself. It is simply that the development and implementation of technology is not idealized — rather, it is there to be turned to best advantage whilst remaining under the control of critical and creative individuals. The potential of computer technology has reached into the imagination of alternative culture: not only is the health food co-op improving its stock control with a business application PC, but the philosopher–prophets are also beginning to spin socio–ecological utopian yarns where computer technology gives everyone the chance to realize creative dreams.

Hedonistic Post-modernism

These anti–ideological, almost decadently cynical youth cultures are defined through outward appearance, through styles mediated by and in fashion, the media and consumerism (cf. Hornstein, 1989; Kellner and Heuberger, 1988; Lenz, 1988; Mattiesen, 1988). The goal is that of distinction from the 'conventional normality' of *Otto Normalverbraucher* (i.e., Joe Bloggs next door). The younger *Schicki-Mickis* (i.e., Sloane Rangers) drink champagne and wear Lacoste (currently!); the older yuppies discuss the movements of the Stock Exchange and share prices. They are generally uninterested in critical reflection and social problems, but are happy to be themselves as they are, gregarious, socially active and looking to make the best of their lives. This group of hedonistic young women and men create and project themselves as the product image of their own advertisement, flirting with commodity aesthetic form and happy to work with styles that have been commercially created or influenced. This is a highly individualistic, mannered culture, but one which fades out existential angst. Its members are suspicious of grand utopian designs, of moral schemes for improving the world, and of demands to change one's lifestyle or standards of living for ecological reasons. They have no intention of letting the muesli brigade disfigure their aesthetic beauty with a dose of moral acid. Social and political engagement meets with their disinterest at best; emancipation is not part of their vocabulary. It is as if they have closed out social problems from their perception, riding a fairytale consumer carousel and seeking to place their lives amidst the ephemeral and glamourous butterflies, as if they were animated copies of glossy advertisements. Even if one is not 'really' successful, one can live the image of success through outward appearance and behaviour, whose style is guided only by one's own personal packaging and the whims of the clique. The motor of the all powerful visual image as cultural expression, so pronounced in these youth cultural circles, would seem to be the very diversification, insecurity, and lack of transparency of social life contexts in the eighties.

Boys on Street Corners

This macho youth culture is particularly conspicuous simply because it occupies — in physical and symbolic form — public spaces, or redefines space as its own territory, defending it against outsiders and intruders (cf. Becker *et al.*, 1984; Lenz, 1988). The young men who belong to it are generally from the urban working classes who transferred to secondary modern or special schools at 12-years-old. They may or may not be unemployed, but they are primarily notorious because they seem to be 'doing nothing' — apart from threatening to cause trouble in the eyes of conventional society. They do indeed sometimes get into trouble as a result of exchanges of aggression between different cliques. Young women can only gain second-class membership, by acknowledging their subordination to, and dependence on, men — especially within couple relationships. This variety of youth culture is collectivist, not individualistic: feelings of 'belonging' are important, and the group presents itself as such in public situations. Members have 'detached' themselves from their families of origin at an early stage, gaining and exercising economic, social and sexual autonomy. Unsurprisingly, such groups are regarded by the wider society (not only by those in power positions) as highly deviant and problematic. The symbolism and practice of physical violence is repellant and incomprehensible to most adults who might be in any position to communicate and intervene.

The Silent Majority?

All the youth cultural groups outlined so far may be interesting and, for different reasons, significant — but the largest group of young people belong to none of them. This 'residual' group is the one which quietly adopts and (largely) reproduces familiar traditions, values and patterns of behaviour in all spheres of life, whose understandings of 'normality' hardly differ from those of adults (cf. Becker *et al.*, 1984; Lenz, 1986 and 1988; Projektgruppe Jugendbüro, 1977). They are family-oriented: ties to parents and relatives are strong, family relationships are harmonious, parental control over their activities is negotiated, and parents are seen as 'setting an example' for their own lives and behaviour. They are institutionally integrated: schooling passes smoothly and successfully, apprenticeships and employment are secured. They take part in a range of organized hobbies, sports and voluntary associations in their communities; they join organized trade unions, political parties and churches. Their adolescence is spent between school, work, peer group and leisure activities, with their families in the backgroud prestructuring and supervising their trajectories. These young people want to get on and fit in, having clear ideas about what they want to aim for at work and in private life. They approach their lives pragmatically, calculating out what the costs and rewards are of conformity and challenge, seeking only to go as far as is necessary to achieve what they want without evoking too much opposition. They may be highly heterogeneous amongst themselves, but on the whole they are uncomplicated, assimilated, and conspicuously inconspicuous! These are the young people adults find it a pleasure to bring up, spend time with, teach and guide. Education, in the best sense of the term, still works here; perhaps we should consider why it does, and build our future perspectives on that, in place of megalomaniac visions of what it is possible for education and educators to achieve.

References

ABBOTT, P. and WALLACE, C. (1988) 'The Family', in BROWN, P. (Ed.) *Beyond Thatcherism*, Milton Keynes, Open University Press, pp. 78–90.

ABEL, T. (1984) 'Ausländer und Sport', *Sportliche Aktivitäten als Freizeitinhalt ausländischer Familien in der Bundesrepublik*, Köln, Pahl-Rugenstein.

ABELS, H., FUCHS, W. and KRÜGER, H.-H. (1988) 'Der Weg durch die Jugendbiographie', *Grounded Arbeiten aus der Sozialforschung*, 4, pp. 1–40.

ABRAMS, P. (1982) *Historical Sociology*, London, Open Books.

AGGLETON, P. (1987) *Rebels Without a Cause*, Lewes, Falmer Press.

ALLATT, P. and YEANDLE, S. (1986) 'It's not fair is it?' in ALLEN, S. *et al.* (Eds) *The Experience of Unemployment*, London, Macmillan, pp. 98–115.

ALLERBECK, K. and HOAG, W.G. (1985) *Jugend ohne Zukunft?* München/Zürich, Piper.

ALTHUSSER, L. (1971) *Lenin and Philosophy and Other Essays*, London, New Left Books.

AMBERT, A. (1986) 'The place of children in North American sociology', *Sociological Studies of Child Development*, 1.

ANDERSON, M. (1980) *Approaches to the History of the Western Family 1500–1914*, London, Macmillan.

ANYON, J. (1983) 'Intersections of gender and class: accommodation and resistance by working-class and affluent females to contradictory sex-role ideologies', in WALKER, S. and BARTON, L. (Eds) *Gender, Class and Education*, Lewes, Falmer Press, pp. 19–38.

APEL, H. (1989) 'Fachkulturen und studentischer Habitus', *Zeitschrift für Sozialisationsforschung und Erziehungssoziologie*, 9, 1, pp. 2–22.

APPLE, M. (Ed.) (1982) *Cultural and Economic Reproduction in Education*, London, Routledge & Kegan Paul.

APPLE, M. (1986) *Teachers and Texts: A Political Economy of Class and Gender Relations in Education*, London, Routledge & Kegan Paul.

ARBEITSGRUPPE PÄDAGOGISCHES MUSEUM (Ed.) (1981) *Hilfe Schule. Ein Bilderlesebuch über Schule und Alltag. Von der Armenschule zur Gesamtschule, 1827 bis heute*, Berlin, Pädagogisches Museum.

ARIES, P. (1962) *Centuries of Childhood*, London, Jonathan Cape.

ARMER. J.M. and MARSH, R.M. (Eds) (1982) *Comparative Sociological Research in the 1960s and 1970s*, Leiden, University of Leiden.

ARNOT, M. and WEINER, G. (1987) *Gender and the Politics of Schooling*, London, Hutchinson/Open University.

ARNOT, M. and WHITTY, G. (1982) 'From reproduction to transformation. Recent radical perspectives on curriculum from the USA', *British Journal of Sociology of Education*, 3, pp. 93–102.

References

ARONOWITZ, S. and GIROUX, H.A. (1986) *Education Under Siege*, London, Routledge & Kegan Paul.

ASHTON, D. and FIELD, D. (1976) *Young Workers*, London, Hutchinson.

ASHTON, D. and MAGUIRE, M. (1983) 'The vanishing youth labour market', *Youthaid Occasional Paper*, 3, London, Youthaid.

ASHTON, D., MAGUIRE, M. and SPILSBURY, M. (1988) *Restructuring the Labour Market*, London, Macmillan.

ASHTON, D. *et al.* (1982) *Youth in the Labour Market*, DOE Research Paper No. 34, Department of Employment.

ASHTON, D. *et al.* (1989) 'The changing structure of the youth labour market', *Labour Market Studies*, Leicester, University of Leicester.

ASTER, R. and KUCKARTZ, U. (1988) 'Jugend und Schule', *Zeitschrift für Sozialisationsforschung und Erziehungssoziologie*, 8, 3, pp. 200–12.

ATWOOD, M. (1986) *The Handmaid's Tale*, Toronto, McClelland and Stewart.

AUERNHEIMER, G. (1988) *Der sogenannte Kulturkonflikt. Orientierungsprobleme ausländischer Jugendlicher*, Frankfurt/M., Campus.

BAACKE, D. (1984) *Die 6-bis 12jährigen. Einführung in Probleme des Kindesalters*, Weinheim/Basel, Beltz.

BAACKE, D. (1987) *Jugend und Jugendkulturen. Darstellung und Deutung*, Weinheim/München, Juventa.

BAACKE, D. and FERCHHOFF, W. (1988) 'Jugendkultur und Freizeit', in KRÜGER, H.-H. (Ed.) *Handbuch der Jugendforschung*, Opladen, Leske + Budrich, pp. 291–325.

BAACKE, D. and HEITMEYER, W. (Eds) (1985) *Neue Widersprüche. Jugendliche in den 80er Jahren*, München, Juventa.

BAACKE, D. and SCHULZE, T. (1979) *Aus Geschichte lernen. Zur Einübung pädagogischen Verstehens*, München, Juventa.

BAACKE, D. and SCHULZE, T. (Eds) (1985) *Pädagogische Biographieforschung. Orientierung, Probleme, Beispiele*, Weinheim/München, Juventa.

BAADER, U. (1979) *Kinderspiele und Spiellieder*, 2 vols., Tübingen, Schloss.

BECK, L. (1988) '"Coughin" up fire: Soundsystems, music and cultural politics', *SE Journal of Caribbean Studies*, 6, 2, pp. 203–18.

BAETHGE, M. (1985) 'Individualisierung als Hoffnung und als Verhängnis', in LINDNER, R. and WIEBE, H.-H. (Eds) *Verborgen im Licht. Neues zur Jugendfrage*, Frankfurt/M., Syndikat, pp. 98–123.

BAETHGE, M. (1988) 'Jugend und Gesellschaft — Jugend und Arbeit' in BENSELER, F. *et al.* (Eds) *Risiko Jugend. Leben, Arbeit und politische Kultur*, Munster, pp. 28–38.

BAETHGE, M. *et al.* (1985) *Jugend, Arbeit und Gewerkschaften*, Opladen, Leske + Budrich.

BAETHGE, M. *et al.* (1988) *Jugend, Arbeit und Identität*, Opladen, Leske + Budrich.

BAETHGE, M., SCHOMBURG, U. and VOSKAMP, U. (1983) *Jugend und Krise — Krise aktueller Jugendforschung*, Frankfurt/M./New York, Campus.

BAGLEY, C. and VERMA, G. (Eds) (1983) *Multicultural Childhood: Education, Ethnicity and Cognitive Styles*, Aldershot, Gower.

BAINS, H. (1988) 'Southall youth: An old-fashioned story' in COHEN, P. and BAINS, H. (Eds) *Multi-Racist Britain*, London, Macmillan.

BALL, S.J. (1981) *Beachside Comprehensive: A Case-Study of Secondary Schooling*, Cambridge, Cambridge University Press.

BALLARD, R. (1982) 'South Asian families', in RAPOPORT, R. *et al.* (Eds) *Families in Britain*, London, Routledge & Kegan Paul.

BALTES, P. and ECKENSBERGER, L.H. (Eds) (1979) *Entwicklungspsychologie der Lebensspanne*, Stuttgart, Klett-Cotta.

BANKS, M., ULLAH, P. and WARR, P. (1984) 'Unemployed and less qualified urban young people', *Employment Gazette*, pp. 343–6.

BARGEL, T. (1979) 'Überlegungen und Materialien zu Wertdisparitäten und Wertwandel in der BRD', in KLAGES, H. and KMIECIAK, P. (Eds) *Wertwandel und gesellschaftlicher Wandel*, Frankfurt/M./New York, Campus, pp. 147–84.

BARLOW, G. and HILL, A. (Eds) (1985) *Video Violence and Children: Report of Findings of an Academic Working Party for the Parliamentary Video Enquiry*, London, Hodder and Stoughton Educational Press.

BARRETT, M. (1980) *Women's Oppression Today*, London, Verso.

BARRETT, M. and McINTOSH, M. (1982) *The Anti-Social Family*, London, Verso.

BARROW, J. (1982) 'West Indian families — an insider's perspective', in RAPOPORT, R. *et al.* (Eds) *Families in Britain*, London, Routledge & Kegan Paul.

BARTON, L. and WALKER, S. (Eds) (1983) *Race, Class and Education*, London, Croom Helm.

BARTRAM, C. and KRÜGER, H.-H. (1985) 'Vom Backfisch zum Teenager — Mädchensozialisation in den 50er Jahren', in KRÜGER, H-H. (Ed.) *Lebensgeschichte und jugendliche Alltagskultur in den 50er Jahren*, Opladen, Leske + Budrich, pp. 84–102.

BATES, I. *et al.* (Eds) (1984) *Schooling for the Dole?* London, Macmillan Youth Questions.

BAUER, K.-O. and BUDDE, H. (1984) 'Schule und Studium: Mehr Berechtigungen, weniger Chancen', in ROLFF, H.-G. *et al.* (Eds) *Jahrbuch der Schulentwicklung*, Volume 3, Weinheim/Basel, Beltz, pp. 76–116.

BAUER, K.W. and HENGST, H. (1980) *Wirklichkeit aus zweiter Hand. Kindheit in der Erfahrungswelt von Spielwaren und Medienprodukten*, Reinbek, Rowohlt.

BAUR, J. (1987) *Körper-und Bewegungskarrieren. Dialektische Analysen zur Entwicklung von Körper und Bewegung im Kindes-und Jugendalter.* (Habilitationsschrift) Paderborn.

BECK, U. (1983) 'Jenseits von Stand und Klasse? Soziale Ungleichheiten, gesellschaftliche Individualisierungsprozesse und die Entstehung neuer Formationen und Identitäten', *Soziale Welt*, Sonderband 2, pp. 35–74.

BECK, U. (1986) *Risikogesellschaft. Auf dem Weg in eine andere Moderne*, Frankfurt/M., Suhrkamp.

BECK, U. (1987) 'Beyond status and class', in MEGA, W. *et al.* (Eds) *Modern German Sociology*, Columbia, Columbia University Press.

BECK, U. and BRATER, M. (1977) *Berufliche Arbeitsteilung und soziale Ungleichheit. Eine gesellschaftlich-historische Theorie der Berufe*, Frankfurt/M., Suhrkamp.

BECKER, H. *et al.* (1984) 'Unterschiedliche Sozialräume von Jugendlichen in ihrer Bedeutung für pädagogisches Handeln', *Zeitschrift für Pädagogik*, 30, 4, pp. 499–517.

BECKER, H., EIGENBRODT, J. and MAY, M. (1984) *Pfadfinderheim, Teestube, Straßenleben. Jugendliche Cliquen und ihre Sozialräume*, Frankfurt/M., Extrabuch Verlag.

BECKER, P. (Ed.) (1982) *Sport und Sozialisation*, Reinbek, Rowohlt.

BECK-GERNSHEIM, E. (1983) 'Vom "Dasein für andere" zum Anspruch auf ein Stück "eigenes Leben"', *Soziale Welt*, 34, 3, pp. 307–40.

BECK-GERNSHEIM, E. (1984) *Vom Geburtenrückgang zur Neuen Mütterlichkeit? Über private und politische Interessen am Kind*, Frankfurt/M., Fischer.

BEECHEY, V. (1978) 'Women and production', in KUHN, A. and WOLPE, A.M. (Eds), *Feminism and Materialism*, London, Routledge & Kegan Paul.

BEECHEY V. (1979) 'On patriarchy', *Feminist Review*, 3.

BEECHEY V. and DONALD, J. (Eds) (1985) *Subjectivity and Social Relations*, Milton Keynes, Open University Press.

BEHNKEN, I., DU BOIS-REYMOND, M. and ZINNEKER, J. (1989) *Stadtgeschichte als Kindheitsgeschichte. Soziale Lebensräume von Kindern in Deutschland und Holland um 1900*, Opladen, Leske + Budrich.

References

BELL, C. and NEWBY, H. (1976) 'Husbands and Wives: The dynamics of the deferential dialectic', in LEONARD, D. and ALLEN, S. (Eds) *Dependence and Exploitation in Work and Marriage*, London, Longman.

BENN, C. and FAIRLY, J. (Eds) (1986) *Challenging the MSC on Jobs, Education and Training: Enquiry into a National Disaster*, London, Pluto Press.

BERG-LAASE, G. *et al.* (1985) *Verkehr und Wohnumfeld im Alltag von Kindern*, Pfaffenweiler, Centaurus.

BERGER, J. (Ed.) (1986) *Die Moderne — Kontinuitäten und Zäsuren, Soziale Welt*, Sonderband 4, Göttingen.

BERGER, P.A. (1986) *Entstrukturierte Klassengesellschaft. Klassenbildung und Strukturen sozialer Ungleichheit im historischen Wandel*, Opladen, Westdeutscher Verlag.

BERLINER GESCHICHTSWERKSTATT e.V. (Ed.) (1985) *Vom Lagerfeuer zur Musikbox. Jugendkulturen 1900–1960*, Berlin, Elefanten Press.

BERNSTEIN, B. (1977) *Class, Codes and Control: Volume 3*, London, Routledge & Kegan Paul.

BERNSTEIN, B. (1982) 'Codes, modalities and the process of cultural reproduction', in APPLE, M. (Ed.) *Cultural and Economic Reproduction in Education*, London, Routledge & Kegan Paul.

BERNSTEIN, B. (1990) *Class, Codes and Control: Volume 4*, London, Routledge & Kegan Paul.

BERTAUX, D. (1981) *Biography and Society*, London, Sage.

BERTRAM, H. (1985) 'Youth 1985: Findings and critique of youth research on the occasion of the International Year of Youth', mimeo, DJI Munich.

BERTRAM, H. (1987a) *Jugend heute. Die Einstellungen der Jugend zu Familie, Beruf und Gesellschaft*, München, DJI.

BERTRAM, H. (1987b) 'Risiko oder Chance: Jugendliche im Wandel der Arbeitsgesellschaft', *Jahresbericht*, München, DJI, pp. 132–45.

BEURET, K. and MAKINGS, L. (1987) '"I've got used to being independent now": Women and courtship in a recession', in ALLATT, P. *et al.* (Eds) *Women and the Life-Cycle*, London, Macmillan, pp. 64–76.

BHACHU, P. (1985) *Twice Migrants: East African Sikh Settlers in Britain*, London, Tavistock.

BHACHU, P. (1988) 'Religious and Cultural Effervescence: Sikhs in the British Diaspora', paper presented at the Conference on Theological and Social Issues in Hindu and Sikh Tradition, Kashmir, Srinigar, pp. 17–21.

BIELEFELD, U., KREISSL, R. and MÜNSTER, T. (1982) *Junge Ausländer im Konflikt. Lebenssituationen und überlebensformen*, München, Juventa.

BILDEN, H. and DIEZINGER, A. (1984) 'Individualisierte Jugendbiografie? Zur Diskrepanz von Anforderungen, Ansprüchen und Möglichkeiten', *Zeitschrift für Pädagogik*, 30, 2, pp. 191–207.

BILDEN, H. and DIEZINGER, A. (1988) 'Historische Konstitution und besondere Gestalt weiblicher Jugend — Mädchen im Blick der Jugendforschung', in KRÜGER, H.-H., (Ed.) *Handbuch der Jugendforschung*, Opladen, Leske + Budrich, pp. 135–55.

BIOS (1988) *Zeitschrift für Biografieforschung und Oral History*, Opladen, Leske + Budrich.

BLOSSFELD, H.-P. (1985) *Bildungsexpansion und Berufschancen*, Frankfurt/M./New York, Campus.

BOCK, U., BRASZEIT, A. and SCHMERL, C. (Eds) (1983) *Frauen an den Universitäten. Zur Situation von Studentinnen und Hochschullehrerinnen in der männlichen Wissenschaftshierarchie*, Frankfurt/M./New York, Campus.

BÖHNISCH, L. (1988) 'Jugend und Konsum: Konsum total?', *Sozialwissenschaftliche Informationen*, 17, 3, pp. 14–19.

BONFADELLI, H. *et al.* (1986) *Jugend und Medien*, Frankfurt/M., Syndikat.

BOOS-NÜNNING, U. (1986) 'Die schulische Situation der zweiten Generation', in

MEYS, W. and SEN, F. (Eds) *Zukunft in der Bundesrepublik oder Zukunft in der Türkei?* Frankfurt/M., Dagyeli Verlag, pp. 131–44.

BORCHERT, K. (1986) 'Soziale Herkunft und berufliche Karriere. Ergebnisse einer Absolventenbefragung an Fachhochschulen', *Zeitschrift für Sozialisationsforschung und Erziehungssoziologie*, 6, 1, pp. 111–27.

BOURDIEU, P. (1974) *Zur Soziologie der symbolischen Formen*, Frankfurt/M., Suhrkamp.

BOURDIEU, P. (1986) *Distinction*, tr. NICE, R., London, Routledge & Kegan Paul.

BOURDIEU, P. (1982a) *Die feinen Unterschiede*, Frankfurt/M., Suhrkamp.

BOURDIEU, P. (1982b) *Entwurf einer Theorie der Praxis*, Frankfurt/M., Suhrkamp.

BOURDIEU, P. (1983) 'Ökonomisches Kapital, kulturelles Kapital, soziales Kapital', *Soziale Welt*, Sonderband 2, pp. 183–98.

BOURDIEU, P. (1985) 'Historische und soziale Voraussetzungen des modernen Sports', *Merkur*, 39, 7, pp. 575–90.

BOURDIEU, P. (1987) *Sozialer Sinn. Kritik der theoretischen Vernunft*, Frankfurt/M., Suhrkamp.

BOURDIEU, P. (1988) *Homo Academicus*, Frankfurt/M., Suhrkamp.

BOURDIEU, P., BOLTANSKI, L., de SAINT MARTIN, M. and MALDIDIER, P. (1981) *Titel und Stelle. Über die Reproduktion sozialer Macht*, Frankfurt/M., EVA.

BOURDIEU, P. and PASSERON, J.D. (1971) *Die Illusion der Chancengleichheit*, Stuttgart, Klett-Cotta.

BOURDIEU, P. and PASSERON, J.D. (1977) *Reproduction in Education, Society and Culture*, London, Sage.

BOWLES, S. and GINTIS, H. (1976) *Schooling in Capitalist America*, New York, Basic Books.

BRAH, A. (1986) 'Unemployment and racism: Asian youth on the dole', in ALLEN S. et al. (Eds) *The Experience of Unemployment*, London, Macmillan, pp. 61–78.

BRAKE, M. (1980) *The Sociology of Youth Culture and Youth Subcultures*, London, Routledge & Kegan Paul.

BRAKE, M. (1985) *Comparative Youth Cultures*, London, Routledge & Kegan Paul.

BRAND, K.-W., BÜSSER, D. and RUCHT, D. (1986) *Aufbruch in eine andere Gesellschaft. Neue soziale Bewegungen in der Bundesrepublik*, Frankfurt/M./New York, Campus.

BRANDT, G. (1984) 'British Youth Caribbean Creole — The politics of resistance', paper presented to the Conference on Languages Without a Written Tradition, Thames Polytechnic.

BRANNEN, J. (1989) *Working Mothers: Ideologies and Experiences*, unpublished ms, University of London Institute of Education, Thomas Coram Research Unit.

BRANNEN, J. and WILSON, G. (Eds) (1987) *Give and Take in Families: Studies in Resource Distribution*, London, George Allen & Unwin.

BRAVERMAN, H. (1974) *Labour and Monopoly Capital*, New York, Capital.

BREYVOGEL, W. and KRÜGER, H.-H. (Eds) (1987) *Land der Hoffnung — Land der Krise. Jugendkulturen im Ruhrgebiet 1900–1987*, Berlin/Bonn, Dietz.

BREYVOGEL, W. (Ed.) (1989) *Pädagogische Jugendforschung*, Opladen, Leske + Budrich.

BRONFENBRENNER, U. (1976) *Ökologische Sozialisationsoforschung*, Stuttgart, Klett-Cotta.

BROPHY, J. and SMART, C. (1981) 'From disregard to disrepute: The position of women in family law', *Feminist Review*, 9, pp. 3–16.

BROWN, P. (1987) *Schooling Ordinary Kids*, London, Tavistock.

BROWN, P. (1988) 'Education and the working class: A cause for concern', in LAUDER, H. and BROWN, P. (Eds) *Education: In Search of a Future*, Lewes, Falmer Press, pp. 1–19.

BROWN, P. (1989) 'Education', in BROWN, P. and SPARKS, R. (Eds) *Beyond Thatcherism*, Milton Keynes, Open University Press, pp. 33–47.

BROWN, P. (1990) 'The third wave: Education and the rise of the parentocracy?', *British Journal of Sociology of Education*, forthcoming.

References

BROWN, P. and ASHTON, D. (Eds) (1987) *Education, Unemployment and Labour Markets*, Lewes, Falmer Press.

BÜCHNER, P. (1983) 'Vom Befehlen und Gehorchen zum Verhandeln. Entwicklungstendenzen von Verhaltensstandards und Umgangsnormen seit 1945', in PREUSS-LAUSITZ, U. *et al.* (Eds) *Kriegskinder, Konsumkinder, Krisenkinder — Zur Sozialisationsgeschichte seit dem Zweiten Weltkrieg*, Weinheim/Basel, Beltz, pp. 196–212.

BÜCHNER, P. (1985) *Einführung in die Soziologie der Erziehung und des Bildungswesens*, Darmstadt, Wissenschaftliche Buchgesellschaft.

BUKAROW, W.D. and LLARYORA, R. (1988) *Mitbürger aus der Fremde. Soziogenese ethnischer Minderheiten*, Opladen, Westdeutscher Verlag.

BUNDESMINISTERIUM FÜR BILDUNG UND WISSENSCHAFT (1986) *Das soziale Bild der Studentenschaft in der Bundesrepublik Deutschland* (11. Sozialerhebung des deutschen Studentenwerks), Bad Honnef, Bock.

BURGOYNE, J. and CLARK, D. (1984) *Making a Go of It. A Study of Stepfamilies in Sheffield*, London, Routledge & Kegan Paul.

BURNETT, J. (1982) *Destiny Obscure: Autobiographies of Childhood, Education and Family from the 1820s to the 1920s*, London, Allen Lane.

BURNHILL, P. and McPHERSON, A. (1984) 'Careers and gender: The expectations of able Scottish school-leavers in 1971 and 1981', in ACKER, S. and WARREN PIPER, D. (Eds) *Is Higher Education Fair to Women?* SRHE and NFER-Nelson, pp. 83–115.

BUSWELL, C. (1989) 'Flexible workers for flexible firms?' in POLLARD, A. *et al.* (Eds) *Education, Training and the New Vocationalism*, Milton Keynes, Open University Press, pp. 165–82.

BUSWELL, J. (1986) 'Employment processes and youth training', in BARTON, L. and WALKER, S. (Eds) *Youth, Unemployment and School*, Milton Keynes, Open University Press.

CAIRNS, E. (1987) *Caught in Crossfire: Children in the Northern Ireland Conflict*, Belfast, Appletree Press.

CAMPBELL, B. (1988) *Unofficial Secrets. Child Sexual Abuse — The Cleveland Case*, London, Virago.

CARBY, H. (1982a) 'Schooling in Babylon', in CENTRE FOR CONTEMPORARY CULTURAL STUDIES (Eds) *The Empire Strikes Back*, London, Hutchinson/CCCS, pp. 183–211.

CARBY, H. (1982b) 'White women listen: Black feminism and the boundaries of sisterhood', in CENTRE FOR CONTEMPORARY CULTURAL STUDIES (Eds) *The Empire Strikes Back*, London, Hutchinson/CCCS, pp. 212–35.

CARTER, M. (1966) *Into Work*, Harmondsworth, Penguin.

CENTRE FOR CONTEMPORARY CULTURAL STUDIES (1982) *The Empire Strikes Back*, London, Hutchinson/CCCS.

CHALLIS, J. and ELLMAN, D. (1979) *Child Workers Today*, Sunbury, Quartermine House in association with the Anti-Slavery Society.

CHARLES, N. and KERR, M. (1987) 'Just the way it is: Gender and age differences in family food consumption', in BRANNEN, J. and WILSON, G. (Eds) *Give and Take in Families: Studies in Resource Distribution*, London, Allen & Unwin.

CHESTER, R., DOGGORY, P. and SUTHERLAND, M.B. (Eds) (1981) *Changing Patterns of Childbearing and Childrearing*, London, Academic Press.

CHILD HEALTH AND EDUCATION STUDY (1970) *Report*, Bristol, University of Bristol.

CHISHOLM, L.A. (1987) *Gender and Vocation*, PSEC Working Papers 1 (new series), London, University of London Institute of Education Post-Sixteen Education Centre.

CHISHOLM, L.A. and HOLLAND, J. (1986) 'Girls and occupational choice: Anti-sexism in action in a curriculum development project', *British Journal of Sociology of Education*, 7, 4, pp. 353–65.

CHISHOLM, L.A. and HOLLAND, J. (1987) 'Anti-sexist action research in school: the

GAOC Project', in WEINER, G. and ARNOT, M. (Eds) *Gender Under Scrutiny: New Enquiries in Education*, London, Hutchinson/Open University Press, pp. 243–257.

CHISHOLM, L.A. and HOLLAND, J. (1988) 'Mädchen und Berufswahl', in WIEBE, H.-H. (Ed.) *Jugend in Europa. Situation und Forschungsstand*, Opladen, Leske + Budrich, pp. 173–87.

CHITTY, C. (1987) (Ed.) *Aspects of Vocationalism*, London, Institute of Education Post 16 Education Centre.

CLARKE, A.M. and CLARKE, A.D. (1976) *Early Experiences: Myth and Evidence*, London, Open Books.

CLARKE, J. et al. (1976) 'Subcultures, cultures and class: A theoretical overview', in HALL, S. and JEFFERSON, T. (Eds) *Resistance Through Rituals*, London, Hutchinson, pp. 9–74.

CLARKE, J. et al. (1979) *Jugendkultur als Widerstand. Milieus, Rituale, Provokationen*, Frankfurt/M., Syndikat.

CLARKE, P. (1977) *Growing Up in Medieval Times*, London, Batsford.

CLARKE, P. (1980) *Growing Up During the Industrial Revolution*, London, Batsford.

CLOUGH, E. et al. (1988) 'Youth Cohort Study: routes through YTS', MSC R and D, 42, *Youth Cohort Series*, 2, Sheffield, MSC.

COCHRANE, R. and BILLIG, M. (1984) 'I'm not National Front myself but . . .', *New Society*, 68, pp. 1121–1258.

COCKBURN, C. (1987) *Two-track Training: Sex Inequalities and the YTS*, Basingstoke, Macmillan.

COFFIELD, F. BORRILL, C. and MARSHALL, S. (1986) *Growing Up At the Margins*, Milton Keynes, Open University Press.

COHEN, P. (1972) 'Sub-cultural conflict and working-class community', *Working Papers in Cultural Studies*, 2, University of Birmingham, Centre for Contemporary Cultural Studies. Reprinted in HAMMERSLEY, M. and WOODS, P. (Eds) *The Process of Schooling*, London, Routledge & Kegan Paul.

COHEN, P. (1984) 'Against the new vocationalism', in BATES, I. et al. (Eds) *Schooling for the Dole?* London, Macmillan Youth Questions, pp. 104–69.

COHEN, P. (1986) 'Rethinking the Youth Question, *PSEC Working Paper 1*, London, University of London Institute of Education Post-Sixteen Education Centre.

COHEN, P. (1988) 'The perversions of inheritance' in COHEN, P. and BAINS, H. (Eds) *Multi-Racist Britain*, London, Macmillan, pp. 9–20.

COHEN, P. and BAINS, H. (Eds) (1988) *Multi-Racist Britain*, London, Macmillan.

COHEN, S. (1980) *Folk Devils and Moral Panics: The Creation of Mods and Rockers*, Oxford, Martin Robertson.

COLEMAN, D. (1988) 'Population', in HALSEY, A.H. (Ed.) *British Social Trends Since 1900*, 2nd ed., London, Macmillan, pp. 36–134.

COLEMAN, J.S. (1986) *Die asymmetrische Gesellschaft*, Weinheim/Basel, Beltz.

COLLINS, R. (1986) *Weberian Sociological Theory*, Cambridge, Cambridge University Press.

COMMISSION FOR RACIAL EQUALITY (1980) *Youth in Multi-Racial Society: The Urgent Need for New Policies*, London, CRE.

CONNELL, R.W. et al. (1982) *Making the Difference: Schools, Families and Social Division*, Sydney, George Allen & Unwin.

CONNELL, R.W. (1983) *Which Way is Up? Essays on Sex, Class and Culture*, Sydney, George Allen & Unwin.

CORRIGAN, P. (1979) *Schooling the Smash Street Kids*, London, Paladin.

COURTENAY, G. (1988) 'Youth Cohort Study: Report on Cohort 1', Sweep 1, MSC R and D, 41, *Youth Cohort Series*, 1, Sheffield, MSC.

CROWE, B. (1983) *Play is a Feeling*, London, Allen & Unwin.

CULLINGFORD, C. (1984) *Children and Television*, Aldershot, Gower.

CZOCK, H. (1988) 'Eignen sich die Kategorien "Kultur" und "Identität" zur Beschreibung der Migrantensituation?' *Informationen zur Ausländerarbeit* 9, 1, pp. 76–80.

DALE, R. *et al.* (Eds) (1981a) *Education and the State Volume 1: Schooling and the National Interest*, Lewes, Falmer Press.

DALE, R. *et al.* (Eds) (1981b) *Education and the State Volume 2: Politics, Patriarchy and Practice*, Lewes, Falmer Press.

DALLA-COSTA, M.-R. (1972) *The Power of Women and the Subversion of the Community*, Bristol, Falling Wall Press.

DANTON, N., AUTONOVSKY, A. and MAOZ, B. (1984) 'Love, war and the life style of the family', in McCLUSKEY, K.A. and REESE, H.W. (Eds) *Life-span Developmental Psychology: Historical and Generational Effects*, New York/London, Academic Press, pp. 143–59.

DAVEY, A, (1983) *Learning to be Prejudiced: Growing Up in Multi-ethnic Britain*, London, Edward Arnold.

DAVIDOFF, L. (1973) *The Best Circles*, London, Croom Helm.

DAVIDOFF, L., L'ESPERANCE, J. and NEWBY, H. (1977) 'Landscape with figures: Home and community in English society', in MITCHELL, J. and OAKLEY, A. (Eds) *The Rights and Wrongs of Women*, London, Penguin, pp. 139–75.

DAVIDOFF, L. and HALL, C. (1987) *Family Fortunes*, London, Hutchinson.

DAVIE, R., BUTLER, N.R. and GOLDSTEIN, H. (1972) *From Birth to Seven*, London, Longmans in association with the NCB.

DAVIES, B. (1986) *Threatening Youth*, Milton Keynes, Open University Press.

DAVIES, L. (1984) *Pupil Power: Deviance and Gender in School*, Lewes, Falmer Press.

DEEM, R. (Ed.) (1984) *Co-education Reconsidered*, Milton Keynes, Open University Press.

DELPHY, C. (1970) 'L'ennemi principal', *Partisans*, pp. 54–55.

DELPHY, C. (1976) 'Continuities and discontinuities in marriage and divorce', in LEONARD, D. and ALLEN, S. (Eds) *Sexual Divisions and Society: Process and Change*, London, Tavistock, pp. 76–89.

DELPHY, C. (1984) *Close to Home: A Materialist Analysis of Women's Oppression*, London, Hutchinson.

DELPHY, C. and LEONARD, D. (1986) 'Class analysis, gender analysis and the family', in CROMPTON, R. and MANN, M. (Eds) *Gender and Stratification*, Cambridge, Polity Press.

DELPHY, C. and LEONARD, L. (1980) *The Family as an Economic System*, unpublished ms, University of Kent.

DELPHY, C. and LEONARD, L. (1990) *Women and the Family*, London, Tavistock.

DEPARTMENT OF EDUCATION AND SCIENCE (1988) *Education Reform Act*, London, HMSO.

DEX, S. (1985) *The Sexual Division of Work*, Brighton, Harvester Press.

DIEZINGER, A., MARQUARDT, R., BILDEN, H. und DAHLKE, K. (1983) *Zukunft mit beschränkten Möglichkeiten*, 2 Bde., München, DJI.

DIGBY, A. and SCARBY, P. (1981) *Children, School and Society in Nineteenth-Century England*, London, Macmillan.

DOBASH, R. and DOBASH, R. (1980) *Violence Against Wives*, London, Open Books.

DOORMANN, L. (Ed.) (1979) *Kinder in der Bundesrepublik*, Köln, Pahl-Rugenstein.

DOUGLAS, J.W.D. (1964) *The Home and the School*, London, MacGibbon & Kee.

DOUGLAS, J.W.D. and BLOOMFIELD, J.M. (1958) *Children Under Five*, London, George Allen & Unwin.

DOUGLAS, J.W.D., ROSS, J.M. and SIMPSON, H.R. (1968) *All Our Future*, London, Peter Davies.

DOWE, D. (Ed.) (1986) *Jugendprotest und Generationskonflikt. Europa im 20. Jahrhundert*, Bonn, Verlag Neue Gesellschaft.

DRECHSEL, R., GÖRS, D., GRONWALD, D. and RABE-KLEBERG, U. (Eds) (1988) *Berufs-*

politik und Gewerkschaften. Gewerkschaftliches Berufsverständnis und Entwicklung der Lohnarbeit. Reihe Forschungsschwerpunkt Arbeit und Bildung, Bd. 9, Bremen.

DRIVER, G. (1982) 'West Indian families', in RAPOPORT, R. *et al.* (Eds) *Families in Britain*, London, Routledge & Kegan Paul, pp. 205–19.

DUNN, G. (1977) *The Box in the Corner: Television and the Underfives*, London, Macmillan.

DUNN, J. (1988) *The Beginnings of Social Understanding*, Oxford, Basil Blackwell.

DUNN, J. and KENRICK, C. (1982) *Siblings*, Glasgow, Grant McIntyre.

DURAND-DROUHIN, J.-L. *et al.* (Eds) (1981/82) *Rural Community Studies in Europe, vol. 1 and 2*, Oxford, Pergamon Press.

DYHOUSE, C. (1981) *Girls Growing Up in Late Victorian and Edwardian England (1860–1920)*, London, Routledge & Kegan Paul.

ECARIUS, J. (1988) 'Feministische Hochschulsozialisationsforschung', *Projekt Studium und Biografie*, 1, pp. 37–47.

ECKENSBERGER, L.H. (1983) 'Interkulturelle Vergleiche', in SILBEREISEN, R.K. and MONTADA. L. (Eds) *Entwicklungspsychologie. Ein Handbuch in Schlüsselbegriffen*, München., Urban & Schwarenberg, pp. 155–64.

ECKENSBERGER, L.H. KREWER, B. and KASPER, E. (1984) 'Simulation of cultural change by cross-cultural research: some metamethodological considerations', in MC-CLUSKEY, K.A. and REESE, H.W. (Eds) *Life-span Developmental Psychology: Historical and Generational Effects*, New York, pp. 73–108.

EEKELAAR, J. and McLEAN, M. (1986) *Maintenance After Divorce*, Oxford, Clarendon Press.

ELIADE, M. (1961) *Das Mysterium der Wiedergeburt. Initiationsriten, ihre kulturelle und religiöse Bedeutung*, Zürich/Stuttgart, Rascher.

ELIAS, N. (1977) *Über den Prozeß der Zivilisation. Soziogenetische und psychogenetische Untersuchungen*. 2 Bde., Frankfurt/M., Suhrkamp.

ELKIND, D. (1981) *The Hurried Child. Growing Up Too Soon*, Reading, Mass.

ENGELBERT, A. (1986) *Lebenssituation von Vorschulkindern*, Frankfurt/M./New York, Campus.

ENGLER, S. (1988) 'Der Raum studentischer Fachkulturen', *Projekt Studium und Biografie*, 2, pp. 25–38.

ERIKSON, E.-H. (1974) *Jugend und Krise*, Stuttgart, Klett-Cotta.

ERLEMANN, C. (1983) 'Frauen in Naturwissenschaft und Technik', in BOCK, U. *et al.* (Eds) *Frauen an den Universitäten*, Frankfurt/M./New York, Campus, pp. 94–105.

ERNST, H. (1982) 'Kindheit. Eine Lebensphase verschwindet', *Psychologie heute* 9, 12, pp. 20–7.

ESSER, H. (1988) *Interethnische Freundschaften*, unpublished ms.

ESSER, H. *et al.* (1986) *Kulturelle und ethnische Identität bei Arbeitsmigranten im interkontextuellen und intergenerationalen Vergleich*, University/Gesamthochschule Essen and Hamburg University.

EWERT, O. (1983) *Entwicklungspsychologie des Jugendalters*, Stuttgart, Kohlhammer.

FAGIN, L. and LITTLE, M. (1984) *The Forsaken Families*, Harmondsworth, Penguin.

FAULSTICH-WIELAND, H. (Ed.) (1987) *Abschied von der Koedukation?* Frankfurt/M., Materialien zur Sozialarbeit und Sozialpädagogik.

FAULSTICH-WIELAND, H. *et al.* (1984) 'Erfolgreich in der Schule, diskriminiert im Beuf: Geschlechtsspezifische Ungleichheiten bei der Berufseinmündung', in ROLFF, H.-G. *et al.* (Eds) *Jahrbuch der Schulentwicklung*, Bd. 3, Weinheim/Basel, Beltz, pp.117–43.

FEIL, C. and FURTNER-KALLMÜNZER, M. (1987) 'Belastungen im Verhältnis zwischen Ausländern und Deutschen — ein Überblick', *Ausländerarbeit und Integrationsforschung. Bilanz und Perspektiven*, München, DJI.

FEMINIST REVIEW (1988) *Family Secrets: Child Sexual Abuse*, Special Issue, 28, Spring.

FEND, H. (1988) *Sozialgeschichte des Aufwachsens. Bedingungen des Aufwachsens und*

Jugendgestalten im 20. Jahrhundert, Frankfurt/M., Suhrkamp.

FERCHHOFF, W. (1985) 'Zur Pluralisierung und Differenzierung von Lebbenszusammenhängen bei Jugendlichen', in BAACKE, D. and HEITMEYER, W. (Eds) *Neue Widersprüche. Jugendliche in den 80er Jahren*, München, Juventa, pp. 46–85.

FERCHHOFF, W. and NEUBAUER, G. (1989) *Jugend und Postmoderne*, München, Juventa.

FERCHHOFF, W. and OLK, T. (Eds) (1988) *Jugend im internationalen Vergleich*, Weinheim/München, Juventa.

FERGUSON, S. (1976) *Growing Up in Victorian Britain*, London, Batsford.

FERRI, E. (1976) *Growing Up in a One-Parent Family*, Windsor, NFER Publishing.

FIELD, F. (1985) *What Price a Child: A Historical Review of the Relative Cost of Dependants*, Policy Studies Institute, Studies of the Social Security System, 8.

FIELD, S. and SOUTHGATE, N. (1982) *Public Disorder*, Home Office Research Study 72, London, HMSO.

FINCH, J. (1983) *Married to the Job*, London, George Allen & Unwin.

FINER REPORT (1974) *Report of the Committee on One-Parent Families*, Cmnd. 5629, London, HMSO.

FINN, D. (1987) *Training Without Jobs: New Deals and Broken Promises*, London, Macmillan.

FIRESTONE, F. (1972) *The Dialectic of Sex: The Case for Feminist Revolution*, London, Paladin.

FISCHER, A., FUCHS, W. and ZINNEKER, J. (1982) *Jugend '81. Lebensentwürfe, Alltagskulturen, Zukunftsbilder*, Opladen, Leske + Budrich.

FISCHER, A., FUCHS, W. and ZINNEKER, J. (1985a) *Jugendliche und Erwachsene '85. 5 Bde.*, Opladen, Leske + Budrich.

FISCHER, A., FUCHS, W. and ZINNEKER, J. (1985b) 'Nachkriegsjugend und Jugend heute — Werkstattbericht aus einer laufenden Studie', *Zeitschrift für Sozialisationsforschung und Erziehungssoziologie*, 5, 1, pp. 5–28.

FITZ, J. (1981a) 'The child as legal subject', in DALE, R. *et al.* (Eds) *Education and the State Volume 2: Politics, Patriarchy and Practice*, Lewes, Falmer Press, pp. 285–304.

FITZ, J. (1981b) *Welfare, the Family and the Child*, Open University Course E353 Unit 12, Milton Keynes, Open University Press.

FITZ, J. and HOOD-WILLIAMS, J. (1982) 'The generation game', in ROBBINS, D. *et al.* (Eds) *Rethinking Social Inequality*, Hampshire, Gower.

FLITNER, A. and HORNSTEIN, W. (1964) 'Kindheit und Jugend in geschichtlicher Betrachtung', *Zeitschrift für Pädagogik*, 10, 4, pp. 311–39.

FOGARTY, M., RAPOPORT, R. and RAPOPORT, R.N. (1971) *Sex, Career and Family*, London, George Allen & Unwin/PEP.

FOGELMAN, K. (Ed.) (1983) *Growing Up in Great Britain: Papers from the National Child Development Study*, London, Macmillan for NCB.

FOGT, H. (1982) *Politische Generationen*, Opladen, Leske + Budrich.

FORSCHUNGSSTELLE FÜR VERGLEICHENDE ERZIEHUNGSWISSENSCHAFT MARBURG (Eds) (1980ff) *Marburger Beiträge zur vergleichenden Erziehungswissenschaft und Bildungsforschung*, München, Minerva.

FOWLKES, M.R. (1980) *Behind Every Successful Man. Wives of Medicine and Academe*, New York, Columbia University Press.

FREEMAN, M.D.A. (1983) *The Rights and Wrongs of Children*, London, Pinter.

FRIEBEL, H. (Ed.) (1983) *Berufliche Qualifikation und Persönlichkeitsentwicklung*, Opladen, Westdeutscher Verlag.

FRIEBEL, H. (1988a) 'Jugend als (Weiter-)Bildungsprozeß (Bundesrepublik Deutschland)', in WIEBE, H.-H. (Ed.) *Jugend in Europa. Situation und Forschungsstand*, Opladen, Leske + Budrich, pp. 121–37.

FRIEBEL, H. (1988b) 'Sozialpolitisierung des Übergangs von der Schule in den Beruf', in DEUTSCHES JUGENDINSTITUT (Ed.) *Berufseinstieg heute*, München, DJI, pp. 31–41.

FRIEBERTSHÄUSER, B. (1988) 'Stand der Hochschulsozialisationsforschung', *Projekt Studium und Biographie*, 1, pp. 17–36.
FROESE, L. (1983) *Ausgewählte Studien zur vergleichenden Erziehungswissenschaft. Positionen und Probleme*, München, Minerva.
FRÖHNER, R. et al. (1965) *Wie stark sind die Halbstarken?*, Bielefeld, M.v.Stackelberg-Verlag.
FUCHS, W. (1983) 'Jugendliche Statuspassage oder individualisierte Jugendbiographie?, *Soziale Welt*, 34, 3, pp. 341–71.
FUCHS, W. (1984) *Biographische Forschung*, Opladen, Westdeutscher Verlag.
FUCHS, W. (1985) 'Jugend als Lebenslaufphase', in JUGENDWERK DER DEUTSCHEN SHELL (Ed.) *Jugendliche und Erwachsene '85. Generation im Vergleich*, 5 vols., Hamburg, Jugendwerk der Deutschen Shell.
FUCHS, W. (1988) *Verlaufsformen der Jugendbiographie*, Kurseinheit 2, Fernuniversität Hagen.
FUCHS, W. and ZINNEKER, J. (1985) 'Nachkriegsjugend und Jugend heute-Werkstattbericht aus einer laufender Studie', *Zeitschrift für Sozialisationsforschung und Erziehungssoziologie*, 5, 1, pp. 5–28.
FULLER, M. (1980) 'Black girls in a London comprehensive', in DEEM, R. (Ed.) *Schooling for Women's Work*, London, Routledge & Kegan Paul, pp. 52–65.
FULLER, M. (1983) 'Qualified criticism, critical qualifications', in BARTON, L. and WALKER, S. (Eds) *Race, Class and Education*, London, Croom Helm, pp. 166–90.
FURLONG, A., CAMPBELL, R. and ROBERTS, K. (1989) 'Class and gender divisions among young adults at leisure', paper presented at the BSA Annual Conference, Plymouth Polytechnic, March.
FYSON, N.L. (1977) *Growing Up in the Eighteenth Century*, London, Batsford.
GADE, A. (1983) *Kultur aus dem Ghetto. Perspektiven einer autonomen Kulturarbeit am Beispiel Frankfurter Ausländervereine*, Magisterarbeit am Institut für Europäische Ethnologie, FB03 der Universität Marburg.
GAISER, W. and MÜLLER, H.-U. (1987) 'Lebenslage und Lebensbewältigung von Jugendlichen und jungen Erwachsenen', in FRIEBEL, H. (Ed.) *Berufsstart und Familiengründung - Ende der Jugend*, Opladen, Westdeutscher Verlag.
GAITANIDES, S. (1983) *Sozialstruktur und 'Ausländerproblem'. Sozialstrukturelle Aspekte der Marginalisierung von Ausländern der ersten und zweiten Generation*, München, DJI.
GANS, H.J. (1988) *Middle American Individualism*, New York, Free Press/Macmillan.
GARRISON, L. (1979) *Black Youth, Rastafarianism and the Identity-crisis in Britain*, London, Acer.
GASKELL, J. (1987) 'Education and the labour market: The logic of vocationalism', in WOTHERSPOON, S. (Ed.) *Sociology of Education: Readings in the Political Economy of Canadian Schooling*, Toronto, Methuen.
GEACH, H. and SZWED, E. (Eds) (1983) *Providing Civil Justice for Children*, London, Edward Arnold.
GENNEP V., A. (1969) 'Initiationsriten' in POPP, V. (Ed.) *Initiation: Zeremonien der Statusänderung und des Rollenwechsels*, Frankfurt/M, Reine Suhrkamp Wissen, Bd.4, Suhrkamp.
GEORGE, V. and WILDING, P. (1972) *Motherless Families*, London, Routledge & Kegan Paul.
GERGEN, K.J. (1982) *Toward Transformation in Social Knowledge*, New York, Springer.
GERGEN, K. J. (1985) 'The social constructionist movement in modern psychology', *American Psychologist*, 40, pp. 266–75.
GEROK, A. (1985) 'Speisung der 5000', in JENS, W. (Ed.) *Studentenalltag*, München, Knaur, pp. 101–8.
GERSHUNY, J. (1981) *Die Ökonomie der nachindustriellen Gesellschaft. Produktion und Verbrauch von Dienstleistungen*, Frankfurt/M./New York, Campus.

References

GESTRICH, A. (1983) *Traditionelle Jugendkultur und Industrialisierung*, Göttingen, SOFI.

GEULEN, D. (1989) *Kindheit: Neue Realitäten und Aspekte*, Weinheim, Deutscher Studienverlag.

GIBSON, S. and BHACHU, P. (1988) 'Ethnicity and school performance: A comparative study of South Asian pupils in Britain and America', *Ethnic and Racial Studies*, 11, 3, pp. 239–62.

GIDDENS, A. (1986) *The Constitution of Sociology*, Cambridge, Polity Press.

GIEHLER, W. and LÜSCHER, K. (1975) 'Die Soziologie des Kindes in historischer Sicht', *Neue Sammlung* 15, 5, pp. 442–63.

GIESECKE, H. (1987) *Die Zweitfamilie. Leben mit Stiefkindern und Stiefvätern*, Stuttgart, Klett-Cotta.

GIESEN, H. *et al.* (1981) *Vom Schüler zum Studenten. Bildungslebensläufe im Längsschnitt. Monographien zur pädagogischen Psychologie*, Bd. 7, München, E. Reinhardt.

GIFFORD, LORD (1986) *The Broadwater Farm, Haringey, Inquiry*, London, HMSO.

GILLIS, J.R. (1980) *Geschichte der Jugend. Tradition und Wandel im Verhältnis der Altersgruppen und Generationen in Europa von der zweiten Hälfte des 18. Jahrhunderts bis zur Gegenwart*, Weinheim/Basel, Beltz.

GILROY, P. (1987) *There ain't No Black in the Union Jack*, London, Hutchinson.

GILROY, P. and LAWRENCE, E. (1988) 'Two-tone Britain: Black and white youth and the politics of anti-racism' in COHEN, P. and BAINS, H. (Eds) *Multi-Racist Britain*, London, Macmillan, pp. 121–55.

GINTIS, H. and BOWLES, S. (1981) 'Contradiction and reproduction in educational theory', in BARTON. L. *et al.* (Eds) *Schooling, Ideology and the Curriculum*, Lewes, Falmer Press.

GIROUX, H. (1983) *Theory and Resistance in Education*, London, Heinemann Education.

GLASER, B. and STRAUSS, A. (1971) *Status Passage*, London, Routledge & Kegan Paul.

GLEESON, G. (Ed.) (1986) *The Growing Child in Competitive Sport*, London, Hodder and Stoughton.

GOLDTHORPE, J. (1980) *Social Mobility and Class Structure in Modern Britain*, Oxford, Clarendon Press.

GOODINGS, L. (Ed.) (1987) *Bitter-Sweet Dreams: Girls' and Young Women's Own Stories*, London, Virago Upstarts.

GORZ, A. (1982) *Farewell to the Working Class*, London, Pluto Press.

GÖTZ von OLENHAUSEN, I. (1987) *Jugendreich — Gottesreich — Deutsches Reich. Junge Generationen, Religion und Politik 1928–1933*, Witzenhausen.

GREVERUS, I.M. (1971) 'Kulturbegriffe und ihre Implikationen, dargestellt am Beispiel Süditaliens', *Kölner Zeitschrift für Soziologie und Sozialpsychologie*, 23, pp. 295–303.

GRIFFIN, C. (1985) *Typical Girls?* London, Routledge & Kegan Paul.

GRIMM, S. (1985) 'Aktuelle Entwicklungstendenzen familialer und schulischer Sozialisation in der BRD', in HRADIL, S. (Ed.) *Sozialstruktur im Umbruch*, Opladen, Leske + Budrich, pp. 287–304.

GROOTINGS, P. (Ed.) (1983) *Youth and Work in Europe. Vol. I: National Reports. Vol. II: Comparative Research and Policy Problems. Vol. III: Bibliography*, European Coordination Centre for Research and Documentation in Social Sciences, Vienna.

GROOTINGS, P. and STEFANOV, M. (Eds) (1988) *Transition from School to Work in Europe*, New York, Routledge Chapman & Hall.

GROSS, P. (1983) *Die Verheißungen der Dienstleistungsgesellschaft. Soziale Befreiung oder Sozialherrschaft?*, Opladen, Westdeutscher Verlag.

HABERMAS, J. (1982) *Theorie des kommunikativen Handelns*, 2 Bde., Frankfurt, Suhrkamp.

HALL, S. and JEFFERSON, T. (Eds) (1976) *Resistance Through Rituals*, London, Hutchinson.

HALL, S., CRICHETER, C., JEFFERSON, T. and CLARKE, J. (1978) *Policing the Crisis, Mugging the State and Law and Order*, London, Hutchinson.

HALL, S., JEFFERSON, T. and CLARKE, J. (1978) 'Youth — a stage in life?', *Youth and Society*, 17, pp. 17–19.

HALSEY, A.H. (1986) *Change in British Society*, 3rd ed., Milton Keynes, Open University Press.

HALSEY. A.H. (Ed.) (1988) *British Social Trends Since 1900*, 2nd revised ed., London, Macmillan.

HAMBURGER, F. (1986) 'Erziehung in der Einwanderergesellschaft', in BORRELLI, M. (Ed.) *Interkulturelle Pädagogik*, Baltmannsweiler, Pädagogischer Verlag, pp. 142–57.

HAMMERSLEY, M. and TURNER, G. (1980) 'Conformist pupils?', in WOODS, P. (Ed.) *Pupil Strategies*, London, Croom Helm, pp. 29–40.

HAMPSON, K. (1980) 'Schools and Work', in PLUCKROSE H. and WILBY, P. (Eds) *Education 2000*, London, Temple Smith, pp. 85–94.

HARBISON, J. and HARBISON, J. (Eds) (1980) *A Society Under Stress: Children and Young People in Northern Ireland*, Shepton Mallet, Open Books.

HARDACH-PINKE, I. (1981) *Kinderalltag: Aspekte von Kontinuität und Wandel der Kindheit in autobiographischen Zeugnissen 1700–1900*, Frankfurt/M./New York, Campus.

HARDACH-PINKE, I. and HARDACH, G. (Eds) (1978) *Deutsche Kindheiten 1700–1900*, Kronberg/Ts., Athanäum.

HARDACH-PINKE, I. and HARDACH, G. (Eds) (1981) *Kinderalltag*, Reinbek, Rowohlt.

HARGREAVES, A. (1982) 'Resistance and relative autonomy theories: problems of distortion and incoherence in recent Marxist analysis of education', *British Journal of Sociology of Education*, 3, pp. 107–26.

HARGREAVES, D. (1979) 'Durkheim, deviance and education', in BARTON, L. and MEIGHAN, R. (Eds) *Schools, Pupils and Deviance*, Driffield, Nafferton, pp. 17–31.

HARGREAVES, D.H. (1967) *Social Relations in a Secondary School*, London, Routledge & Kegan Paul.

HARMS, G. *et al.* (1985) *Kinder und Jugendliche in der Großstadt*, Berlin, FIPS.

HARRIS, C. (1983) *The Family and Industrial Society*, London, George Allen & Unwin.

HARRIS, C.C. (1977) 'Changing conceptions of the relation between family and societal form in Western society', in SCASE, R. (Ed.) *Industrial Society: Class, Cleavage and Control*, London, George Allen & Unwin.

HARRIS, C.C. *et al.* (1987) *Redundancy and Recession in South Wales*, Oxford, Basil Blackwell.

HARTMANN, J. (1987) 'The impact of new technologies on youth-parent relations in contemporary societies: the trend for individualization', paper presented to the CFR/CYR International Seminar-Young People and their Families, Freising/München.

HARTWIG, H. (1980) *Jugendkultur. Ästhetische Praxis in der Pubertät*, Reinbek, Rowohlt.

HAUßER, K. (1987) 'Zum Identitätskonzept in der Ausländerforschung', *Ausländerarbeit und Integrationsforschung*, München, DJI.

HAYES, L. (1989) '"One of us would do something": Gender and the long term obligations of young people to their family', paper presented to the BSA Annual Conference, Plymouth Polytechnic, March.

HAZEKAMP, J. MEUS, W. and TE POEL, Y. (Eds) (1988) *European Contributions to Youth Research*, Amsterdam, University of Amsterdam Press.

HEBDIGE, D. (1976) 'Reggae, Rasta and Rudies', in HALL, S. and JEFFERSON, T. (Eds) *Resistance Through Rituals*, London, Hutchinson, pp. 135–53.

HEBDIGE, D. (1979) *Subcultures: The Meaning of Style*, London, Methuen.

HEBDIGE, D. (1981) 'Skinheads and the search for white working class identity', *New Socialist*, 1, pp. 39–41.

HECKMANN, F. (1981) *Die Bundesrepublik — ein Einwanderungsland?* Stuttgart, Klett-Cotta.

HEINZ, W. (1987) 'The transition from school to work in crisis: coping with threaten-

ing unemployment', *Journal of Adolescent Research*, 2, 2, pp. 127–41.
HEINZ, W. (1988) 'Übergangsforschung — Überlegungen zur Theorie und Methodik', DEUTSCHES JUGENDINSTITUT (Ed.) *Berufseinstieg heute*, München, DJI, pp. 9–29.
HEINZ, W. et al. (1985) *'Hauptsache eine Lehrstelle'. Jugendliche vor den Hürden des Arbeitsmarkts*, Weinheim/Basel, Beltz.
HEINZE, T., KLUSEMANN, H.-W. and SOEFFNER, H.-G. (1980) *Interpretationen einer Bildungsgeschichte. Überlegungen zur sozialwissenschaftlichen Hermeneutik*, Bensheim, päd extra.
HELLFIELD V., M. (1987) *Bündische Jugend und Hitlerjugend. Zur Geschichte von Anpassung und Widerstand 1930–1939*, Witzenhausen, Verlag Wissenschaft und Politik.
HELSPER, W. (1987) 'Selbstkrise und Individuationsprozeß. Zur Bedeutung des Imaginären in der Selbstgenese. Überlegungen zu einer vernachlaßigten Dimension der Subjecktivität', Dissertation, Universität Marburg.
HELSPER, W. (1988) 'Jugend und Schule', in KRÜGER, H.-H. (Ed.) *Handbuch der Jugendforschung*, Weinheim/Basel, Beltz, pp. 249–72.
HENGST, H. (1981) 'Tendenzen zur Liquidierung von Kindheit', in HENGST, H. et al. (Eds) *Kindheit als Fiktion*, Frankfurt/M., Suhrkamp. pp. 11–72.
HENGST, H. et al. (1981) *Kindheit als Fiktion*, Frankfurt/M., Suhrkamp.
HENGST, H. (ed.) (1985) *Kindheit in Europa. Zwischen Spielplatz und Computer*, Frankfurt/M., Suhrkamp.
HENN, F. and WERKMANN, M. (1985) *Migrations- und emigrationsbedingte Konflikte junger Türkinnen*, Diplomarbeit, Institut für Erziehungswissenschaft, Universität Marburg.
HENNE, H. (1986) *Jugend und ihre Sprache. Darstellung. Materialienkritik*, Berlin, de Gruyter.
HENNIG, U., KEIM, K.D. and SCHULZ zur WIESCH, J. (1984) *Spuren der Mißachtung. Zum Verhältnis von Jugendproblemen und Stadtstruktur*, Frankfurt/M., Campus.
HENRIQUES, J. et al. (Ed.) (1984) *Changing the Subject: Psychology, Regulation and Subjectivity*, London, Methuen.
HENTIG V., H. (1976) *Was ist eine humane Schule?* München, Hanser.
HERGET, H., SCHÖNGEN, K. and WESTHOFF, G. (1987) *Berufsausbildung abgeschlossen — was dann? Ergebnisse einer Längsschnittuntersuchung zum übergang der Jugendlichen nach Abschluß einer betrieblichen Berufsausbildung in das Beschäftigungssystem*, Berichte zur beruflichen Bildung, H 85, Berlin.
HERMANNS, H. (1987) 'Developments in family and youth, indicating and favouring changes in the relationship between young people and their parents', paper presented to the CFR/CYR Intenational Seminar — Young People and their Families, Freising/Munich.
HERON, L. (Ed.) (1985) *Truth, Dare or Promise: Girls Growing Up in the Fifties*, London, Virago.
HERRMANN, U. (1984) 'Aufwachsen im Dorf — "dortmals". Versuch einer historischen Rekonstruktion', in WEHLING. H.-G. (Ed.) *Auf dem Lande leben*, Stuttgart, Kohlhammer, pp. 111–25.
HEßLER, M. and RILLING, E. (1987) *Jugenddelinquenz und Integration junger Ausländer. Teil 2*, Berlin, Publikationen der FHSVR.
HEWITT, R. (1982) 'White adolescent Creole users and the politics of friendship', *Journal of Multilingual and Multicultural Development*, 3, 3, pp. 217–32.
HEWITT, R. (1986) *White Talk Black Talk. Inter-racial Friendship and Communication Amongst Adolescent*, Cambridge, Cambridge University Press.
HEWITT, R. (1989) 'Creole in the classroom: Political grammars and educational vocabularies', in GRILLO, R. (Ed.) *Social Anthropology and the Politics of Language*, Sociological Review Monograph 36, London, Routledge, pp. 126–44.
HISTORISCHES MUSEUM FRANKFURT (1984) *Spielen und Lernen. Spielzeug und Kinderleben*

in Frankfurt 1750–1930, Kleine Schriften des Historischen Museums Frankfurt, 22, Frankfurt/M.

HOBSBAWM, E. (1989) *Politics for a Rational Left*, London, Verso.

HODGE, R. and TRIPP, D. (1986) *Children and Television: A Semiotic Approach*, Oxford, Polity Press.

HOFFMANN, L. (1987) 'Die Sache mit der Mentalität. Braucht man soziokulturelles Hinterwissen, um Ausländer zu verstehen?' *sozial extra*, 11, 10, pp. 42–3.

HOGAN, D. (1982) 'Education and class formation: the peculiarities of the Americans' in APPLE, M.W. (Ed.) *Cultural and Economic Reproduction in Education*, London, Routledge & Kegan Paul, pp. 32–78.

HOGGETT, B.M. (1981) *Parents and Children* 2nd ed., London, Sweet and Maxwell.

HOLLAND, J. (1989) 'Girls and occupational choice: In search of meanings', in POLLARD, A. *et al.* (Eds) *Education, Training and the New Vocationalism*, Milton Keynes, Open University Press, pp. 129–47.

HOLT, J. (1964) *How Children Fail*, New York, Pitman.

HONIG, M.-S. (1988) 'Kindheitsforschung: Abkehr von der Pädagogisierung', *Soziologische Revue*, 11, 2, pp. 169–78.

HOOD-WILLIAMS, J. (1984) 'The family: Demographic trends', *The Social Science Teacher*, 14, 1, pp. 4–7.

HOPPE, F. (1985) 'Weit entfernt, die Welt zu verändern', in JENS, W. (Ed.) *Studentenalltag*, München, Knaur, pp. 12–20.

HORNSTEIN, W. (1965) *Vom 'Jungen Herrn' zum 'Hoffnungsvollen Jüngling' Wandlungen des Jugendlebens im 18. Jahrhundert*, Heidelberg, Quelle & Meyer.

HORNSTEIN, W. (1985a) 'Jugend '85 — Strukturwandel, neues Selbstverständnis und neue Problemlagen', *Mitteilungen aus der Arbeitsmarkt- und Berufsforschung*, 18, 2, pp. 157–66.

HORNSTEIN, W. (1985b) 'Jugend. Strukturwandel im gesellschaftlichen Wandlungsprozeß', in HRADIL, S. (Ed.) *Sozialstruktur im Umbruch*, Opladen, Leske + Budrich, pp. 323–42.

HORNSTEIN, W. (1988) Strukturwandel der Jugendphase in der Bundesrepublik Deutschland, mimeo, München.

HORNSTEIN, W. (1989) 'Auf der Suche nach Neuorientierung: Jugendforschung zwischen Ästhetisierung und neuen Formen politischer Thematisierung der Jugend. Über einige Tendenzen in der Jugendforschung', *Zeitschrift für Pädagogik*, 35, 1, pp. 107–25.

HORNSTEIN, W., SCHEFOLD, W., SCHMEISER, G. and STACKEBRANDT, J. (1975) *Lernen im Jugendalter. Ergebnisse, Fragestellungen und Probleme sozialwissenschaftlicher Forschung*, Stuttgart, Klett-Cotta.

HOYLES, M.J.A. (1977) *Television and Children*, London, New University Library.

HOYLES, M. and EVANS, P. (1989) *The Politics of Childhood*, London, Journeyman Press.

HRADIL, S. (Ed.) (1985) *Sozialstruktur im Umbruch*, Opladen, Leske + Budrich.

HUBER, L. (1980) 'Sozialisation in der Hochschule', in HURRELMANN, K. and ULICH, D. (Eds) *Handbuch der Sozialisationsforschung*, Weinheim/Basel, Leske + Budrich.

HUBER, L. *et al.* (1983) 'Fachcode und studentische Kultur — Zur Erforschung der Habitusbildung in der Hochschule', in BECKER, E. (Ed.) *Reflexionsprobleme der Hochschulforschung. Beiträge zur Methodendiskussion*, Weinheim/Basel, Beltz, pp. 144–68.

HÜBNER-FUNK, S. (1985) *Youth Research in the FRG 1975–1985: Report and Selected Bibliography*, München, DJI.

HUMPHRIES, S. (1977) *Hooligans or Rebels? An Oral History of Working-Class Childhood and Youth 1889–1939*, Oxford, Basil Blackwell.

HUMPHRIES, S., MACK, J. and PERKS, R, (1989) *A Century of Childhood*, London, Sidgwick and Jackson.

References

HURRELMANN. K. (1976) *Sozialisation und Lebenslauf*, Reinbek. Rowohlt.
HURRELMANN, K. (Ed.) (1986) *Koedukation — Jungenschule auch für Mädchen?*, Opladen, Leske + Budrich.
HURRELMANN, K. (1987) 'Mit 16 fängt das Leben, aber auch das Alkoholkonsum an', *Frankfurter Rundschau*.
HURRELMANN, K. *et al*. (1985) *Lebensphase Jugend*, Weinheim/München, Juventa.
HURRELMANN, K. *et al*. (1988) 'Die psychosozialen "Kosten" verunsicherter Statuserwartungen im Jugendalter', *Zeitschrift für Pädagogik*, 34, 1, pp. 25–44.
HURRELMANN, K. and ENGEL, U. (1989) *The Social World of Adolescents: International Perspectives*, Berlin.
HURRELMANN, K. and HEITMEYER, W. (1988) 'Sozialisations- und handlungstheoretische Ansätze in der Jugendforschung', in Krüger, H.-H. (Ed.) *Handbuch der Jugendforschung*, Opladen, Leske + Budrich, pp. 47–70.
HURRELMANN, K. and ULICH, D. (Eds) (1980) *Handbuch der Sozialisationsforschung*, Weinheim/Basel, Betz.
HUTSON, S. and JENKINS, R. (1987) 'Coming of age in South Wales', in ASHTON, D. and BROWN, P. (Eds) *Education and Economic Life*, Lewes, Falmer Press.
INGHAM, M. (1981) *Now We Are Thirty: Women in the Breakthrough Generation*, London, Eyre Methuen.
INLEBY, J.D. (1986) 'Development of social context', in RICHARDS, M. and LIGHT, P. (Eds) *Children of Social Worlds*, Oxford, Polity Press.
INSTITUT FÜR ARBEITSMARKT- UND BERUFSFORSCHUNG (Ed.) (1980) *Jugendliche beim Übergang in Ausbildung und Beruf*, Nürnberg, IAB.
INSTITUTE OF MANPOWER STUDIES (1989) *How Many Graduates in the 21st Century? The Choice is Yours*, IMS Report No. 177, Brighton, University of Sussex.
INTERNATIONAL SOCIOLOGICAL ASSOCIATION RESEARCH COMMITTEE 34: SOCIOLOGY OF YOUTH (Ed.) (1985ff) *International Bulletin for Youth Research*.
INTERNATIONALE KONFERENZ DES 'RESEARCH COMMITTEE ON POLITICAL EDUCATION' DER 'INTERNATIONAL POLITICAL SCIENCES ASSOCIATION' (1988) *Political Socialisation of the Young in East and West. Proceedings*, Köln, 8–13 March, Frankfurt/M., IPSA.
JACKSON, C. (1985) *Who Will Take Our Children? The Story of the Evacuation in Britain 1939–1945*, London, Methuen.
JACKSON, S. (1982) *Childhood and Sexuality*, Oxford, Basil Blackwell.
JAIDE, W. (1988) *Generationen eines Jahrhunderts. Wechsel der Jugendgenerationen im Jahrhunderttrend. Zur Geschichte der Jugend in Deutschland 1871–1985*, Opladen, Leske + Budrich.
JENCKS, C. (Ed.) (1982) *Sociology of Childhood: Essential Readings*, London, Batsford.
JENKINS, R. (1982) 'Pierre Bourdieu and the reproduction of determinism', *Sociology*, 16, pp. 270–81.
JENKINS, R. (1983) *Lads, Citizens and Ordinary Kids*, London, Routledge & Kegan Paul.
JENNINGS, P. and DURRAN, M. (1986) *Children of the Troubles: Growing Up in Northern Ireland*, Basingstoke, Marshall Pickering.
JOERGES, B. (1981) 'Berufsarbeit, Konsumarbeit, Freizeit. Zur Sozial- und Umweltverträglichkeit einiger struktureller Veränderungen in Produktion und Konsum', *Soziale Welt*, 32, 2, pp. 168–95.
JONES, G. (1986) *Youth in the Social Structure: Transitions to Adulthood and Their Stratification by Class and Gender*, Ph.D. thesis, University of Surrey.
JONES, G. (1987) 'Young workers in the class structure', *Work, Employment and Society*, 1, 4, pp. 487–508.
JONES, G. (1988) 'Integrating process and structure in the concept of youth: a case for secondary analysis', *Sociological Review*, 4, pp. 706–32.

JONES, G. and WALLACE, C. (1988) 'Changing patterns of the life course in youth: Britain', unpublished ms.

JONES, S. (1988) *Black Culture, White Youth: The Reggae Tradition from JA to UK*, London, Macmillan.

JUGENDWERK DER DEUTSCHEN SHELL (Ed.) (1977) *Jugend in Europa. Ihre Eingliederung in die Welt der Erwachsenen. Eine vergleichende Analyse zwischen der Bundesrepublik Deutschland, Frankreich und Großbritannien*, 3 Bde., Hamburg.

JUGENDWERK DER DEUTSCHEN SHELL (Ed.) (1981) *Jugend '81. Lebensentwürfe, Alltagskulturen Zukunftsbilder*, 3 Bde., Hamburg.

JUGENDWERK DER DEUTSCHEN SHELL (Ed.) (1985) *Jugendliche und Erwachsene '85. Generationen im Vergleich*, 5 Bde., Hamburg.

KAGAN, J. and MOSS, H.A. (1983) *Birth to Maturity*, 2nd ed., New Haven/London, Yale University Press.

KALPAKA, A. (1986) *Handlungsfähigkeit statt 'Integration'. Schulische und außerschulische Lebensbedingungen und Entwicklungsmöglichkeiten griechischer Jugendlicher*, München, DJI.

KAMINSKI, G. and MAYER, R. (1984) *Kinder und Jugendliche im Hochleistungssport*, Schorndorf, Hofmann.

KAUFMANN, F.-X. and LÜSCHER, K. (1979) 'Wir brauchen eine Politik für Kinder', *Neue Sammlung*, 19, 2, pp. 222–33.

KELLNER, H. and HEUBERGER, F. (1988) 'Zur Rationalität der "Postmoderne" und ihrer Träger', *Soziale Welt*, Sonderband 6, pp. 325–37.

KELLY, G.P. and NIHLEN, A.S. (1982) 'Schooling and the reproduction of patriarchy: unequal workloads, unequal rewards', in APPLE, M. (Ed.) *Cultural and Economic Reproduction in Education*, London, Routledge & Kegan Paul, pp. 162–80.

KENNISTON, K. (1970) 'Youth as a stage of life', *American Scholar*, 39, 4, pp. 631–54.

KILCHENSTEIN, T. (1987) 'Gemeinsam Fußball spielen ist einfacher als miteinander leben. Sport als Integrationsfaktor?', *Ausländerkinder*, 7, 32, pp. 57–66.

KING, R. (1971) 'Unequal access in education: Sex and social class', *Social and Economic Administration*, 5, pp. 167–75.

KLAGES, H. (1984) *Wertorientierungen im Wandel*, Frankfurt/M./New York, Campus.

KLEFF, H.G. (1985) *Vom Bauern zum Industriearbeiter. Zur Kollektiven Lebensgeschichte der Arbeitsimmigranten aus der Türkei*, Mainz/Ingelheim, Monthano.

KLEIN, J. (1965) *Samples from English Culture*, Vols. 1 and 2, London, Routledge & Kegan Paul.

KLEMM, K. (1987) 'Die Bildungsbe(nach)teiligung ausländischer Schüler in der Bundesrepublik', *Westermanns Pädagogische Beiträge*, 39, 12, pp. 18–21.

KLEMM, K. and KOCH, H. (1984) 'Schule und Arbeitsmarkt', in ROLFF, H.-G, et al. (Eds) *Jahrbuch der Schulentwicklung*. Vol. 3, Weinheim/Basel, Beltz, pp. 44–75.

KLEWES, J. (1983) *Retrospektive Sozialisation. Einflüsse Jugendlicher auf ihre Eltern*, Weinheim/Basel, Beltz.

KNOLL, J.H. (1980) *Erwachsenenbildung und berufliche Weiterbildung in der Bundesrepublik Deutschland*, Grafenau, Expert Verlag.

KOEBNER, T., JANZ, R.-P. and TROMMLER, F. (Eds) (1985) 'Mit uns zieht die neue Zeit'. *Der Mythos Jugend*, Frankfurt/M., Suhrkamp.

KOHLI, M. (Ed.) (1978) *Soziologie des Lebenslaufs*, Darmstadt/Neuwied, Luchterhand.

KOHLI, M. (1985) 'Die Institutionalisierung des Lebenslaufes. Historische Befunde und theoretische Argumente', *Kölner Zeitschrift für Soziologie und Sozialpsychologie*, 37, pp. 1–29.

KOHLI, M. (1986a) 'Gesellschaftszeit und Lebenszeit', *Soziale Welt*, 4, pp. 183–208.

KOHLI, M. (1986b) 'Der Lebenslauf im Strukturwandel der Moderne', *Soziale Welt*, Sonderband 4, pp. 183–208.

KOHR, H.-U., KRIEGER, R. and RÄDER, H.-G. (1983) *Reproduktion von Gesellschaft. Jugend-Partizipation-Politische Bildung*, Weinheim/Basel, Beltz.

253

References

KOMMISSION DER EUROPÄISCHEN GEMEINSCHAFTEN (Ed.) (1982) *Die jungen Europäer. Situationsstudie über die 15- bis 24jährigen in den Ländern der Europäischen Gemeinschaft*, Brüssel.

KORNSTADT, H.-J. and TROMMSDORFF, G. (1984) 'Erziehungsziele im Kulturvergleich', in TROMMSDORFF, G. (Ed.) *Jahrbuch für Empirische Erziehungswissenschaften*, Düsseldorf, Cornelsen Schwan-Girardet.

KRAPPMANN, L. and OSWALD, H. (1983) Beziehungsgeflechte und Gruppen von gleichaltrigen Kindern in der Schule', in NEIDHARDT, F. (Ed.) *Soziologie der Gruppe*, Sonderheft 25 der Kölner Zeitschrift für Soziologie und Sozialpsychologie, pp. 420–50.

KRECKEL, R. (Ed.) (1983) 'Soziale Ungleichheiten', *Soziale Welt*, Sonderband 2, Göttingen.

KRÜGER, H.-H. (1985) *'Die Elvis-Tolle...' Lebensgeschichte und Jugendliche Alltagskultur in den 50er Jahren*, Opladen, Leske + Budrich.

KRÜGER, H.-H. (1988a) 'Einleitung', in KRÜGER, H.-H. (Ed.) *Handbuch der Jugendforschung*, Opladen, Leske + Budrich, pp. 1–11.

KRÜGER, H.-H. (1988b) 'Geschichte und Perspektiven der Jugendforschung', in KRÜGER, H.-H. (Ed.) *Handbuch der Jugendforschung*, Opladen, Leske + Budrich, pp. 13–26.

KRÜGER, H.-H. (1988c) 'Theoretische und methodoloigische Grundlagen der historischen Jungendforschung', in KRÜGER, H.-H. (Ed.) *Handbuch der Jugendforschung*, Opladen Leske + Budrich, pp. 207–30.

KRÜGER, H.-H., ECARIUS, J. and WENSIERSKI V., H.-J. (1988) 'Alterskonzepte in der biographischen Rekonstruktion von Jugendlichen', *Grounded. Arbeiten aus der Sozialforschung*, 4, pp. 41–57.

KRÜGER, H. (1986) 'Die Segmentierung des Berifsbildungssystems — eine bildungspolitische Barriere für Marktpositionen weiblicher Arbeitskräfte', in RUDOLPH, H. *et al.* (Eds) *Berufsverläufe von Frauen*, München, Juventa.

KRUMREY, H.-V. (1984) *Entwicklungsstukturen von Verhaltensstandarden. Eine soziologische Prozeßanalyse auf der Grundlage deutscher Anstands- und Manierenbücher von 1870 bis 1970*, Frankfurt/M., Suhrkamp.

KUMAR, K. (1986) *Prophecy and Progress*, London, Pelican.

LABOUR MARKET QUARTERLY REPORT (LMQR) Sheffield, The Training Agency Employment Department Group, MSC.

LACEY, C. (1970) *Hightown Grammar*, Manchester, Manchester University Press.

LAING, R.D. (1976) *The Politics of the Family*, Harmondsworth, Penguin.

LAING, R.D. and ESTERSON, A. (1964) *Sanity, Madness and the Family*, London, Tavistock.

LANG, S. (1985) *Lebensbedingungen und Lebensqualität von Kindern*, Frankfurt/M., Campus.

LANGER, I. (1987) 'Familie im Wandel', *Frauenforschung*, 5, 1/2, pp. 165–88.

LASCH, C. (1977) *A Haven in a Heartless World*, New York, Free Press.

LASH, S. and URRY, J. (1987) *The End of Organized Capitalism*, Cambridge, Cambridge University Press.

LASLETT, P. (1971) *The World We Have Lost*, 2nd ed., London, Methuen.

LAU, E. and KELCHNER, M. (1927) 'Die jugendliche Arbeiterschaft und die Arbeitslosigkeit' in THURNWALD, R. (Ed.) *Die neue Jugend. Forschungen zur Völkerpsychologie und Soziologie*, Bd. 4, Leipzig, Barth, pp. 321–40.

LAUDER, H. and BROWN, P. (Ed.) (1988) *Education: In Search of a Future*, Lewes, Falmer Press.

LEDIG, M., NISSEN, U. and KREIL, M. (1987) *Kinder und Wohnumwelt. Eine Literaturanalyse zur Straßensozialisation*, München, DJI.

LEES, S. (1986) *Losing Out: Sexuality and Adolescent Girls*, London, Hutchinson.

References

LENZ, K. (1986) *Alltagswelten von Jugendlichen: Eine empirische Studie über jugendliche Handlungstypen*, Frankfurt/M./New York, Campus.
LENZ, K. (1988) *Die vielen Gesichter der Jugendlichen. Jugendliche Handlungstypen in biografischen Portraits*, Frankfurt/M./New York, Campus.
LEONARD, D. (1980) *Sex and Generation*, London, Tavistock.
LEONARD, D. and HOOD-WILLIAMS, J. (1988) *Families*, London, Macmillan.
LEONARD, D. and SPEAKMAN, M. (1986) 'Women in the family: Companions or caretakers?' in BEECHEY, V. and WHITELEGG, E. (Eds) *Women in Britain Today*, Milton Keynes, Open University Press, pp. 8–76.
LEONTJEW, A.N. (1982) *Tätigkeit, Bewußtsein, Persönlichkeit*, Köln, Pahl Rugenstein.
LEVY, R. (1977) *Der Lebenslauf als Statusbiographie*, Stuttgart, Enke.
LEWIN, K. and SCHACHER, M. (1981) *Studienberechtigte 79 — Studien- und Berufswahl im Wandel. Bestandsaufnahme und Vergleich mit Studienberechtigten 76. HIS-Hochschulplanung*, Bd. 35, Hannover, HIS.
LIDDIARD, M. and HUTSON, S. (1989) 'Homeless and vulnerable? A study of young people in Wales', paper presented to the BSA Annual conference, Plymouth Polytechnic, March.
LIEBAU, E. (1982) 'Das Jugendbild der Politik', *Neue Sammlung*, 5, pp. 438–458.
LIEBAU, E. and HUBER, L. (1985) 'Die Kulturen der Fächer', *Neue Sammlung*, 25, 3, pp. 314–49.
LIEGLE, L. (1987) *Welten der Kindheit und Familie. Beiträge zu einer pädagogischen und kulturvergleichenden Sozialisationsforschung*, Weinheim, Juventa.
LIMBACH, J. (1986) 'Wie männlich ist die Rechtswissenschaft?' in HAUSEN, K. and NOWOTNY, H. (Eds) *Wie männlich ist die Wissenschaft?* Frankfurt/M., Suhrkamp, pp. 87–107.
LINDNER, R. (1983) 'Straße — Straßenjunge — Straßenbande. Ein zivilisationstheoretischer Streifzug', *Zeitschrift für Volkskunde* 79, 2, pp. 192–208.
LINDNER, R. et al. (1976) *Freizeit im Arbeiterviertel. Ästhetik und Kommunikation.* 7, 24.
LINDNER, R. and WIEBE, H.-H. (Eds) (1985) *Verborgen im Licht. Neues zur Jugendfrage*, Frankfurt/M., Syndikat.
LIPP, W. (1979) 'Kulturtypen, kulturelle Symbole, Handlungswelt. Zur Plurivalenz von Kultur', *Kölner Zeitschrift für Soziologie und Sozialpsychologie*, 31, pp. 450–84.
LLEWELLYN, M. (1980) 'Studying girls at school: The implications of confusion', in DEEM, R. (Ed.) *Schooling for Women's Work*, London, Routledge & Kegan Paul, pp. 42–51.
LONEY, M. (1979) 'The politics of job creation', in CRAIG, G., MAYO, M. and SHARMAN, N. (Eds) *Jobs and Community Action*, London, Routledge & Kegan Paul.
LOPÉZ-BLASCO, A, (1983) *Sozialisationsprozesse und Identitätskrise spanischer Jugendlicher in der Bundesrepublik Deutschland*, München, DJI.
LUKES, S. (1984) 'The future of British Socialism?' in PIMLOTT. B. (Ed.) *Fabian Essays in Socialist Thought*, London, Heinemann, pp. 269–83.
LUNDGREEN, P. (1977) 'Historische Bildungsforschung', in RÜRUP, R. (Ed.) *Historische Sozialwissenschaft*, Göttingen, Vandenhoeck & Ruprecht, pp. 96–126.
LUNDGREEN, P. (1980) *Sozialgeschichte der deutschen Schule im Überblick. Teil 1: 1770–1918, Teil 2: 1918–1980*, 2 Bde., Göttingen, Vandenhoeck & Ruprecht.
LÜSCHER, K. (1975) 'Perspektiven einer Soziologie der Sozialisation. Die Entwicklun der Rolle des Kindes', *Zeitschrift für Soziologie*, 4, 4, pp. 359–79.
LÜSCHER, K. (Ed.) (1979) *Sozialpolitik für das Kind*, Stuttgart, Klett-Cotta.
LÜSCHER, K. et al. (Eds) (1988) *Die 'postmoderne' Familie. Familiale Strategien und Familienpolitik im Übergang*, 2 Bde., Konstanz, Universitätsverlag.
LUTZ, J. et al. (1983) *Jugendsubkulturen — Produktionsstätten von Identität — Orte der sozialen Reproduktion. Ethnographische Studie einer Clique von Arbeiterjugendlichen*,

Diplomarbeit Institut für Erziehungswissenschaft der Universität Marburg.

MAC AN GHAILL, M. (1989) *Young, Gifted and Black*, Milton Keynes, Open University Press.

MACDONALD, M. (1980) 'Socio-cultural reproduction and women's education', in DEEM, R. (Ed.) *Schooling for Women's Work*, London, Routledge & Kegan Paul.

MACDONALD, M. (1981) 'Schooling and the reproduction of class and gender relations', in DALE, R. *et al.* (Eds) *Education and the State Volume 2: Politics, Patriarchy and Practice*, Lewes, Falmer Press, pp. 159–78.

MCGRATH, K. (1973) 'Survey on pocket money', *Where*, 77, pp. 78–82.

MCINTOSH, M. (1978) 'The state and the oppression of women', in KUHN, A. and WOLPE, A.M. (Eds) *Feminism and Materialism*, London, Routledge & Kegan Paul, pp. 254–89.

MCKEE, L. and O'BRIEN, L. (Eds) (1982) *The Father Figure*, London, Tavistock.

MACLENNAN, E. (1982) *Child Labour in London*, London, Low Pay Unit.

MACLENNAN, E., FITZ, J. and SULLIVAN, J. (1985) *Working Children*, London, Low Pay Unit.

MACLEOD, M. and SARAGA, E. (1988) 'Challenging the orthodoxy: Towards a feminist theory and practice', *Feminist Review*, 28, pp. 16–55.

MCROBBIE, A. (1978) 'Working class girls and the culture of femininity', in CCCS WOMEN'S STUDIES GROUP (Ed.) *Women Take Issue*, London, Hutchinson, pp. 96–108.

MCROBBIE, A. (1980) 'Settling accounts with subcultures', *Screen Education*, 34, pp. 37–50.

MCROBBIE, A. and GARBER, J. (1976) 'Girls and subcultures: An exploration', in HALL, S. and JEFFERSON, T. (Eds) *Resistance Through Rituals*, London, Hutchinson, pp. 209–27.

MCROBBIE, A. and MCCABE, T. (Eds) (1980) *Feminism For Girls: An Adventure Story*, London, Routledge & Kegan Paul.

MCROBBIE, A. and NAVA, M. (Eds) (1984) *Gender and Generation*, London, Macmillan Youth Questions.

MAHONY, P. (1985) *Schooling for the Boys?* London, Hutchinson Explorations in Feminism.

MANNHEIM, K. (1927) 'The problem of generations', in KECSKMETI, P. (Ed.) (1952) *Essays on the Sociology of Knowledge*, London, pp. 276–320.

MANNHEIM, K. (1928) 'Das Problem der Generationen', *Kölner Vierteljahreshefte für Soziologie*, 7, 2, pp. 157–85, 3, pp. 309–30.

MARSDEN, D. (1969) *Mothers Alone*, London, Allen Lane.

MARSH, R.M. (1967) *Comparative Sociology: A Codification of Cross-Sectional Analysis*, New York, Harcourt.

MARSHALL, G., NEWBY, H., ROSE, D. and VOGLER, C. (1988) *Social Class in Modern Britain*, London, Hutchinson.

MARSHALL, T.H. (1950) *Citizenship and Social Class*, Cambridge, Cambridge University Press.

MARSLAND, D. (1987) 'Introduction: Education and youth', in MARSLAND, D. (Ed.) *Education and Youth*, Lewes, Falmer Press, pp. 1–20.

MARTIN, N. *et al.* (1976) *Understanding Children Talking*, Harmondsworth, Penguin.

MASSEY, D. (1985) 'Geography and class', in COATES, D. *et al.* (Eds) *A Socialist Anatomy of Britain*, Cambridge, Polity Press.

MATHIEU, N.-C. (1977) *Ignored by Some, Denied by Others*, London, WRRC Explorations in Feminism.

MATTIESEN, U. (1988) 'Outfit und Ich-Finish. Zur beschleunigten Wandlungstypik der gegenwärtigen Bekleidungsmoden', *Soziale Welt*, Sonderband 6, pp. 414–48.

MATZA, D. (1964) *Delinquency and Drift*, Englewood Cliffs, NJ, Prentice Hall.

MATZA, D. (1969) *Becoming Deviant*, Englewood Cliffs, NJ, Prentice Hall.

MAUSE DE, L. (Ed.) (1977) *Hört ihr die Kinder weinen. Eine psychogenetische Geschichte der Kindheit*, Frankfurt/M., Suhrkamp.

MAUSS, M. (1970) *The Gift*, London, Routledge & Kegan Paul.

MAYALL, B. and PETRIE, P. (1983) *Childminding and Day Nurseries: What Kind of Care?* London, Heinemann Educational.

MEAD, M. (1970) *Jugend und Sexualität in primitiven Gesellschaften*, 3 Bde., München, dtv.

MEGA, W. *et al.* (Eds) (1987) *Modern German Sociology*, New York, Columbia University Press.

MEHLER, F. (1986) 'Jugendsubkulturen und Jugendkultur', *deutsche jugend*, 34, 7–8, pp. 304–10.

MEHRLÄNDER, U. (1983) *Türkische Jugendliche — keine beruflichen Chancen in Deutschland?* Bonn, Neue Gesellschaft.

MEHRLÄNDER, U. (1986) *Forschungsbericht. Situation der ausländischen Arbeitnehmer und ihrer Familienangehörigen in der Bundesrepublik Deutschland. Repräsentativuntersuchung '85*, Hrg. v. BMAS, Bonn.

MERTENS, D. and PARMENTIER, K. (1982) 'Zwei Schwellen — acht Problembereiche. Grundzüge eines Diskussions- und Aktionsrahmens zu den Beziehungen zwischen Bildungs- und Beschäftigungssystem', in MERTENS, D. (Ed.) *Konzepte der Arbeitsmarkt- und Berufsforschung. Eine Forschungsinventur des IAB*, Beitr 70, Nürnberg, pp. 357–96.

MERTENS, G. (1977) 'Strukturen türkischer Migrantenfamilien in ihrer Heimat und in der Bundesrepublik Deutschland', in MERTENS, G. and AKPINAR, Ü. (Eds) *Türkische Migrantenfamilien*, Bonn, Verband der Initiativen in der Ausländerarbeit, pp. 9–134.

METZ-GÖCKEL, S. (1987) 'Licht und Schatten der Koedukation', *Zeitschrift für Pädagogik*, 33, pp. 454–74.

MICHEL, K.M. (1986) 'Über das Verhältnis von Jugendkultur und Offizialkultur', in DEUTSCHER WERKBUND E.V./WÜRTTEMBERGISCHER KUNSTVEREIN (Ed.) *Schock und Schöpfung. Jugendästhetik im 20. Jahrhundert*, Darmstadt/Neuwied, Luchterhand, pp. 12–15.

MIHELIC, M. (1984) *Jugoslawische Jugendliche. Intraethnische Beziehungen und ethnisches Selbstbewußtsein*, München, DJI.

MILLER, F.J.W. (1974) *The School Years in Newcastle upon Tyne 1952–62*, Oxford, Oxford University Press.

MILLER, F.J.W. *et al.* (1960) *Growing Up in Newcastle upon Tyne*, Oxford, Oxford University Press for the Nuffield Foundation.

MILLETT, D. (1970) *Sexual Politics*, New York, Doubleday.

MILNER, D. (1983) *Children and Race: Ten Years On*, London, Ward Lock Education.

MITCHELL, A. (1985) *Children in the Middle: Living Through Divorce*, London, Tavistock.

MITCHELL, J. and OAKLEY, A. (Eds) (1977) *The Rights and Wrongs of Women*, London, Penguin.

MITTERAUER, M. (Ed.) (1983) *Damit es nicht verlorengeht*, Köln/Wien.

MITTERAUER, M. (1986) *Sozialgeschichte der Jugend*, Frankfurt/M., Suhrkamp.

MOLNAR, P. and ZINNEKER, J. (forthcoming) 'Jugend in Westdeutschland und in Ungarn 1984/85', in OLK, T. (Ed.) *Sozialer Wandel der Lebensphase Jugend in interkultureller Perspektive*, Weinheim/München, Juventa.

MOOSER, J. (1983) 'Auflösung des proletarischen Milieus', *Soziale Welt*, 34, 3, pp. 270–306.

MORRIS, A. and GILLAR, H. (Eds) (1983) *Providing Criminal Justice for Children*, London, Edward Arnold.

MORRIS, L. (1984) 'Redundancy and patterns of household finance', *Sociological Review*, 32, 3, pp. 503–23.

References

MORRIS, L. (1985) 'Local social networks and domestic organization: A study of redundant steel workers and their wives', *Sociological Review*, 33, 2, pp. 327–42.

MUCHOW, H.H. (1959) *Sexualreife und Sozialstruktur der Jugend*, Reinbek, Rowohlt.

MÜHLFELD, C. *et al.* (1987) *Lebenzusammenhang und planung der zweiten Generation türkischer Arbeitsmigranten*, Bamberg, Bayerisches Statasministerium für Arbeit und Sozialordnung.

MÜLLER-SPUDE, G. *et al.* (1985) 'Geschlechtsrollenkonflikte. Untersuchungen zur schulischen und familialen Situation türkischer Berufsschülerinnen', in ARABIN, C. *et al.* (Eds) *Türkischer Frauenalltag in Heimat und Fremde, Kasseler Materialien zur Ausländerpolitik*, 4, Kassel, Gesamthochschule.

MUNGHAM, G. and PEARSON, G. (Eds) (1976) *Working Class Youth Culture*, London, Routledge & Kegan Paul.

MÜNCHNER STADTMUSEUM (Ed.) (n.d.) *Vater, Mutter, Kind. Bilder und Zeugnisse aus zwei Jahrhunderten*, München, Süddeutscher Verlag.

MURCH, M. (1980) *Justice and Welfare in Divorce*, London, Sweet and Maxwell.

MURCOTT, A. (1983) '"It's a pleasure to cook for him": Food, mealtimes and gender in some South Wales households', in GAMARNIKOW, E. *et al.* (Eds) *The Public and the Private*, London, Heinemann.

MURDOCK, G. and McCRON, R. (1976) 'Consciousness of class and consciousness of generation', in HALL, S. and JEFFERSON, T. (Eds) *Resistance Through Rituals*, London, Hutchinson, pp. 192–208.

MURRAY, J. (1988) 'Life after Henry Ford', *Marxism Today*, October, pp. 8–13.

MUSIAL, M. (1982) 'Jugendbewegung und Emanzipation der Frau', Dissertation, Essen, Universität-Gesamthochschule.

MUTSCHLER, S. (1983) 'Ländliche Kindheit in Lebenserinnerungen. Familien- und Kinderleben in einem württembergischen Arbeiterbauerndorf um die Jahrhundertwende', Dissertation, Tübingen, Universität.

NATIONAL CHILD DEVELOPMENT STUDY (1958) *Report*, London, City University.

NATIONAL ECONOMIC DEVELOPMENT OFFICE (1989) *Defusing the Demographic Timebomb*, London, NEDO Books.

NEIDHARDT, F. (1987) 'Jugend im Spiegel von Umfrageforschung und Statistik', mimeo, Köln, Forschungsinstitut für Soziologie.

NEUE GESELLSCHAFT FÜR BILDENDE KUNST E.V./STAATLICHE KUNSTHALLE BERLIN (Ed.) (1980) *Die gesellschaftliche Wirklichkeit der Kinder in der bildenden Kunst*, Berlin, Elefanten Press.

NEULOH, O. and ZILIUS, W. (1982) *Die Wandervögel*, Göttingen, Vandenhoek und Ruprecht.

NEUMANN, K. (Ed.) (1981) *Kindsein*, Göttingen, Vandenhoek und Ruprecht.

NEW, C. and DAVID, M. (1985) *For the Children's Sake: Making Childcare More Than Women's Business*, Harmondsworth, Penguin.

NEWBY, H. (1977) *The Deferential Worker*, London, Allen Lane.

NEWBY, H. *et al.* (Eds) (1985) *Restructuring Capital: Recession and Reorganization in Industrial Society*, London, Macmillan.

NEWSON, J. and E. (1963) *Patterns of Infant Care in an Urban Community*, London, George Allen & Unwin.

NEWSON, J. and E. (1968) *Four Years Old in an Urban Community*, London, George Allen & Unwin.

NEWSON, J. and E. (1976) *Seven Years Old in the Home Environment*, London, Hutchinson.

NEWSON, J. and E. (n.d.) *Childhood into Adolescence*, unpublished ms.

NEWSON, J., NEWSON, E. and BARNES, P. (1977) *Perspectives on School at Seven Years Old*, London, George Allen & Unwin.

NIESSEN, M. and PESCHAR, J. (Eds) (1982a) *Comparative Research and Education. Strategy and Applications in Eastern and Western Europe*, Oxford, Oxford University Press.

NIESSEN, M. and PESCHAR, J. (Eds) (1982b) *International Comparative Research. Problems of Theory, Methodology and Organization in Eastern und Western Europe,* Oxford, Oxford University Press.

NIESSEN, M., PESCHAR, J. and KOURILSKY, C. (Eds) (1984) *International Comparative Research. Social Structures and Public Institutions in Eastern and Western Europe,* Oxford, Pergamon Press.

NIETHAMMER, L. (Ed.) (1979) *Wohnen im Wandel. Beiträge zur Geschichte des Alltags in der bürgerlichen Gesellschaft,* Wuppertal, Hammer.

NIETHAMMER, L. (Ed.) (1980) *Lebenserfahrung und kollektives Gedächtnis. Die Praxis der 'Oral History',* Frankfurt/M., Suhrkamp.

NOBLE, G. (1975) *Children in Front of the Small Screen,* London, Constable.

OECD (1985) *Education in Modern Society,* Paris, OECD.

OERTER, R. (Ed.) (1985) *Lebensbewältigung im Jungendalter,* Weinheim, Edition Psychologie.

OFFE, C. (1983) 'Arbeit als soziologische Schlüsselkategorie', in MATTHES, J. (Ed.) *Krise der Arbeitsgesellschaft,* Frankfurt/M./New York, Campus, pp. 38–65.

OFFE, C. (1985) *Disorganized Capitalism,* Cambridge, Cambridge University Press.

OFFICE OF POPULATION CENSUSES AND SURVEYS (1981) *General Household Survey 1979,* London, HMSO.

OFFICE OF POPULATION CENSUSES AND SURVEYS (1982) *General Household Survey 1980,* London, HMSO.

ÖKER, T. and ÖNAL, R. (1986) 'Soziokulturelle Arbeit mit Einwandererjugendlichen', *Informationsdienst zur Ausländerarbeit,* 2, pp. 85–9.

OLBRICH, E. and TODT, E. (1984) *Probleme des Jugendalters. Neuere Sichtweisen,* Berlin, Springer.

OLK, T. (1985) 'Jugend und gesellschaftliche Differenzierung — Zur Entstrukturierung der Jugendphase', *Zeitschrift für, Pädagogik,* 31, pp. 290–301.

OLK, T. (1986) 'Jugend und Gesellschaft. Entwurf für einen Perspektivenwechsel in der sozialwissenschaftlichen Jugendforschung', in HEITMEYER, W. (Ed.) *Interdisziplinäre Jugendforschung,* Weinheim/München, Juventa, pp. 41–62.

OLK, T. (1988) 'Gesellschaftstheoretische Ansätze in der Jugendforschung', in KRÜGER, H.-H. (Ed.) *Handbuch der Jugendforschung,* Opladen, Leske + Budrich, pp. 113–34.

OPIE, I. and OPIE, P. (1969) *Children's Games in Street and Playground,* Oxford, Clarendon.

OSWALD, H., KRAPMANN, L. and FRICKE, C. (forthcoming) *Alltag der Schulkinder. Methoden und Ergebnisse eines qualitativen Forschungsprojektes über Kinder zwischen sechs und zwölf Jahren.*

PAHL, R. (1984) *Divisions of Labour,* Oxford, Basil Blackwell.

PAHL, R. (1988) 'Some remarks on informal network, social polarization and the social structure', *The International Journal of Urban and Regional Research.*

PARKER, H., BAKX, K. and NEWCOMBE, R. (1988) *Living with Heroin,* Milton Keynes, Open University Press.

PARSONS, K. (1988) *Young People: Trainers and Trainees,* various mimeos, Plymouth, Polytechnic South West.

PARSONS, T. (1951) *The Social System,* New York, Free Press.

PAYNE, J. (1987) 'Does Unemployment Run in Families?' *Sociology,* 21, 2, pp. 199–214

PEARSON, G. (1976) 'Paki-bashing' in a north east Lancashire cotton town: A case study and its history, in MUNGHAM, G. and PEARSON. G. (Eds) *Working class Youth Culture,* London, Routledge & Regan Paul, pp. 48–81.

PEARSON, G. (1983) *Hooligans,* London, Macmillan.

PEARSON, G. (1987) *The New Heroin Users,* Oxford, Basil Blackwell.

PEISERT, H. (Ed.) (1984) *Studiensituation und studentische Orientierung. Eine empirische*

References

Untersuchung im WS 1982/83. Bundesminister für Bildung und Wissenschaft, Bonn.

PEISERT, H. *et al.* (1981) *Abiturienten und Ausbildungswandel*, Weinheim/Basel, Beltz.

PERKS, R. (Ed.) (1987) 'Childhood', special issue of *Oral History*, 15.2, Autumn, Dept of Sociology, University of Essex.

PIACHAUD, D. (1981) *Children and Poverty*, Poverty Research Series, 9, London, Child Poverty Action Group.

PIACHAUD, D. (1982) *Family Incomes Since the War*, Study Committee on the Family, Occasional Paper 9.

PIAGET, J. (1953) *The Origin of Intelligence in the Child*, London, Routledge & Kegan Paul.

PIEPER, M. (1978) *Erwachsenenalter und Lebenslauf. Zur Soziologie der Altersstufen*, München, Kögel.

PINCHBECK, I. and HEWITT, M. (1969) *Children in English Society: Vol 1 — From Tudor Times to the Eighteenth Century; Vol 2 — From the Eighteeth Century to the Children's Act 1948*. London, Routledge & Kegan Paul.

POLLOCK, L. (1983) *Forgotten Children: Parent-child Relations from 1500–1900*, Cambridge, Cambridge University Press.

POLLOCK, L. (1987) *A Lasting Relationship: Parents and Children over Three Centuries 1600–1900*, London, Fourth Estate.

POPP, V. (Ed.) (1969) *Initiation: Zeremonien der Statusänderung und des Rollenwechsels*, Reihe Suhrkamp Wissen, Bd. 4, Frankfurt/M., Suhrkamp.

PORTELE, G. (1985) 'Habitus und Lernen', *Neue Sammlung*, 25, 3, pp. 93–113.

POSTMAN, N. (1982) *The Disappearance of Childhood*, New York, Delacorte Press.

POSTMAN, N. (1983) *Das Verschwinden der Kindheit*, Frankfurt/M., S. Fischer.

PREUSS-LAUSITZ, U. *et al.* (Eds) (1983) *Kriegskinder, Konsumkinder, Krisenkinder — Zur Sozialisationsgeschichte seit dem Zweiten Weltkrieg*, Weinheim/Basel, Beltz.

PREUSS-LAUSITZ, U. (1987) *Wandlungstendenzen in der institutionalisierten Erziehung, insbesondere der Schule*. Vortrag in der evangelischen Akademie Hofgeismar, MS.

PRICE, R. and BAIN, G.S. (1988) 'The labour force', in HALSEY, A.M. (Ed.) *British Social Trends Since 1900*, 2nd revised ed., London, Macmillan, pp. 162–201.

PROJEKTGRUPPE JUGENDBÜRO (1975) *Die Lebenswelt von Hauptschülern. Ergebnisse einer Untersuchung*, München, Juventa.

PROJEKTGRUPPE JUGENDBÜRO (1977) *Subkultur und Familie als Orientierungsmuster*, München, Juventa.

PRYCE, K. (1979) *Endless Pressure*, Harmondsworth, Penguin.

RABE-KLEBERG, U. and ZEIHER, H. (1984) 'Kindheit und Zeit. Über das Eindringen moderner Zeitorganisation in die Lebensbedingungen von Kindern', *Zeitschrift für Sozialisationsforschung und Erziehungssoziologie*, 4, 1, pp. 29–43.

RAFFE, D. (1984) 'The transition from school to work and the recession: evidence from the Scottish School Leavers Surveys, 1977–1983', *British Journal of Sociology of Education*, 5, 3, pp. 247–65.

RAFFE, D. (1986) 'Change and continuity in the youth labour market', in ALLEN, S. *et al.* (Eds) *The Experience of Unemployment*, London, Macmillan, pp. 45–60.

RAFFE, D. (1988a) 'Going with the grain: Youth training in transition', in BROWN, S. (Ed.) *Education in Transition*, Edinburgh, Scottish Council for Research in Education, pp. 110–23.

RAFFE, D. (Ed.) (1988b) *Education and the Youth Labour Market*, Lewes, Falmer Press.

RAFFE, D. and COURTNEY, G. (1988) '16–18 on both sides of "the border"', in RAFFE, D. (Ed.) *Education and the Youth Labour Market*, Basingstoke, Falmer Press, pp. 12–39.

RAMPTON, M. (1987a) 'Uses of English in a multilingual British peergroup', Ph.D. thesis, University of London Institute of Education.

RAMPTON, M. (1987b) *A Non-Educational View of ESL in Britain*, Adolescents and

Language Use Working Papers No. 1, Sociological Research Unit, University of London Institute of Education.

RANG, B. (1981) 'Zur Diskussion um "Schulstress" in der Geschichte des deutschen Bildungswesens', in ZIMMER, G. (Ed.) *Persönlichkeitsentwicklung und Gesundheit im Schulalter*, Frankfurt/M./New York, Campus, pp. 214–37.

RANSON, S., TAYLOR, B. and BRIGHOUSE, T. (1986) *The Revolution in Education and Training*, Harlow, Longman.

RAPOPORT, R.N. et al. (Eds) (1982) *Families in Britain*, London, Routledge & Kegan Paul.

RAPOPORT, R., RAPOPORT, R.N. and STRELITZ, S. (1977) *Fathers, Mothers and Others*, London, Routledge & Kegan Paul.

RASCHKE, J. (1985) *Soziale Bewegungen. Ein historisch-systematischer Grundriß*. Frankfurt/M./New York, Campus.

RAUSCHENBACH, B. (1988) *Was ist an dem heuristischen Konzept der Selbständigkeit in besonderer Weise gegenwartsbezogen?* Berlin, MS.

REES, T.L. and ATKINSON, P. (Eds) (1982) *Youth Unemployment and State Intervention*, London, Routledge & Kegan Paul.

REILLEY, D. (1983) *War in the Nursery*, London, Virago.

RERRICH, M.S. (1983) 'Veränderte Elternschaft — Entwicklungen in der familialen Arbeit mit Kindern seit 1950', *Soziale Welt*, 34, 4, pp. 420–49.

REULECKE, J. (1987) 'Probleme einer Sozial- und Mentalitätsgeschichte der Nachkriegszeit', *Geschichte des Westens*, 2, 1, pp. 7–25.

RICH, J. (1968) *Interviewing Children and Adolescents*, London, Macmillan.

RICHARDS, M. (1982) *The Integration of a Child into a Social World*, Cambridge, Cambridge University Press.

RICHARDS, M. and DYSON, M. (1981) *Separating Parents and Their Children: A Pilot Study*, unpublished ms.

RICHARDS, M. and DYSON, M. (1982) *Separation, Divorce and the Development of Children: A Review*, mimeo, Child and Development Group, University of Cambridge.

RICHTER, J. (1984) *Das Geraniengefängnis*, Hamburg, Rowohlt.

RILEY, D. (1983) *The War in the Nursery: Theories of the Child and Mother*, London, Virago.

ROBERTS, K. (1968) 'The entry into employment: an approach towards a general theory', *Sociological Review*, 16, 2, pp. 165–84.

ROBERTS, K. (1983) *Youth and Leisure*, London, George Allen & Unwin.

ROBERTS, K. (1984) *School Leavers and their Prospects*, Milton Keynes, Open University Press.

ROBERTS, K. (1989) 'ESRC — Young people and society' in COSIN, B. et al. (Eds) *School, Work and Equality*, Milton Keynes, Open University Press, pp. 263–86.

RODAX, K. and SPITZ, N. (1982) *Soziale Umwelt und Schulerfolg*, Weinheim/Basel, Beltz.

ROLFF, H.-G. and ZIMMERMANN, P. (1985) *Kindheit im Wandel. Eine Einführung in die Sozialisation im Kindesalter*, Weinheim/Basel, Beltz.

ROSENMAYR, L. (1986) 'Über Familien in den Strukturumbrüchen heute', *Archiv für Wissenschaft und Praxis in der sozialen Arbeit*, 17, 1, pp. 48–73.

ROSSER, C. and HARRIS, C. (1965) *The Family and Social Change*, London, Routledge.

ROTH, L. (1983) *Die Erfindung des Jugendlichen*, München, Juventa.

ROWNTREE, R. (1901) *Poverty: A Study of Town Life*, London, Macmillan.

RUTTER, M. and MADGE, N. (1976) *Cycles of Disadvantage*, London, Heinemann for the DHSS.

SACK, H.-G. (1980) 'Jugend, Sportverein und sozialer Wandel', in QUELL, M. (Ed.) *Sport, Soziologie und Erziehung*, Berlin, Bartels & Warnitz, pp. 52–82.

SACK, H.-G. (1986) 'Zur Bedeutung des Sports in der Jugendkultur. Eine Reanalyse

References

der Studie Jugend '81', in PILZ, G.A. (Ed.) *Sport und Verein*, Reinbek, Rowohlt, pp. 114–31.

SAMUEL, L. (1983) 'The making of a school resister: A case study of Australian working class secondary schoolgirls', in BROWNE, R.K. and FOSTER, L.E. (Eds) *Sociology of Education*, 3rd ed., Sydney, Macmillan, chapter 34.

SANDER, U. and VOLLBRECHT, R. (1987) *Kinder und Jugendliche im Medienzeitalter*, Opladen, Leske + Budrich.

SAUL, K., FLEMMING, J., STEGMANN, D. and WITT, P.-C. (Eds) (1982) *Arbeiterfamilien im Kaiserreich. Materialien zur Sozialgeschichte in Deutschland 1871–1914*, Königstein/Ts., Athenäum.

SCARMAN, LORD (1982) *The Brixton Disorders: 10–12 April 1981*, Harmondsworth, Penguin.

SCARRE, G. *et al.* (Eds) (1989) *Children, Parents and Politics*, Cambridge, Cambridge University Press.

SCHELSKY, H. (1957) *Die skeptische Generation. Eine Soziologie der deutschen Jugend*, Düsseldorf/Köln, Diederichs.

SCHERER, K.-J. (1988) *Jugend und soziale Bewegung. Zur politischen Soziologie der bewegten Jugend in Deutschland*, Opladen, Leske + Budrich.

SCHIFFAUER, W. (1983) *Die Gewalt der Ehre, Erklärungen zu einem türkisch-deutschen Sexualkonflikt*, Frankfurt/M., Suhrkamp.

SCHIFFAUER, W. (1987) *Die Bauern von Subay. Das Leben in einem türkischen Dorf*, Stuttgart, Klett-Cotta.

SCHLUMBOHM, J. (1981) '"Traditionale" Kollektivität und "moderne" Individualität: Einige Fragen und Thesen für eine historische Sozialisationsforschung. Kleines Bürgertum und gehobenes Bürgertum Deutschlands im späten 18. Jahrhundert als Beispiel', in VIERHAUS, R. (Ed.) *Bürger und Bürgerlichkeit im Zeitalter der Aufklärung. (Wolfenbütteler Studien zur Aufklärung, Bd. 8)*, Heidelberg, Schneider, pp. 265–320.

SCHLUMBOHM, J. (Ed.) (1983) *Kinderstuben. Wie Kinder zu Bauern, Bürgern, Aristokraten wurden, 1700–1850*, München, dtv.

SCHLÜTER, A. (1986) *Neue Hüte — alte Hüte? Gewerbliche Berufsbildung für Mädchen zu Beginn des 20. Jahrhunderts — zur Geschichte ihrer Institutionalisierung*, Düsseldorf, Schwann.

SCHNEIDER, H. (1985) *Studentenbefragungen in der Bundesrepublik Deutschland*, Pfaffenweiler, Centaurus.

SCHNITZLER, K. (1983) *Das soziale Bild der Studentenschaft in der Bundesrepublik Deutschland — Ergebnisse der 10. Sozialerhebung des Deutschen Studentenwerks im Sommersemester 1982*, Bad Honnef, Bock.

SCHOLL, V. (1985) 'Ein Beispiel', in JENS, W. (Ed.) *Studentenalltag*, München, Knaur, pp. 77–84.

SCHOOLS HEALTH EDUCATION UNIT (1988) *Schoolchildren and Drugs*, Exeter, University of Exeter.

SCHRADER, A., NIKLES, B.W. and GRIESE, H.M. (1986) *Die zweite Generation. Sozialisation und Akkulturation ausländischer Kinder in der Bundesrepublik*, Königstein/Ts., Athenäum.

SCHULZ, W. (1983) 'Von der Institution "Familie" zu den Teilbeziehungen zwischen Mann, Frau und Kind. Zum Strukturwandel von Ehe und Familie', *Soziale Welt*, 34, 4, pp. 401–19.

SCHWARZ, K. (1984) 'Eltern und Kinder in unvollständigen Familien', *Zeitschrift für Bevölkerungswissenschaft*, 10, 1, pp. 3–36.

SEABROOK, J. (1982) *Working Class Childhood*, London, Gollancz.

SEABROOK, J. (1987) 'Bringing up baby to enjoy the wealth of the nation', *The Guardian*, 24 August, p. 20.

SEBBA, M. (1987) 'London Jamaican and Black London English', in SUTCLIFFE, D. and WONG, A. (Eds) *The Language of Black Resistance*, Oxford, Basil Blackwell.

SEIDENSPINNER, G. and BURGER, A. *Mädchen '82*, München, DJI.

SEYFARTH-STUBENRAUTH, M. (1985) *Erziehung und Sozialisation in Arbeiterfamilien im Zeitraum 1870 bis 1914 in Deutschland*, 2 vol, Frankfurt/M./Bern/New York, Lang.

SHARPE, S. (1976) *Just Like a Girl*, London, Pelican.

SHAW, J. (1981) *Family, State and Complusory Education*, Open University Course E353 Unit 13, Milton Keynes, Open University Press.

SHEPHERD, P. (1985) 'The National Child Development Study: An introduction to the background of the study and the methods of data collection', *Working Paper No. 1*, NCDS User Support Group, City University.

SHIPMAN, M.D. (1972) *Childhood: A Sociological Perspective*, Windsor, NFER.

SHORTER, E. (1983) *Die Geburt der modernen Familie*, Reinbek, Rowohlt.

SIEDER, R. (1984) 'Geschichten erzählen und Wissenschaft treiben. Interviewtexte zum Arbeiteralltag', in BOTZ, G. and WEIDENHOLZER, J. (Eds) *Mündliche Geschichte und Arbeiterbewegung*, Wien, Böhlau, pp. 203–32.

SIEDER, R. (1986) '"Vata, derf i aufstehn?" Kindheitserfahrungen in Wiener Arbeiterfamilien um 1900', in EHALT, H.-C., HEIß, G. und STEKL, L. (Eds) *Glücklich ist, wer vergißt. . . . Das andere Wien um 1900*, Wien, Böhlau, pp. 39–89.

SIEDER, R. (1987) *Sozialgeschichte der Familie*, Frankfurt/M., Suhrkamp.

SILBEREISEN, R.K. and MONTADA, L. (Eds) (1983) *Entwicklungspsychologie. Ein Handbuch in Schlüsselbegriffen*, München, Urban + Schwarzenberg.

SIMON, B. (1988) *Bending the Rules: The Baker 'Reform of Education'*, London, Lawrence & Wishart.

SINUS-INSTITUT (1984) *Jugendforschung in der Bundesrepublik*, Opladen, Leske + Budrich.

SINUS-INSTITUT/INFRATEST SOZIALE FORSCHUNG (1982/3) *Veränderungen in der Motivationsstuktur Jugendlicher und junger Erwachsener*, 6 volumes, Heidelberg.

SKOLNICK, A. (1974) 'The limits of childhood', *Law and Contemporary Problems*, 39, pp. 38–77.

SMALL, P. (1984) *Police and People in London*, London, Policy Studies Institute.

SMART, C. (1984) *The Ties that Bind*, London, Routledge & Kegan Paul.

SMITH, D. (1981) 'New movements in the sociology of youth', *British Journal of Sociology*, 32, pp. 239–51.

SOLOMOS, J. (1985) 'Extended review: Youth training, unemployment and state policies' *Sociological Review*, 83, 2, pp. 343–53.

SOLOMOS, J. (1988) 'Institutionalized racism: Policies of marginalization in education and training', in COHEN, P. and BAINS, H. (Eds) *Multi-Racist Britain*, London, Macmillan, pp. 156–94.

SOMMERVILLE, C.J. (1982) *The Rise and Fall of Childhood*, Beverly Hills, CA., Sage.

SPECHT, F. and WEBER, M. (Eds) (1981) *Kinder in unserer Gesellschaft*, Göttingen, Vandenhoeck & Ruprecht.

SPEIER, M. (1976) 'The child as conversationalist: Some culture contact features of conversational interactions between adults and children', in HAMMERSLEY, M. and WOODS, P. (Eds) *The Process of Schooling*, London, Routledge & Kegan Paul, pp. 98–103.

SPENDER, D. and SARAH, E. (Eds) (1980) *Learning to Lose: Sexism and Education*, London, The Women's Press.

SPRINGHALL, J. (1986) *Coming of Age: Adolescents in Britain 1860–1960*, Dublin, Gill & Macmillan.

STACEY, M. (1960) *Tradition and Change*, Oxford, Oxford University Press.

STAMBOLIS, B. (1982) *Der Mythos der jungen Generation. Ein Beispiel zur politischen*

References

Geschichte der Weimarer Republik (Diss.), Bochum.

STATHAM, J. (1986) *Daughters and Sons: Experiences of Non-sexist Childraising*, Oxford, Basil Blackwell.

STATISTISCHES BUNDESAMT (Ed.) (1987) *Datenreport 2. Zahlen und Fakten über die Bundesrepublik Deutschland*, Bonn.

STEEDMAN, C. (1982) *The Tidy House: Little Girls' Writing*, London, Virago.

STEEDMAN, C. URWIN C. and WALKERDINE, V. (1985) *Language, Gender and Childhood*, London, Routledge & Kegan Paul.

STEGMANN, H. (1987) 'Das duale System in den 90er Jahren. Ausbildungs- und Beschäftigungschancen der geburtsschwachen Jahrgänge', *Recht der Jugend und des Bildungswesens*, 31, 6, pp. 423–41.

STERN, H.L. and ALEXANDER, R.A. (1977) 'Cohort, age and time of measurement: Biomorphic considerations', in DATAN, N. and REESE, H. (Eds) *Life Span Developmental Psychology* Dialectic Perspective on Experimental Research, New York, Academic Press.

STRIKSRUD, A. (Ed.) (1984) *Jugend und Werte. Aspekte einer Politischen Psychologie des Jugendalters*, Weinheim/Basel, Beltz.

STRAUBE, H. (1987) *Türkisches Leben in der Bundesrepublik*, Frankfurt/M./New York, Campus.

STÜWE, G. (1982) *Türkische Jugendliche. Eine Untersuchung in Berlin-Kreuzberg*, Bensheim, päd. extra.

SUTCLIFFE, D. (1982) *British Black English*, Oxford, Basil Blackwell.

SUTCLIFFE, D. (1984) 'British Black English and West Indian Creoles' in TRUDGILL, P. (Ed.) *Language in the British Isles*, Cambridge, Cambridge University Press.

SUTTON-SMITH, B. (1986) *Toys as Culture*, New York, Gardner Press.

SZWARTZ, D. (1981) 'Class educational systems and labour markets', *Archives — European Journal of Sociology*, 22, pp. 235–53.

SZALAI, A. et al. (1972) *The Use of Time. A cross-national Comparative Survey of Daily Activities of Urban and Suburban Populations in Twelve Countries*, The Hague, Mouton.

SZALAI, A., PETRELLA, R., ROKKAN, S. and SCHEUCH, E.K. (Eds) (1977) *Cross-National Comparative Survey Research. Theory and Practice*, Oxford, Pergamon.

TAYLOR, I., WALTON, P. and YOUNG, J. (1973) *The New Criminology*, London, Routledge & Kegan Paul.

TENFELDE, K. (1982) 'Großstadtjugend in Deutschland vor 1914. Eine historisch-demografische Annäherung', *Vierteljahresschrift für Sozial- und Wirtschaftsgeschichte*, 69, 2, pp. 182–218.

TEUTEBERG, H.A. and WISCHERMANN, C. (Eds) (1985) *Wohnalltag in Deutschland 1850–1914. Bilder-Daten-Dokumente*, Münster, Coppenrath.

THATCHER, M. (1987) Interview with Douglas Keay, *Women's Own*, 31 October.

THOMPSON, E.P. (1977) *The Making of the English Working Class*, Harmondsworth, Penguin.

THOMPSON, T. (1981) *Edwardian Childhoods*, London, Routledge & Kegan Paul.

TROMMSDORFF, G. (Ed.) (1988) *Sozialisation und Kulturvergleich*, Stuttgart, Enke.

TROTHA, V., T. (1982) 'Zur Entstehung von Jugend', *Kölner Zeitschrift für Soziologie und Sozialpsychologie*, 34, pp. 79–97.

TROYNA, B. (1979) 'Differential commitment of ethnic identity by Black youths in Britain', *New Community*, 17, 3, pp. 406–14.

TROYNA, B. (Ed.) (1987) *Racial Inequality and Education*, London, Tavistock.

TROYNA, B. and CASHMORE, E. (1982) *Black Youth in Crisis*, London, Allen & Unwin.

TURNER, G. (1983) *The Social World of the Comprehensive School: How Pupils Adapt*, London, Croom Helm.

TWENHÖFEL, R. (1984) 'Kulturkonflikt und Integration. Zur Kritik der Kulturkonflikt-these', *Schweizerische Zeitschrift für Soziologie*, 10, 2, pp. 405–34.

VOGES, W. (Ed.) (1987) *Methoden der Biographie- und Lebenslaufforschung*, Opladen, Leske + Budrich.

WAKEFORD, J. (1969) *The Cloistered Elite: A Sociological Analysis of the English Boarding School*, London, Macmillan.

WALFORD, G. (1986) *Life in Public Schools*, London, Methuen.

WALKER, S. and BARTON, L. (Eds) (1983) *Gender, Class and Education*, Lewes, Falmer Press.

WALKER, S. and BARTON, L. (Eds) (1986) *Youth, Unemployment and Schooling*, Milton Keynes, Open University Press.

WALKERDINE, V. (1983) 'It's only natural: Beyond child-centred pedagogy', in WOLPE, A.M. and DONALD, J. (Eds) *Is There Anyone Here From Education?*, London, Pluto Press.

WALKERDINE, V. (1987) 'Sex, power and pedagogy', in ARNOT, M. and WEINER, G. (Eds) *Gender and the Politics of Schooling*, London, Hutchinson/Open University, pp. 166–74.

WALKERDINE, V. and LUCEY, H. (1989) *Democracy in the Kitchen*, London, Virago.

WALLACE, C. (1987) *For Richer, For Poorer*, London, Tavistock.

WALLACE, C. (1989) 'Youth', in BURGESS, R. (Ed.) *Investigating Society*, London, Longman.

WALTER, H. and OERTER, R. (Eds) (1979) *Ökologie und Entwicklung. Mensch-Umwelt-Modelle in entwicklungspsychologischer Sicht*, Donauwörth, Auer.

WALVIN, J. (1982) *A Child's World: A Social History of English Childhood 1800–1914*, Harmondsworth, Penguin.

WALZ, H.D. (1980) *Sozialisationsbedingungen und Freizeitverhalten italienischer Jugendlicher*, Müchen, DJI.

WARD, C. (1978) *The Child in the City*, London, Architectural Press.

WATTS, A.G. (1978) 'The implications of school-leaver unemployment for careers education in schools', *Journal of Curriculum Studies*, 10, pp. 233–50.

WATTS, A.G. (1987) 'Beyond unemployment? Schools and the future of work', *British Journal of Educational Studies*, 35, pp. 3–17.

WATTS, A.G. (1983) *Education, Unemployment and the Future of Work*, Milton Keynes, Open University Press.

WEBER, M. (1968) *Economy and Society*, New York, Bedminster Press.

WEBER-KELLERMANN, I. (1979a) 'Die gute Kinderstube. Zur Geschichte des Wohnens von Bürgerkindern' in NIETHAMMER, L. (Ed.) *Wohnen im Wandel. Beiträge zur Geschichte des Alltags in der bürgerlichen Gesellschaft*, Wuppertal, Hammer, pp. 44–64.

WEBER-KELLERMANN, I. (1979b) *Die Kindheit. Kleidung und Wohnen, Arbeit und Spiel. Eine Kulturgeschichte*, Frankfurt/M., Insel.

WEBER-KELLERMANN, I., EICKE-JENNEMANN, D. and FALKENBERG, R. (1985) *Der Kinder neue Kleider. Zweihundert Jahre deutsche Kindermoden in ihrer sozialen Zeichensetzung*, Frankfurt/M., Insel.

WEIGEL, S. (1986) 'Die Verdoppelung des männlichen Blicks und der Ausschluß von Frauen aus der Literaturwissenschaft', in HAUSEN, K. and NOWOTNY, H. (Eds) *Wie männlich ist die Wissenschaft?* Frankfurt/M., Suhrkamp, pp. 43–61.

WEINER, G. and ARNOT, M. (Eds) (1987) *Gender Under Scrutiny: New Inquiries in Education*, London, Hutchinson/Open University Press.

WEITZMAN, L. (1985) *The Divorce Revolution: The Unexpected Social and Economic Consequences for Women and Children in America*, New York, Free Press.

WERNER, H. (1957) *The Comparative Psychology of Mental Development*, New York, Free Press.

WHITTY, G. (1985) *Sociology and School Knowledge*, London, Methuen.

WIEBE, H.-H. (Ed.) (1988) *Jugend in Europa. Situation und Forschungsstand*, Opladen, Leske + Budrich.

References

WILD, R. (1987) *Die Vernunft der Väter. Zur Psychographie von Bürgerlichkeit und Aufklärung in Deutschland im Beispiel ihrer Literatur für Kinder*, Stuttgart, Metzler.

WILKINS, F. (1979) *Growing Up Between the Wars*, London, Batsford.

WILKINSON, M. (1981) *Children and Divorce*, Oxford, Basil Blackwell.

WILLIS, C. (1983) *The Use, Effectiveness and Impact of Police Stop and Search Powers*, Home Office Research Unit, London, HMSO.

WILLIS, P. (1977) *Learning to Labour*, Farnborough, Saxon House.

WILLIS, P. (1978) *Profane Culture*, London, Routledge & Kegan Paul.

WILLIS, P. (1986) 'Unemployment: The final inequality', *British Journal of Sociology of Education*, 7, 2, pp. 155–69.

WILLIS, P. (1988) *Unemployment and Youth in Wolverhampton*, Wolverhampton, Social Services.

WOODS, P. (1983) *Sociology and the School: An Interactionist Viewpoint*, London, Routledge & Kegan Paul.

WOUTERS, C. (1979) 'Informalisierung und Prozeß der Zivilisation' in GLEICHMANN, P. *et al.* (Eds) *Materialien zu N. Elias' Zivilisationstheorie*, Frankfurt/M., Suhrkamp, pp. 279–98.

WRENCH, J. (1986) 'YTS, racial inequality and the trade unions', *Policy Papers in Ethnic Relations*, 6, Centre for Research in Ethnic Relations, University of Warwick.

WRENCH, J. and LEE, G. (1983) 'The subtle hammering — Young Black people and the labour market', in SMITH, D. and TROYNA, B. (Eds) *Education, Race and the Labour Market*, Leicester, NYB.

WRINGE, C. (1981) *Children's Rights: A Philosophical Study*, London, Routledge & Kegan Paul.

WYNN, M. (1972) *Family Policy: A Study of the Economic Costs of Rearing Children and their Social and Political Consequences*, Harmondsworth, Penguin.

YAKUT, A., REICH, H.H., NEUMANN, U. and BOOS-NÜNNING, U. (1986) *Zwischen Elternhaus und Arbeitsamt. Türkische Jugendliche suchen einen Beruf*, Berlin, Express Edition.

ZEIHER, H. (1983) 'Die vielen Räume der Kinder. Zum Wandel räumlicher Lebensbedingungen seit 1945', in PREUSS-LAUSITZ, U. *et al.* (Eds) *Kriegskinder, Konsumkinder, Krisenkinder — Zur Sozialisationsgeschichte seit dem zweiten Weltkrieg*, Weinheim/Basel, Beltz, pp. 176–95.

ZEIHER, H. (1988) 'Verselbständigte Zeit — Selbständigere Kinder?', *Neue Sammlung*, 28, 1, pp. 75–92.

ZEIHER, H. and ZEIHER, H. (1987) *Lokale Umwelt und Eigeninitiative in der Tageslaufgestaltung zehnjähriger Kinder*, mimeo, Berlin.

DIE ZEIT (1989) 'Arbeitszeit und Arbeitsleistung', Daten der Dresdner Bank/Bundesvereinigung der deutschen Arbeitgeberverbände, 43–20, October.

ZIEHE, T. (1988) 'Wie man es im Kopf aushält. Strukturen des Alltagswissens Jugendlicher', *Pädagogik*, 40, 3, pp. 11–14.

ZIEHE, T. and STUBENRAUCH, H. (1982) *Plädoyer für ungewöhnliches Lernen. Ideen zur Jugendsituation*, Reinbek, Rowohlt.

ZINNEKER, J. (1981) 'Jugend '81. Portrait einer Generation', in JUGENDWERK DER DEUTSCHEN SHELL (Ed.). *Jugend '81, Bd. 1*, Hamburg, pp. 80–114.

ZINNEKER, J. (1985a) 'Jugend der Gegenwart — Beginn oder Ende einer historischen Epoche?', in BAACKE, D. and HEITMEYER, W. (Eds) *Neue Widersprüche. Jugendliche in den 80er Jahren*, Weinheim/München, Juventa, pp. 24–46.

ZINNEKER, J. (1985b) 'Die Jugendstudien von Emnid/Shell 1953–1955', in JUGEND WERK DER DEUTSCHEN SHELL (Ed.) *Jugendliche und Erwachsene '85: Generationen im Vergleich*, Opladen, Bd. 3, pp. 409–80.

ZINNEKER, J. (1985c) 'Kindheit, Erziehung, Familie', in JUGENDWERK DER DEUTSCHEN SHELL (Ed.) *Jugendliche und Erwachsene '85. Generationen im Vergleich*, Opladen, Bd. 3, pp. 97–292.

Zɪɴɴᴇᴋᴇʀ, J. (1986) 'Jugend im Raum gesellschaftlicher Klassen. Neue überlegungen zu einem alten Thema', in Hᴇɪᴛᴍᴇʏᴇʀ, W. (Ed.) *Interdisziplinäre Jugendforschung*, Weinheim/München, Juventa, pp. 99–132.

Zɪɴɴᴇᴋᴇʀ, J. (1987) *Jugendkultur 1940–1985*, Opladen, Leske + Budrich.

Zɪɴɴᴇᴋᴇʀ, J. and Mᴏʟɴᴀʀ, P. (1988) 'Lebensphase Jugend im historisch-interkulturellen Vergleich', in Fᴇʀᴄʜʜᴏғғ, W. and Oʟᴋ, T. (Eds) *Jugend im internationalen Vergleich*, Weinheim/München, Juventa, pp. 181–206.

Zᴏʟʟ, R. (1988) '*Nicht so wie unsere Eltern*'. *Ein neues kulturelles Modell?* Wiesbaden/ Opladen, Westdeutscher Verlag.

Notes on Contributors

Georg Auernheimer is Professor of Didactics and Educational Theory at the University of Marburg. His research interests for many years have focused upon intercultural education.

Michael Brake is Head of the Social Studies Department at the Polytechnic of North London. He is well-known for his work in youth cultural studies, criminology and social policy.

Phillip Brown is Lecturer in the Department of Sociology at the University of Kent at Canterbury. His current writing addresses the politics of educational reform and economic change.

Peter Büchner is Professor of Education at the University of Marburg. As a sociologist of education, he is particularly interested in the sociology of childhood and in schooling structures.

Lynne Chisholm is Lecturer in Curriculum Studies and Sociology of Education at the University of London Institute of Education. Her research interests lie in exploring educational-occupational links, youth transitions and gender.

Steffani Engler is a Research Officer on the DFG-funded project 'University Study and Biography' located at the University-Polytechnic of Siegen, and is especially interested in youth socialization processes.

Wilfried Ferchhoff is Professor of Pedagogics at the University of Bielefeld, working in the field of youth cultural studies and social pedagogics.

Roger Hewitt is Senior Research Officer in the Sociological Research Unit at the University of London Institute of Education, currently directing an ESRC-funded project on oral communication.

John Hood-Williams is Lecturer in Social Studies at Thames Polytechnic. His research is placed within a critical analysis of family and childhood in contemporary society.

Gill Jones is Research Officer at the Centre for Educational Sociology at the University of Edinburgh, with a particular interest in family and youth research.

Helga Krüger is Professor of Sociology and Education at the University of Bremen. She conducts research into family, youth and gender questions within the University's Centre for Research in Work and Education and the DFG-funded research programme 'Status Passages and Life Risks'.

Heinz-Hermann Krüger is Lecturer in Education at the University of Dortmund. He has conducted a number of sociohistorical and cultural studies of West German youth, and is well-known for his research into fifties youth culture.

Diana Leonard is Senior Lecturer in the Department of Policy Studies at the University of London Institute of Education, with particular specialisms in women's studies and the sociology of the family.

Claire Wallace is Senior Lecturer in Social Studies at Polytechnic South West, Plymouth, and her research work focusses on youth transitions.

Jürgen Zinneker is Professor for Social Pedagogics at the University-Polytechnic of Siegen. He has conducted large-scale surveys into the attitudes and lifestyles of young West Germans, and is currently engaged in charting indicators of social and cultural change.

Index

absenteeism 67
acid house 224
adolescence 20
  in FRG in 1950s 105–8
  in FRG in 1980s 108–11
  see also youth
age patriarchy 163–9
alcohol 218
alienation 132, 204–5
Apple, M 55
apprenticeships 122, 123, 126, 172
Asian youth 188–90
  Bhangra music 189–90
  self assertion 189
  social mobility 189
attachment theory 59
Auernheimer, Georg 9, 10, 197–212
autonomy 83

Beck, V 134–7
  see also individualization, theory
Bernstein, B 163, 164, 166
Bhangra music 189–90
biographies 18
  biographization 28, 77
  changes in, in FRG 71–84
  collective, of a generation 78–80
  construction 7–8
  early acquisition of independence 82–4
  individual class biographies 140–4
  mapping across transitions 8
  see also employment biographies:
    individualization
Birmingham Centre for Contemporary
  Cultural Studies *see* Centre for
    Contemporary Cultural
    Studies (Birmingham)

Bourdieu social reproduction *see* social
  reproduction theory
Bourdieu's habitus concept 37, 178–9
  see also habitus
Brake, Michael 10, 213–25
British Movement 186
Brown, Phillip 8, 85–103
Büchner, Peter 6, 7, 71–84

Centre for Contemporary Cultural
  Studies (Birmingham) 6, 22, 35, 193
  commercial distortion 231
  youth cultural studies 35, 231
cheekiness 167
Chicago ecological research 214
  new Chicago school 215
Child Development Research Unit
  (Nottingham) 58
child-centredness 164
childhood
  as career 166–7
  family and 21
Childhood and Sexuality (Jackson) 60
childhood studies 58–70
  anthropological studies of
    communities 61–2
  attachment theory 59
  children's work 67–8
  divorce 61
  families and 20, 21, 61, 62
  feminism and 62–3
  history of childhood 60
  in FRG 71–84
  in UK 58–70
  individualization process 77–8
  interviewing difficulties 59
  leisure and 68

Printed in the United Kingdom
by Lightning Source UK Ltd.
114458UKS00002B/90

9 781850 006510